MIRRORS OF DESTRUCTION

War, Genocide, and Modern Identity

OMER BARTOV

OXFORD
UNIVERSITY PRESS

OXFORD

UNIVERSITY PRESS

Oxford   New York

Athens   Auckland   Bangkok   Bogotá   Buenos Aires   Cape Town   Chennai
Dar es Salaam   Delhi   Florence   Hong Kong   Istanbul   Karachi   Kolkata
Kuala Lumpur   Madrid   Melbourne   Mexico City   Mumbai   Nairobi   Paris
São Paulo   Shanghai   Singapore   Taipei   Tokyo   Toronto   Warsaw

and associated companies in
Berlin   Ibadan

Copyright © 2000 by Oxford University Press, Inc.

First published in 2000 by Oxford University Press, Inc.
198 Madison Avenue, New York, New York 10016
www.oup.com

First issued as an Oxford University Press paperback, 2002

Oxford is a registered trademark of Oxford University Press.

Library of Congress Cataloging-in-Publication Data
Bartov, Omer.
Mirrors of destruction : war, genocide, and modern identity / Omer Bartov.
    p.   cm.
Includes bibliographical references and index.
ISBN 0–19–507723–7; 0–19–515184–4 (pbk.)
1. Holocaust, Jewish (1939–1945)—Historiography.   2. Genocide.   3. Ethnicity.
4. World War, 1914–1918—Influence.   5. France—History—20th century—Historiography.
6. Holocaust, Jewish (1939–1945)—Public opinion.   7. Public opinion—Germany.
8. Memory.   I. Title
D804.348 B37   2000
940.53'18'072—dc21   99–039974

9 8 7 6 5 4 3 2 1

Printed in the United States of America
on acid-free paper

IN MEMORIAM

Yehudit Bartov,
1924–1998

Acknowledgments

This book was written over the span of several years. At times it seemed that it would never be completed. Now that it is done, I feel that there is much more that could have been said, read, and written on this topic. Yet it does represent my thinking at this point in time and will hopefully be of some use to others who are grappling with the realities of our century as it comes to a close.

On the way I accumulated more debts than I could possibly acknowledge without providing a long list of names. I would thus like to thank all those who have read and commented on drafts of papers, published articles, lectures, reviews, and all other thoughts and ideas I sent their way verbally, electronically, or on paper. One of the more elevating experiences I had in writing this often depressing book was to confirm the tremendous value of an ongoing intellectual exchange with friends and colleagues ranging well beyond the academic politics and gossip that seem to take up so much of our time and energy. In particular I wish to thank the National Endowment for the Humanities for a research fellowship during 1996–97 and Rutgers University for granting me sabbatical leave during 1995–96. Without these two years of leave, I would not have been able to complete this book. My wife, Li Wai-yee, has her own books to write and our daughter, Shira, and my son, Raz, thankfully have more enjoyable things on their minds than war and genocide, as they forge their own identities. But without them, I would not have had the courage to stare at the Gorgon's face. I dedicate this book to my mother, whose life spans not only much of this century's sorrow and pity but also its hope and glory, from Buczacz in Polish Ukraine to Kibbutz Ein Ha-choresh in Israel. She taught me more than I ever admitted during her lifetime. *Tehi nishmatah tserurah bi-tsror ha-chayim.*

Some sections of this book include revised versions of previously published articles and chapters in edited volumes. I wish to thank the editors and publishers of the following publications for allowing me to reprint them here, either in part, whole, or expanded form. These are, in order of appearance in the book: "Martyrs' Vengeance: Memory, Trauma, and Fear of War in France, 1918–1940," in *The French Defeat of 1940: Reassessments,* ed. Joel Blatt (Providence and Oxford: Berghahn Books, 1998), pp. 54–84; "The Proof of Ignominy: Vichy France's Past and Present," *Contemporary European History* 7/1 (1998): 107–131; "Trauma and Absence: France and Germany, 1914–45," in Time to Kill: The Soldier's Experience of War in the West 1939–1945, ed. P. Addison and A. Calder (London: Pimlico Press, 1997), pp. 347–58; "Trauma and Absence," part II, in *European Memories of the Second World War,* ed. H. Peitsch, C. Burdett, C. Gorrara (New York and Oxford: Berghahn Books, 1999), pp. 258–71; "Defining Enemies, Making Victims: Germans, Jews, and the Holocaust," *American Historical Review* 103/3 (June 1998): 771–816; "The Lessons of the Holocaust," *Dimensions* 12/1 (1998): 13–20; "Kitsch and Sadism in Ka-Tzetnik's Other Planet: Israeli Youth Imagine the Holocaust," *Jewish Social Studies* (spring 1997): 42–76.

All translations in this book are mine, unless otherwise noted.

Contents

MIRRORS OF DESTRUCTION

Introduction

This book is a study in perceptions. Its central focus is the Holocaust, but rather than providing a narrative of the event, its goal is to examine the manner in which a variety of perspectives on violence have molded European views and redefined individual and collective identities in a process of emulation, mutual reflection, and distortion. Hence the book is conceived somewhat as a hall of mirrors wherein repeated images, seen from different angles, provide a prism through which we can distill a clearer understanding of the origins, nature, and impact of the atrocity that occurred in the heart of our civilization and has become the defining event of the twentieth century.

What concerns me most is the moment of encounter. When we look into a mirror, we see our own reflection; but when we see ourselves reflected in another person's eyes, our mutual gaze transforms a mere impression into an event. History is all about this encounter, the moment in which impression is transformed into event. Yet the history of the Holocaust is conventionally written from only one perspective, either that of the killer or that of the victim. A narrative of the past that remains within the bounds of a single perspective is an incomplete history, for it lacks precisely that moment of encounter from which events are born. In his contemplation on Auschwitz, the writer-survivor Ka-Tzetnik (Yehiel Dinur) recounts just such a moment, as he stares into the eyes of the SS man sending him to the gas chamber and realizes that had their roles been reversed no disruption to the scheme of the universe would have occurred. It is at this point, forty years after the event, that he gains an understanding of the Holocaust that no amount of obsessively retelling his own perspective had hitherto afforded.[1]

Just as vampires were declared inhuman by dint of lacking a reflection, so, too, we are deprived of our humanity when it is no longer reflected in the eyes of the beholder. Elie Wiesel writes that as he looked at the mirror for the first time just after being liberated from the camps he could not reconcile his reflection with his self-awareness; the dead face that stared at him from the mirror remained etched on his mind for the rest of his life.[2] Robert Antelme recounts that camp inmates would look at themselves in a broken mirror, trying, increasingly in vain, to recognize their individual humanity in facial features that progressively came to resemble those of their comrades, as the deprivations and brutalization they endured eroded their unique physical characteristics.[3] Yet the mirror is also the instrument of knowledge: the Taoist sage uses his heart as a mirror to transcend subjectivity and reflect everything, even if, since the mirror reflects only phenomenal reality, it is just the first step on the path to understanding. Conversely, mirrors lead to madness, a descent into total subjectivity by passing over to the other side of the glass. When Alice in *Through the Looking Glass* crosses over to the other side of the mirror, she enters the world of her own imagination; she steps into herself to discover the horrors and fantasies, passions and fears that could not be reflected on the surface of the glass.

In the first part of this century, European images and practices of violence produced an increasingly destructive dynamic of imitation, distortion, and radicalization. At the fulcrum of these mirroring images of destruction is the Holocaust, as reality and fantasy, as past event and historical burden. In a century characterized by a quest for perfection, stark reality and intoxicating illusion became each other's distorted reflection. Utopia has been the engine of our epoch's aspirations and disillusionments, violence and annihilation. As utopians smashed their way through sordid reality, the utopias they established contained mere fragments of past ideals. Nazism's racial utopia was the genocide of the Jews. But as we contemplate the Holocaust through the mirror of time, the seeming madness of the event makes it appear increasingly unreal; for in order to imagine ourselves into that world, we must cross over to a universe that inverted the very notion of a shared humanity.

The twentieth century has been the site of a titanic struggle over competing conceptions of humanity. This struggle was waged not merely in the minds of intellectuals and in university lecture halls but also in the popular media and on the streets of great cities, on battlefields, and in concentration camps. Its roots can be traced at least as far back as the French Revolution and European colonialism, and it was neither limited to the world wars nor to the West, although much of its ideological baggage originated in Europe. It was, and in parts of the world still remains, a conflict over abstract ideas grafted onto conventional struggles for power and hegemony and carried out with the destructive weapons of modern technology. In essence our century has tried to define what and who is human, and then to set rules as to how human beings should live in society and who must be excluded from it altogether. Looking at themselves in the mirror, or seeing themselves reflected in others' eyes, people asked: Am I a human? Are they human? The answers to such questions were not necessarily the outcome of philosophical contemplation, nor did they result simply in further intellectual discussion. Rather, they engendered a destructive urge that wiped out vast numbers of human beings and ravaged whole countries, while also releasing tremendous creative energies. The rationale for this surge of violence was the need to define or redefine, maintain or drastically change individual and collective identity. Yet it was this very process of unmaking and remaking humanity—whereby each annihilatory bout and its requisite multitude of tortured and mutilated individuals, each assertion of impossible atonement, each new march along the narrow path between utopia and hell was a mirror image of all that had preceded it, in reality and imagination—that made for the appearance of new and unforeseen identities forged in the crucible of destruction.

Over the past couple of decades increasing attention has been devoted to the violent legacy of Western civilization and especially to European imperialism, the world wars, the crimes of Communism, and the Holocaust. In many ways, the following pages are part of this ongoing discussion. At the same time, however, this book attempts to provide a very different perspective on an issue that has become increasingly controversial, namely, the centrality of the Holocaust for our era. In recent years, a growing number of commentators have expressed criticism of what appears to them as an undue, disproportionate, and even distorting emphasis on the genocide of the Jews. The German historians' controversy of the mid-1980s, for instance, focused on the relative importance of the Holocaust, its centrality for the course of German history, and the extent to which it could be construed as a singular, unprecedented event.[4] Even more recently, a number of French scholars and intellectuals have argued that the excessive preoccupation with the genocidal policies of the Nazi regime has diverted attention from other cases of mass murder both in the past and in the present.[5]

My own intention is not to argue directly with such opinions. Rather, I am interested in examining the crucial relationship between war, genocide, and modern identity. Within the European context—as well as its various offshoots in other parts of the world—there can be no doubt that the Holocaust is, both historically and as a historical burden, an event of unparalleled importance. This is precisely why so much intellectual energy and ingenuity was required by those who have tried to contextualize, relativize, or marginalize it. Yet I am not making a plea here for the centrality of the Holocaust, since this appears to me far too obvious to merit much discussion. Rather, my main argument is that we cannot understand the manner in which individuals; ethnic, religious, and ideological groups; and nations perceive themselves or interact with others, without considering the impact of our century's preoccupation with violence. This does not mean that all societies are influenced to the same extent by wars and genocides, nor that other, nonviolent, indeed wholly antiviolent and humanistic undertakings in the past hundred years are any less central to many nations and civilizations. It is my assertion, however, that the project of remaking humanity and defining identity has been at the core of this century, and that much of this project was characterized by a tremendous destructive urge followed by a long and as yet uncompleted process of coming to terms with the disasters it has produced and is still producing in many parts of the world.

In other words, while this book is devoted primarily to German, French, and Jewish discourses on war, genocide, and identity, and therefore refers extensively to the Holocaust, this should in no way be seen as an attempt to diminish the importance of other genocides and cases of mass murder or their role in defining individual and group identities. Conversely, although my focus on these nations is partly due to my greater familiarity with their history, it is also rooted in my belief that the Holocaust is indeed a crucial event for Western civilization, and that however much we learn about other instances of inhumanity, we cannot avoid the fact that this genocide, in the heart of our civilization, perpetrated by one of its most important nations (with the collaboration or complicity of many others), can never be relegated to a secondary place. This fact as such has nothing to do with "victimology" and everything to do with grasping the potentials of the world in which we live and the culture we share. It is for this reason, too, that I find debates over the "uniqueness" of the Holocaust unhelpful. A historical event can only be understood within its context, just as its significance can be grasped only at some historical distance.

Even in this narrower framework, I do not intend to provide a historical narrative or a comprehensive analysis of all that might be involved in this process. Rather, I propose four distinct but related discussions, each of which has a direct bearing on the book's main argument. First, I explore the glorification of war, violence, and genocide. Here, most clearly, identity is seen as the product of violent action against groups defined as outside the national, racial, or ideological collectivity. Second, I discuss the disillusionment from violence and destruction. Such disillusionment may revise perceptions of the past and thereby also redefine identity, but it can also lead to competition over representations of this past and thus threaten to undermine any solid sense of identity. Moreover rejection of violence may either limit its impact or allow it to operate unchallenged: collaboration with oppression in the name of nonviolence. Third, I turn to the impact of constructing elusive enemies, namely, those who defy clear definitions of identity and therefore become the focus of anxiety and aggression. Elusive enemies are a crucial component of modern war and genocide, and their persistence after the event, precisely because they can never be identified, makes for the perpetuation, though often in a highly altered form, of past phobias and violent urges. Finally, I analyze the predilection toward apocalyptic visions and the relationship between utopia and violence. Here we find elements of the previous three perspectives in a more radical but also more hopeful form: violence is glorified but must lead to the end of history; disillusionment is the engine of action rather than passivity, rebellion rather than submission; elusive enemies are the objects of destruction but their disappearance ensures purity and relief from anxieties of pollution. In this context humanity's greatest aspirations, highest virtues, most generous instincts and most enchanting visions become part and parcel of an apocalyptic upheaval of boundless devastation and atrocity. It is this legacy of hope and disillusionment, beauty and terror, sacrifice and murder that the following pages attempt to explore.

1

FIELDS OF GLORY

It is commonly assumed, at least in the West, that the glorification of war is a thing of the past. Even more prevalent is the assumption that such war-related phenomena as expulsions and deportations, ethnic cleansing and mass rape, massacre and genocide would be universally condemned in any civilized country. Indeed, such condemnation is viewed as a mark of civilization, and groups or nations that still conduct policies of this nature are considered to be, by definition, beyond the pale. And yet, only a few decades ago, war was seen by most Europeans as a glorious undertaking, and many of the actions we would describe today as war crimes were celebrated as an inherent part of the conduct of war and the consolidation of victory or, at the very least, were perceived as regrettable but unavoidable features of modern warfare.

That non-Western nations, countries that straddle the ill-defined line between Europe and Asia, and a variety of despicable regimes, have engaged in the recent past or are still engaged today in widespread crimes and abuses of human rights is, of course, readily conceded. Yet such crimes have rarely led to their expulsion from the international community. Since the end of World War II, the collapse or disintegration of such regimes was more often the result of their own incompetence or self-destructive dynamics, and at best of indirect international pressure. Hence the main difference between the first and the second parts of this century is not so much that war has lost its potential to inspire self-glorification, and certainly not that war has been any less murderous. Indeed, the ratio of innocent civilians killed in war has grown progressively since 1914. The difference is that following the devastation of World War II, Western nations have had both less inclination and less need to fight each other; when they did go to war, it was against non-Western lands, and it was the latter that took the main brunt of human and material destruction.

The Spirit of 1914

Thoughts of war throughout history and in many civilizations have revolved around two contradictory, though not perforce mutually exclusive, sets of images. The first postulated war as an elevating, heroic experience. The second described war as a site of destruction and desolation. This polarity between the portrayal of war as an occasion for humanity to express its nobility and its perception as providing the opportunity for human savagery is thus deeply embedded in culture and civilization.

During the last two centuries, however, major transformations in demographic patterns and social organization, in politics and industry, and in science and technology have had an immense impact on the practice and theory of war, as well as on its imagery and mythology. The availability of unprecedented quantities of ever more effective weapons, along with seemingly unlimited and increasingly pliable human reserves, and the growing capacity to mobilize these resources by the modern industrialized nation-state, greatly enhanced war's destructive potential. This was a prospect both terrifying and exhilarating, repulsive and fascinating. It has evoked the wildest fantasies and the most nightmarish visions. Characteristically for an age of rapid changes, the reality of total war and genocide consistently remained one step ahead of its image. Ours is a century in which man's imagination has been conducting a desperate race with the practice of humanity. And precisely because the mind could no longer catch up with man-made reality, it conjured up visions of the future that surpassed all known forms and dimensions of destruction and thereby created the preconditions for even greater suffering, pain, and depravity.

What is most crucial about Europe's first industrial war in 1914–18 is not the enthusiasm with which its outbreak was greeted in the major combatant nations. To be sure, even if the extent of what has come to be called "the spirit of 1914" has been somewhat exaggerated, one cannot ignore the fact that youthful volunteerism, mass industrial mobilization, intellectual and academic propagandistic engagement, and political consensus all combined to provide the early phases of the war with a bizarre mixture of anxiety and elation, a festive atmosphere permeated with premonitions of disaster.[1] However much disillusionment was to set in during the latter parts of the war, this was still an extraordinary expression of devotion not merely to the nation but also to the notion of war itself as a noble, purifying, and elevating experience. Yet in some ways, this early phenomenon harks back to the past; what makes World War I into the true baptism by fire of the twentieth century is not the high spirits of 1914 but the grim reality that followed.

If World War I is remembered primarily for the continuous front of trenches that stretched all the way from the Swiss border to the Atlantic, another crucial factor of the fighting was, in fact, the growing porousness of the boundaries between soldiers and civilians both as combatants and as targets of destruction. Civilians had been the main victims of war often in the past, but none of the great cataclysms of destruction in previous centuries could compare in sheer scale and lasting impact to 1914–18. For while vast numbers of men were transformed into soldiers, all other civilians became exposed to the human, economic, and psychological cost of total war. The war invaded the most remote corners of the land, and the huge conscript armies at the front contained members of every social stratum and region of the country. This was truly a war of nations, and for this reason none of the major participants was spared its consequences.

Soldiers' Glory

The enthusiasm of the first months of the war was rooted in an imagery of military glory that bore no relationship to the reality of the battlefield. The splendid bayonet charge over a field of flowers that so many soldiers had been taught to expect did not materialize.[2] Instead, green fields were transformed into oceans of mud, frontal attacks ended up as massacres, great offensives rapidly ground to a bloody halt, and heroic gestures were soon replaced by grim determination and a desperate will to survive. Yet as the huge, arrogant armies burrowed underground into a maze of trenches filled with slime and excrement, rats and rotting body parts, the soldiers began to construct their own vision of glory, distinct both from the romantic images of the past and from the discredited chauvinistic eyewash of the propagandists in the rear. This new vision, unique to the age of total war, has become part of the manner in which we imagine destruction; aestheticized and cherished, it motivated another generation of young men to fight and die, and enabled the veterans of previous wars to make a kind of peace with their memories of massacre. Given the right political and cultural context, however, this vision has also come to serve as a crucial component of our century's genocidal predilections, facilitating a metamorphosis of values and perspectives in which the annihilatory energy of modern war was portrayed as generating great creative powers, and the phenomenon of industrial killing was perceived as a historical necessity of awesome beauty.[3] The Great War's new fields of glory were the breeding ground of fascism and Nazism, of human degradation and extermination, and from them sprang the storm troops of dictatorships and the demagogues of racial purity and exclusion. In a tragic process of inversion, the true comradeship and sacrifice of millions of young men was perverted into hate and destruction. The new vision of war that emanated from the trenches of 1914–18 ensured that our century's fields of glory would be sown with the corpses of innocent victims and the distorted fragments of shattered ideals.

Contemptuous of the idealized images of war that bore no relationship to the fighting as they knew it, resentful of the staff officers' sheltered lives behind the front and the civilians in the rear, the troops developed a complex subculture all of their own making. Exemplified in frontline journals for their own consumption, a vocabulary that only they could understand, and a new kind of sarcasm and black humor, this was a state of mind that combined a good measure of self-pity with immense pride in their ability to endure inhuman conditions for the sake of a nation seemingly ignorant of and indifferent to their terrible sacrifice. This camaraderie of the combat troops was shared by soldiers on both sides of the line, and while it had some common features with the mentality of all armies in history, the crucial difference was that most of these men were conscripts who would return to civilian life as soon as the fighting ended—if they were lucky enough to survive.[4] The first months of the war had decimated the professional formations and the traditional officer corps of all combatant nations, not least because they could not adapt to the new conditions on the battlefield without fundamentally changing those very attitudes that had previously ensured their elite social status. Soon they were replaced by a new breed of combat officers who shared the emerging ethos of the battle-hardened conscripts and were socially less remote from them.

Patriotism at the front differed from the rhetoric of the rear, and no one was more aware of this than the soldiers themselves. They had gone to war to serve and save their country, but not only was this nothing like the war they had expected, the country too seemed to take a very different shape when seen from the perspective of the trenches. The camaraderie that helped them endure the front also created and made a virtue of the difference between them and that part of the nation that had stayed behind. Theirs was not the naive heroism extolled by the propagandists, but one born of suffering and pain, horror and death. To be sure, most soldiers had but the vaguest notion of how the nation should be transformed once they returned from the front, but they increasingly felt that it was their right and duty to bring about far-reaching changes, rooted, first and foremost, in the trench experience.

By now we have become used to thinking of World War I as the moment in which innocence was forever shattered. We are haunted by the image of millions of devoted, unquestioning, patriotic, young men being led to senseless slaughter, betrayed by their elders. The Western Front has come to epitomize the notion of war as a vast arena of victimhood. That all this sacrifice was in vain is underlined by the aftermath of the war. We recall the broken promises and despair, the soldiers who instead of returning to a "land fit for heroes" were abandoned to unemployment, destitution, and physical and mental decay. Hence, it is argued, both the apathy and the extremism, the conformism and the violence that were characteristics of the postwar era.[5] But the very attitudes toward violence and the perceptions of destruction that emerged among the soldiers during the war as a means to endure it were ultimately at the root of the even greater horror and devastation of the next war. The images of violence and fantasies of destruction that became so prevalent during the interwar period were directly related to the reality and trauma of the front experience in 1914–18. It was these fantasies that played such a major role in the enactment of genocide two decades later. Ironically, the same mechanism that helped soldiers survive one war created the necessary mind-set for mass murder. A crucial component of this mechanism was the frontline notion of soldiers' glory.

Glory at the front meant enduring the most degrading, inhuman conditions, under constant threat of death and while regularly killing others, without losing one's good humor, composure, and humanity. It meant discovering the ability to switch between being a helpless prey and a professional killer, and acting as a loving son, father, and husband, radically separating the atrocity at the front from the normality of the rear, indeed making this very separation into a badge of honor and a key for survival. For one had to survive not only the fighting but also the homecoming. The true accomplishment of the frontline troops was not merely to tolerate this unbearable, schizophrenic condition but to glorify it, to perceive it as a higher existence rather than a horrifying state of affairs that could not be evaded. To be sure, many soldiers were incapable of this transformation of perception. But such World War I *mussulmen* (originating in the German word for Moslem, this term was commonly used by Nazi–concentration camp inmates to describe the most emaciated among them), walking dead who had lost all desire to survive, were normally doomed if they were not taken out of the line in time. To be saved from drowning, soldiers had to rely on the glory they had fabricated of which the essence was to construe atrocity as an elevating experience, one which was to be simultaneously celebrated, kept apart from personal relationships in the rear, and used as a tool to change the universe that had made it possible. And because such notions of wholesale future transformation were entertained within a context of vast devastation, they were inevitably permeated by an imagery of destruction.

When the war finally ended, the veterans felt an even greater urge to endow it with meaning. This does not mean that all of them glorified the war, but by and large most seem to have glorified their own and their comrades' experience even when they rejected the war itself. Here was a paradox of significant import, since opposition to war, even pacifism, shared one important element with extremism and militarism, namely, the glorification of the individual soldier, whether as a ruthless fighter or as a hapless victim. Some hoped that the shared fate of the veterans would become a formula for unity, for domestic and international peace. But as we know, precisely the opposite happened, not least because what all these soldiers had in common more than anything else was years of fear and atrocity, killing and mutilation. This was a treacherous foundation for peace.[6]

Unknown Soldiers

During the interwar period all political and ideological trends drew on the legacy of World War I for their own, often wholly contradictory purposes, since this rich source of violent images and metaphors of destruction proved to be highly malleable. But the fact that the memory of mass killing was widely employed by such divergent interests introduced a violent dimension to postwar political discourse, channeling it toward a constant preoccupation with human and material devastation. To be sure, the glorification of war after 1918 took many forms. The most visible and emotionally most potent was the commemoration of fallen soldiers. Significantly, even when such public symbols of mourning expressed implicit or, less frequently, explicit criticism of the war, they simultaneously strove to endow the death of the soldiers with a higher meaning and thereby ended up obscuring that the war had largely been an affair of senseless slaughter. Sacrifice was thus glorified while its context was refashioned in a manner that would enhance the nobility of its victims. Since commemoration is more about instilling the past with sense and purpose than with simply remembering it, the official remembrance of millions of fallen young men could not help but provide the war, in which their lives were squandered, with a retrospective meaning for the benefit of the living.[7]

The investment of death in war with meaning can be accomplished by both generalizing and individualizing it. In giving war a unique moral significance, the fallen soldier can be presented as having sacrificed himself for a greater cause: death is glorified by the context in which it occurred, abstract principles and entities are valued higher than individual lives. Hence mourning will focus on the service rendered by the dead for the nation's historical mission and future; rather than being deprived of its sons, the nation is enriched by those who die for it. Conversely, by concentrating on individual devotion, suffering, and sacrifice, the fallen glorify the cause and endow it with deeper meaning because they had given their lives for it. Here mourning will focus on individual qualities as an example to be followed by others. Put differently, in the former case the soldier is an extension of the nation, in the latter the nation is an extension of the soldier who embodies its very best essence. Rhetorically, one might either say that great nations produce heroic sons or that heroic soldiers deserve a nation fit for their sacrifice.

In the wake of World War I, both modes of mourning and ascribing meaning to death were common features of the vast and unprecedented wave of commemoration that swept through Europe, although the balance between the two varied from one nation to the next.[8] Yet even while public commemoration naturally tended to emphasize collective sacrifice for the national cause, it seemed to be increasingly informed by a quest for a new type of individual heroism. This synthesis between the collective and the particular was directly related to the emergence of mass society, vast conscript armies, and total war, a context in which there was no more room for the traditional hero, whose ultimate sacrifice was inscribed on his fate and inherent to his existence. World War I ushered in the glorification of the rank and file, expressed in such countries as Britain and France in the erection of national memorials for the unknown soldier. Here was a figure that represented both the individual and the mass: glorified by the nation, he also stood for the multitudes sent out to die and quickly forgotten. He thus gave a face to anonymity, personifying and glorifying precisely those masses that had no place in public memory; in other words, in being remembered, the unknown soldier legitimized forgetting.[9]

The figure of the unknown soldier thus made possible a shift from the inflated and largely discredited rhetoric of the abstract nation to the individual, yet presented the individual as a soldier who by definition had no specific traits and features, and who consequently embodied the nation after all. For all that was known about this "unknown" figure was his status as soldier, his gender, and his nationality (or "race"). Through him the nation could represent itself as a site of resurrection, returning from the Valley of Death thanks to the sacrifice of its sons. It was this identification of the living nation with its anonymous but glorified fallen soldiers that provided a means to come to terms with the trauma of war, and normalized the haunting images of the dead returning from the endless cemeteries in which they now resided, because the longing for the return of the fallen was mixed with a good deal of shame and trepidation. At the end of the war, people wanted to return to normality as soon as possible, to bury the dead and then to go on with life. Yet the presence of so much death and mourning also gave rise to a wave of mysticism, spiritualism, and occultism. The unknown soldier fulfilled the requirement of both focusing on the suffering and sacrifice of the individual, for which a powerful need existed, and of distancing oneself from any particular fallen member of family or community. The final death of the soldier was thus acknowledged through this familiar yet unknown figure safely and irrevocably locked in a national sepulcher.

Significantly, Germany did not erect a tomb for the unknown soldier; unlike France and Britain, Germany could not come to terms with the trauma of war through a symbol of final and irredeemable death.[10] Rather, many Germans hoped to overcome defeat by continuing the struggle; for this purpose, the dead could not be locked away, since they still had a role to play in urging the living to win back victory. In France and Britain, the glory of the unknown soldier, confined as he was to his tomb, was a matter of the past, and thereby helped the rest of the nation to get on with the present. In Germany, the unburied unknown soldier continued to roam the old battlefields and to march in the cities, reminding those who might have forgotten that his mission must still be accomplished. In France and Britain, especially the former, the specter of the fallen served as a warning that such slaughter should never be allowed again. But in Germany, the pain and sorrow of mourning was increasingly oriented to the future, and loss could not be accepted precisely because of the refusal to come to terms with the past. Ultimately, it was one of those surviving unknown soldiers who claimed to embody the nation and persuaded increasing numbers of Germans that he indeed personified its fate and would mold its future.

Adolf Hitler was one of millions of unknown veterans, who, unlike their fallen comrades, had urgent material and psychological needs. Glorifying the dead came more cheaply than caring for the living, many of whom had been physically and mentally mutilated at the front. Interwar European politics, society, and culture were deeply influenced by the massive presence of former soldiers, who often felt abandoned and misunderstood by the civilian environment to which they returned. Indeed, it was precisely the difficulties of social and economic reintegration in countries still reeling from the human and material costs of total war that stimulated the urge among the veterans to realize those vague but powerful aspirations they had forged during the war, and to translate their discovery of comradeship and sacrifice in the trenches to the realities of life after the disaster. The story of post-1918 Europe is thus largely about the cleavage between those who "had been there" and those who had not; it is a tale of rage and frustration, resentment and disillusionment.[11]

If most soldiers returning from the war wanted to pick up their lives where they had left them before they marched off to the trenches, this was rarely possible. Both they and their societies had been irreversibly transformed during the war years, and the idealized prewar world was as far from the present as the front had been from the rear.[12] Postwar Europe had neither the resources nor the skills to deal with the mental needs of men exposed to the horrors of sustained industrial warfare. Hence the tendency of veterans to organize their own associations, which provided them with psychological support and served as pressure groups on governments to meet the economic and the political demands of those whose sacrifice for the nation endowed them with a moral weight well beyond their numbers. Here the veterans could rekindle the comradeship that had sustained them at the front, mourn their fallen comrades and celebrate their sacrifice, and shelter from what they deemed to be an alienated society, impatient to put the war behind it, and unwilling to heed its lessons. In contradistinction to the state's glorification of the dead, the veterans associations glorified their war experience, which they both represented as incommunicable and as having tremendous political import for postwar society. Beyond this vague but powerful notion that society had to be radically transformed, these associations often embraced very different political stances, ranging from pacifism to Communism and fascism, and depending largely on the national, political, and economic context in which they functioned. But what they all had in common was the sense that they had learned something in war that could not be grasped by those who had not been there. Hence their effort not only to endow the war with meaning but to employ their shared experience as a tool to mold the future.

The Community of Suffering

The interplay between veterans associations, state policies, and individual mourning worked to create different attitudes toward war in France and Germany.[13] Paradoxically, while defeated Germany ultimately came to celebrate war as an occasion for individual and collective glory, in victorious France its perception as a site of personal and national suffering only intensified. The strand of veterans' conceptualizations of the front as an opportunity to surpass the individual and discover the community of battle and fate *through* common sacrifice became increasingly prevalent in Germany; whereas in France it was the veterans' insistence on their right and duty to fight *against* war, having seen its true face and realized its inhumanity, that won the day. Thus the aftermath of World War I produced two kinds of (imagined) communities, whose common experience was articulated very differently, and whose glorification in their respective countries lent a great deal of weight to national perceptions of destruction. The French *community of suffering* was unified by common pain and sorrow, bound together by horror, determined to prevent such wars from ever happening again. The German *battle community* was united through sacrifice and devotion to a common cause, the comradeship of warriors, and the quest to extend its newly found values to postwar civilian society. Both creatures of war, the community of suffering envisions a future without international conflict, whereas the battle community perceives the front as a model for posterity. For both the present is a battleground between past trauma and future hopes, but they pull in opposite directions. Imbued with a missionary zeal, the one fights for prevention, the other for reenactment. For the one, war is hell; for the other, it is destiny. For the French, the front equals senseless destruction; for the Germans, the destruction of others would bring about their own resurrection. The community of suffering glorifies endurance and survival; the battle community ennobles comradeship and death.

The *anciens combattants* (French war veterans) venerated soldiers and abhorred war. This had a major impact on French conduct during the interwar period and following the debacle of 1940. The inability to envision another war as anything but an even worse butchery than 1914–18 was embodied by Marshal Henri Philippe Pétain, the single most influential military figure in France throughout these years. A staunch advocate of defensive strategy during the 1920s and 1930s, Pétain eventually formed the collaborationist Vichy regime. If he personified the glory of World War I as the "victor" of the Verdun bloodbath in 1916, Pétain owed much of his popularity, and his promotion to supreme commander of the army, to his acceptance of soldiers' demands to cease suicidal frontal attacks in the wake of the disastrous Chemin des Dames offensive and the subsequent mutiny of 1917.[14] Consequently, Pétain came to be seen as a soldiers' general, who, like so many of the men under his command, refused to contemplate the prospect of yet another massacre.

For most of the French, therefore, the ultimate justification for World War I was that it would remain *la der des ders,* the war that put an end to all wars. To be sure, not everyone shared this view; there were those who glorified war as the supreme test of individual manhood and national greatness, and as the appropriate arena for purging undesirable weaklings and foreigners and elevating the warrior to his rightful position in society and politics. But such fascist aestheticization of destruction and promotion of the warring state was relatively rare among interwar veterans, soldiers, politicians, and intellectuals alike, both on the Right and the Left.[15] Ironically, following the debacle of 1940, fascists and pacifists alike could be found among the collaborationists. The near unanimous support for Vichy and collaboration with the Germans in the first months after the debacle had a variety of reasons, ranging from admiration for Nazi Germany and contempt for the decadent republic, to a sincere belief that it was better to make peace with the devil than to continue the war. It took the combined effects of mass deportations of Jews, beginning in summer 1942, the German occupation of the Free Zone in November of the same year, and especially growing economic hardship and the forced conscription of labor to Germany in 1943 to finally tarnish the glory of Pétain and all that he stood for. It was only at this point that France's fields of glory came to be increasingly populated by the Resistance, personified by yet another soldier, General Charles de Gaulle.[16]

The Battle Community

Germany experienced the aftermath of World War I as an unmitigated disaster. Apart from the tremendous cost in lives, the Reich's overseas empire was lost along with large tracts of its European territories, the Kaiser was gone, and the newly established Weimar Republic signed what most Germans considered a humiliating peace treaty that compelled it to pay huge reparations and severely restricted its military. The sailors' and soldiers' mutinies, the revolutions in Berlin and other cities, the ensuing civil strife and spiraling inflation, all made for a picture of chaos and disintegration. And yet, from the midst of despair, a new notion of German glory and greatness began to emerge. Central to this process were not only the veterans associations but even more important the Freikorps formations, paramilitary units that roamed Germany in the early years of the postwar period, composed of former soldiers and youngsters who had just missed service in the war. Engaged in vicious fighting against their domestic enemies in the cities and their foreign enemies along the former Reich's eastern frontiers, these heirs of a long freebooter tradition attributed their despair to peacetime conditions rather than to the suffering of war and perceived their identity as meaningful only within the context of the *Kampfgemeinschaft*. On one level, this "battle community" was constituted only of one's direct comrades in the unit; but on a more abstract level, it included all those multitudes of men who had shared the same frontline experiences and came to see the world, and their role in it, through the prism of struggle, sacrifice, and destruction. Furthermore, the *Kampfgemeinschaft* soon came to be defined in a manner that excluded from it those veterans who embraced different political views or were not considered "truly" German. This referred mainly to the Jews, whose own nationalist veterans association consequently became increasingly isolated. Conversely, the battle community included men who had not taken part in the war and shared the front experience by sheer force of their convictions and imagination, combining the requisite physical qualities with a similar view of the world. Thus the *Fronterlebnis,* the experience of the front, was not an objective event, but rather, as Ernst Jünger called it, an "inner experience" (*inneres Erlebnis*) available only to those of the right persuasion, sensibilities, and ultimately "race," and containing the potential of being extended in time well beyond the war generation. The postwar conceptualization of the *Kampfgemeinschaft* therefore became the core of the *Volksgemeinschaft,* the national, or "racial" community whose frontlines were populated by the battle-hardened political soldiers of the extreme right and the fledgling Nazi movement. For these men, Germany's fields of glory led from the trenches of 1914–18 to the struggle of the *Volk* for its future greatness, to be waged with equal devotion and comradeship, sacrifice and ruthlessness.[17]

The notion of destruction was of course central to this worldview in its many variations; shared in the 1920s by a relatively small but growing minority, by the 1930s it was widely disseminated as a central tenet of the Nazi regime. The terrible devastation of World War I, while it justified calls for retribution, was also perceived as clearing the way for a better future, not least because it made for the emergence of a "new man" out of the debris of the past, a warrior much better equipped for the tasks of a new Germany.[18] Intoxicated by the reality and aesthetics of destruction, these men saw war as a sure instrument to sweep away the weak and the degenerate, making room for the brave and the pure. The trenches had taught humanity that life is war and war is life, that violence brought out the best qualities in man, and that only the ruthless application of violence would propel one to the higher spheres of existence. The fact that many Germans were just as terrified and disgusted by the carnage of the war as other Europeans only served to enhance the vehemence with which such views were propagated. Moreover, this powerful undercurrent of extremism reflected a far more prevalent preoccupation with violence on both sides of the political divide, ranging from the conservatives to the Communists. Even the most explicit antiwar imagery of such artists as Otto Dix and George Grosz reveals a brutal strain, a fascination with depravity, mutilation, and inhumanity generally absent from representations of war in France.

This is of course most evident in German World War I veteran Ernst Jünger, the tone and ideological import of whose writings on the war distinguishes them from most other popular accounts of life and death in the trenches. Thus, for instance, French writer Henri Barbusse's novel *Under Fire* (1916) presents the war in collective moral and political terms: the slaughter at the front heralds the beginning of a new world in which the downtrodden rise against the powerful and establish universal social justice, thereby finally bringing an end to war and suffering. A compatriot of Barbusse, Roland Dorgelès strikes a more melancholy chord in his wartime novel *Wooden Crosses* (1919). Here, too, the close-knit group of soldiers is extolled, but not only does the author lament its progressive destruction at the front, he also follows its survivors as they find themselves denied or abandoned by their loved ones in the rear and rejected by an indifferent postwar world. This atmosphere of regret and disillusionment also characterizes German veteran writer Erich Maria Remarque's best-seller, *All Quiet on the Western Front* (1929), as well as his subsequent, less well-known novels on the "lost generation." While Remarque's celebration of comradeship demonstrates his affinity with the exponents of the *Kampfgemeinschaft,* his focus is the loss of innocence, as the group of comrades is decimated and the individual is mentally and physically annihilated. It is, indeed, through the prism of Remarque's tale of heroes betrayed and victimhood uncompensated that generations of readers first encountered the carnage of 1914–18.

Jünger is an entirely different case. His *Storm of Steel* (1922) is an acute and powerful portrayal of the emergence of the new, modern warrior, from the mechanical and faceless destruction in the trenches. He does not lament his fallen comrades and feels no regret for the loss of innocence. For Jünger the individual is wholly autonomous; and it is during the war, in the midst of devastation, that he discovers his freedom, his inner strength and "essence," and rises from the destruction whole and purified. But in Jünger's universe, World War I is only the point of departure, a necessary baptism by fire in which he acquires knowledge about himself and humanity that must then be employed by, indeed imposed on, the postwar world, as his later writings indicate. In some respects, Jünger's new man is the embodiment of the Nazi ideal; yet his early rejection of the *Kampfgemeinschaft,* bred by his individualistic heroism and innate elitism, made him into an ambivalent and somewhat skeptical observer of the fictions and realities of the emerging *Volksgemeinschaft.* Nevertheless Jünger relished his iconic status in Nazi imagery and rhetoric, and was in turn fascinated by the Third Reich's immense destructive energies. His long-term impact on subsequent generations, however, should be sought in his ability for detached observation of unmediated horror and his curious mix of cold reason and almost uncontrollable passion in the face of destruction, a state of mind that came to be idealized by the Wehrmacht's combat officers and even more so by the SS. Because of Jünger's fascination with naked violence, the pleasures of causing and submitting to pain, he straddles the line between nihilism, fascism, and postmodernism, articulating the enormous appeal of modern industrial destruction as event and image, memory and anticipation: destruction on such a monumental scale that it fills one with awe, even while being devoured by it.

War Imagined

As in France, Germans too associated traditional military glory with generals; but the circumstances of war and politics were meanwhile radically transformed. During the last two years of the war, Germany was largely controlled by Field Marshal Paul von Hindenburg and General Erich Ludendorff, whose "silent dictatorship" combined tradition and modernity.[19] Seen by the conservatives after the fall of the monarchy as an ersatz Kaiser, Hindenburg had the same predilection as Pétain to "make a gift of his person" by offering himself as Germany's savior in time of war and crisis, even if it meant returning from retirement on the brink of senility. But unlike Pétain, his paternalism was geared to conquest and expansion, not to preventing yet another slaughter. Nor was he a soldiers' general; to the contrary, he helped launch the career of the man he derisively called the "Bohemian corporal," who personified the frontline soldier yet eventually became supreme commander of the army. Moreover, Pétain had no Ludendorff at his side—for Ludendorff was a man who formulated and strove to implement the concept of total war on the military, political, psychological, and economic fronts during World War I (ultimately articulated in his 1935 book, *Total War*), along with such officers as General Wilhelm Groener and Colonel Max Bauer.[20] Both a relentless technician and a political extremist, Ludendorff made up for the qualities lacking in Hindenburg, behind whose stature as Prussian warlord he devised modern warfare. It is no coincidence that Ludendorff appears again on the scene during Hitler's Munich Beer Hall Putsch of 1923 (in which he showed more courage than his Nazi colleagues).[21] For him war was destiny, all encompassing and unavoidable, but rather than a mythical, chivalrous encounter, it had to be waged by mobilizing all the energy and organizational sophistication of the modern industrial state. Behind him was a younger generation of gifted staff officers who emerged in the 1930s as Hitler's generals. Professional, modern in outlook, and ruthless, these men were dedicated to making a new kind of war that would reverse the outcome of 1914–18 and reconceptualize the relationship between war and the state.[22] And behind them was an even younger group of men, many of whom had missed service in the war, who became the chief organizers of the Nazi police state and the genocide of the Jews, both of which they deemed an essential component of winning the next war.[23]

To be sure, World War I had produced a whole crop of young officers devoted to designing a new type of modern, violent, and decisive warfare: De Gaulle in France, Basil Liddell Hart and J. F. C. Fuller in Britain, M. N. Tukhachevskii in the Soviet Union, and Guilio Douhet in Italy. To some extent, this seemed a reasonable reaction to the terrible stalemate on the Western Front. Indeed, along with the expanded use of aircraft and armor, new strategies and tactics were already being developed and partly employed in the latter phases of the war. These included Ludendorff's infiltration tactics, using storm battalions (of which Jünger was a member) that prefigured future elite units, Marshal Ferdinand Foch's similar offensive tactics, and Fuller's brilliant though unrealized "Plan 1919," which in many ways heralded the Wehrmacht's Blitzkrieg strategy twenty years later. But in Germany the notion of combining new strategies with a total reorganization of state and society went much further, thanks to the traditionally greater role of the army in politics and the continuing influence of military elites in the Weimar Republic, the intellectual glorification and aestheticization of battle, the powerful urge to reverse the humiliating outcome of the war, and the rampant extremism and violence of the republic's early and final years. The progression from Alfred von Schlieffen's concept of a *Vernichtungsschlacht* (battle of annihilation) in the early 1900s to the realities of *Vernichtungskrieg* (war of extermination) in the 1940s was neither inevitable nor, in retrospect, entirely fortuitous.[24] The German concept of war as an exercise in total destruction emanated from a complex of ideas about the relationship between the individual and the collective; it postulated the militarization of society and the organization of the state as a tool for waging war.[25] Such ideas were not foreign to other countries. But in the initial phases of World War II, the Nazi state and the Wehrmacht employed them better than anyone else. By the end of the war, however, all major combatant nations had learned the rules of total destruction. The Third Reich was crushed by enemies who had acquired its own methods of waging war, and if they did not match the Nazi dedication to extermination, they could muster far greater resources of men and matériel. The devastation of Europe and the murder of millions of citizens was testimony to the triumph of the new concept of war.

The Nazis gave the veterans a new sense of pride in the war they had lost and promised those who had missed the fighting their share of glory in a future struggle that would make Germany great again. Much as racist and eugenicist ideas were crucial to its ideology, Nazism must be viewed within the context of the war's traumatizing effects as well as with the notion of the "new man" that sprouted out of the trenches. All other attempts to endow the carnage of 1914–18 with a higher meaning were ultimately appropriated and put to political use by the Nazis, and no one was more adept at this than Hitler. For millions of Germans, Hitler came to symbolize the unknown soldier of World War I. It is no coincidence that during World War II he donned a simple uniform rather than fabricating an elaborate generalissimo's costume, thereby underlining his affinity with the *Frontschweine* ("grunts") on the line. Hitler was the soldier who had come back from the dead, from anonymity and oblivion, from neglect and abandonment. What Hindenburg failed to understand was that this contemptible corporal represented for innumerable forgotten soldiers the kind of leader who knew what they had been through, spoke their language (admittedly with an Austrian accent), shared their phobias and prejudices, and yet proved that it was possible to survive, rise to prominence, and ultimately wreak vengeance on all those foreign and domestic enemies at the root of the inexplicable catastrophe that had deprived their sacrifice and devotion of all sense and meaning. It was the Führer who resurrected Germany's fields of glory by personifying the forgotten soldier and acting out his rage and frustration.[26]

The Honor of Faith

Following Hitler's "seizure of power" (which he actually attained by being appointed chancellor by the president as leader of the largest party in parliament), the new Wehrmacht, established in March 1935 as a conscript army in defiance of the Versailles Treaty, began the process of binding together all these different strands: the Prussian tradition represented by Hindenburg and the conservative elite; the technological, technocratic, and organizational concepts of Ludendorff and his ambitious young disciples; the veterans' ethos of the *Kampfgemeinschaft;* and Hitler's notion of the "new man," the resurrected unknown soldier, committed to the destruction of Germany's domestic and foreign, political and "biological" enemies who had allegedly stabbed Germany in the back on the brink of victory in 1918. The new leaders of the Wehrmacht had all been junior and middle-ranking officers in World War I. Devastated by the defeat, they had spent the intervening years vegetating in unpromising careers in the Weimar Republic's 100,000-man Reichswehr, dreaming of the day of reckoning.[27] Now their time had come; given the opportunity of personal advancement and national aggrandizement by Hitler, they were not about to relent. In complete agreement with the Führer, they were convinced that as a precondition for victory they had to instill a new spirit into their fresh recruits, combining traditional patriotism

with National Socialist teaching, a glorification of war and a determination to wipe out the enemy at home and abroad.[28]

The extraordinary motivation and resilience of the Wehrmacht
during World War II was thus a function of its perception of war as
an opportunity to rectify the errors of 1914–18 and redress the abom-
ination of defeat. But unlike the French, who envisioned the next
war as a repetition of the last, German conduct took a radically different course. Paradoxically, while French war plans were based on
a perfectly rational analysis of 1914–18, the German tendency to take
the Great War's myth of the battle community at face value contributed in no small measure to the Wehrmacht's élan.[29] To be sure,
many practical lessons from 1914–18 were applied to tactics and strategy in World War II. But the emphasis on re-creating a tight-knit
community of warriors, wholly dedicated to its members and to the
nation, became a fundamental tenet in the organization and indoctrination of the Wehrmacht, while the belief that the army had been
betrayed by the "November criminals" of 1918 introduced a unique
brutality and vindictiveness to military conduct. Moreover both the
motivation and the ruthlessness of the soldiers were tremendously
influenced also by Hitler's repeated references to himself as a frontline soldier who had firsthand knowledge of the realities of combat,
as well as by his much publicized obsession with annihilating both real
and imaginary enemies. His impact on the troops was manifested by
their devotion to him until very late in the war, just as much as by their
massive participation in the implementation of Germany's policies of
subjugation, devastation, plunder, and extermination. Hitler represented to the troops both their fathers, mythologized as the heroic
and tragic warriors of World War I, and themselves, the hopeless,
desperate, and tough *Landser* (simple soldiers), wreaking revenge on
a "world of enemies." Remarkably, despite his extremely rare visits to
the front, Hitler was increasingly seen by the troops as their only true
(but omnipotent) representative in the Reich's leadership.[30]

There is an understandable reluctance to concede that German
soldiers fought out of conviction, that they truly believed themselves
to be part of a glorious, "world-historical" undertaking. Many prefer
to view them as coerced by a dictatorial regime, united by fear of their
superiors and enemies, and motivated by loyalty to their "primary
group" and a sheer will to survive. All such explanations have one
thing in common—they largely ignore the troops' own self-perception
and understanding of their actions. For whatever the purchase of
various theories on motivation, one crucial element in the reality of the
war was the manner in which it was perceived and interpreted by

those who made it happen. What we need to understand is that the Wehrmacht's soldiers saw the world through very different eyes from our own. Our disbelief that acts of murder, wanton destruction, and ruthless plunder could be perceived as glorious may reflect our humanistic sentiments, but also exposes the limits of our moral universe and imagination: the troops' distorted perceptions cannot be retroactively corrected by our own.

If after World War I the reality of defeat was repressed by a great deal of talk about the community of battle, the army's complicity in criminal actions was obscured after 1945 by a rhetoric of suffering and victimhood. To be sure, in the 1950s German mainstream magazines still carried pictures of handsome, tired, but undefeated officers and men, revealing a male ideal that for a while continued to compete with the new image of youthful rebels popularized by Hollywood melodramas.[31] But such representations of heroic soldiers were gradually relegated to publications for veterans and military history buffs. The conventional image that came to dominate the German media and scholarship in the early postwar decades was of the simple soldier as an increasingly disillusioned victim of circumstances beyond his control, fighting a hopeless battle against unequal odds, and in no way responsible for the crimes committed "behind the army's back" by the SS and the Gestapo. Speaking of the war as a glorious undertaking became highly unfashionable, although the fighting against the Red Army always retained a certain aura of desperate resistance to evil.[32]

Yet during the war things appeared very differently. There is little doubt that not all the men who served in the Wehrmacht sympathized with the regime or wanted to fight. Many combat soldiers shared the sentiment of their World War I predecessors that the ample propaganda material disseminated to their units was mere eyewash concocted by people who had never been to the front. But the majority of the troops did not fight with such remarkable determination merely as cynical survivalists. As their own letters, diaries, frontline journals, and memoirs clearly indicate, they were strongly motivated by an image of battle as a site of glory precisely because it was harsh, pitiless, and deadly.[33] That their sacrifice was not given sufficient public recognition after the war embittered many of them.[34] But postwar testimonies and accounts, interviews and oral histories, and public and private encounters have repeatedly demonstrated over the years that veterans still cherish their memory of the good and glorious fight and feel offended, challenged, and enraged when it is suggested that they were part of a vast criminal undertaking.[35] The

longevity of this resistance to the overwhelming evidence of the
Wehrmacht's crimes tells us a great deal about the efficacy of the
soldiers' self-perception, their view of the enemy, and their understanding of Germany's mission in determining their conduct and
molding its memory.

In trying the grasp how glory on the battlefield was conceptualized, we must understand that conventional distinctions between
heroism and comradeship, and what we would normally describe as
atrocities and war crimes, were not perceived in the same manner
at the time (although individual soldiers occasionally did make such
distinctions). Especially during the war against the Soviet Union,
and in the latter phases of the war in other parts of Europe, soldiers
were told and in most cases seem to have believed that fighting enemy troops was as honorable as murdering political commissars,
massacring Jews, wiping out villages in acts of collective punishment,
and shooting outright or starving to death prisoners of war.[36] As
early as 1939 the Wehrmacht's leadership insisted that the honor of
the German officer depended on his firm National Socialist bearing
(*Haltung*), and as of summer 1941 the implications of this were manifested on a vast scale. By the end of the war, Germany's fields of glory
were strewn with the corpses of its political and "biological" enemies.
Repeatedly exhorted to remember that this was a war of ideologies
aimed at exterminating the Judeo-Bolshevik enemy who had caused
the collapse of 1918, and that taking pity on seemingly innocent victims was tantamount to betraying the *Volk* (nation or race), the troops
came to view their criminal actions as the very essence of military
glory, as exacting a just and necessary retribution for past defeats and
humiliations and thereby ensuring the final victory.

As the war wore on, it is true that anything that smacked of propaganda emanating from the "green desks" of staff officers in the rear
or Goebbels's ministry was viewed with suspicion by the troops. Yet
those elements of the regime's ideology and policies that coincided
with the views and prejudices internalized by the troops even before
their conscription were not thought of as propaganda, but rather as
accurate statements about and actions relevant to their role and mission in the war. Hence soldiers' letters to family and friends described
their actions at the front in almost identical terms to those employed
by the regime's propaganda. Most revealingly, the troops' perception
of the enemy as diabolical led them to ascribe their own atrocities
to Bolshevik savagery and Jewish criminality, and to portray mass
killings of civilians as a glorious final reckoning with foes who had
been poised to inflict untold barbarities on the German *Volk*. While

the army tried to justify its actions also with conventional arguments, citing security concerns, partisan activity, and civilian resistance, one is struck by the extent to which soldiers expressed pride and satisfaction in finally being able to destroy their enemies, be they soldiers, prisoners, civilians, or, provoking the greatest glee, Jewish men, women, and children. It was at this point that massacre and glory became synonymous.[37]

In the case of the SS, the equivalence of genocide and glory was the very core of its identity. The motto of the Black Corps was "SS man, Your Honor is Loyalty" (*SS-Mann, Deine Ehre heisst Treue*). The German term *Treue,* which also means faith, crucially linked personal honor with an unflinching devotion to Hitler's person and Weltanschauung. And since the Führer was said to have ordered the extermination of the Aryan race's enemies, perpetrating mass murder was transformed into a glorious enterprise. Heinrich Himmler was well aware of the implications of this breathtaking moral inversion. Speaking to SS leaders in October 1943, he noted that the glory of the SS consisted in its ability to carry out genocide while remaining clean and decent; the task was not merely to kill efficiently but to guard against the damage that such actions may cause to the organization's moral fiber. Hence, while genocide was an honorable undertaking, its victims threatened morally to pollute the SS even as they were being massacred. In Himmler's logic, murdering women and children was virtuous, making a personal profit from such actions despicable. Precisely because both Himmler and his audience knew that in reality organized and unauthorized robbery of the victims was an institutionalized component of the "Final Solution," Himmler's rhetoric revealed an awareness of his revolutionary reconceptualization of glory well beyond its mundane manifestations. This concept's long-term polluting effects on humanity as a whole cannot be overestimated. No amount of erasing the traces by exhuming and cremating the murdered, bulldozing the death camps, and planting forests over mass graves would purge our moral universe of this redefinition of ethics and decency.[38]

If World War I had replaced the old notion of chivalry with the sustained industrial killing of nameless soldiers, Nazi Germany invented the glorification of systematic industrial killing of civilians. By now what bound the soldiers together more than their *Kampfgemeinschaft* and its extension in an ostensible *Volksgemeinschaft,* was their awareness of belonging to a *community of murder,* attested to implicitly and explicitly both by the leadership of the Reich and by many of its citizens and soldiers. With defeat looming on the horizon, the knowledge of complicity in horrendous crimes only exacerbated fears of ultimate retribution. But alongside the bonding effects of shared guilt (accompanied by frantic attempts to waive responsibility) came the construction of genocide as a liberating, redemptive act whose centrality for the salvation of humanity need only be recognized by other nations to release the perpetrators from accusations of murder: the realization that even in defeat, Germany had purged the world of the evil that had threatened its very existence.[39] It is this presentation of depravity as morality, guilt as honor, atrocity as heroism, and genocide as redemption that continues to haunt our civilization long after the destruction of Nazism.

In Quest of Glory

World War II was the scene of destruction on an unprecedented scale: from Leningrad to Stalingrad, Warsaw to Auschwitz, Nanjing to Okinawa, Rotterdam and Coventry to Dresden and Hiroshima, the world was seized by a paroxysm of self-obliteration that no single mind could grasp nor could the wildest fantasies encompass. Everywhere millions of soldiers and civilians were burning, torn to shreds, asphyxiated, gassed. And yet in the midst of the horror, almost as if it were the moving engine of this universal *Totentanz,* everyone claimed their share of glory: the soldiers charging the enemy or defending the homeland, the citizens of bombed cities holding out amongst the ruins, the Nazis purging the world of evil, the Jews rising up against their murderers. In this infernal landscape, one nation's damnation was another's redemption, as humanity seemed to seek salvation in the flames of hell.

Once the killing was over, the glory of mutual destruction began to unravel; now new positions had to be staked. For a moment, perhaps, both victors and vanquished were beset by a sense of shame in view of so much human and material devastation. But shame is politically useless and psychologically debilitating. Politics could not stand still, people had to be fed, cities had to be rebuilt, and individual and national identity had to be reconstructed. Hence apologies were (and are still being) made, rationalizations offered, brave new visions propagated, and refashioned unifying fears whipped up. If some of the old enthusiasm was gone, it was still better to seek new fields of glory in the future than to be paralyzed by the horrors of the past.

What made glory such an ambiguous concept in postwar France was not only that many "resisters of the eleventh hour" had previously worked for Vichy but also that the relationship between victimhood, collaboration, and heroism turned out to have been much more problematic than initially conceded. The massacre at Oradour-sur-Glane, which has come to symbolize German barbarism and French martyrdom, is a good example. This punitive action by the Waffen-SS division Das Reich, in reaction to a minor partisan attack, reflected the routinized brutality of a formation that had recently arrived from the Eastern Front, where the Wehrmacht had massacred the inhabitants of tens of thousands of villages and towns. Yet in France, Oradour was the exception rather than the rule, and even its own inhabitants, like those of most other French towns, had hoped to survive the war unscathed. Indeed, as was subsequently the case in several other European communities that had experienced the same fate, rage against the perpetrators was accompanied by a residue of bitterness against the partisans who had allegedly brought about the massacre by attacking the Germans in the first place. The moral ambiguity inherent to this process of rewriting the heroic narrative of resistance to occupation was recently reflected in Tzvetan Todorov's study of the bloodbath that resulted from the takeover of the town of Saint-Amand by the Resistance, an event which to his mind demonstrates the moral equivalence between the resisters and the Milice, the fascist militia of Vichy.[40] Yet such assertions can only serve to justify the passivity of the bulk of the population. Conversely, the paradigmatic narrative of French victimhood at Oradour was confused by the discovery that some of the soldiers involved in the massacre were Alsatians conscripted into the Waffen-SS. Consequently, the French court's decision to hand out lighter sentences to these men than to their German comrades established a distinction between French complicity in murder and Nazi criminality, which ultimately enabled far more influential collaborators to escape justice.[41] It's little wonder that the narrative of France's glorious uprising against the Germans gradually dissipated over the following two decades.

France soon found itself embroiled in very different types of inglorious wars. While colonial conflicts had evolved their own rules and practices over decades of empire building that predated the German occupation, in postwar France it became increasingly difficult to justify the continued subjugation of other peoples while simultaneously celebrating the nation's own liberation from foreign occupation. That the French government employed mainly professional soldiers and mercenaries in the bitter and merciless war in Indochina indicated its realization that much of the population in metropolitan France was either indifferent or opposed to the fighting there. Nor did the disastrous defeat at Dien Bien Phu in 1954, which put an end to the war, add to the popularity of colonial conflicts. The Algerian War was even more complex and contentious, since that former colony, which had been made part of metropolitan France, was inhabited not only by a large indigenous Arab and Berber population but also by hundreds of thousands of French citizens, many of whom had been living there for generations (and were in fact mostly of Italian, Spanish, and Jewish Sephardi extraction).[42] Unable to suppress the FLN (Front de Libération Nationale) uprising with regular forces, the French government resorted to employing conscripts, thereby transforming a colonial war into a national endeavor, about whose goals and methods there was little consensus. Although it was fought in the name of French prestige and world status, as well as for the sake of the colons, the Algerian War brought to France little glory and a great deal of domestic strife. While suppressing a national liberation movement was ideologically repugnant to growing circles in France, abandoning a million *pieds-noirs* (Algerian-born French persons) to Algerian nationalists was also morally distasteful. And if military reverses in operations against Algerian irregulars were humiliating to an army still smarting from the debacles of 1940 and 1954, the practice of torture and collective punishment by elite paratrooper units was unacceptable to many who recalled the brutal methods used by the Germans against the Resistance. The struggle in Algeria could not be won without conscripts; but once they were brought in, the war was doomed, since compulsory service unleashed much greater opposition, just as Vichy's declaration of compulsory labor in Germany had rapidly swelled the ranks of the Resistance in 1943.[43]

Thus the Algerian War became a domestic conflict over what constituted French identity and greatness, glory and honor.[44] Both sides spoke in the name of France's role in the world as a great civilization. But the intellectuals who led a growing movement of protest saw this role as facilitating national independence for colonized peoples. Conversely, the nationalists, who included both the military and not a few patriots identified with the Left, such as the future president François Mitterrand, argued that France could accomplish its civilizing mission only by maintaining its status as a great power, for which holding on to Algeria was essential. Once several renegade colonels threatened to topple the regime at home in the name of greatness and glory, however, it became clear that the complex legacy of Vichy still haunted French politics, since this act brought to mind de Gaulle's own claim that his rebellion against Pétain in 1940 was justified by the higher mission of preserving France from betrayal by its own leaders and reasserting its historical greatness. The question as to who was committing treason—the government that "betrayed" the nation or the rebels who fought to "save" it—raised first after the debacle, was thus posed again in 1961. By now, of course, de Gaulle was on the other side of the barricades, committed to saving France by surrendering Algeria, and it was precisely his prestige as the "liberator" of the nation from its domestic and foreign enemies that enabled him to pull it off. What this struggle within a struggle demonstrated was that two decades after the debacle France had still not found for itself new and more appropriate fields of glory, nor had reached a consensus over what national glory actually meant. One of de Gaulle's greatest achievements was to rationalize this last humiliating defeat and final retreat from imperial grandeur as another instance of French glory, and to set France on a course of modernization and adjustment to new circumstances from which it has benefited ever since.[45]

In 1962 France finally emerged from almost three decades of civil strife and foreign wars, starting with the February 1934 extreme right attack on the National Assembly that provoked fears of an imminent fascist putsch, through the years of division under the Popular Front, the appeasement of the late 1930s, Vichy and the Occupation, the Liberation and the purges, all the way to the wars of decolonization. Even if we stretch this period back to 1914, and extend it forward to encompass the students' revolt of 1968, we can say that many of its protagonists—be they ordinary citizens and soldiers, or prominent politicians, generals, and intellectuals—experienced much or all of it in their lifetime. These were the years of French ignominy and discontent, and they left an ambivalent legacy whose deep imprint can still be felt today. Such an inextricable mix of courage and betrayal, devotion and opportunism makes it exceedingly difficult to look back with a sense of pride or to anticipate the future with confidence. And yet, as it experienced a remarkable economic, political, and cultural revival following the end of the Algerian War, France sought for itself a new sense of purpose and identity rooted in visions of a technologically streamlined future and representations of a glorious past.[46] Ultimately it was the resistance to foreign occupation in 1940–44, and especially the great sacrifice of 1914–18, that were most frequently cited as edifying examples.[47] That these past fields of glory were also sites of mass killing and genocide has meant that France's identity remained infused with memories of atrocity, even though they were invariably interpreted to suit differing ideological or particularist agendas.

The Shield of Honor

For postwar Germans the years of the Third Reich and the devastation of the war were so overwhelming that the more distant events of World War I were often allotted the role of mere historical background to the catastrophe of Nazism.[48] Indeed, precisely this inescapable presence of Nazism has motivated some German scholars and politicians to insist that in order to face the future, their nation had to be given a usable past. And since Hitler's Reich could not be wished out of history, the common strategy to come to terms with its legacy was to relativize it, either by reference to other criminal regimes and genocides, or by shifting the focus to the allegedly positive elements in Nazi society and rejecting the centrality of the Holocaust. Seen by its promoters as a crucial precondition for reestablishing what they deemed a missing sense of national identity, this exercise in rewriting the past unleashed the so-called *Historikerstreit* (historians' controversy) of the mid-1980s.[49] Interestingly, however, while in the early postwar decades German educators often preferred to avoid teaching the Nazi period altogether, rather than confronting its moral dilemmas (and their own complicity), in the 1990s both scholarly and public attention has not only refocused on the Third Reich and the war but has for the first time begun to shift toward a recognition of the pivotal role of the Holocaust in understanding Hitler's Germany.[50] In the wake of reunification, the hopes expressed by some conservative circles that the past would somehow be finally normalized were dashed, and a new generation of scholars is now engaged in a relentless effort to reconstruct its historical realities.

For Germans the transition from national self-glorification in victory to a status of international disgrace in defeat was even more radical and traumatic than in France. To be sure, even during the war many soldiers and civilians remarked that if Germany lost the war, the victors would exact terrible retribution.[51] This anticipation of revenge reflected an internalization of the Nazi line that especially the Jews, who "lurked behind" both the Bolsheviks and the Western "plutocracies," had always wanted to destroy Germany and therefore had to be exterminated. But it also revealed an understanding that Germany was indeed perpetrating horrific crimes that would not go unpunished in case of defeat. As long as the war lasted, the expectation that Germany would be subjected to the same brutalities it had perpetrated on others had a largely galvanizing effect. This inverted view of reality, whereby Germany's most helpless victims were perceived as the greatest threat to its existence, was of course

the result of years of Nazi propaganda, whose own efficacy was derived from deeply rooted antisemitic prejudices in wide sectors of the
German population.[52] Hence, in the last years of the war, a good measure of agreement existed between those increasingly numerous
Germans who knew that crimes were being perpetrated "in their
name" (as the saying went after the war) and the regime that ordered
these policies.[53] Indeed, as I noted above, this circular argumentation
created a bond—often insufficiently recognized—between the regime
and the population, based on the awareness of complicity in crime.

The last years of the Third Reich were experienced and remembered by most Germans as a period of murderous air raids and disastrous defeats, fear and destruction, horror and disillusionment. Yet
the soldiers who fought to the bitter end, the workers who kept producing armaments, the civilians who held out in bombed out cities,
let alone the organizers and perpetrators of genocide, were anything
but hapless victims of forces beyond their control. The defeat of the
Reich was so costly both to its enemies and to its defenders, and was
delayed beyond hope for the vast majority of Jews under Nazi rule,
because the Germans resisted it with great determination, while only
a marginal minority tried to rid the nation of its criminal leadership.
By the latter part of the war, most Germans had become convinced
that they were fighting for their very survival; hence their courage
and self-sacrifice, which was construed at the time, and often subsequently, as a glorious manifestation of a united national will to ward
off destruction by a "world of enemies." Hence, too, the glorification
of genocide, which was subsequently mostly denied or repressed. That
so many memoirs, popular histories, films, and pulp fiction, as well as
more respectable scholarly works, have described the barbarous fighting in the East as constituting a bulwark against "Asiatic barbarism,"
and have insisted on distinguishing between this glorious page in
German history and the genocidal policies that were prolonged by the
army's tenacity, merely indicates the extent to which Nazi propaganda both influenced and reflected widely held public sentiments.[54]
Conversely, while shock and despair, suffering and pain were keenly
felt by Germans at the end of the war, shame seems to have been
largely absent from the emotional landscape of the population.[55]

In 1918 Germans were shocked to discover that the war they were
supposed to be winning had been lost; consequently, they sought the
reason for defeat in treachery at home rather than in enemy superiority. In 1945 the totality of defeat left no room for doubt that its main
cause was overwhelming Allied preponderance. But besides being
forced to recognize the limits of their power, Germans were also

deprived of honor by their foes, who insisted on invalidating the moral value of their sacrifices by asserting that they had served an evil cause. The glorious defense of the homeland was now presented as shameful and incriminating support for a genocidal regime. Vanquished and occupied, struggling to survive in a devastated land, bereft of both basic food staples and political leadership, Germany's population was now expected to acknowledge its complicity in murder. For many young soldiers and Hitler Youth members, the Führer's suicide—and in some cases, however implicitly, the confirmation of rumors about the death camps—was experienced as the "collapse of a whole world."[56] In other words, if 1918 was traumatic because it shattered the glory of national unity—and created the myth of domestic betrayal—1945 was traumatic because it shattered the glory of dedication to a cause and created the myth of obedience and victimhood.

Following the debacle of 1940, most French were initially far too preoccupied with survival to be concerned with the reasons for the defeat, the true nature of Vichy, or the fate of the Jews. So, too, following the "catastrophe" of 1945, Germans were primarily engrossed in fending for themselves. But while the Third Republic had been largely discredited long before the defeat, many Germans had continued believing in Hitler well into the war; hence both his suicide and the criminality of his regime were exceedingly difficult to accept. It seemed therefore best simply not to discuss the issue; instead Germans concentrated on clearing the rubble from their cities and in the process surreptitiously buried the debris of their former beliefs and convictions.[57]

Graves dug in a hurry tend to be shallow; as the seasons change, the corpses may resurface. The thousands of German soldiers killed in Stalingrad still reappear every thaw on the old battlefields, serving as a rich source of souvenirs for the local population.[58] The SS exhumed untold numbers of its Jewish victims in order to erase all signs of its crimes by cremating the bodies; but a genocide on this scale could not be concealed.[59] The Wehrmacht was more successful in covering up its crimes under the facade of a honorably fought patriotic war, not least because most Germans, as well as their new Western Allies, had an interest in preserving this image. But while one tended to remember the statement by the conspirators of July 20, 1944, that they were striving to save the army's shield of honor, one tended to forget that they had resorted to conspiracy and assassination precisely because they could not expect the support of their troops and fellow officers in an open rebellion against Hitler. By then the army's honor

FIGURE 1. Ambiguous heroism. Statue in Berlin commemorating the July 20, 1944, bomb plot against Hitler. Plaques by the monument assert that the conspirators "died for Germany," "did not endure the shame," and gave their lives "for freedom, justice, and honor."

had already been irredeemably tarnished, yet most soldiers and civilians perceived the plot as high treason.[60] The paradoxical outcome was that the conspirators were subsequently presented as a shining example of the officer corps' moral fiber (fig. 1), whereas their complete isolation within their own profession and the population at large was mostly repressed.[61]

From this perspective we can say that the army's shield of honor was more than a metaphor. Considering that close to twenty million men served in its ranks, the Wehrmacht truly represented German society, and its veterans became the founding generation of the two postwar German states. No wonder that the exhibition on the crimes of the Wehrmacht touring Germany and Austria since the mid-1990s has aroused a great deal of anger among conservative circles, who strongly oppose its assertion that there was nothing glorious about Germany's war of extermination in the East and its deep involvement in the Holocaust.[62] To be sure, over the years Wehrmacht veterans have often complained that having first been deceived by the Nazi regime, they were then disowned and rejected by postwar society, without sufficient recognition of their devotion to their comrades, the homeland, and Western civilization as a whole (as its protectors from "Asiatic Bolshevism"). The fact is, however, that the full extent of the Wehrmacht's unsavory record was not exposed for several decades after the end of the war, and even today new documentation on its crimes is still being uncovered.

German attempts to come to terms with the Nazi period were closely linked to the quest for a glorious past. The tortuous nature of this process reflected not only the scarcity of past virtue but also contemporary domestic and foreign politics. Both German leaders and their Western colleagues wanted the Federal Republic to join the emerging anti-Communist coalition as part of Germany's reintegration into the international community. But popular suspicion of Germany in the West and the reluctance of many Germans to become part of a new military alliance made it necessary to create an image of the past that balanced outright rejection of Nazism with empathy for the suffering and sacrifices of the German people. By distancing the Nazi regime from the population, and associating the hardship of the latter with the crimes of the former, Germany was ultimately presented as Hitler's victim, the (Western) Allies as its liberators from Nazi tyranny, and Communism as the continuation of Nazi practices and the perpetual enemy of Germany and democracy. German glory became grounded both in suffering (from war and tyranny) and in opposition to evil (by creating a bulwark against Communism and trying to unseat Hitler). Moreover Hitler was said to have "seized power" rather than gained the support of much of the public, and the genocide of the Jews was described as having been unknown to the German people although falsely presented by the regime as perpetrated in their name. It was thanks to this image that Germany could be reintegrated into Europe as a member of the community of victimhood and heroism. Ironically, the Nazis had used a similar image to legitimize genocide, arguing that Germany had been the victim of the Jews and that Hitler was determined to save the

Reich and the rest of the world from the evil of Judeo-Bolshevism. The difference was, of course, that after the war the glorification of suffering served as a tool for integration rather than confrontation. However, while it contributed to the normalization of the present, it also distorted the past by blurring the distinction between complicity in murder and the victimhood of the murdered.[63]

The tendency to lump together all victims of Nazism and war has been an integral feature of German politics and commemoration. Following German reunification, for instance, the Neue Wache Monument in Berlin was rededicated (after a public controversy) to "the victims of war and tyranny." Thus a direct association was made between Jews murdered in the camps, soldiers who followed Hitler, and civilians killed in the aerial bombing offensive against *Judenrein* (Jew free) cities. Similarly, on the occasion of the fiftieth anniversary of the destruction of Dresden, German President Roman Herzog spoke of that city's fate as an example of suffering and victimhood that could provide the basis for solidarity between the German victims of war and the victims of German genocide. By asserting the unifying effects of victimhood, Herzog ignored the causal links between the stance of the German population and the genocide of the Jews, and between Germany's war of aggression and the bombing of its cities. Instead, he implied that since all victims are by definition innocent, none of them can be burdened with responsibility for victimizing others.[64] The equalizing effects of shared suffering were also employed as a means for reconciliation by American president Ronald Reagan during his 1985 visit to the German military cemetery in Bitburg, where he asserted that German soldiers buried there (who include members of the Waffen-SS) had also been victims of Hitler's regime. Reagan's reluctant visit to the concentration camp Bergen-Belsen, added to his schedule after a good deal of public pressure, only underlined the association between German victims and the victims of the Germans.[65] In this manner the glorification of murder by the Nazis was rescripted as a glorification of suffering: in the first case the killers were glorious avengers of their victimhood; in the second they became helpless victims of the forces of darkness. As for their own victims, they played at best a secondary role in this drama of German fate and destiny, a largely glorious, if also tragic, tale of suffering, survival, and reconstruction. What remained unanswered was who, after all, was not a victim, save for Hitler and his "criminal clique"?

Another case in point is the reestablishment of the military in West Germany. At the end of the war, it seemed inconceivable to Germans and foreigners alike that the armed forces, which had served as Hitler's instrument of conquest and annihilation, would ever be reconstituted. But history knows no *Stunde Null* (zero hour). The wartime tensions between the Western Allies and the Soviet Union culminated in the division of Europe and the Cold War, whose threat was exacerbated by the introduction of nuclear weapons. In these circumstances it seemed impossible to keep Germany disarmed. Chancellor Konrad Adenauer quickly grasped that rearmament presented the Federal Republic with a golden opportunity to reintegrate into the international community as an equal partner. The Western Allies, for their part, hoped to enhance their military capabilities and to draw the line between democracy and Communism on German soil. Despite a fair amount of public opposition both in Germany and abroad, just ten years after the end of World War II, the new Bundeswehr was established without any major hitches.[66]

Although within a few years it became one of the best military organizations in Europe, the Bundeswehr, whose command cadres were recruited from among veterans of the Wehrmacht, was faced with a difficult dilemma. For the new national army was called on to reflect the Federal Republic's asserted status as the sole legitimate successor state of historical Germany and simultaneously to demonstrate a total break with everything that German militarism and Nazism had stood for. This led to the introduction of *Innere Führung* (literally, "inner leadership"), according to which the army would serve as a school of democracy and citizenship to its conscripts, rather than foster blind obedience and political extremism. In this manner the Bundeswehr hoped to maintain the traditional role of the army in Germany as the "school of the nation" but to drastically transform the content of its teaching so as to bring it in line with Western values and political concepts. However, if the rigidly hierarchical structure and disciplinary needs of any army are hardly conducive to democratic thinking, in the Bundeswehr matters were further complicated by the assumption that esprit de corps and motivation must be established on the firm foundation of the German military tradition. Interpretations of the army's heritage obviously depended on one's political stance, and those who supported its continued glorification argued that it was precisely traditional values that had made the Wehrmacht immune to Nazism and thus a "haven" from Hitler's regime. Though entirely false, this assertion fit nicely into the ruling conservative elite's depiction of Nazism as an example of the dire consequences that can be expected from breaking with the "good old" tradition of clearly defined gender roles in the family, adherence to religious faith, respect to authority, and patriotism. Hence the Bundeswehr could insist on Germany's past military glory as a model for its new recruits, while rejecting any suggestion that the Wehrmacht had been implicated in the regime's criminal policies. That the Red Army remained Germany's main enemy made it all the easier to draw positive links between the Bundeswehr and the Wehrmacht as fulfilling the role of a "bulwark against Communism," and to repress the army's past or at least relativize it by reference to Soviet criminality.[67] By now, of course, the passage of time and the end of the Cold War have facilitated a much more open public discussion of the Wehrmacht's inglorious past. Yet Germany has also seen a great deal of opposition to such alleged attempts to "besmirch" the army's shield of honor. More than half a century after the fall of the Third Reich and a decade after reunification, the myth of the Wehrmacht's "purity of arms" still plays an important role in the ongoing process of constructing postwar German national identity.[68]

The agreement to pay restitution to the victims of the Holocaust constituted another facet of this same process. Politically, the decision on *Wiedergutmachung* by the Adenauer administration had the same rationale of legitimizing the new German state, this time by means of partial, and strictly financial, atonement for the crimes of its predecessor. For obvious reasons the Federal Republic was loath to accept direct responsibility for acts committed by Hitler's Germany; and yet it maintained unbroken links with a good share of the Third Reich's legislative and administrative legacy, and employed numerous former Nazis as civil servants. This delicate balance between continuity and change made it necessary to settle the issue of the genocide of the Jews without alienating the survivors while avoiding any pronouncements or steps that might undermine the legitimacy of the new German state. The restitution agreement accomplished this by compensating the Jews for what was never accepted as more than crimes committed "in the name of the German people." Although Adenauer's opponents argued that his decision implied accepting a measure of responsibility, in fact it was precisely this ambivalence that facilitated the new state's integration both into the course of German history and into the international community, making for the historical and political legitimacy it required to normalize its existence. Moreover, by ostensibly compensating the victims of another state and regime, postwar Germans acquired a new sense of self-respect and national honor, while non-Germans, including many Jews, also saw this act with a measure of appreciation. To be sure, many Holocaust survivors viewed restitution merely as an attempt by Germany to wash its hands of guilt with bribes of money, and in Israel the decision to accept reparations led to widespread demonstrations and riots that came close to toppling the government. Conversely, in Germany the argument could be heard that having squeezed so much money out of German pockets the Jews were no longer in a position to make any further moral demands on postwar Germany or to accuse it of the sins of the Third Reich. But overall Adenauer's policy proved a resounding success, all the more remarkable considering its inherent contradictions. If the Bundeswehr's *Innere Führung* enabled it to rely on the German military tradition without tarnishing its newly forged shield of honor, the policy of *Wiedergutmachung* enabled the Federal Republic to construct itself as the successor state of historical Germany without being tainted by the crimes of its predecessor.[69]

To be sure, as numerous observers have noted over the years, the past—by which is meant the Nazi past—will not pass. Indeed, despite some predictions to the contrary, more than a decade after the *Historikerstreit* German debates on the Third Reich have lost none of their vehemence. Both those who insist that Germans must finally put the past behind them and those who urge to recognize the centrality of the Holocaust for German history are ultimately concerned with the impact of the nation's heritage on its contemporary self-perception and politics. This question came up with particular intensity following reunification, when West Germans showed remarkable zeal in purging East Germany of what some called the Communist equivalent of Nazi ideological and institutional pollution.[70] By piling up the fresh debris of Communism over the rotting remnants of the Third Reich, it seemed for a while that these two very different systems would become indistinguishable, indeed, that the more recent injustices of the former would obscure the mass crimes of the latter. One had the impression that in purging Communists accused of victimizing Germans, the Federal Republic was trying to compensate for its failure to punish the Nazi murderers of an incomparably larger number of non-Germans, non-"Aryans," "asocials," and the "unfit." Yet this last effort to domesticate and make political use of victimhood failed once more, as a new debate over the complicity of the German population in the genocide of the Jews demonstrated the extent to which the Holocaust has remained, or rather become, the crucial point of departure for any attempt to construct a modern German identity rooted in history.

This does not mean that there is any consensus on the place of the Holocaust in, or its importance for, German history, but only that by now no debate on the German past can avoid confronting this event.

Indeed, at the root of the German controversy over Daniel Jonah Gold-hagen's book *Hitler's Willing Executioners* was a question that went well beyond the actual events of the Holocaust, concerning as it did the very foundations of a culture that ultimately produced genocide.[71] Here the public was compelled to face up not only to the horror of mass murder by "ordinary men" (or Germans) but also to inquire after its links to precisely those more glorious aspects of the past that were employed as positive reference points in the creation of a post-Nazi nation. What threatened the conceptualization of German identity as an expression of national history was the argument that German culture had long been imbued with antisemitism and had developed "eliminationist" traits and genocidal predilections before Hitler ever appeared on the scene. This was also the reason for the endorsement of the book by the sociologist Jürgen Habermas, who has argued for years that German identity must be based not on the past but rather on loyalty to its democratic constitution.[72] Hence too the universal acclaim with which the simultaneous publication of Victor Klemperer's diaries was greeted.[73] A converted and patriotic German Jew, Klemperer managed to remain in Germany through-out Hitler's twelve-year rule largely thanks to his "Aryan" wife. This posthumously published day-by-day account of life in the Third Reich revealed the complexities of German society and prejudices that Gold-hagen's simplistic portrayal had obscured. Moreover, Klemperer's allegiance to German culture, despite his personal experiences, ful-filled a deep need in contemporary German readers, for in a painfully paradoxical manner, pride in German culture was now legitimized by a representative of those who had been brutally deprived of any share in it. To be sure Klemperer's diaries also demonstrated in great detail the penetration of Nazi ideas into society and the progressive marginalization of German Jews long before the Holocaust. From this perspective his account could also have been the cause of pro-found shame, for his refusal to give up the one thing that could not be taken away from him, his pride in his identity, tells us more about his own courage than about his society's virtues. But this aspect of the diaries was given less prominence in the public discussion of the book: this is merely another way of saying that shame and glory are in the eyes of the beholder.

2

GRAND
ILLUSIONS

Fantasies of glory breed traumatic disillusionment. Opening the century with a wave of exhilaration, World War I swiftly
transformed Europe's mental landscape into a site of mourning and
anxiety, loss and trauma. First the scar of trenches stretching across the
continent and then the vast, symmetrical cemeteries, which rendered
a semblance of aestheticized order to the slaughter, have become
embedded in Europe's collective consciousness. The illusion of glory
became the reality of atrocity. And yet disillusionment from romantic
visions of heroism and sacrifice was accompanied by even grander,
more reckless, and more destructive illusions. The carnage and genocide of World War II that followed did more than shatter the dreams
of military and national greatness; it dealt a lethal blow to the very idea
of shared humanity. Having torn out of its midst millions upon millions of its own people, inverted and perverted every value and belief,
exploited to the limit humanity's willingness to sacrifice itself for a
higher cause in order to perpetrate the most heinous crimes, the war
has left us with a legacy of gaping absences of memory and identity,
culture and biography. Half a century later we are still groping for a
way to come to terms with the belated effects of this trauma, even as
its last witnesses are leaving the stage. Bereft of heroes and ideals, we
are haunted by nightmares of catastrophe, as the gallant tales of the
past turn out to have been nothing but smoke and mirrors.

The Widow's Lament

On December 13, 1927, at 10:15 A.M., Marie-Pauline Murati, a war
widow, attempted to kill the mayor of Toulon, Emile Claude, in the

course of an interview in his office at the town hall. According to the account given by M. Berry, the head clerk at the mayor's office, Mme Murati was the last of three ladies to have been shown into M. Claud's office that morning. Mme Murati, thirty-five years old, entered the office leaving the door ajar. M. Berry, however, who was still on the landing, pushed the door shut for reasons of discretion.

As he did so he heard the sound of quick steps, followed by calls for help from M. Claude. M. Berry pushed the door open, entered the room, and was confronted by an unexpected and tragic spectacle: Mme Murati, clutching a long knife in her hand, was ferociously striking M. Claude on his face, neck, and chest. The mayor, covered with blood, tried to escape the attacker, but she chased him around his desk, arm raised in the air. At this point M. Berry leaped at the would-be assassin, immobilized her, and, following a fierce struggle, managed to disarm her. "Unfortunate woman! What are you doing?" he reportedly said to her. Beside herself, her hands red with blood, Mme Murati cried at him, "Let me go! Let me go!" M. Claude, blinded by the blood streaming from one of his wounds, now approached the woman and asked her: "What have I done to you?" to which she responded furiously: "I've been martyred for too long, it's become a scandal. That's what it is!" "Better say that it's an assassination!" M. Berry said to her, at which point the woman suddenly turned pale and fell unconscious on the carpet.

Though stabbed four times, M. Claude swiftly recovered from his injuries. Mme Murati, it was reported, had acted under the spell of a mental crisis, or temporary insanity, to which she had frequently succumbed since the death of her husband, a lieutenant in the colonial infantry, from wounds sustained in battle. While Mme Murati was held in detention and undergoing mental examination by the forensic pathologist Doctor Ernest Rapuc, a search of her domicile uncovered letters written by her to the public prosecutor (the equivalent of a district attorney), and several journalists, in which she wrote: "I pass my days crying; I have looked for the reason in vain. I finally know that it is because strange things are happening in Toulon, and it is necessary to punish the abusers and defend the truth."[1]

In 1927 the film *Napoléon vu par Abel Gance* was first screened. But the images that haunted Mme Murati were most probably not those of Gance's celebrated triptych, which in a fit of (artistic) rage he had once tried to destroy. Napoleon's melancholy and tragic greatness as seen by this proponent of artistic suffering does not seem to have been of central concern to the French of the interwar period. Rather, it was images of meaningless, horrible death, boundless, inexplicable suffering, inarticulate rage, madness, and violence that surfaced in innumerable forms and means of expression during an era of recovery from one massacre and growing anxiety with the approach of another. This was not a good time for Napoleon, not even when projected on three screens simultaneously. It was a time of guilt, accusation, and fear. Gance's *J'accuse* (1919), with its terrifying image of dead soldiers rising from their graves, and Raymond Bernard's *Les Croix de bois* (1931), based on the novel by Dorgelès, in which a soldier becomes mad at the moment of attack, reflected much better the atmosphere of the period and people's attitudes to war.[2]

These were not merely artistic hallucinations and creative fantasies. World War I had produced a reality that few minds of the belle Epoque could have conjured up. Both the nature and the scale of the killing stretched the boundary between sanity and madness, perception and distortion to the limit. Mme Murati's fit of rage and madness, whatever its specific causes, must be viewed within the context of postwar (and interwar) France. Strange things were happening in Toulon; perhaps the strangest of all was the attempt to go back to normality, to forget the events and erase the images that had scarred the consciousness of so many Europeans in the slaughterhouse of the front. Was a war widow's plea for attention to her suffering madder than society's indifference? Was her violence less legitimate than that which had taken so many lives only a few years before?[3]

Strange Defeat

The main illusion of the interwar period in France was that another war could somehow be averted.[4] Since the debacle of 1940 the central question has been, What brought about the collapse? Here two views dominate. The first argues that the debacle, and everything that flowed from it, was a more or less inevitable consequence of attitudes and events in the previous two decades, as suggested already during the Occupation by Marc Bloch.[5] The second denies any determinism in France's collapse, stresses the patriotism and willingness of most Frenchmen to defend their country in 1939–40, and either implies or explicitly asserts that Vichy and the Collaboration were an aberration not representative of the vast majority of the population or of the general sweep of French history.[6]

Further complicating the issue is the fact that while fascists on both sides of the Rhine had attributed the defeat to the alleged decadence of the republic, the French generals disseminated the myth that the debacle had been the inevitable outcome of the army's material and technological inferiority. The prewar prime minister, Edouard Daladier, rejected the latter argument outright. As he wrote in his prison cell during the Occupation, it was precisely those "pathetic old officers," such as Pétain, who had "betrayed the trust we placed in them" by their "opposition to armored divisions" and their "belief in fixed fortifications." And yet, much as he derided the generals, Daladier viewed the larger context of the debacle through the prism of France's reaction to World War I, writing that the republic had transformed the commemoration of the Armistice into "a funeral rite," and had made the Arc de Triomphe into "little more than a glorified sepulcher" surrounded by "a crowd huddled in meditation, as if at graveside."[7] Indeed, even the victory parade of 1919 began with the march of the wounded—many of whom were horribly mutilated.[8] Soon thereafter France became dotted with innumerable memorials that acted more as sites of mourning than as reminders of triumph. Sculptures of dead and dying soldiers, such as we find in Domme, Lilas, Levallois, and countless other locations, reflect a general public perception of war as an event of mass death.[9] No wonder then that while Daladier perceived Vichy as the creature of a conspiracy by "the men of February 6," who "took their revenge by surrendering in Bordeaux," and "handed France over to the Germans so as to finish off the Republic," he also had no doubt that the success of this "plot" was facilitated by the widespread pacifist sentiment in interwar France.[10]

This view is shared by several scholars who have recently written on this period. Philippe Burrin traces French accommodation during the Occupation to the rifts of the 1930s. It was then, he argues, that the country's cohesion was undermined, that fear of war created a "pacifist depression," and that growing xenophobia and antisemitism were accompanied by a remarkably "unaggressive attitude" toward the Nazis.[11] If the French entered the war filled with angst rather than determination, the trauma of defeat and the wholly unanticipated occupation only enhanced their bewilderment. Accommodation was thus the expression of both mental attitudes and political opinions already present in France before the debacle, ranging from separatism, antirepublicanism, a longing for national renewal, outright fascism, integral pacifism, and sheer opportunism. While preventing the formation of a united front, these competing dispositions and ideologies created a space for collaboration with the Germans and for the brutal persecution of France's perceived domestic enemies.

Similarly, Eugen Weber endorses Bloch's view that the passage from the glory of World War I to the confusion, turmoil, and ultimate paralysis of the interwar period lay at the roots of the "strange defeat." Weber notes that for the "pacifists of the Left and Right" the "real enemies of peace . . . were inside France: in parliament, in government, and among those Jews and refugees who sought to embroil the country in war with Germany."[12] It was this view of the enemy as being installed within the nation, that eventually led some pacifists to see the German occupation as an occasion to purge France of its domestic foes. At a time of economic crisis and unemployment, this attitude bred prejudice and intolerance. While the Right had a long tradition of antisemitism, dating back to the 1880s, the climate of the 1930s offered the Left, too, as Weber writes, "licit opportunities for xenophobia and patriotic ire." And since "Jews had long been the resident alien par excellence," and in France "were associated with the German enemy," anti-Jewish outbursts occurred already in the 1920s and were greatly exacerbated by the waves of refugees from Germany after Hitler's "seizure of power" in 1933.[13] Thus Jews and refugees became synonymous in the public mind, foreigners in general were seen as polluting the nation and taking away jobs from honest Frenchmen, and antisemitism became increasingly prevalent in the last years of the republic.[14]

To be sure, for all its fear of war, economic hardship, resentment of foreigners, political instability and corruption, France did not turn to fascism. While the mass of the print media was on the Right, and an array of antirepublican and quasi-fascist or paramilitary organizations flourished, when push came to shove in the street fighting of February 6, 1934, what died was not democratic rule but the future of fascism in France (until the German occupation). The riots made possible the formation of the Popular Front and demonstrated the limits of fascism—an inherently aggressive and militaristic movement—in a nation imbued with pacifist and defensive attitudes. This, however, made for a major reorientation of political attitudes in the mid-1930s, whereby right-wing nationalists shifted to an antiwar posture, while the Left became increasingly militant. The possibility of national unity vanished when the Right joined the pacifists in viewing their main threat as the socialists and Communists whose destruction must be achieved even at the cost of collaboration with France's foreign foes. As each political camp harbored its own illusions, the increasing politicization and polarization of society, the timidity and lack of enterprise of the military (whose concepts of

warfare remained firmly anchored in the experience of World War I)
and the shortage of manpower caused by the "hollow years" of low
birthrate that resulted from the losses in 1914–18 combined to enhance the political paralysis and domestic tensions that prevented the
nation from preparing for confrontation with Germany.

The central paradox of French society in the 1930s was that it maintained an obsessive public discourse on war yet was tremendously reluctant to prepare for it. Thus, for instance, while aerial warfare was
anticipated to bring about a universal apocalypse, hardly anything
was done to create civil defense or to build an air force capable of
stopping enemy aircraft. As Alain put it, "The essence of tragedy is
the expectation of catastrophe." Hence we find Julian Green writing
in his *Journal* in 1930 that everyone was talking about the next war:
"In salons, in cafés, that is all that one hears with the same tone of
horror." In 1932 he notes, "The madness . . . consists of expecting the
war for the end of the week. For the last four years we have lived in
this nightmare of fear." Henri de Montherlant, who claimed to be
kept awake at night by thoughts of war, asserted that most people
around him "do not give a damn. . . . they know there is a menace . . .
but bury their heads in the sand"; and Jean de Pange noted that "all
France [is] obsessed by the thought of German aggression." That was
the atmosphere in which France erected the Maginot Line, the vast
chain of fortifications that only trapped its soldiers underground and
channeled the German Panzer divisions to a scantily protected invasion route that should have surprised nobody, using tactics and war
machines already known since at least the Polish campaign of the
previous year. This was, as Weber says, "the war that nobody wanted";
it was also one that nobody had prepared for, despite the fact that
everyone talked about it.[15] Moreover, while some believed that the war
had been fought against the wrong enemy, others insisted that it should
not have been fought at all, and others still maintained that the defeat was the consequence of a domestic conspiracy by the opposite
political camp. One can hardly think of a more propitious climate for
the installation of a regime in France that declared its determination
both to collaborate with the Germans and to totally change the nature
of French politics and society.

Notably, it was during the 1930s that the social-revolutionary
pacifist optimism represented by Barbusse was replaced by much
darker visions, as the French remembered the death and desolation
of 1914–18 with even greater intensity in view of the shattered hopes
for a better world and fears of yet another war. This was well reflected
in Jean Renoir's film *The Grand Illusion* (1937), which is both about

World War I as an event that brutalized even the most noble spirits, and a devastating critique of the interwar years, made even more explicit in Renoir's *The Rules of the Game* (1939). Hardly in line with his commitment to the *cinéma engagé* of the Popular Front, Renoir makes a powerful statement on the disintegration of French society in the wake of disaster, while simultaneously painting a nostalgic, if also ironic picture of the old codes of conduct and honor, decency and courage, that were irretrievably lost in the war. Renoir may be politically on the side of Maréchal (Jean Gabin), but he laments the disappearance of such men as the French aristocrat de Boeldieu (Pierre Fresnay), or the physical and mental distortion of his German counterpart von Rauffenstein (Eric von Stroheim), two men who have more in common with each other, both socially and spiritually, than with their respective underlings. Gabin wins, but his victory is finally not that of his class, but of his type, of the tough survivors, of the fittest. Neither courage, nor justice, appear victorious, but raw instincts, physical strength and will power. These, combined with the now rotten and degenerate remnants of the old society, and quasi-pathetic arrivistes characterized by the Jew Rosenthal (Marcel Dalio), ultimately create the world of *The Rules of the Game,* a Ship of Fools whose passengers dance away the night as it irrevocably goes under.[16]

Renoir's films mirrored the increasing preoccupation in 1930s France with the nature of the next war. Here was a perplexing image with neither clear-cut boundaries nor easily identifiable foes, where domestic strife overlapped with international conflict, and the identity of friends and enemies alike became progressively elusive. Torn over opposing prognoses of and preventive measures against future military confrontation, the French conducted a debilitating battle among themselves over the shape of their society and the implications of destruction. As the turmoil at home and the dangers abroad intensified, France began to imagine war as an apocalyptic event that, rather than bring about the end of armed conflict, would wipe out civilization itself. In the last prewar years, a cacophony of voices competed over the implications of this predicted catastrophe: Would it sweep away the old and prepare a clean slate for the construction of a "brave new world," a "workers' paradise," or a "racial utopia"? Or would it irreversibly annihilate humanity altogether? Was universal apocalypse an event to be anticipated with revolutionary fervor or should it be prevented even at the price of submitting to evil?

That the conflicting images of war and anticipations of disaster that wreaked havoc in 1930s France coalesced into an initially almost uniform support for, or acquiescence with, Vichy and the Occupation demonstrates the extent of overlap between warring political camps in this respect. On both extremes of the ideological spectrum, those who hoped to build a new world on the ruins of the old found their loyalties stretched between allegiance to the *patrie* (homeland) and attraction to foreign paragons and allies. Resentful of the republic and fascinated with fascism, the radical Right found it difficult to oppose Germany in defense of a system it no longer supported. The Communists, for their part, were torn between animosity to the Right and the military establishment, and obedience to the conflicting orders of the Kremlin—which first declared war on fascism and then signed a treaty with Hitler. Similarly, the New Pacifism of the interwar years, which proclaimed absolute opposition to war, even at the price of national capitulation, both employed a terminology of violent conflict at home and prepared for collaboration with the foreign enemy.[17]

What is so striking about representations of war in France of the *entre-deux-guerres* is that beyond their heavy emphasis on mourning for the fallen of 1914–18, they frequently imply the need to avoid another war at any cost. It is here that the ideological divide almost totally vanishes, as it did, for similar reasons, in the early months following the debacle. For such representations reflect the widespread illusion that anything, including defeat, occupation, and collaboration, is better than another slaughter. This was of course the message of the endless lists of names inscribed on hundreds of memorials in the towns and villages of France. But the dead were mobilized by every political cause and fear of war became a potent weapon in the hands of all parties. Thus, for instance, a poster protesting the Allies' demand from France to pay back its war debts, depicts a dead soldier rising from his tomb with the question: "In your calculations, have you included the price of my blood and that of my comrades?" A right-wing election poster in 1928 warns that a victory by the Left would encourage "Hindenburg the God of war"—seen marching ahead of massed artillery and warplanes—to launch war, just as Bethmann-Hollweg had done following the elections of 1914. Yet while throughout the interwar period the Right played on the public's fear of war, it proposed no alternative to confronting a future enemy invasion. This had a devastating effect on public morale, since neither the Right nor the Left appeared able or willing to contemplate the actual possibility of war but merely used it as a threat and a warning. Moreover, the boundaries between foreign and domestic conflict were intentionally blurred. Thus, in a mid-1920s election

FIGURE 2. Internal conflict as extension of foreign threat. "Les Jeunesses Patriotes
are building the ramparts that will stop the revolutionary hordes." Right-wing
poster, mid-1920s.

poster, the extreme right-wing league, Les Jeunesses Patriotes, presents itself as manning the ramparts, flying the flag of "Social Peace,"
while defending the fortress from the charging "revolutionary hordes"
(fig. 2).[18]

This kind of rhetoric intensified during the 1930s, when the
danger of a new war increased and the domestic conflict became ever
more vicious. Following the riots of February 6, 1934, the socialist
party's daily, *Le Populaire,* appeared with the headline "Fascism Will
Not Pass!" equating the radical Right, which included many war veterans, with the *Boches* (Germans) against whom the slogan "they will
not pass!" was used in 1914–18.[19] Thus the Left, too, presented domestic opponents as equivalent to the foreign threat. Conversely, the
Popular Front came to be seen by the Right as even more menacing
than the Germans, while simultaneously being charged with wishing
to bring about war. Innumerable political posters now depicted the
anticipated war in the form of German bombers destroying France,
implying thereby that the Right would prevent a conflict that France
could not conceivably win (fig. 3).[20] This right-wing defeatism in
the guise of anti-Left sentiments is probably the best indication of
the crisis of French society on the eve of the debacle. The bizarre

consensus between the Left and the Right that was at the root of the strange defeat is perfectly encapsulated in a 1938 poster issued by the fascist journal *Je suis partout,* where a morose *poilu* (ordinary soldier), faced with the demand to "Die for the Soviets! Die for the Negus! Die for Red Spain! Die for China! Die for the Czechs! Die for the Jews!" responds by saying: "Thank you, I'd rather: 'live for France!'"[21] This is the atmosphere of fear and defeatism depicted so well in Jean-Paul Sartre's novel on the war scare of 1938, *The Reprieve.* For such fascist opposition to war was not substantially different from the attitude expressed in a 1939 trade union poster, portraying the workers of Europe united behind the slogan "Enough!" (with war and arms production).[22] It was this same slogan that united French, German, and Italian pacifist veterans who gathered at Douaumont, by Verdun, in 1936, in an antiwar demonstration. Four years later these same German workers were dictating terms to their French comrades.

It was the illusion of peace that led Félicien Challaye, one of the leaders of French pacifism, to declare in March 1936 that the pacifists "want nothing to do with war, even that which is baptized antifascist and revolutionary" and to insist, following the debacle, on the "duty to collaborate with Germany."[23] On the other extreme of the political map, the Jeunesses Patriotes proclaimed in its leaflets: "Le Communisme, violà l'Ennemi!" (Communism, this is the enemy!), while the new fascist league La Solidarité Française warned that the red fascism of social-Communist Judeo-freemasons posed a deadly threat to freedom, the family, and the nation and that it was about to bring revolutionary tyranny to France as it had to central Europe and Russia.[24] War was thus conceived as a struggle between competing forces inside France, all of which, for one reason or another, feared or rejected the idea of military confrontation with a foreign enemy and vented their rage by combating each other. The term *pacifism* is perhaps somewhat misleading in this context, since even the most militant pacifists were willing to fight those who in their opinion were *French* proponents of war. *Blood, sacrifice,* and *destruction* were terms on everyone's lips. War became a general obsession, perhaps even greater than in Germany in the late 1930s; and yet it was civil war that everyone spoke of, whether in order to prevent another catastrophe such as that of 1914–18 or to ward off a Franco-Bolshevik uprising. There is little doubt that the ample evidence of the price of war throughout France did its share in diminishing the public's willingness to take part in another massacre. At the same time the fact that the fear of war did not facilitate domestic reconciliation, but rather introduced a new violence to political and intellectual discourse, in-

FIGURE 3. Fear of war as component of domestic politics. "If the
Front Commun [Popular Front] attacks . . . Hitler [will] attack
France!" Right-wing poster, mid-1930s.

dicates the brutalizing impact of 1914–18 on French society. That the
abhorrence of foreign war reached such dimensions in France is
quite laudable; that it ultimately led not only to military defeat but
also to collaboration with the Nazis is a trauma that France is still
trying to overcome.

The Grand Illusion

The "somber years" of France under German occupation, stretching
from the debacle of May-June 1940 to the Liberation in summer 1944,

are now viewed as having played a crucial role in France's postwar politics, self-perception, and historiography.[25] Yet the burden of that past still makes for a tendency to avoid some of its murkier aspects. This has to do both with the illusions that Vichy itself had fostered and with the myth constructed after the Liberation, one of whose main components was the denial that those very same wartime illusions had ever existed.

The difficulties involved in writing the history of that traumatized and fractured society are reflected in the competing narratives of the period. Was France a victim of Nazi conquest and rule, of its own decadence and corruption, or of the cataclysms of modern history? Conversely, were the French by and large passive, not to say indifferent bystanders, concerned primarily with their own safety, while much of the rest of the world went up in flames and some of their own neighbors were deported to death camps? Is there, indeed, any sense at all in talking about "France" and "the French" during those years, and if not, what are the implications of denying the national solidarity and identity of the population?[26]

Between 1940 and 1944 France was geographically divided into an occupied and a "free zone." The latter, however, was ruled by an authoritarian dictatorship and was under the influence of the Germans even before they occupied it in November 1942. Whereas Pétain's regime hoped radically to transform French life and politics, the Nazi occupation of France was far more benevolent than their occupation of Eastern Europe, excluding, of course, the treatment meted to the Jews and the Resistance. If the majority of the French quickly came to reject both the German occupation and the Vichy regime, they were also not keen to see the Third Republic restored. Germany's astounding victory left a profound impression on the population, while Pétain's promise to rebuild the nation, made at a time of distress and anxiety, provided Vichy with an initial capital that cannot be dismissed when gauging contemporary French attitudes. Both the Germans and Vichy exploited and exacerbated the prejudices and animosities that characterized French society in the 1930s, thereby making the transition to foreign rule and domestic dictatorship appear all the more necessary.

While the initial compliance with Vichy and the Occupation is closely linked to prewar conflicts and perceptions, the ultimate resistance to German rule and to Pétain's regime must be analyzed within the larger social, economic, and political context and cannot be reduced to a mere expression of patriotism and sacrifice. Resistance expanded as a reaction to the growing brutality of the authorities, to increasing indications that Germany might lose the war, and, most important, to the compulsory recruitment of labor to German factories. Just as crucial is the fact that much of the resistance was directed at Vichy, rather than the Germans. In the climate of violence and vengeance that characterized the death throes of Vichy and the Third Reich, liberation from foreign rule and civil war between competing organizations and ideologies became inextricably mixed. No wonder that Vichy's ambivalent legacy and the imperfect *épuration* that followed it have made coming to terms with those years exceedingly difficult.

Immediately after the war, Charles de Gaulle successfully installed the first narrative of the Occupation, asserting that the vast majority of the French had heroically resisted the Germans and eventually liberated themselves from Nazi rule. While it might have been necessary in order to facilitate France's recovery, this version of the past both marginalized the fate of the Jews and served to reintegrate and legitimize some of Vichy's worst henchmen. Beginning in the 1970s, a new narrative slowly emerged, arguing that most of the French had either collaborated with the Germans, supported Vichy, or simply protected their own interests and well-being; in some instances even the Resistance was portrayed as far less heroic than previously thought. Between the first screening of Marcel Ophuls' *The Sorrow and the Pity* in 1969 and the publication of Henry Rousso's *The Vichy Syndrome* in 1987, this narrative became increasingly prevalent, although not hegemonic.[27] The publicity surrounding the cases of Klaus Barbie, René Bousquet, Paul Touvier, and Maurice Papon, and the revelations about François Mitterrand's dubious past have added to the sense of confusion and opaqueness, ambiguity and discomfort evoked by those four dark years.[28] As the reality of Vichy recedes into the past, it is increasingly recognized as a profound moral fiasco with far-reaching consequences for the identity of postwar France.

The nature and stakes of the conflict were identified by some very early on. Former prime minister Edouard Daladier, incarcerated by Vichy and later the Germans following the armistice, had a clearer perception of reality from the confines of his prison cell than many of France's politicians, generals, and bishops. As he wrote in the fall of 1941, "Only the outcome of the war is of real concern. If Germany should be victorious . . . I would just as soon not survive, just as soon not have to witness the moral decline and the decay that would result."[29] Later, on hearing about "the existence of crematoriums and the experiments with various gasses they perform on prisoners," he noted that "centuries of effort and progress have been wiped out" by

Nazi crimes and this war of "mass destruction."[30] Conversely, as early as November 1940, he commented that the Germans "would prefer a policy of 'collaboration,' to use the term in vogue in the French press," since "this would guarantee Germany control over our principal industries . . . and reduce France to the state of a colony or a protectorate." As Daladier clearly understood, this would be a far more effective policy than outright annexation, because it "undermines virtually all the material and moral reasons for revenge."[31] He also realized, however, that in the long run, any promoter of collaboration would be seen as "a servile partisan of surrender, a traitor . . . who is organizing France so that the Krauts can squeeze the most out of her."[32] Hence his belief that France would eventually reject that "bunch of incompetent fools and traitors" who had "handed [her] over to the enemy."[33] Indeed, throughout his years in prison, Daladier was constantly preoccupied with recovering the moral fiber of the French nation and always on the lookout for signs of unity and patriotism. On hearing reports in 1942 of demonstrations on July 14 in French cities, he delighted in this proof of the "deep-seated feelings of rebellion and the growing sense of a veritable and profound national unity that extends from Communist workers to Catholics." This "greatest national movement in all of French history" appeared to him as evidence that "our defeat was a necessary step for us, but not at all in the way it is presented by Pétain and his cliques of hypocrites and traitors."[34] While he recognized that the deportations of Jews and the executions of Communists demonstrated that the "National Revolution has planted its roots in blood and infamy," he nevertheless lauded the clergy who "have condemned the barbaric anti-Semitic acts that are being committed."[35]

Indeed, although Daladier damned Vichy and the collaboration, he shared with de Gaulle the desire to reestablish France's glory and the illusion that by and large the French had acted honorably at a time of crisis and distress. For this reason he reacted with pride to news of French resistance and exclaimed that now "people admit to having underestimated the French," since France has "once again become, in Churchill's words, 'one of the world's leading powers.'"[36] This same logic led him to insist that the purges be swift and reasonable. "Of all the wounds," he wrote, "this is the most painful and the most grievous of all, which is why it should be lanced, without delay, so that the healing process might begin."[37] Despite his ready acknowledgment of "the horrors of the concentration camps," he showed little inclination to associate them with French complicity.[38] Always the politician, he looked forward to the future and thereby ultimately came to share the myths and illusions of the post-war period.

To be sure many of Vichy's most objectionable aspects, of which the deportations of the Jews were doubtlessly the worst, can be partly ascribed to the condition of German occupation under which this regime operated. But the myth of the resistance denied both the re-sponsibility of Vichy for the anti-Jewish policies it initiated of its own accord and the responsibility of "France" for Vichy. Over the past two decades a growing number of (initially, mainly foreign) studies have amply documented Vichy's anti-Jewish legislative initiatives and ultimate willing complicity in Nazi genocidal policies.[39] In reaction to this accusatory literature, other scholars now urge a more nuanced view of French conduct. One representative of this approach is John F. Sweets, who has argued that as of a relatively early phase, "most French people were unwilling to accept the ideology and programs associated with Vichy's National Revolution"; that Vichy's henchmen were untypical of the population as a whole; that the brutal practices of the Milice in its war on "Communism, Gaullism, the Jewish lep-rosy, [and] Freemasonry," merely reflected "the violent temperament and unsavory character of some of its members"; and that officials charged with Jewish affairs were "hoodlums, thugs, [and] brutes of the most despicable sort."[40] While obviously partly true, such argu-ments neglect to note that Pétain's promises to cleanse France of "for-eign elements" and purge it of the corrupt practices associated with the republic struck a powerful chord with many French. Indeed, one is reminded here of early assertions made in Germany about Nazi per-petrators. Moreover, as Sweets himself concedes, young men often joined the Milice for the same reason that others joined the Resis-tance, namely to escape compulsory labor in Germany; fighters in both groups commonly hailed from the same communities and social classes.[41] Similarly, just as the architects of the "Final Solution" came from the top echelons of German society, so, too, the functionaries of Vichy stemmed from the established French elites; and as we now know, a significant number of perpetrators on both sides of the Rhine swiftly reintegrated into postwar society, more often than not in lead-ing bureaucratic, administrative, and business positions.[42]

A case can be made for the somewhat apologetic-sounding argu-ment that the Germans' "relative lack of success" in perpetrating geno-cide in France "testifies to . . . the far wider network of support avail-able after the German occupation of the south."[43] Yet while many brave individuals helped the victims, the murder of some 76,000 Jews living in France could not have been accomplished without the close collaboration of the French authorities and at least part of the population. That most French policeman acted "with a conviction that they were behaving as responsible professionals fulfilling their duty" only shows that they were not much different in this sense from their German counterparts.[44] Similarly, and again not unlike the German case, the ineffectiveness of protests against deportations of Jews derived from the alleged "legality" of these measures, as well as from most people's preoccupation with their own problems. In fact new evidence continues to support Robert Paxton's well-known assertion that public opinion "offered a broad basis of acquiescence within which active participation in the Vichy regime was made legitimate."[45] For if there were indeed "symptoms of systematic distrust and indifference," the population on the whole manifested little active opposition to the roundups of Jews;[46] and if disillusionment with Vichy became increasingly widespread, until very late in the war the French were also keenly aware that theirs was the only major European country to have largely avoided devastation. In the meantime people tried to make the best of a bad situation, showing the Germans what Sweets calls a "modicum of civility," which is why German soldiers remembered service in France as a one of the most pleasant experiences of the war.[47] Indeed, in the region of Clermont-Ferrand that Sweets has closely examined, he found that "throughout most of the occupation relations were relatively good between the French and the Germans. Until the summer of 1944" (when the Allies landed) and despite the "limited number of troops at their disposal," the Germans "do not seem to have felt threatened" in "accomplishing their basic missions at Clermont, those of pacification and of securing production for the war economy." This comes very close to accepting Paxton's argument that French *attentisme,* a "wait-and-see attitude," made them into "'collaborators' in the functional sense." No wonder that Clermont's population could congratulate itself after the war that except for "certain measures against their Jews . . . for the most part . . . the region had been spared the flagrant atrocities" that occurred in other areas.[48]

We are often prone to the illusion that spiritual leaders are endowed with moral courage and disinterested humanism. Hence the long-held myth concerning the role of the clergy in Vichy. Yet as W. D. Halls has recently shown in devastating detail, the Catholic Church was already highly critical of the republic in the 1930s, expressed vehement opposition to the Left, and, especially after the establishment of Léon Blum's Popular Front government, became increasingly imbued with antisemitism, an attitude further encouraged by the Pope's silence on Germany's racist policies. No wonder that Catholic leaders were attracted to Pétain's mélange of quasi-fascist authoritarianism and reactionary rhetoric, encapsulated in the slogan "Travail, Famille, Patrie" (Work, Family, Homeland). The fact is that many Christians perceived the debacle of 1940 as confirmation of France's moral decline, corruption, and the "corrosive" influence of secularism, described by Cardinal Verdier as the equivalent of German racism. Only an alliance between the Church and Pétain seemed to offer salvation from the Godlessness that had almost caused the nation's extinction. Paul Claudel celebrated the delivery of France from anti-Catholic "teachers, lawyers, Jews, Freemasons . . . universal suffrage and Parliamentarism;" Archbishop Feltin asserted that the debacle facilitated undertaking "the task of inner regeneration;" and Monsignor Caillot saw it as putting an end to the "evil parenthesis" between the Revolution and 1940, in which the Freemasons and the Jews had introduced the separation of Church and state. As Halls remarks, it almost seemed as if God had sided with Nazism in order to purify France.[49]

Church leaders took an active part in propagating Pétain's status as the savior of France. As Cardinal Gerlier declared, "Pétain is France, and France, today, is Pétain!"[50] The ecclesiastical adulation of "le Maréchal-Christ" (the Marshal-Christ) peaked with the German invasion of the Soviet Union in 1941, described by Cardinal Baudrillat as a "noble common enterprise," in which the soldiers of the Légion des Volontaires Français (LVF) were fighting as "the crusaders of the twentieth century."[51] In late 1941 the prefects still reported excellent relations with the clergy, and on May Day 1942, just before the mass deportations of Jews began, Cardinal Suhard declared his "undying attachment" to Pétain. Indeed, even while the Hierarchy protested the deportations, Church leaders insisted that they had "nothing in common with that strange adventurer de Gaulle" and warned that the liberation of political prisoners and Jews in North Africa were a dire indication of what might be expected from an Allied victory.[52] This was no case of political opportunism, but rather of ideological connivance. Even the Protestant Pastor Boegner believed that there was a "Jewish problem," and many others supported the enactment and implementation of "grave" but "justifiable" measures against the "pernicious power" of the Jews. How such policies could be accomplished on the basis of "the rules of charity and justice" was less obvious. Cardinal Gerlier tried to square the circle by arguing that while anti-Jewish measures were not unjust, they lacked "justice and clarity," while the Archbishop of Toulouse somewhat lamely asserted that the "Jews are men and women." But Gerlier soon qualified his protest by acknowledging that "the French authorities have a problem to resolve."[53] As Halls notes, "Even before the storm raised by their protests had died down bishops were again lavish in their expressions of loyalty to the Marshal."[54]

Among the lower clergy there were many instances of moral and physical courage. Some Protestant communities stood out in particular; the people of Le Chambon sheltered 1,000 Jews and smuggled another 4,000 across the border.[55] Priests in the rural areas often supported the Resistance and helped those persecuted by the Germans, who retaliated by executing 216 priests and seven pastors.[56] But the anti-Jewish stance of the Church leadership reflected a wider sentiment. Halls comments that "for some Frenchmen, including some Christians, the Jews served as a convenient scapegoat for the defeat of 1940." This in turn was related not merely to economic resentment but to a long antisemitic tradition, exacerbated first by the Great Depression and the influx of refugees during the 1930s and then by Vichy and German incitement. While Church leaders "did not foresee the terrible consequences that flowed from their attitude" of identifying a "Jewish problem," they were definitely in a position to observe the cruelty and brutality of the regime they supported.[57] Yet instead of criticizing German atrocities, the Church indulged in recriminations against the Allies and the Resistance. Père Roguet called the Allies "assassins and butchers," Monsignor Duparc spoke of their "barbarism," Cardinal Liénart characterized their actions as "carnage," Cardinal Suhard condemned their "atrocities" and "crimes," and Monsignor Piguet spoke of the "cataclysms of extermination" the Allies allegedly perpetrated. French resisters were similarly described by Liénart as "terrorists," whose actions were called "banditry" by Monsignor Le Bellec and "criminal" by Monsignor Choquet.[58] Conversely, as late as January 1944, Liénart thanked the Germans for their "correct and benevolent" behavior, "professed understanding" for their need to "occasionally . . . bear down severely," and promised "to pacify the population and exhort it to act correctly." When German units massacred ninety villagers near Lille in April as collective punishment for the derailment of a train, Liénart "enjoined silence." Cardinal Suhard was just as obliging; described by the Germans as "anxious to depoliticize his clergy," he was praised for having "genuinely sought a *modus vivendi* with the occupying forces," which obviously manifested his "disposition to collaborate."[59]

If the Church supported collaboration, many of the extremists in Vichy were products of Christian education. While Catholic resisters described themselves as rebels against their superiors, Halls identifies "a distinctly Catholic element" in collaborationist institutions. The Milice especially "attracted many young men from the Catholic bourgeoisie" and from Action Catholique, whose explicit goal was to fight "pagan Freemasony," destroy Bolshevism, and "save" France from the Jews. This "instrument of Nazi brutality" was, writes Halls, an "offshoot of an organization intensely patriotic and loyal, often commanded by young officers with a strongly religious upbringing."[60] All of which indicates that we are dealing here not merely with the dire effects of the Church's silence, recently acknowledged by its leadership, but with a significant degree of congruity with Vichy. If Philippe Henriot—whose "great influence over Catholic opinion" derived from his "impeccable . . . Catholic credentials"—was dedicated "to reconcile national socialism and the Church," the majority of the bishops greatly preferred Vichy to the republic, openly advocated collaboration, and can therefore not be acquitted of complicity in its policies.[61] The illusion that any sort of harmony could be found between the *'principes chrétiens'* (Christian principles) of the Church and the *'idées maîtraisse'* (governing ideas) of the Révolution Nationale led to association with genocide. Nor did the Church have the moral courage to recognize this fatal "error" after the Liberation; by assuming a posture of "injured innocence," the Church perpetuated the illusion of ignorance and resistance and further discredited its claim as the nation's moral guide.[62]

Nevertheless, if Vichy strove to create the illusion of enthusiastic support and de Gaulle fabricated the myth of universal resistance, thanks to Philippe Burrin's research we now know that most of the French "lived through the occupation with the sole preoccupation of 'getting through it.'"[63] Between the two extremes of resistance and collaboration, and following an initial period in which submission to the occupiers was the rule and collaboration was perceived as "participating in a common task," the majority of people chose to accommodate themselves to the situation and simply wait things out.[64] While the men of Vichy "accepted defeat so easily" because "mentally they were ready both to switch direction in the country's external policies and also to change its internal structures," the enthusiasm with which they were greeted was generated by an almost total rejection of the Third Republic and by the shock of military collapse.[65] To be sure, if at the beginning there were very few signs of hatred against the *Boches*, whose military prowess and orderly, "correct" behavior were often admired, the prevailing mood of resignation and acceptance— even among future resisters—gradually changed in the fall of 1940.

And yet, as Burrin notes, this "did not resolve the confusion in people's minds and still left room for a widespread desire for accommodation."[66]

Ultimately, German economic exploitation and Vichy's increasingly authoritarian rule made the French perceive the policies of collaboration as placing them between "a boot and a bottom."[67] Yet while the regime clung to the illusion of sharing power in a German-dominated Europe and was "carried away by scenarios whose realism was daily shrinking away to nothing," the Germans were pleased to find that the cooperation of the French on all levels of society "almost exceeded what was to be expected from the administration of an occupied country."[68] Thus the French contributed massively to the German war effort even as Vichy pursued its claim to sovereignty by doing the dirty work for the Germans, including political repression, ideological persecution, and eventual acceptance of German methods in dealing with the "Jewish question." Burrin notes, "No knife was being held to Vichy's throat" during the mass deportations of 1942, yet "without the cooperation of the police, the SS were paralyzed." To the contrary, Pierre Laval's advocacy of "national prophylaxy" demonstrated that in Vichy "*raison d'état* was stiffened by ideological complicity."[69]

Collaboration by the regime depended on the public's focus on material self-interest. To be sure, support for Vichy was "fragile, shaky, and dwindling." At the same time, the population's remarkable passivity was fostered by uncertainty, the hardships of daily life, and the repressive policies of Vichy and the Germans. Indeed, because the regime persecuted mainly Jews and Communists, the public attitude can be defined as "complicit resignation."[70] Some people retreated into silence and avoidance of contact with the Germans; but the conduct of many others made the occupiers feel anything but unwelcome. Educated men and women found their counterparts among the Germans, and numerous French celebrities socialized with the occupiers. For those of a less intellectual taste, there were other distractions. At the liberation, between 10,000 and 20,000 women were punished for liaisons with Germans, and a "minimum of several tens of thousands of French women engaged in sexual relations with the occupiers," producing some 50,000 to 70,000 children. Denunciations, reported by prefects to have reached flood levels in the autumn of 1941, constituted yet another form of instrumental contact with the Germans.[71]

Not surprisingly, the business elites were particularly quick to adapt. By 1944 the majority of French industrial undertakings were working for the Reich, with some 14,000 French firms taking German orders of either civilian or military nature.[72] Banks swiftly struck deals with the Germans and just as expeditiously began directing large funds to the Resistance with the turn of the tide in 1944.[73] Lower down on the social scale, at least 10,000 Frenchmen became temporary managers of some 40,000 despoiled Jewish businesses. As for labor, by 1944 half a million French men and women were employed by the Wehrmacht or the Todt Organization, with a total of at least 200,000 citizens volunteering for work in Germany and another 200,000 prisoners of war held in Germany willingly converting to the status of workers. The German firm IG Farben employed French workers at its plant in Auschwitz.[74]

While all this activity was going on, increasing numbers of French children and adults began learning German. The Berlitz language school increased its enrollments from 939 adult students of German in 1939, to 7,920 in 1941; the German Institute in Paris from a few hundreds in the 1930s, to 15,000 by 1942, mostly taught by French instructors. Altogether, some 30,000 students took courses at the German Institute; the majority were adult members of the urban middle class and the liberal professions, with a total of about 100,000 French people learning German during the Occupation.[75] This in turn reflected the accommodation of the intellectual and academic elites. Institutions of higher education, ranging from the Collège de France to practically all universities, rapidly and voluntarily purged themselves of their Jewish members, without any registered public protests by the professors.[76] The prominent historian Lucien Febvre demanded the resignation of Marc Bloch, the Jewish coeditor and cofounder of their journal *Annales,* so as to save it from being banned. While Bloch joined the Resistance and was executed by the Germans, Febvre continued to edit the journal—which in no way promoted resistance—from the safety of his country house.[77] Similarly, such respectable French publishers as Gallimard purged their lists of Jewish authors and turned to publishing texts by German racial ideologues and French collaborators. Nor did many renown French writers desist from having their works published during the Occupation, including Louis Aragon, Georges Bataille, Simone de Beauvoir, Maurice Blanchot, Albert Camus, Paul Claudel, Marguerite Duras, Paul Éluard, François Mauriac, Jean Paulhan, Romain Rolland, Jean-Paul Sartre, and Paul Valéry. Marcel Aymé wrote for the fascist antisemitic journal *Je suis partout,* Mauriac contributed to the collaborationist *Nouvelle Revue Française,* Camus cut out a chapter on Franz Kafka from *Le Mythe de Sisyphe* to have it published in 1942,

Antoine de Saint-Exupéry paid a quasi-official visit to Germany to promote the translations of his books there, and Aragon excised references to Heinrich Heine and the Dreyfus Affair from his writings to facilitate their publication in Germany. Other artists followed suit. Jean Cocteau expressed admiration for Hitler, Abel Gance made a friendly visit to wartime Germany, and Pierre Fournier gave concerts in the Reich. That some of these men and women eventually ended up in the Resistance only highlights the moral confusion and the depth of accommodation that characterized the French intelligentsia in the first years of the Occupation.[78]

Created by men who deluded themselves that they could turn the clock back to the ancien régime while simultaneously finding a place for France in a Nazi-dominated Europe, Vichy was supported or at least tolerated by a population that strove to keep out of harm's way and pursue its economic or intellectual interests in conditions of relative safety. As these illusions were shattered, the Resistance emerged as a means to transform France and purge one's conscience and record. The eventual failure of the resisters to create a new postwar society, the rapid return to normality and the reintegration of the old elites, along with the resisters' urge to legitimize their own newlywon positions of power and influence made it appear necessary to mask the sins of the past and the sordid reality of the present with a new myth of glorious self-liberation. To be sure, while committed collaboration, in Burrin's words, was both "engendered by society" and ultimately "tore itself away from society," there was also a good deal of heroism and sacrifice, although some of it was in the service of evil.[79] But France under the Germans was characterized primarily by accommodation to a generally unpleasant condition and a reluctance to fight against what was finally recognized as a criminal regime obsessed with murdering a host of helpless victims. And if the purges affected no less than 150,000 people, we should note that in 1944 no less than four million French citizens were working directly for the Germans in one capacity or another. Hence one must agree with Burrin that "deliberate, voluntary accommodation extended well beyond the circle of those punished in the purges," even if "the great majority of French people had no faith in collaboration and wanted none of it."[80] This is a hard truth to swallow; no wonder that, even fifty years after the event, it could only be expressed so bluntly by a Swiss historian.

Self-liberation was thus the final illusion of the Occupation and the founding myth of postwar France. But if it failed to liberate the French from the ghosts of the past, this was also liberation from an ambiguous, often troubling event, whose legacy consisted not only of mirth and hope but also of pity and sorrow. For the Jewish survivors of the camps, as Primo Levi wrote, "the hour of liberation was neither joyful nor lighthearted. For most it occurred against a tragic background of destruction, slaughter, and suffering . . . which seemed definitive, past cure." Indeed, "leaving the past behind . . . almost always . . . coincided with a phase of anguish."[81] Such camp survivors rarely experienced a sense of triumph when their liberators appeared at the gate, nor for many years thereafter, as they learned of their personal losses and tried to come to terms with the universal wound the Nazis had inflicted on humanity.[82] Binjamin Wilkomirski, whose book on a childhood spent entirely in the camps appears to have been a work of fiction rather than an authentic memoir, nevertheless captures the sense of being denied the very awareness of liberation. As he notes in the closing pages of the book, he (or his protagonist) learned of it only years later, as a high school student in Switzerland, when his class was shown documentary footage of the Holocaust. While to others it appeared almost inconceivable, to him these were scenes of his childhood memories. Then, however, "came something so unexpected as to be unreal, that I knew nothing about: . . . the liberation of the camps. . . . And everywhere, over and over again, faces transfixed with happiness at being liberated . . . I was there too, in a camp, and I didn't see anything. No one freed us, and nobody brought us food, and nobody tended us. . . . Nobody ever told me the war was over. Nobody ever told me that the camp was over, finally, definitely over."[83]

The liberation of France, comments H. R. Kedward in a new collection of essays he coedited with Nancy Wood, was "a complex amalgam of opening and closure," whose protagonists "looked backward as well as forward." Whereas "scores of resisters . . . closed a chapter in their own lives at the moment of liberation," others climbed onto the "Resistance bandwagon" or used "acts of resistance as a personal *point de départ*," or point of departure, in their postwar careers. While we should not underestimate "the human immensity of the struggle to close the door firmly on Nazism," we can also recognize now the explanatory limitations of the Resistance narrative.[84] Indeed, even the heroism of the resisters was never unambiguous. As was revealed in the film *Au coeur de l'orage* (*In the Midst of the Storm*), released in 1948 but understandably shelved shortly thereafter, this attempt to glorify the Resistance in the Vercors region unwittingly displayed the vanity and incompetence of the fighters and the calamity they brought down on the surrounding communities by provoking murderous acts of collective punishment by the Germans.[85] Similarly, the studies presented in the Kedward and Wood collection complicate the portrayal of the Resistance as an instance of "pure" French heroism by showing the active participation of immigrant Jewish groups in the fighting, as well as demonstrating that while women retained a gendered view of their role in the Resistance, Jewish women resisters became also increasingly aware of the tension between their "Frenchness" and "Jewishness."[86] We also learn that contrary to the myth of police participation in the liberation of Paris, in fact, "most policemen carried out . . . orders" to deport Jews "even after obedience to Vichy had ceased to be automatic,"[87] and that while the educational establishment rewrote children's stories in a manner consistent with Vichy's ideology, following the Liberation these same writers hastily adapted such books to the myth of the Resistance.[88]

The Liberation saw a resumption of the wars over French identity, in which the recovery of freedom was accompanied by recrimination and violence. Thus, while many women "emerged from the war with new and important rights," and "with an increased awareness of their own potential,"[89] this process also exacerbated the crisis of masculine identity, rooted in the double failure of French men to defend the *patrie* and provide for their families.[90] The mass phenomenon of *les femmes tondues* (the shearing of women's hair for alleged association with the enemy), which obviously also had a basis in reality, can simultaneously be seen as a male reaction to the fact that "women's new-found independence and importance during the war—in economic life and in Resistance activity especially—contrasted sharply with the humiliation of French men."[91] On a more elevated level, while the Liberation was expected to release creative spirits from the stranglehold of tyranny, French literary and intellectual culture remained haunted by the ghosts of collaboration and complicity, not least because the purges had cast a dubious light on the role of intellectuals during the Occupation. Thus, for instance, Jean Paulhan, who rightly criticized the hypocrisy of the *épuration* of the intellectuals, had served during the Occupation as editor of Pierre Drieu La Rochelle's collaborationist *Nouvelle Revue Française.*[92] Similarly, the Paris trial of Otto Abetz, Nazi sympathizer and German ambassador to France before and during the Occupation, gingerly avoided mention of his embarrassing links with the French intelligentsia, even while his defense ironically presented him as a proponent of Franco-German reconciliation.[93] Even more disturbing was the attempt by collaborationist French pacifists to justify their activities by both denying the genocidal character of the Nazi regime and charging the Allies with employing Hitlerian methods against the Germans.[94]

The manner in which the contested memory of the Liberation continues to feature in the French discourse on the twentieth century can be gauged from the recent discussion of Alain Resnais's classic *Hiroshima, mon amour* (1959) by the philosopher Alain Brossat. Resnais made an analogy between a young woman whose head was shaven for a love affair with a German soldier and a Japanese man from Hiroshima. For Brossat this "symbolic equivalence" consists in the fact that both are survivors of a catastrophe struggling to emerge from the "tyranny" of a cataclysmic memory.[95] As Nancy Wood perceptively notes, Brossat presents "modern History" as having "inflicted the 'grand' and 'infinitesimal' legacies of catastrophe." Such an "analogy of 'survivorship,'" she writes, "potentially embraces all of us who must live under History's tyrannous shadow." And since "we are all nominated as History's 'survivors,' we risk losing sight altogether of the specific sufferings of real survivors of this century's catastrophes."[96] In other words the assertion of universal victimhood releases us all from responsibility for past and present sins.

This specific case indicates a peculiar French manner of linking the nation's past to the catastrophic events of this century. While Resnais's earlier *Night and Fog* (1955) presents the suffering in the Nazi camps as universal, avoiding any mention of the Jews and implying that the victims were primarily (French) political resisters, *Hiroshima, mon amour* focuses on an innocent French victim of history's cataclysmic events, for which Hiroshima serves merely as a backdrop. The victims of history are thus either those who fought against evil or those whose innocent love was destroyed by "heroes without imagination," as the French heroine of *Hiroshima, mon amour* describes the patriots who shaved her hair.[97] Significantly, the script for the film was written by Marguerite Duras, whose memoir *La Douleur* (translated as *The War*, 1985) is about her own suffering while awaiting the return of her husband from Nazi captivity; deeply concerned with her own pain, she desists from any reference to the genocide of the Jews. Just as interesting is the fact that the man she waits for is Robert Antelme, the author of *L'espèce humaine* (*The Human Species*, 1947), a haunting memoir about political inmates in the Nazi camps, frequently cited as the paradigmatic depiction of *French* suffering under the Germans.[98]

The perception of France as a heroic, tragic victim of uncontrollable outside forces and as the conscience of civilization, which is still prevalent in certain intellectual circles, has made for a muddled

discourse on catastrophe and identity. Illusory resemblance may have
a liberating effect of its own. As could be seen in an academic conference at the Sorbonne in 1997, the mere use of the term *camps* can
facilitate false analogies between genocide and ethnic cleansing,
colonialism and postcolonialism, persecution and prejudice, immigration and cultural hegemony, while totally avoiding any discussion
of French complicity in the genocide of the Jews.[99] Similarly, the
frequent analogy between Antelme and Primo Levi (which Antelme
himself would have strongly rejected) tends to obscure the fact that
while only a fraction of the 76,000 Jews deported from France survived the camps, well over half of a roughly equal number of French
political deportees managed to return.[100] In this sense concern for the
victims of history can serve to avoid confrontation with the more
troubling episodes in one's own national past.

The continuing evolution of intellectual thinking in this direction
can be gleaned from Brossat's most recent book, *L'épreuve du désastre*
(*The Proof of Disaster*).[101] Brossat argues that "the prevailing contemporary propensity to perceive extremity and catastrophe as strictly a
matter of the past" prevents those who "only stress the singularity"
of the Shoah from recognizing that "the Palestinian camps are in-
exorably linked to the Jewish disaster." Hence, he concludes, "our relationship to catastrophe remains essentially under the tyrannical hold
of a double bind: . . . so long as the plunder and oppression of the
Palestinians appears as compensation for the crime of Auschwitz;
so long as the 'uniqueness' of the Nazi crimes serves *also* as the alibi
for the avoidance, indeed the uninhibited negation of the Soviet extermination or the colonial atrocities—the life without end of catastrophe will continue to pierce the flesh of the democratic order as it
expands throughout the world."[102] In other words it is the insistence
on the Nazi genocide of the Jews and the singularity of Auschwitz
that perpetuates the presence of evil in the world. Hence, if we only
spoke less about the Jews and "their" Shoah, the lot of humanity
would be greatly ameliorated. This final illusion about the beneficial
effects of repression indeed indicates that *France's* "relationship to
catastrophe remains essentially under the tyrannical hold of a double
bind," whose parameters, however, are the debilitating impact of
1914–18 and the complicity of Vichy in the murder of the Jews. It is
the illusion that one can somehow compensate for one's own crimes by
reference to the injustice of others that has led to "the life without end
of catastrophe." For France's "proof of disaster" is the moral debacle
of Vichy; that should be the *point de départ* for all attempts to dispel
the illusions of the past and to resist the obfuscation of the present.

The Competition of Victims

In January 1998 the French daily *Le Monde* published an attack by the writer Henri Raczymow against what he called the "ever more prevalent trend of historical, literary, and moral thinking that considers any crime as having the same value [*vaut*] as another, any victim as having the same value as another." Raczymow argued that "this current is not made up of negationists (those who negate the reality of the gas chambers), but much more, it appears, of people who are exacerbated by the claim—made by Jews—about the absolute uniqueness of the Shoah, its incommensurability, its incomparability."[103] The article was primarily a response to a statement made by the historian Stéphane Courtois, whose preface to the recently published volume *Le livre noire du communisme* (*The Black Book of Communism*) included the assertion that "the death from hunger of the child of a Ukrainian Kulak intentionally driven to starvation by the Stalinist regime 'has the same value' [*vaut*] as the death from hunger of a Jewish child driven to starvation by the Nazi regime."[104] In turn Raczymow's article provoked Catherine Coquio, professor of comparative literature at the Sorbonne, to charge him with implying that "the life of a child in one place is not worth [*vaut*] the same as that of a child in another place."[105] Tzvetan Todorov, whose new book, *Les Abus de la mémoire* (*The Abuses of Memory*), was also criticized by Raczymow, responded by rejecting the notion of uniqueness altogether.[106] To support his assertion, Todorov argued that even Vassili Grossman, coeditor with Ilya Ehrenburg of the original *Black Book* on the Nazi genocide of the Jews, had drawn a parallel between Nazi and Soviet criminality when he wrote that "the Germans say: The Jews are not human beings. That's what Lenin and Stalin say: The Kulaks are not human beings." For Todorov, since "every human being has the same price," there is no point in asserting that one crime is "worth" more than another. Rather, what is identical in all genocides is that on the "moral plane" they are "'worth' . . . absolute condemnation."[107]

Neither the participants in this debate, nor other scholars criticized by Raczymow—who included the Belgian sociologist Jean-Michel Chaumont, author of *La Concurrence des victimes* (*The Competition of Victims*)—are historians of the Holocaust.[108] Indeed, this was not a controversy about the Holocaust, but rather about the meaning, memory, and political use of crimes against humanity. (See fig. 4 for the twisted memory of victims in an almost "judenfrei" Poland.) Nor did Raczymow's insistence on the uniqueness of the Holocaust have anything to do with his alleged insensibility to the suffering endured

FIGURE 4. The hate of victims. Monument to the victims of the Płaszów concentration camp near Kraków, Poland. Hebrew inscription calls to avenge the spilled blood. Graffiti made in the 1990s: "You fucking Jews, you and your Christ."

by millions of people in numerous other mass crimes. His argument was about the reluctance of French intellectuals to focus on the Holocaust as an event in its own right, especially since France itself—including many of its intellectuals at the time—had played a much greater role in that very specific event than they wish to concede. The arguments leveled against him merely proved his point. For rhetorical assertions regarding the suffering of children constitute precisely the kind of abuse of memory against which Todorov himself has rightly warned. The individual suffering of innocents under any regime and in any historical context does not tell us a great deal about the political circumstances in which it occurs; but it can serve as a device to relativize or normalize the past, as the example of the German *Historikerstreit* in the mid-1980s had already shown. Suffering is never relative, but its assertion does not suffice to distinguish one event from another nor to make one "better" or "worse." Just as Todorov's attempt to recover the existence of "moral life in the concentration camps" in his book *Facing the Extreme* fails to distinguish between Hitler's and Stalin's camps,[109] so, too, in his polemic with Raczymow, he neglects to cite Grossman's reaction on returning to his liberated birthplace in 1943: "There are no Jews in Ukraine. Nowhere . . . in none of the cities, hundreds of towns, or thousands of villages will you see the black, tear-filled eyes of little girls; you will not hear the sad voice of an old woman; you will not see the dark face of a hungry baby. All is silence. Everything is still. A whole people have been brutally murdered."[110] Thus the *Black Book of Communism* is indeed part of a larger trend. François Furet, the late historian of the French revolution and a former left-winger turned conservative, also attempted to resurrect the claim that Communism and Nazism were inherently the same in his book *The Passing of an Illusion*.[111] To be sure France has produced several subtle and sophisticated analyses of genocide, the most recent of which is Yves Ternon's *L'État criminel* (*The Criminal State*).[112] Yet it is works such as Courtois's edited volume, whose very title presents it as a "response" to the alleged overemphasis on the Holocaust, that arouse most interest in the public, by asserting that while there was no inherent difference between Nazi and Communist crimes, the latter were worse simply because of their supposedly greater scale. What is hardly ever mentioned in this debate is that it was Communist Russia, not the French intelligentsia, that destroyed Nazism and thereby facilitated the liberation of France.

From this perspective one can argue that France remains torn between trying to come to terms with is own ignominious legacy and asserting its status as the center of European civilization and the conscience of humanity. In the process the Holocaust is either shoved aside and ignored, or is presented as an obstacle to humanizing contemporary politics. A rather different perspective on this same issue has been recently offered by Éric Conan and Henry Rousso in their study *Vichy: An Ever-Present Past.* The authors' main argument, with which Robert Paxton wholeheartedly agrees in his foreword to the English translation, is that rather than failing to come to terms with the past, over the last fifteen years France has become obsessed with it. In a sense, Rousso's "Vichy syndrome" has come to haunt the nation with a vengeance. Moreover, the authors believe that, especially thanks to the manner in which it is practiced, this preoccupation with the past has by now become largely counterproductive. The insistence on the "duty to remember," they claim, has made it impossible to face the future; instead of facilitating action against contemporary problems and injustices, the politics of memory obstruct and distort French perceptions of the present. Nor does remembering mean the same as knowing; references to the past are often made and exploited by those wholly ignorant of its realities. Hence the plea by Conan and Rousso to declare a "right to forget," so as to be able to get on with life in the present, and to insist on the "duty to know," so that memory can be replaced by knowledge of the past, whose production is primarily the task of the historian.[113]

The difficulty is that one cannot forget what one does not remember and that knowledge about the past in France is still scarce, fragmented, biased, and selective. To be sure, in Germany, too, ignorance about the actual practice of genocide was for long obscured by empty clichés and more or less sincere expressions of grief. Both nations have still not fully worked out what led them to turn against part of their own population, and this failure cannot but have ramifications for more recent outbreaks of xenophobia and struggles over definitions of national identity. It is not that one can face up to the present only by forgetting the past, but rather that as long as one does not face up to the past it will keep happening in the present. Yet both Germans and French have long refused to acknowledge that what made those "somber years" unique in their respective national histories was above all the genocide of the Jews. France's ambiguous past has made this process all the more difficult, since it straddles the boundary between complicity in murder, resistance to Nazism, and helpless victimhood. This ambivalence has enabled "negationism" and "revisionism" to gain some intellectual respectability in France.[114] For the Holocaust remains an obstacle to the perception of France as charged with

a "civilizing mission" and is thus an object of (possibly often unconscious) resentment. Hence the bizarre argument that the genocide of
the Jews diverts attention from "human" suffering and victimhood,
which now seems to have replaced the previous focus on the martyrdom of the "truly" French political resisters.

This is not to deny that an obsessive preoccupation with remembering can obscure both the realities of the past and the problems of
the present. Rousso and Conan are quite right to argue that France
will internalize an awareness of its own role in genocide, not through
public scandals but by careful and responsible research, study, and
teaching. As long as the past remains a dark secret, it will keep haunting the present. The assertion of the German "revisionists" in the
1980s that the burden of the past made it impossible for Germany
to forge a new national identity was ultimately answered with an
increased effort by younger German scholars to learn about Nazism
and the Holocaust rather than to put it aside. So, too, in France a
growing recent effort to excavate the troubled years of the Occupation will eventually enable it to forge for itself a national identity
rooted in knowledge and understanding, not in empty rhetoric and
recriminations.

Memories of War

The publication in 1990 of Jean Rouaud's novel *Les Champs d'honneur*
(*Fields of Glory*) caused a major sensation on the French literary scene.
Within four months the book sold over half a million copies in France
and was in the process of translation into fifteen languages.[115] Over-
night the thirty-eight-year-old Rouaud was transformed from an
anonymous newsstand employee in the nineteenth arrondissement
into the winner of a prestigious literary prize, the Prix Goncourt,
and was celebrated as one of the most important literary "discoveries"
of contemporary French letters. Indeed, since the publication in 1970
of Michel Tournier's novel *Le roi des aulnes* (*The Ogre*), no book had
received such unanimously enthusiastic praise from French critics.[116]

Rouaud's rise to fame must be understood within the context of
modern France's preoccupation with memory, both as mental process
and as literary and scholarly trope. To be sure, memory is a vague,
indeed unusable category if left to its own devices. Personal memories
are often nothing more than a mélange of endless trivia, occasionally
brushing with events and personages of a more general interest. In
order to gain greater universal relevance, memory therefore needs
organization, direction, guidance, and meaning. No wonder that the

first and most powerful analysis of collective memory was written during the interwar period, in a France haunted by the proximity of total war and devastation, and by the vast abyss that 1914–18 had torn between the present and the prewar past, transformed in a series of brutal, bloody battles into a dim, far-off, sentimental memory of a lost world. Nor is it mere coincidence that both the sociologist Maurice Halbwachs, who had coined and analyzed this concept, and the historian Marc Bloch, who had pioneered the study of collective mentalities and the role of fraud and error in history, became victims of a historical moment in which a regime determined to "correct" the memory of the past had occupied a nation unable to be reconciled with its own memories of that same event.[117]

The trauma of World War I had a profound effect on European conceptualizations of history and memory: visions of the future were permeated by images of the past, some lamentably lost in time, others etched in the mind as moments of horror and destruction, marking an irreparable break that inevitably diminished trust in progress. It is worth noting, for instance, that the greatest French novel of the century, Marcel Proust's *Remembrance of Things Past,* written before, during, and after World War I, was a series of ruminations, on a vast scale, about time lost—that is, about the inability ever to recapture and recreate the past. Significantly, Proust's relentless efforts to grasp the fleeting images of things lost were interrupted by war and illness, and finally by death. As he wrote in December 1919, "The war prevented me from receiving the proofs; now my illness prevents me from correcting them." Eventually, much of his oeuvre was published posthumously, thereby transforming the memory of the author's own existence into a final "thing" both remembered and lost.[118]

If it is difficult to establish the links between collective and individual experiences and memories, the traumatic events of this century cannot be understood without reference to their effects on the individual. As Halbwachs has argued, "While the collective memory endures and draws strength from its base in a coherent body of people, it is individuals as group members who remember."[119] Conversely, individual recollection is formed by a collective imagery of the past. Thus Lewis A. Coser notes Halbwachs's accomplishment in recognizing that "our conceptions of the past are affected by the mental images we employ to solve present problems, so that collective memory is essentially a reconstruction of the past in the light of the present. . . . Memory needs continuous feeding from collective sources and is sustained by social and moral props."[120] It is precisely in this sense that we should understand the enthusiastic reception of

Fields of Glory as indicative of France's contemporary perception of World War I as the key event of the century. For Rouaud constructs a sentimental, lightly humorous, comforting, and soothingly continuous narrative of a French family of the lower Loire from 1912 to 1987, only to wreck that fabricated world in the last pages of the novel, revealing the "real" memories of a family never recovered from the trauma of war, the blood bond of death and procreation, the links between generations that still carry the memory of a devastation they had never experienced. This is a novel, therefore, about the tenuous balance between memory and forgetting on which individual and collective identity is based, and about the effects of that link on a single, "representative" French family. It is this odyssey between personal, family and historical memories, between the superficial narrative of this troubled century and the hidden diaries and skeletons that fill its closets, which was shared by so many French readers of Rouaud's novel. And it was as part of that same fascination with this century's first collective trauma that only a few months before the novel was published French cinemas began screening Bertrand Tavernier's *La vie et rien d'autre* (*Life and Nothing But*), which is similarly preoccupied with the complex links between personal mourning and official commemoration, physical and psychological devastation, and the unquenchable urge for life in the aftermath of World War I.

The German memory of this century is organized around a different event. Hence, while Rouaud and Tavernier *focus* on the trauma of 1914–18, German director Edgar Reitz begins his sixteen-hour cinematic saga *Heimat* (1984) at the *end* of the war and represents the interwar years as still part of the sentimental memory of things now long vanished. The pastoral, idyllic existence of his imaginary village is finally wiped out only during the modernization that followed in the wake of Germany's far more disastrous defeat in World War II. Even if we discount Reitz's obsession with anti-Americanism and the ills of modernity, his film reflects the fact that for most Germans the Nazi era has displaced World War I as the central trauma of the century. In Germany, then, *Vergangenheitsbewältigung* (coming to terms with the past) must begin with the Third Reich, even if some scholars have traced its origins to the Wilhelmine Empire. Conversely, French confrontations with the past often begin with World War I, even if its impact is eventually read into explanations of more recent and morally more troubling episodes. Postwar German youths grew up surrounded by the debris of Hitler's thousand-year Reich; French youths, even in the most remote villages, were in daily contact with memorials of World War I. In both nations the victims of

1939–45 retain an ambivalent status, not least because of the tendency
to blur the distinction between them and the perpetrators. Yet the
Federal Republic formally accepted responsibility for the atrocities
committed "in the name of the German people" and has spent much
of the postwar period trying to figure out what precisely is meant by
this formulation. France has commemorated the fallen soldiers—
along with the often more numerous "executed" and "deported"
political and "racial" victims—of World War II on small plaques
attached to World War I memorials or discreetly placed at street corners and bridges, parks and squares. There is no physical, plastic
presence to remind one of Vichy that even faintly resembles the massive memorials and vast cemeteries of 1914–18, or that has the same
effect as the concentration camp sites in Central and Eastern Europe.

Almost a generation before *Fields of Glory,* Tournier's *The Ogre* was
concerned with another war, another devastation, another (but not
unrelated) perversity. The novel was part of the complex process of
coming to terms with defeat, humiliation, and collaboration; it also
reflected the renewed fascination with an evil of the more recent past.
Neither sentimental, nor moralizing, nor edifying, *The Ogre* is a deeply
disturbing, ambivalent, unremitting work, in some ways closer to
Günter Grass's *The Tin Drum* (1959) than to contemporary French
novels. And just like Grass, Heinrich Böll, Siegfried Lenz, and other
German novelists of that generation, Tournier does not try to recreate
or recapture a lost past, but rather grapples with a personal and collective recollection, painful, troubling, unresolved, burdened with
guilt and apologetics, resentment and self-contempt. What *The Ogre*
does have in common with other French (and German) attempts to
confront the legacy of Nazism is that it constitutes a reckoning with
an evil not wholly spelled out and with complicity not entirely conceded. The memory of those most directly subjected to that evil has
for long remained the domain of others. This memory may be mythical and exotic, as in André Schwarz-Bart's *The Last of the Just* (1959);
alienated and ironic, as in Romain Gary's *King Solomon* (1979); obsessed and tormented, as in Boris Schreiber's *La descente au berceau*
(*The Descent to the Cradle,* 1984). It is increasingly now the borrowed,
reconstituted memory of a second generation, as in Patrick Modiano's
La Place de l'étoile (1968), Henri Raczymow's *Writing the Book of
Esther* (1985) and Robert Bober's *What News of the War?* (1993). These
are memories of the Jewish victims (and their descendants), whose
family roots often reach back to other, far off, now extinct worlds.
They are about destruction and survival, and about becoming French
and yet remaining Jewish, often without knowing or remembering

what being Jewish actually means. Significantly, the most remarkable cinematic representation of memory made in recent years, French Jewish filmmaker Claude Lanzmann's *Shoah* (1985), is about the *Jewish memory* of the Holocaust—with the role of the French in the event largely left out. Conversely the most influential film on *France's* complicity in Nazi policies, French Jewish filmmaker Marcel Ophuls's *The Sorrow and the Pity* (1969), is a *documentary.*

By contrast, in postwar Germany representations of Nazism have been very much concerned with the *German* memory of the period, and especially of the war; but this is mainly a memory of German victimhood.[121] The role of Germany's victims has been primarily to function as an absent entity that provides an unspoken model of victimhood in representations of German suffering, as can be seen, for instance, in Alexander Kluge's film *The Patriot* (1979).[122] Hence, until recently, both in France and in Germany the memory of national suffering displaced the memory of the nation's victims. French memories of victimhood focus on World War I and the Resistance, while German recollections of suffering are primarily concerned with the latter phases of World War II. In both cases, however, the genocide of the Jews is both a symbol of absolute victimhood and an obstacle to the recreation of national identity rooted in a sense of shared catastrophe; it must be constantly alluded to without being directly associated with the nation's own past traumas. For this reason the officially acknowledged (annihilated) existence of Germany's victims disappears from view into a self-contained box that can be more easily related to other cases of atrocity and murder perpetrated by other regimes and nations than to those specifically implicated in the genocidal policies of the Nazi regime and its collaborators.

If the trauma of 1914–18 determined French anticipations of war in the next twenty years, the war that eventually came was nothing like what had been expected. The debacle, Occupation, and collaboration became yet another traumatic memory, too close and too ambiguous to be confronted head-on. Hence World War I, now rapidly receding into the past, became a tempting site of remembrance, and the interwar ambiguity about its meaning was replaced by an imagery of national solidarity. Of the two traumas, then, the more distant was preferred. To be sure, coming to terms with the memory of 1914–18 eventually led back to the debacle and Vichy, tracing the path from one trauma to the next. For the roots of Vichy are indeed to be found in World War I, just as present-day France cannot be understood without reference to Vichy. But the memory of Vichy still retains the quality of a political time bomb. In a nation whose previous president was both a socialist, a former Vichyite, and a youthful member of a militant right-wing organization, and where calls for redefining the nation and enhancing Frenchness are accompanied by growing xenophobia, it may seem comforting to remember a distant war in which true patriots died in vast numbers for the homeland.[123] But just as German claims of victimhood can no longer erase the memory of genocide and former chancellor Helmut Kohl's repeated reference to his "grace of late birth" has failed to detach his nation from its history, so, too, the immense sacrifice of France in World War I can no longer obscure the "somber years" of Vichy.[124]

Memories of Absence

In *The First Man* the forty-year-old Albert Camus visits for the first time the grave of the father he had never known.[125] Prompted by the coincidence that his childhood mentor lives in the vicinity, this late encounter also fulfills his mother's oft-repeated wish that he go up to the grave she had been unable to see. But as he stands there, many years older than his father had been when he was killed in the battle of the Marne in 1914, he is filled with a sudden urge to find out more about this man who died for France only a few days after he had set foot on its soil for the first time in his life. Yet no one remembers. The mother has long forgotten, not only because so many years have passed but also, as he says, because the poor are too preoccupied with making a living, with surviving from day to day. "Remembrance of things past," writes Camus, "is just for the rich. For the poor it only marks the faint traces on the path to death."[126] And besides, she cannot read and write, and is hard of speech and hearing. Upon meeting his father for the first time, Camus is confronted with his absence. For a brief moment he is there, and the next he is gone again. Searching for the lost memory of his father, Camus discovers instead his own childhood, recalling how his teacher would read aloud to the class from Roland Dorgelès's *Wooden Crosses*. Not long after this encounter, the old teacher presents him with a copy of that same book as a final farewell gesture.[127] Having previously had only the most tenuous link to World War I, Camus's visit to the grave invests it with a deeply personal meaning, across two generations and another world war.

There is a remarkable similarity between Camus's recently published, unfinished autobiographical novel, found by his side when he was killed in a car crash at the age of forty-seven in 1960, and Georges Perec's semiautobiographical novel *W or The Memory of Childhood*, published in 1975, just seven years before Perec's death at the age of forty-six.[128] Perec visits his father's grave for the first time when he is twenty years old. A mere toddler when his father was killed in 1940 during the German attack on France, Perec has very few memories of him. And it takes yet another twenty years for him to begin consciously searching for his childhood, when he is, just as Camus was at the outset of his own quest, forty years old. But while Camus must reinvent his childhood because the people who could tell him about it are inarticulate and stricken by poverty, hard work, and mental and physical handicaps, Perec cannot return to his childhood's scenes because the people who accompanied him there were taken away from him and killed. Camus's mother lives in a distant, unreachable world, staring out of the window without a word; Perec's mother was deported to Auschwitz when he was six. He asserts, "I have no childhood memories,"[129] but he writes to save the absent, the parents whose disappearance erased his memory of childhood: "I write because they left in me their indelible mark, whose trace is writing. Their memory is dead in writing; writing is the memory of their death and the assertion of my life."[130]

This loss of parents, of childhood, of memory is bound together with war and atrocity. Here the destruction of human beings leads to the erasure of their memory, indeed, even the erasure of the survivors' memories and, in a different, perverse manner, also that of the perpetrators (the memory of their deeds, the memory of their victims). No one remembers. Yet everyone remembers. But the memory of everyone is also the memory of no one; it is the illusion of remembrance. As Perec writes, up to his twelfth year, he could hardly remember anything: "I took comfort in such an absence of history." This absence protected him from his own history. Not remembering was an avoidance of pain. The answers to his history were "a different history, History with a capital H . . . : the war, the camps." History, he thought, had an "objective crispness," an "apparent obviousness," an "innocence"; whereas his own history, "the story of my living, my real story, my own story," was "presumably . . . neither crisp nor objective, nor apparently obvious, nor obviously innocent."[131] Hence the memory, or rather the knowledge of History, can also serve as a refuge from the memory of one's own, one's private history; it is the illusion of History. But Perec can hardly escape History's reach into his own personal tale, for the private has been swallowed up and devoured, and all that is left are fragments that can be put together this way or that, not knowing what belongs where, for the instructions, the guides, have all disappeared. Thus he flees to his imaginary, and increasingly monstrous W, the dreamland of his childhood

transformed in his adult imagination into a land of sports and inhumanity, progressively taking the shape of the Nazi "concentrationary universe."

Having once escaped from his home(land) to France, the nation
to which he feels a cultural allegiance, Camus now seeks the path
back to Algeria, the site of childhood's physical pleasure of life and
nature, the land of the "first man." Yet there is no return, for he can
no longer communicate with the "first men" of his life, his long-dead,
silent father, or his inarticulate, worn out uncle. Having been touched
by civilization, he is now a foreigner in his own land, on the eve of
yet another bout of war and atrocity, the bitter and bloody struggle
between France and Algeria, which will destroy his homeland (for
him) once and for all. Thus Perec and Camus return to the scene of
the crime, to the physical traces of death, the father's grave, the war,
and from those sites of past slaughter they seek a passage to their
childhood, the houses where they were raised, the streets through
which they ran as children. It is a belated return, long postponed,
painful, almost paralyzing, but by opening up the possibility of memory, it also makes life possible, for it provides the capacity to think of
the future and its own still unrealized memory. We have emerged
from a century saturated with the memories of shattered childhoods,
lost parents, devastation on an unimaginable scale.[132] The memory of
the destruction may be so unbearable, so debilitating and wrought
with despair, that we are often tempted to forget. But absence of
memory makes life equally unbearable, for it is lived in an incom-
prehensible, uncharted void, without hope of a future. We remember
so as to be able to forget and forget only to remember all over again.

We remember. But memory is an elusive entity, and the human
mind is never the same. What some remember, others forget; what
some excavate, others cover up. Memory can liberate; it can also be
buried under its own weight. The memory of the past will always
extend into the future, always threaten to monopolize our hopes and
aspirations. And so we mold and twist it to fit our needs, and project
that newly fashioned image forward, making it into a distorting mirror of imagined, fabricated recollections.

One of the most striking features of World War II is that both
Germans and Jews remember it as an event of mass victimization.
The perpetrators may be remembered, but they rarely record their
memories, or do not remember themselves as perpetrators, or claim
to be victims. To be sure, the sites of German and Jewish victimization are different. Germans remember bombing raids and rapes, murderous battles and cruel captivity. Jews remember starving ghettoes,

inhuman camps, and mass murder.[133] Hence, with a few sinister exceptions such as Rudolf Höss and Franz Stangl, the scene is emptied of memories by the agents of destruction.[134] While evil reigns supreme, its messengers are faceless; they wear the dull mask of Adolf Eichmann in the glass cage.[135] Both German and Jewish memories negotiate between recollection and repression. But the former repress the memory of complicity, since it delegitimizes their assertion of victimhood and undermines their identity, whereas the latter repress the memory of atrocity, since it makes life after the disaster unthinkable.[136] In the process the numbers of the victims are enormously expanded, while the numbers of the perpetrators drastically diminish. To the outsider the two groups may appear identical, not because they share a common fate or memory but because of their self-perception as victims.

Memory is conditioned by the relationship between past events and present circumstances. More durable than the ephemeral events it remembers, it is also malleable, unstable, and fragile. When the past is violent and traumatic, both memory and forgetting are crucial for coming to terms with the present. But when the event is also permeated with loss and absence, identity itself is deprived of coherence and constantly threatens to disintegrate. A few memoirs of Germans who served the Nazi regime while opposing it and of Jews who survived the Holocaust by ceasing to be Jewish may illustrate this process. These memoirs all reconstruct the memory of childhood and youth from a distance of several decades and, while keenly aware of the menacing implications of the past for the present, nevertheless retain a measure of optimism, rooted in their writers' personal survival from destruction of inconceivable dimensions. But these are the stories of ruptured lives and double identities: their protagonists are complicit nonconformists, dissemblers of faith, traitors of lost causes and shattered allegiances. They expose the facility to assume contradictory identities in time of crisis and the immense difficulty of sorting them out once it is over. They belie the very notion of a "true" or "authentic" self even as their authors strive to re-create it through the very act of narrating their lives. For the attempt to record traumatic memory is hampered by the narrators' precarious identity and the need to purge the narration of precisely those elements that made past events unendurable. Trauma, in this sense, cannot be overcome by confronting its unexpunged reality but by constructing a bearable image of it. But because it is incomplete and unstable, this image remains a constantly threatening presence in the mind, the site of a daily struggle to keep together a self unable to look into the mirror lest it reveal what must not be allowed to resurface. The fragmented record of atrocity is thus made of the loss and absence produced by physical and mental destruction and by the inability to confront it in its entirety and yet survive its memory.[137]

This is also the point at which we begin to distinguish between German and Jewish memory. The writer Heinrich Böll was raised in a Catholic family that sustained and supported him in his inner resistance to Nazism and his decision not to join the Hitler Youth. In his memoir *What's to Become of the Boy?* (1981), he describes the roots of his courageous postwar moral stance and his opposition to all forms of hypocrisy and control, the seeds of his independent, unconventional Catholicism that made him into a thorn in the flesh of the conservatives and the Left alike.[138] But during the war years, as we know, the boy becomes a soldier, reluctant to serve the Führer, but brave and resolute all the same, so much so that he returns to the front even after being wounded several times in combat. In this memoir, Böll does not reach his army service, but other quasi-autobiographical stories, mostly written in the immediate aftermath of the war, focus on that experience, as in *A Soldier's Legacy* and *The Train Was on Time.*[139] The gist of Böll's perspective on the war as a site of victimhood is succinctly summarized in Henri Plard's blurb on the latter's 1972 German edition: "There are authors who grant war an apparent nobility, others, who have known the humor and rough joys of warriors. In none of Böll's writing can one find even the most qualified approval of war; nowhere does man appear there as anything but its victim."[140] Böll evokes painful, tormenting memories, yet he also cleanses them of all that would have made them unbearable and thus impossible to tell. By concentrating on his own and his comrades' suffering, he leaves out the annihilated presence of their innumerable, truly innocent victims. His is, finally, a memory of moral courage and victimhood—or perhaps of the courage of victimhood—in a world remembered as demanding ever more human sacrifice, yet humanized by moments of love and devotion. This is a memory more suited to serve the future than to excavate the past. The hero may die, but his humanity is preserved; and if he survives, the memory of his true faith and conscience sustains his future existence, if only because he remembers himself always as victim, never as perpetrator.[141]

Otl Aicher's memoir *Innenseiten des Krieges* (*War from Within*, 1985) has much in common with Böll's recollections.[142] Raised in a Lutheran environment and inclined to unconventional theological ruminations, Aicher refuses to join the Hitler Youth. Consequently, he is ostracized by the authorities and barred from taking the *Abitur* (matriculation examination). While he despises the military establishment, declines an officer's commission with the argument that the junior officers are "Nazis without party membership cards,"[143] and attempts to avoid frontline service, he in fact spends much of the war in combat zones. Similarly, despite some vague references to Nazi atrocities, Aicher relativizes them by enumerating all other massacres in human history. His memoir is a strange but not an uncharacteristic mélange of anti-Nazi sentiments and complicity, of recriminations—especially of the German bourgeoisie—and assertions of personal integrity. Painful recollections are qualified by Aicher's self-perceived role in the period. Ultimately he can live with his memories because, just like Böll, he was sufficiently part of the system not to be persecuted and destroyed by it, and sufficiently apart from it to feel redeemed by his refusal to share the sentiments of his environment. Both were, in a sense, "inner émigrés"; hence, too, the title of Aicher's memoir. But both, perhaps due to their upbringing and nature, could not desist from active participation, even if they were in total disagreement with the larger scheme of things. Thus Aicher can direct the Wehrmacht's guns at the Russians in his capacity as an artillery observer and yet feel that he is not "really" part of the Nazi war machine. He can perceive himself as a close friend of Hans and Sophie Scholl—leaders of the White Rose resistance group uncovered and executed by the Nazi authorities—and yet escape arrest by the Gestapo in a somewhat unlikely episode that finds him part, but not a full member, of the resistance. Ultimately, Aicher will enjoy a long and successful postwar career in Germany, even if, like Böll, he bitterly criticizes "the State" and most of what it stands for. But for all its disturbing complacency, his memoir also betrays deeply repressed feelings of guilt and self-doubt, of which the author himself seems mostly unaware.

When the memory of Holocaust survivors comes, it is a memory of loss and separation, absence and uprooted identity, repressed, fragmented, traumatic. All the more so in the case of converted children, whose unrecoverable memory, if it finally resurfaces, threatens to undermine their last remaining, fragile refuge, that third, postwar identity, constructed with great care and pain. "An adult conversion," writes Saul Friedländer in *When Memory Comes,* "may be a purely pro forma affair . . . or it may be the result of a spiritual journey that ends in a decision freely made; nothing disappears, yet everything is transformed: the new identity then changes one's former existence into a prefiguration or a preparation." But for him, a child whose parents were determined to save at any price, conversion had a much deeper, traumatic, enduring meaning: "The rejection of the past that was forced upon me was neither a pro forma affair—for my father had promised not only to accept my conversion but to assure me a Catholic education if life resumed its normal course—nor, of course, the result of a spiritual journey. The first ten years of my life, the memories of my childhood, were to disappear, for there was no possible synthesis between the person I had been and the one I was to become."[144]

Friedländer's life was saved through conversion. But this spelled an irreparable loss of parents and childhood, of self; spiritually, it was the equivalent of a child's hell. Having escaped from the Catholic boarding school to which his parents had sent him, and before being taken back, never to see his parents again, the child clings to the bars of his father's hospital bed. "How did my parents ever find the courage to make me loosen my hold, without bursting into sobs in front of me?" He does not know, he does not remember: "It has all been swept away by catastrophe, and the passage of time. What my father and mother felt at that moment disappeared with them; what I felt has been lost forever, and of this heartbreak there remains only a vignette in my memory, the image of a child walking back down the rue de la Garde, in the opposite direction from the one taken shortly before, in a peaceful autumn light, between two nuns dressed in black."[145]

Shlomo Breznitz parted from his parents at the entrance to the Catholic orphanage, where he was to remain with his older sister. As he writes in his memoir *Memory Fields* (1993): "The final farewell was brutally brief. We all knew what it meant and said nothing to each other. The tears of all four mixed on our faces, and even after they left I could feel the taste of salt on my lips. That was the last material remnant, and for a while I tried to distinguish between mother's and father's salt. . . . Did my official admission into the orphanage mean that I had become an orphan?"[146]

For Friedländer and Breznitz, their previous Jewish identity is a threat, a hidden blemish not to be revealed, the cause of endless anxiety and shame, but also their only link to their childhood, their parents. To survive, perhaps also to make up for their lost identity, both excel in their religious studies as children and youths. After the war Breznitz is told by his mother—who returns from the camps—that the local bishop had protected him precisely because he knew that the boy was Jewish and admired his extraordinary skill in memorizing Latin prayers. Hence both the facility to remember foreign texts and the ability to repress the memory of past identity had been instrumental to his salvation. Friedländer discovers his identity through a Jesuit teacher just as he is about to be launched on a promising career in the clergy. By now the war is over, but he is ignorant of what had happened. They stand under a painting of Christ on the Cross: "'Didn't your parents die at Auschwitz?' Father L. asked. What did this name mean? Where was Auschwitz? He must have understood then that I knew nothing of the extermination of the Jews: to me, the death of my parents was enveloped in vague images, indistinct circumstances that bore no relation to the real course of events. And so, in front of this obscure Christ, I listened: Auschwitz, the trains, the gas chambers, the crematory ovens, the millions of dead. . . . " The Father tells him further about antisemitism: "For the first time, I felt myself to be Jewish—no longer despite myself or secretly, but through a sensation of absolute loyalty. It is true that I knew nothing of Judaism and was still a Catholic. But something had changed. A tie had been reestablished, an identity was emerging, a confused one certainly, contradictory perhaps, but from that day forward linked to a central axis of which there could be no doubt: in some manner or other I was Jewish—whatever this term meant in my mind."[147]

Friedländer's reconversion to Judaism is not the product of memory. In some ways, he, too, is an "imaginary Jew," as Alain Finkielkraut, member of a younger generation of French Jews and the child of immigrants from Poland, had described himself.[148] His rediscovered identity is based on defiance, not on familiarity, on absence, not presence. But for Friedländer it springs from sudden confrontation with the facts of the past. And with that knowledge, he says, ultimately comes memory. But is it knowledge that makes the need to remember so urgent or is it memory—however fragmented—that endows knowledge with this and no other meaning, that redefines him as a Jew? Is knowledge not Perec's History with a capital H, the History that *protects* him from his own past, and that must be discarded, made into an adult's version of a child's nightmare of atrocity (in that imaginary land of W), so as to make room for his private, unique memories?

"As a child who happened upon the wrong place at the wrong time, caught in the whirlpool of events, I too became one of the centers of the earthquake," writes Breznitz.[149] "I was born in Prague at the worst possible moment, four months before Hitler came to power," writes Friedländer at the opening of his memoir.[150] This was bad timing because vast numbers of children became victims of the Nazi murder machine. It was also bad timing because the few who survived were left with gaping absences, not only of parents and siblings but of the memory of their own childhood, of their identity, which became split into disparate fragments and had to be put together again and again in different and contradictory versions. These are the unbearable memories that need to be repeatedly juggled and rearranged, day in day out, in a perpetual struggle to preserve a reconstituted identity. For even as memory comes, it always slips back into the abyss. "For many years my memories of those times played tricks on me," writes Breznitz. "While some could always be recalled, others were more elusive, surfacing for a moment, tempting me to chase them, and then disappearing again without a trace. And there was a third kind of memory, whose existence was evidenced by the deep voids in the story of my childhood. As if it too had been buried under the debris of the earthquake. For too long it remained beyond my reach, its secrets locked behind the faithful bars of repression."[151] Can one ever reach back with any kind of clarity or certitude? Can one express these recovered memories in words? For Friedländer the text of his own memoir is "very far removed . . . from my memories, and even my memories retrieve only sparse fragments of my parents' existence, of their world, of the time when I was a child." But precisely because of this loss and absence, precisely because only a few, fragile memories remain in his mind, Friedländer, just like Perec, feels compelled to write. Not because he remembers well, but because he remembers at all; not because of the need to describe a rich, multifaceted past, but because of the urge to save even a fragment of biography from that vast absence before it too recedes into total oblivion: "I must write, then. Writing retraces the contours of the past . . . it does at least preserve a presence, and it enables one to tell about a child who saw one world founder and another reborn."[152]

Böll and Aicher experience the trauma of war, devastation, and the destruction of the world into which they were born. They must rebuild their lives and forge for themselves new identities from the debris of fallen friends, shattered cities, discredited beliefs. Their return to the homeland is a difficult journey, but a possible one. They retain their language, their family, their landscapes. Böll once wrote that at times he failed to comprehend how he could live in Germany.[153] And indeed, throughout his life he was a harsh and demanding critic of his society. Yet he became and remained a German author, deeply rooted in his culture, honored and respected by many readers. He and his generation underwent a deep trauma, but if there was an absence, if many members of their age group felt that with the collapse of the Third Reich and Hitler's suicide their whole world had broken apart, they could at least pick up the pieces and march on into a new future in the old land and culture. To be sure, some regions of Germany were torn away, and many millions pushed out; but the bulk of Germany remained to flourish again.

This return to the homeland is barred to Camus. While he experiences the trauma of World War I only vicariously through the loss of his father, the path back home is no longer open to him; he must remain in the land he adopted without ever fully belonging to it. Although Perec does not leave his homeland, he must lead his life without a memory of childhood, for the loss of his parents has deprived him of his own past; he must reconstruct the lost years from material remains, houses, streets, photographs, and each time he tells a different tale, for no one remembers. Friedländer has lost both the sites and the memory of childhood; along with Perec and Breznitz, his survival in conversion links the loss of childhood with a new faith and identity, belied once more with his final salvation. In *Wartime Lies,* Louis Begley recounts survival through deceit, after which his protagonist can no longer trust the distinction between truth and lies, and must settle on one of several optional identities.[154] So, too, Breznitz and Friedländer must re-create themselves, with few points of reference and only shards of memory. But the blank spaces on which their new selves are established force them to search for the past, to travel to their place of origin, to reconstruct in their minds the universe and people they had lost. Their new identity is an act of choice and reason, not of faith and memory, and as such it is always fragile and tenuous. They are there, and yet they are not. Their survival is a cause for hope, but unlike their German counterparts, it is grounded in despair, for they are always perched over an abyss that makes them homeless in their own selves. As their memoirs alternate between "now" and "then," they relate to the present as a focus of coherence, a scrap of firm ground to which memory can be anchored. Yet behind this illusory solidity we sense the anxiety of recollected identities on the verge of disintegration, the orphaned memories of solitary children. Theirs is a daily struggle with memory, with what it remembers and what it forgets. And always there remains the fear of plunging into the void of oblivion.

3

ELUSIVE
ENEMIES

The discourse on enemies and victims, its effects on our conduct in and perceptions of war and genocide, and the extent to which such perceptions have in turn redefined our views of victim-hood and identity can be viewed as among the most crucial issues of this century. This is an important key to understanding German self-perceptions and attitudes toward Jews; French conduct in the "somber years" and subsequent conceptualizations of the nation; and Jewish self-definitions and views of real and perceived enemies. But in the larger context, the relationship between enemies and victims has broad implications for grasping the phenomenon of modern genocide, for while it molds national and individual identities, it also retains a persistently pernicious potential that has often led to obfuscation, repression, and violence, rather than understanding and reconciliation. At the end of the twentiety century, we need to ask whether we have succeeded in breaking out of the vicious circle of defining enemies and making victims, which has characterized a great deal of the last hundred years and has been at the root of so much violence and bloodshed. Since historians have been implicated in much of this discourse in the past, they would do well to think about its ramifications for their own time as well.

Border Cases

World War I came at the end of a long process of domestic consolidation and outward expansion of the great European powers. Indeed, among the most distinct features of the new nation-state were the eradication of inner resistance to its claim to sovereignty and control and the ceaseless striving to expand either its proper borders or its overseas empire. This in turn tended to create a mechanism of self-definition and legitimization based on two mutually dependent conceptual and material requirements, namely, the need to define enemies and the urge to make victims, even if the intensity and severity of its application depended on specific circumstances in each individual state. From the state's point of view, those seen as belonging to it had to be integrated, either willingly or by coercion, whereas those seen as not belonging to it had to be excluded or eliminated, no matter whether they wished to belong to it or not.[1] Hence the definition of both foe and friend, compatriot and nonpatriot entailed the making of victims, that is, compelling people to conform to a definition they might not share, based on categories imposed on them by a larger community or a political regime.

The process of state formation in Europe was of course riddled with ambiguities and contradictions, occasionally leading to eruptions of violence and destruction. There were "border cases" along the frontiers of states as well as in the heartland. The identities of the Alsatians and the inhabitants of the Pyrenees, for instance, kept shifting for several centuries, as was the case with some of the peoples living along the eastern and expanding borders of the old and new German empire. Such groups could be defined either as enemies or as members of the national community, depending on changing political circumstances, military conquests, ideological determinants, and economic requirements. French peasants were in the process of becoming "Frenchmen" throughout the latter part of the nineteenth century, while the inhabitants of the numerous states and principalities that eventually made up the newly unified German Reich were similarly undergoing a process of "Germanization." If the Third Republic refashioned the notion of "true France," the German Empire appropriated and expanded the concept of *Heimat* (home, birthplace, homeland).[2] In the course of this process, some ethnic, religious, and linguistically distinct minorities within these large entities retained an especially ambiguous status. Paradigmatic of such ambiguity were the Gypsies and the Jews.

Of these two groups, the Gypsies presented less difficulties of definition, since they remained the domestic outsider par excellence, neither wishing nor being allowed to join the national community. No wonder that such terms as *German* or *French Gypsies*, or, for that matter, the very word *Gypsy* (or *Zigeuner* or *tsigane*) to designate the Sinti (German Gypsies) and Roma (the ethnic group as a whole) in the first place, tell us very little about the self-perceptions of the group. Instead, these terms reflect the long-standing prejudices in Europe and the growing inability of national communities to deal with those who remained outside of the consensus, fitting into none of the increasingly established categories of class, ethnicity, language, or residence.[3] The Jews were a more difficult case. On the one hand, their legal emancipation coincided with the political, constitutional, and administrative emergence of the modern nation-state, as was the case in revolutionary France and, in the following century, with the establishment of the German Reich. On the other hand, it was this very same process that brought about a profound transformation in the age-old anti-Jewish prejudices of Christian Europe to modern political and racial antisemitism. Unlike the Gypsies, who appear to have largely preferred to retain their traditional way of life, the Jews experienced a massive process of "coming out of the ghetto," motivated both by the state's lifting of legal restrictions on occupation and residence, and by the Jews' growing urge to achieve political and economic integration into gentile society, not least in order to improve their often wretched material conditions. And yet the parallel effort by increasingly assimilated Jewish communities to retain some features of their specific identity and some links to their coreligionists across national borders made them into a symbol of the "insider as outsider." Thus the Jews served as both proof of and metaphor for the immense integrative powers of the new nation-state; simultaneously, they came to symbolize its exclusionary potential.[4] Ambiguous identities produced tremendous social, political, and psychological tensions, which in turn made for that complex relationship between creativity and disintegration, ingenuity and annihilation, so typical of our century. In this sense, the Jews can be seen as the paradigmatic example of the preoccupation with identity and solidarity, exclusion and victimization that numerous states or at least some of their agencies have manifested in the modern era.

As it consolidated its domestic and international status, the nation-state was simultaneously beset by visions of decadence and degeneration, chaos and anarchy, disintegration and subversion, invasion and destruction. Europe on the eve of World War I was a society haunted by inarticulate fears and anxieties just as much as it was propelled forward by a fervent faith in progress and science. The hard-won domestic unity seemed to symbolize and facilitate the eternal grandeur of the nation; paradoxically, it also appeared to be in imminent danger of social, political, and moral upheaval. A source of confidence and security, the national community also generated anxieties about its potential dissolution, seemingly under attack from all quarters:

organized labor "from below," destabilization of traditional gender roles "from within," and deterioration of international relations "from without." Moreover, confidence in European superiority vis-à-vis the rest of the world, rooted in the newly conquered vast colonial empires, was undermined by fears about the West's vulnerability to infiltration by other races and civilizations and alarm about the biological degeneration of the white race.[5]

The New Solidarity

With the outbreak of World War I, it seemed at first that rumors of approaching internal disintegration had been greatly exaggerated, as all the aggressive potential of fear and anxiety and the dehumanizing and demonizing imagery of prewar domestic enemies were mobilized against the foreign enemy at the gate. The German *Burgfrieden* (civil peace) and the French *union sacrée* (sacred union) were explicit attempts to create solidarity at home (declaring an end to parliamentry strife) by focusing attention on the danger from without. Moreover, those sectors of society which had remained to a greater or lesser degree excluded from the nation, such as the socialists, the Jews, and the Catholics (who carried the memory of the *Kulturkampf* in Germany and of the separation of Church and state in France), along with other regional and ethnic minorities still not wholly integrated into *la Grande Nation* or the Reich, rallied to the flag in a show of patriotism meant to legitimize them as full members of the national community. Similarly, disgruntled intellectuals, skeptical bohemians, disengaged artists, and detached scholars, some of whom had already undergone a "nationalist revival" in the years immediately preceding the war, now seized the opportunity of this uplifting event of cataclysmic military confrontation and took up the national cause.[6] If the enemy was now clearly defined and easily identifiable, so, too, the victims of the war were obviously all those who fought for one's own nation. For a moment, then, the fog and confusion of war was accompanied by a miraculous clarification of identities.

Yet as the casualties mounted at the front and deprivation and mourning increased in the rear, the classifications of foe and friend, victim and perpetrator began shifting once more. This was a fundamental transformation, occurring simultaneously with the unprecedented expansion of the state's powers of mobilization and production, control and surveillance, propaganda and coercion. It has had far-reaching consequences for the rest of the twentieth century.

While propaganda and the brutalizing effects of the fighting enhanced a view of the world as divided between demonic foreign enemies and one's own victimized nation, the peculiar conditions in the trenches of the Western Front created a sense of solidarity between the fighting troops on both sides of the line and a growing resentment of the rear. Moreover, the scope and relentlessness of this new type of industrial killing also created a sense of breathless, if often morbid, fascination and, for some, even an overpowering enchantment and intoxication with the horror being perpetrated on the battlefield. The soldiers could thus both hate the war and experience a sinister attraction to its desperate camaraderie and ruthless, indifferent, wholly unambiguous, outright destructiveness; they could both hate the men across no-man's-land and appreciate that they alone could empathize with their own predicament, due to that bond of blood and suffering that had been sealed between them. The "real" enemy was therefore to be found in the rear, among the staff officers, the noncombatants, the politicians and industrialists, even the workers in the factories, all those who were perceived as having shirked the fighting and thus having excluded themselves from that community of battle increasingly celebrated by the fighting troops. This was a grim, probably inevitable glorification of one's helplessness, of pain and death, just as much as of heroism and sacrifice; it was, that is, a glorification of victimhood.

The community of solidarity both crossed over the border and shrank into itself. Precisely by fighting the enemy across the line, combat soldiers shared a frontline solidarity and a sense of alienation from their respective civilian hinterlands. This imaginary battle community continued to exert a tremendous influence on postwar society long after the fighting had ceased. Made of embittered and at times silent, at other times rebellious and violent survivors of the front, this community was torn between a desire to be reintegrated into society and a sense of being separated from those who had not been "there." This sense of separation was mythologized by certain extremist organizations as an insurmountable barrier, more difficult to traverse than even the no-man's-land into which the soldiers had stared with horror from both sides of the front for four long years.[7]

A sense of victimhood and alienation breeds an urge to look for culprits, for those who had perpetrated the slaughter and in the process both eschewed the suffering and profited from it. Hence the transformation of frontline solidarity into a quest for the "true" enemy, the "real" cause of evil. And because the evil was so keenly felt and of such vast dimensions, so, too, should be the punishment of the guilty. And yet the identity of that "true" enemy remained elusive, making for still greater rage and frustration, expressed in both passivity and listlessness, violence and brutality. If the foreign enemy had become one's comrade in suffering, if the glorious war for which one had sacrificed so much had been in vain, and if patriotism had been whipped up by a lying propaganda machine run by gutless intellectuals safely closeted in the rear, then how was one to make sense of it all?[8]

Disaster can be more easily confronted if traced to a cause, human culprits, superhuman agency, and natural forces. Destruction may not always be rooted in identifiable evil, but it often creates imaginary carriers of perdition. Scapegoats have the advantage of being readily accessible and defenseless, and if slaughtering them may not prevent future catastrophe, it can have a powerful psychological effect. For bewilderment and inaction in the face of catastrophe sap the will to hold out, while identifying a cause and acting against it helps cope with trauma, creating the illusion of fighting back and generating the energy and determination needed to ensure survival. Hence imagination and metaphor are crucial in liberating people from the perceived stranglehold of uncontrollable, invincible forces. In other words, the aftermath of disaster may have fewer devastating psychological and physical consequences for survivors if they can, in turn, victimize their real or imaginary enemies.

Disintegration

The search for those guilty of the massacre in the trenches, the "real" enemy, began in Germany even before the deteriorating military situation at the front and its ultimate collapse made for open accusations of subversion against those least capable of defending themselves. The legend of the "stab in the back" (*Dolchstoßlegende*) was preceded by the notorious "Jew count" (*Judenzählung*) of 1916, an official inquiry aimed at gauging the alleged underrepresentation of Jews in the army. If, before the war, many generals had feared that the growing numbers of working-class recruits affiliated with the Social Democratic Party (SPD) would undermine the army's reliability as a tool against social unrest, during the war the notion of casting doubt on the loyalty of millions of fighting soldiers stemming from the lower classes would have obviously been counterproductive and might have seriously demoralized the troops. But turning against the Jews, a numerically almost irrelevant minority actually striving to demon-

FIGURE 5. Dying for the Fatherland. Tombstone of soldier fallen in 1918 at the Jewish cemetery in Breslau, Germany (now Wrocław, Poland).

strate its loyalty to the regime by dying with frightening zeal at the front, was an almost foolproof way to direct the people's growing anger and frustration away from the political and military leadership without undermining morale (an old method employed often enough in Russia by the czarist regime). Out of a community of about half a million, some twelve thousand German Jews were killed in the war (fig. 5). Yet reports by Jewish soldiers indicate that they were encountering antisemitism even among their own comrades, a sentiment also reflected in the diaries and correspondence of the officer corps, some of whose members eventually became Hitler's generals in the next war.[9] In this respect the legendary battle community (*Kampfge-meinschaft*) was already in the process of becoming a racial or people's community (*Volksgemeinschaft*), from which the Jews were excluded by definition. The rapid and vast growth of the populist, ultrana-tionalist, and antisemitic Vaterlandspartei (Fatherland Party) during the latter part of the war, is also instructive in this context. The do-mestic enemy, whose presence could explain the military disaster and whose elimination would herald national salvation, was thus be-coming an indispensable factor in the national imagery even before the fighting finally ended.[10]

The German sailors and soldiers who rebelled against their com-manders were primarily motivated by a desire to put an end to the pointless carnage at the front and the Navy's plan of a suicidal attack against the British. The widespread disenchantment among the troops would indicate that, by the last phase of the war, the myth of the battle community hardly expressed the rank and file's perception of reality. But revolutionary situations are a highly fertile breeding ground for fantasies and distorted perceptions. The legacy of the immediate postwar years in Germany was one of seething animosities and mutual victimization, violence and terror, all crucial elements in the subsequent rise of the Nazi Party. The extremists on both the Left and the Right, but also to some extent the more moderate liberals and socialists, tended to view their political opponents as sworn en-emies; the militants also often perceived themselves as victims. It is true that the Weimar Republic provided more opportunities for Ger-man Jews than ever before in the past, as can be seen from the grow-ing prominence of Jews in the arts, academe, the media, and politics. At the same time, however, the 1920s were also a period of growing antisemitism, in which the Jews came to be viewed by much of the radical and conservative Right as the main cause and beneficiary of the military disintegration and the collapse of the imperial regime and all it had stood for. The impact of this atmosphere on German Jewry was just as significant, although reactions were anything but unified. Some Jews turned to accelerated assimilation, others sought to recover their Jewish identity, still others made efforts to emigrate, but most were aware of the mixed signals given them by gentile society and beset by a sense of crisis.[11] Conversely, if the socialists could be ac-cused of adhering to a pernicious ideology, the working class as such could never take the place of the nation's foreign enemies, since the future army expected to undo the humiliation of the Versailles *Diktat* (the peace terms dictated to Germany) would eventually be raised from its ranks. To be sure, the carriers of "Bolshevism" had to be eliminated, but their followers were to be won over, not destroyed. Those on the lookout for domestic enemies needed a target group that would be both sufficiently visible and more or less universally disliked, perceived as both all-powerful and numerically marginal so that its elimination from society would not have a major detrimental effect on the nation, both an easy target for victimization and generally accepted as the chief instigator of its persecutors' own victimhood. An enemy, that is, whose very persecution would serve to manifest the power and legitimacy of the victimizer, while simultaneously allowing the persecutor to claim the status of the "true" (past, present, and potentially future) victim.[12]

While in Germany the aftermath of World War I unleashed new destructive energies, in France it hindered a unified resistance to future foreign threats and ultimately played an important role in French reactions to defeat and occupation in 1940. The mutiny of 1917 in the French army did not bring about a collapse of the front and, at least overtly, was not politically motivated. But the refusal of numerous battalions to participate in any more suicidal attacks reflected the transformation of the old *élan,* the spirit of the *offensive à outrance* (all-out offensive) into a grim determination to hold back the Germans and survive in the trenches. Indeed, long before the mutiny, the troops began a complex process of largely unspoken negotiations with their frontline officers regarding the manner in which the fighting should be conducted. Now the generals and politicians in the rear also had to accept the limits of the troops' willingness to follow orders. This meant that if, in one sense, France as a nation was still seen as Germany's victim, in another, more direct and intimate sense, the soldiers also saw themselves as the victims of their own amorphous authorities, against whose whims and ignorance of frontline reality they had a right to protect themselves even as they continued to defend the country from foreign invasion.[13]

France held out to the end, despite the simmering anger of the troops, the waves of strikes in industry, political crises and changes of government, and very much thanks to the final massive involvement of American troops.[14] Since France won the war, there was no need to look for the agents of disintegration, as happened in Germany. But the terrible price of victory was not blamed only on the Germans. While Georges Clemenceau and Philippe Pétain purged the rear and the front of "defeatist" elements and could thereby claim to have overcome the crisis and ensured France's survival, the growing realization during the interwar years of the devastation that 1914–18 had wrought on a whole generation, made the French extremely wary of

anyone suspected of preparing yet another war. The question was not
so much who was guilty of the previous war, but rather, against whom
would or should the next war be fought, whose interests would it
serve, and who was inciting the population to take part in another
bout of mutual slaughter. In other words France became increasingly
involved in searching for those elusive agents of future catastrophe,
perceived as domestic warmongers and their alleged foreign allies,
whose identity depended on the ideological stance and prejudices of
the beholder. This both reflected and further propelled a deepening
social and political rift in the nation that only enhanced the fear of
another major war. If in Germany initial disintegration was followed
by a redefinition of enemies and a determination to destroy them
both at home and abroad, France was too preoccupied with arguing
over the identity of its domestic enemies to perceive the real danger
across the Rhine. Finally, following the debacle of 1940, Vichy collaborated with the German occupiers in seeking out and annihilating those domestic enemies identified by the Nazis and their French
counterparts as the agents of national decomposition. Hence, while
Germany extended its domestic conflict to the international scene,
France imported its foreign enemy to settle a domestic dispute.[15]

In Quest of the Elusive Enemy

France of the 1930s presents a fascinating example of confused, over-
lapping, and often contradictory perceptions of enemies and victims.
This was reflected in the bizarre combination of ideological dogmatism
and fluidity, whereby unrelenting pacifists advocated collaboration,
adherents of communism or socialism turned to militant populism
and fascism, intellectuals were transformed into demagogues and
bullies, and mainstream republicans were converted into putschists.[16]
The ambiguity of French politics extended well beyond the interwar
period and the Occupation into the Fourth Republic and its ultimate
demise in the wake of the Algerian crisis. But in the midst of the
social and ideological turmoil of the 1930s, and under the impact of
the Great Depression and France's decline as a world power, most
political camps came to share the view that rather than being the victors of World War I, they had in fact become its victims. This transformation of self-perception from the vanquishers of the enemy to
its victims was of course related to the fear of even greater destruction
in a future war. Yet since the superiority of the most likely foreign
enemy was readily recognized, the fear of war only enhanced ani-

mosities toward its alleged domestic advocates. Hence precisely those who supported resistance to foreign threats were labeled as the enemy's allies, while those who supported compromise, appeasement, and eventually collaboration, claimed to be true patriots. Not only did this skewed reasoning blur the distinction between homemade and external enemies, it severely paralyzed politics by making resistance to invasion into treason, and resistance to war into an act of national loyalty. Moreover, as fears of yet another slaughter grew, the advocates of compromise on the international front became increasingly supportive of active domestic suppression of those who called to prepare the nation for war. This anxious, often paranoid search for the nation's "true" enemies was made all the more bitter by mutual accusations of paving the path for another mass murder of a new generation of French youth, whose numbers were already depleted by the butchery of their potential fathers in 1914–18.[17]

United by their fear of war, the French were thus split on what to do about it. The lessons drawn by the socialists and communists from events in Germany were that the Left must unite against the threat of domestic fascism. Hence the precarious coalition of the Left and the moderate center was achieved by postulating the existence of an enemy within the nation who shared the interests and ideology of the foreign foe. Moreover, even this alliance included a powerful communist component whose willingness to tone down its revolutionary, antidemocratic rhetoric in view of the more immediate danger of fascism, reflected rather than diminished its subservience to Moscow's changing policies. In fact only the socialist party was willing to stand firm against the Right and at the same time to protect the democratic system, since the pragmatist Radical Party had no qualms about changing coalition partners in mid stride as long as it could maintain its position at the center of national politics. If the logic of the Popular Front was to confront the putschist tendencies manifested on February 6, 1934, to protect the working class from exploitation by big capital and to prepare for international conflict, its price was to institutionalize a national split that haunted the country until well after the Liberation. For now the Right could unite against what it saw as the greatest threat to the nation, namely the policies of the Left, rather than the emergence of Hitler. The Left, which had previously opposed war as serving the interests of capitalism, now pushed for rearmament; whereas the Right, which had traditionally advocated maintaining France's stature as a great European and colonial power, now charged the Left with provoking war in service of foreign interests, such as the

Soviet Union and Britain, and of real or alleged "foreigners" resid-
ing in France, such as the Jews and a variety of political refugees from
Germany, Italy, and Spain.[18]

In France, then, fear of war and domestic turmoil made for the
construction of an array of enemies over whose identity there could
be no agreement. Conversely, in 1930s Germany, as politics came
under the tyrannical rule of Nazism and the mobilization of society
for war became state policy, the identity of the nation's primary enemy was dictated from above, albeit drawing on an increasingly widespread popular prejudice. To be sure, France too revealed a growing
predilection to view those most vulnerable to attack, namely the Jews,
as its primary, though elusive, domestic and foreign enemy. But while
antisemitism intensified in the 1930s, nourished as it certainly was
by much older anti-Jewish sentiments, France also produced impres-
sive manifestations of resistance to this easy solution for its seemingly
intractable problems. The infamous battle cry of the Right, "better
Hitler than Blum," also signified the fact that the leader of the Popular Front, and for a while the Prime Minister of France, was a Jew,
at a time when the expansion of antisemitism throughout the continent made such an appointment unthinkable in most other European
countries. Conversely, Léon Blum's political prominence enabled the
antidemocratic forces in France to identify not only the Left but the
republican tradition itself, with Jewish influence, an argument repeatedly made during Vichy. It is also true that among France's intellectual circles, antisemitic sentiments were anything but rare, ranging
from Louis-Ferdinand Céline's rabid calls to slaughter the Jews to
André Gide's ambivalent comments on the "Jewish question." Yet
Blum's substantial electorate seemed impervious to this rhetoric. And
if the deep rift between the rejection of antisemitism by the working
class and the socialists, and the right-wing and Catholic growing enchantment with it, was symptomatic of the disintegration of French
politics, it also indicates that unlike Germany, 1930s France never
reached a consensus on "the Jew" as the nation's main enemy and victimizer. In other words, just as the French could not agree on what
was to be done about the approaching war, so, too, they failed to
agree on the status of the Jews.[19] And if Vichy tried to realize the
aspirations of French antisemites to eliminate the Jews from society,
it is clear that its anti-Jewish policies did not have the unifying ideological and political effect they achieved in Germany. Indeed, despite
a widespread indifference to the fate of the Jews in occupied France,
the radicalization of antisemitic policies by Vichy and its collaboration
on this issue with the Nazis did eventually contribute to popular

resentment and opposition, even if it was not the primary cause. In Vichy, then, the prewar condition of disunity soon prevailed, thereby making everyone—Jew or gentile—into a potential enemy; conversely, in Nazi Germany the utopia of racial purity focused attention on every individual's potential Jewish heritage.[20] It is for this reason that far more French Jews could remain patriotic both during and after the war than was the case in Germany, despite some notable exceptions on both sides of the Rhine.[21]

If the inability to agree on the identity of the enemy in France hampered its preparation for war and resistance to occupation, it also ultimately prevented it from wholeheartedly engaging in the fantasy of redemptive antisemitism and from remaining blind to the folly of collaboration.[22] Under Pétain the question quickly arose as to who was the enemy and who the savior. Initially, it was Pétain who had saved the nation at its darkest hour from its domestic and foreign enemies by striking a deal with the victorious Germans and setting out to eliminate those who had allegedly brought about the debacle. By the time of the Liberation, however, it was the rebel Charles de Gaulle, described by Vichy as chief of the nation's domestic enemies and ally of its foreign foes, who was now hailed as the savior of *la Grande Nation*. Now Pétain was declared the chief of the nation's domestic enemies and the leader of its collaboration with the Germans, even if this view was qualified by his record as the more or less undisputed savior of World War I. These shifts reflected, of course, the transformation in people's perceptions of the foreign enemy. If the Germans were first viewed as the enemy, then as occupiers, then as allies, and finally as agents of crime and destruction, the British (and later the Americans) were first allies, then enemies, then liberators, even if they also became agents of destruction. Moreover, while the French had collaborated to avoid becoming the victor's victims, they felt betrayed when the Germans nevertheless increasingly victimized them. Similarly, while they felt betrayed by Britain in 1940, the French were grateful for their liberation by the Western Allies, embarrassed by their relatively marginal contribution to it, and embittered by the devastation it brought in its wake. Hence another reason for the myth of the Resistance. Finally, while French authorities during the Occupation produced an array of victims, especially Jews and resisters, by the end of the occupation the French perceived themselves as victims of war, fate, and injustice. Here the Resistance played a more crucial role in organizing and normalizing the memory of the past than it had in influencing the course of events. At this point there was no room for the argument that some members of the nation might have been victimized more than others. And although the French wars of identity, along with those of decolonization, were far from over, the notion of elusive enemies was gradually supplanted by the idea of universal victimhood, which paradoxically made specific, individual victims into an increasingly elusive entity.[23]

The Elusive Enemy Found

Toward the end of the 1920s, and with much greater vehemence following Hitler's nomination as chancellor in 1933, increasing numbers of Germans began to identify the Jews as their most pernicious domestic foe. And precisely because the Jews were the elusive enemy by definition they served as a metaphor for all other domestic and foreign opponents of the nation (and the regime that claimed to represent it), making it appear possible to wipe out political opposition without casting doubt on the inherent unity of the *Volk*. Hence the image of "the Jew" as constructed by the regime played an important role in consolidating the Nazi state and preparing it for the existential struggle for which Hitler had always striven.[24]

While a consensus over the identity of the enemy was being reached, however, his elusive nature, as presented by the regime, meant that he might lurk everywhere, not only in one's social environment but even as a constant threat to each individual's alleged Aryan purity. Paradoxically, just as the Reich was declared progressively *judenrein* (Jew-free), the specter of Jewish presence seemed to haunt people's imagination all the more. It was as if the Jews had simply gone underground or had merged into the innocent Aryan population so well that they might be discovered even among Hitler's most obedient followers. At the same time, "the Jew" came to represent also the entirety of Germany's foreign foes, serving as the incarnation of Bolshevism and plutocracy just as much as the cause of the "stab in the back" and all the misfortunes that followed it. Hence individual psychological anxiety, domestic social threats, and foreign military opponents were all merged into the image of that elusive yet all-powerful enemy, "the Jew."[25]

The image of "the Jew" as the state's most insidious enemy by dint of being both distinctly and irreversibly alien and capable of such mental and physical dissimulation that made him appear "just like us" was a legacy of late-nineteenth-century political and racial antisemitism. The rapid transformation of European society in the wake of the industrial revolution, whose immediate outcome for much of the population was often poverty, disorientation, and fear, created the need to isolate and identify the evil forces lurking behind such an un-precedented upheaval. Simultaneously, the emancipation of the Jews, which, along with industrialization, accompanied the creation of the new nation-state, while providing the Jews with new opportunities, created unease and animosity within a gentile population still per-meated by anti-Jewish prejudices.[26] And since the Jews appeared to be the main beneficiaries of the process, they quickly came to be iden-tified as the instigators of the suffering it caused. Thus, especially among the threatened old middle class of small shopkeepers and ar-tisans, the argument could be made that by putting the Jews "back in their place" all the confounding and wretched realities of modern-ization would go away and the good old order would return.

If the new economic forces were anonymous and faceless, Jewish emancipation and assimilation created a new kind of Jew who could no longer be identified as such with the same ease as in the past. Seem-ingly indistinguishable from his gentile neighbors, "the Jew" as an identifiable "other" was disappearing, at the same time as his power, according to the antisemitic logic, was expanding immeasurably. Modernity and the Jews thus shared the same elusive qualities and could be presented as inextricably linked. To be sure, a rather signif-icant leap of the imagination was needed in order to conclude that an international Jewish conspiracy was at work, where "real" Jews, stripped of their modern, emancipated garb, were plotting in the dark to take over the world. But in both popular and elite circles, the idea was gaining ground that behind the mask of the new Jew lurked the "Asiatic" features of the proverbial Jew of medieval lore and Chris-tian imagery. And, as in all nightmares, this elusive enemy generated much greater anxiety than the easily identifiable one. The notion that the enemy is among us yet cannot be unmasked has always been the stuff of fear and paranoia and the cause of destructive imaginings and violent eruptions.[27]

Modernity brought with it also a belief in science and progress, accompanied by fears of physical and mental degeneration. Scientific racism soon asserted that humanity was divided into higher and lower species, thereby positing racial purity as a goal and miscegenation as racial pollution. According to the skewed logic of racial hygiene, the Jews were both the lowest and most insidious race and the most zeal-ous guardians of their own racial purity, even as they threatened to contaminate the higher races with inferior blood. Yet the same sci-entists who claimed to have identified the different strands of the human race were haunted by the protean nature of "the Jew" and his ability to defeat scientific diagnoses. This implied that every individual was potentially a carrier of precisely those Jewish qualities one was striving to eliminate, that is, that everyone was suspect of belonging to the enemy's camp without even being aware of it. Indeed, anti-semitism was imbued with this fear of "the Jew within," just as the glorification of masculinity was undercut by anxieties regarding one's feminine predilections. The most nightmarish vision of the elusive enemy was to discover that he was none other than oneself.[28]

World War I strengthened the state's ability to identify, control, and supervise its population to an unprecedented degree; it thereby also greatly contributed to the spread of anxiety about the presence of a seemingly inexhaustible number of elusive enemies in society's midst. The modern surveillance techniques developed in that period were designed to acquire *knowledge* about the population, *influence* it in ways deemed necessary by the regime, and *eradicate* domestic enemies. This does not mean, of course, that such techniques and policies were employed in the same manner everywhere, and there is a vast difference in the development of surveillance in the Soviet Union, Fascist Italy, and subsequently Nazi Germany versus interwar France and Britain. Yet the potential was definitely there, expressed, for instance, in postal control, mass public opinion surveys, lists of political suspects to be arrested at a time of emergency, and even the proliferation of popular fiction and film on spies, treason, and in-filtration of the state by foreigners disguised as patriots. Indeed, by acknowledging the difficulty of identifying the enemy within, the emerging surveillance state, which reached its fully fledged form in the Third Reich and Stalinist Russia, asserted that anyone was a po-tential foe, however well integrated and assimilated he or she seemed to be. A society of doppelgängers, where each individual might dis-cover in himself an unknown Mr. Hyde or be metamorphosed over-night into a repulsive insect was also one being prepared to apply the most powerful insecticides to rid itself of its perceived monstrous traits.[29]

The Enemy Within

Obsession with "the Jew within" was also the lot of many assimilated and even baptized Jews, who often internalized the antisemitic im-agery of their environment and consequently held a highly ambivalent perception of their own identity. This could be expressed in self-torment and ultimate self-destruction, as was illustrated, for instance, in the case of Otto Weininger, whose study *Sex and Character* (1903) presented Judaism as an extreme manifestation of the "feminine principle," about to clash with Aryanism, the manifestation of the "masculine principle." For Weininger, Zionism embodied all that was good and noble in the Jewish soul, but he predicted its defeat from within by Judaism, which would return the Jews to their natural place: destruction and the Diaspora. Rejected by Sigmund Freud, obsessed by the "Jewish principle" within himself (which led him to convert to Protestantism in 1902), and devastated by the cool reception of his book (which subsequently became a sensational best-seller), the twenty-four-year old Weininger shot himself in the same room where Beethoven had died.[30]

But the notion of "the Jew within" was also, of course, apparent in the thinking of the fledgling Zionist movement. For the Zionist desire to create a "new Jew" in his own (home)land was accompanied by urgent calls to purge the Jews of what had made them into a Diaspora people, or of what the Diaspora had made of them, namely, those same insidious traits proclaimed by the antisemitic movement, which both created the occasion for Zionism and provided it with much of its anti-Diaspora rhetoric. Zionism pledged not only to take the Jews out of the Diaspora but also to take the Diaspora out of "the Jew." The assimilated Jew's "discovery" of his monstrosity or abnormality lay in his awareness of the discrepancy between his alien "essence" and his conventional outer appearance, whereby he ended up as neither Jew nor gentile. For just as the Jews were abandoning most, but not quite all, of what had made them into Jews, and saw themselves as almost, but not wholly, indistinguishable from their environment, they were increasingly reminded that it was precisely these remnants of their identity that made them appear all the more suspect to the rest of society. The proverbial "self-hating Jew" was predicated on this condition of almost yet not quite complete assimilation. And the solutions to this predicament were either self-annihilation, whether by physical or cultural suicide, or self-assertion, whether by return to Jewish tradition or by Jewish nationalism.

If, in Germany, many gentiles both before and after World War I could still say that some of their best friends were Jews, many German Jews discovered that some of *their* best friends still preserved antisemitic sentiments. Indeed, the elusive social enemies of the Jews were precisely those liberals who, while supporting Jewish emancipation and integration, insisted that they must eventually disappear as a distinct religious or ethnic category. This meant in turn that, especially in Central Europe, Jews in this period were torn between the desire to enter into gentile society as equals and a reluctance or inability wholly to give up their own sense of history and identity.

Tragically, just as German and Austrian Jews were desperately and often creatively seeking a solution to this dilemma, their environment was rapidly edging toward a total rejection of the Jewish-German symbiosis for which they had striven.[31]

Exterminating the Elusive

For Hitler the destruction of the Jews was a sine qua non, a fundamental precondition for the re-creation of the Germans as an Aryan master race in a new thousand-year Reich. What he meant by his calls for eliminating the Jewish influence in Germany may have changed over the years, but he always maintained that "Judaism" must be removed, uprooted, or annihilated in order to preserve Germany from degeneration and decline. This was an extreme position, espoused even in the 1920s by a relatively small minority. Hitler himself was hardly in a position to envision Auschwitz when he wrote *Mein Kampf* (1925). But many others of his generation in Germany and elsewhere were haunted by exterminatory fantasies. Moreover, if most Germans in the 1920s were probably not particularly preoccupied with the "Jewish question," antisemitic sentiments of varying intensity were becoming increasingly prevalent in the Weimar Republic, fed by economic hardship and political turmoil in the aftermath of the war and soon thereafter the Great Depression.

The tendency to perceive the Jews as somehow related to all the evils that beset postwar Germany greatly facilitated the Nazi party's antisemitic propaganda and the popular appeal of the Third Reich's subsequent anti-Jewish policies. Eventually, it meant that the regime never faced any difficulties in recruiting personnel to organize, administer, and perpetrate genocide, and could count on the implicit support for, or at least general indifference to, these policies by the rest of the population. This was achieved in part thanks to the regime's ability to present the Jews as the real, albeit elusive, enemy lurking behind all other evils that plagued Germany. Thus, while widespread circles in Germany saw Communism and Bolshevism as the greatest domestic and foreign danger, the Nazi argument that the Jews were the "real" instigators of Bolshevism could both popularize antisemitism and offer the not insignificant minority of Communist Party supporters in Germany a convenient rationale to rejoin the emerging racial community (*Volksgemeinschaft*) as they "liberated" themselves from Jewish influence. Similarly, by arguing that plutocracy was also part of a Jewish world conspiracy, the Nazis could attract at least some members of the working class (and apparently more than has been estimated until recently) without thereby antagonizing big capital and industry, on whose cooperation Hitler's expansionist policies were largely dependent. The argument that Hitler had played down antisemitism in the years immediately preceding and following his nomination as chancellor because it was far less popular than his promises of economic recovery and national reassertion is insufficient. Rather, the very image of "the Jew" as the "real" but elusive enemy of the German nation enabled the regime to maneuver between contradictory ideological assertions and policies. Hence antisemitism, even when it was least discussed, served along with economic anxiety and hardship, fear of revolution, a longing for national unity and greatness, and a generally xenophobic climate as an important adhesive that kept together an otherwise incoherent and irreconcilable ideological hodgepodge.[32]

The elusive and yet ubiquitous presence attributed to the Jews by the regime played an even more important role in creating an inverted perception of victimhood throughout the Nazi era. While the regime glorified both nation and race, it invariably presented Germany as a victim of its enemies, among whom the Jews stood out most prominently. In January 1939 Hitler "prophesied" that if the Jews were once more to unleash a war aimed at the "Bolshevization of Europe," this time their attempt to victimize the Germans would lead to their own annihilation. He never budged from this position, asserting in his testament that it had indeed been the Jews who had caused the destruction of his thousand-year Reich.[33] The impact of this view can be seen just as clearly in individual Germans' perceptions of reality. Soldiers tended to ascribe massacres perpetrated by their own units to Jewish criminality, even when the actual victims of such atrocities were Jews, and civilians in the rear similarly attributed the destruction of cities by aerial bombing to Jewish thirst for revenge. Indeed, fear of "Jewish" retribution was very much at the back of Germany's stubborn resistance in the last and desperate months of the war, when the invading "Asiatic hordes" in the East and the *Materialschlacht* (war of attrition) in the West were presented as an expression of the Jewish will for world domination.[34]

In this context, it should be stressed that, even while they were murdering Jews in unprecedented numbers, many of the perpetrators perceived themselves as acting in their own defense against their past and potential victimizers. That the Jews *appeared* defenseless and helpless seems only to have enhanced the need among the perpetrators to view themselves as the "real" victims and those they murdered as the culprits. The children, if allowed to survive, would take revenge; the women would bear more children; the elderly would tell the tale. Hence Germany's misfortune could only end by means of a terrible, final sólution, whose execution merely proved the German nation's determination to survive against all odds and enemies. As early as October 10, 1941, the commander of the Sixth Army, Field Marshal Walther von Reichenau, called upon his troops to understand that killing the Jews was "a harsh, but just atonement of Jewish subhumanity."[35] By October 4, 1943, Heinrich Himmler spoke to a gathering of SS soldiers in Posen of "the extermination of the Jewish people" as an action that "appalled everyone, and yet everyone was certain that he would do it the next time if such orders should be issued and it should be necessary." And at a meeting of army generals in Sonthofen on May 5, 1944, Himmler further elaborated:

> You can understand how difficult it was for me to carry out this military (*soldatisch*) order which I was given and which I implemented out of a sense of obedience and absolute conviction. If you say: "We can understand as far as the men are concerned but not about the children," then I must remind you of what I said at the beginning. In this confrontation with Asia we must get used to condemning to oblivion those rules and customs of past wars which we have got used to and prefer. In my view, we as Germans, however deeply we may feel in our hearts, are not entitled to allow a generation of avengers filled with hatred to grow up with whom our children and grandchildren will have to deal because we, too weak and cowardly, left it to them.[36]

While it is impossible to establish how many Germans shared this view, indeed, what proportion of the population was even aware of the Holocaust, it would appear that it was prevalent among those directly involved in perpetrating genocide. Recent research on some of the most important sites of the Holocaust has amply documented the extraordinary extent to which all representatives of the Reich were involved in the killing of Jews and has shown the intentional selection of known antisemites to positions of power in such territories. This massive participation in genocide has also led these scholars to conclude that both Germans not directly involved in the killing and the population in the rear could not have possibly remained unaware that mass murders were taking place, although precise details were not always known.[37] Moreover, the kind of reasoning reflected in the statements made by Reichenau and Himmler had much deeper roots. The fact that the genocide of the Jews was planned and executed by German bureaucrats, soldiers, and policemen, just as much as the manner in which it was both carried out and rationalized, tells us a great deal about the crucial role played by the fabricated image of the

elusive enemy in preparing German society to take the path to inhumanity and barbarism. It could be argued that the very notion of elusive enemies—who especially in the German case were invariably
the Jews—is a crucial precondition for atrocity and genocide, since
it postulates that the people one kills are never those one sees but
merely what they represent, that is, what is hidden under their mask
of innocence and normality. Thus the encounter of Germans with
"authentic" Jews in Poland and Russia, who conformed to the antisemitic imagery of a traditional garb and way of life, only confirmed
the suspicion that "their" German Jews were merely hiding behind
a westernized facade. Moreover, even these Polish and Russian Jews
were not the old men, women, and children they appeared to be but
pernicious enemies in no way different from fanatic Red Army commissars and vicious partisans. When Franz Stangl, the death camp
commander, was asked by Gitta Sereny how he had felt about killing
children, though he himself was a father, he said that he "rarely saw
them as individuals. It was always a huge mass . . . they were naked,
packed together, running, being driven with whips." On another occasion, he noted that on reading about lemmings he was reminded
of Treblinka.[38]

Central to the worldview and functioning of the Third Reich was
the assertion that its elusive enemies were both ubiquitous, indestruc-
tible, and protean. That is why Nazism was not only committed to
killing all the Jews but was predicated on the assumption that there
would always be more "Jews" to kill. This is the crucial link between
the "euthanasia" campaign and the Holocaust, quite apart from the
well-documented fact that the killing of the mentally and physically
handicapped, which began before the "Final Solution," provided the
expertise and experience, as well as the crews and the psychological
make-up, necessary for the launching of a vast genocidal undertaking.[39] For if there was always a fear of "the Jew within," the urge to
cleanse society of all deformity and abnormality was truly a promise
of perpetual destruction. In this quest for perfection, everyone was
potentially tainted, and no proof of ancestry could protect one from
allegations of pollution. Even in a totally *judenrein* universe, the definition of *health* could always exclude more and more members of
society, whose elimination would promise a better future for the rest.
The boundless definition of *purity* thus made for an endless pool of
potential victims certain to feed the nihilistic dynamics of Nazism for
as long as it survived self-annihilation. Nor has this urge for purity
and health in modern civilization wholly disappeared with the final
destruction of the Nazi regime.

Ubiquitous Victims

The ubiquity of perpetrators and victims, and the frequent confusion between them, is at the core of the destructive energy characteristic of modern genocide, taking place as it does within an imaginary universe that encompasses every single individual in a cycle of devastation and murder. And, since a neutral position is no longer available, both individuals and collectives will naturally tend to present themselves as victims. Thus the unique features of the Nazi genocidal enterprise illustrate an important characteristic of state-organized industrial killing, whereby the fabrication of elusive enemies makes everyone into a potential victim and the assertion of elusive perpetrators makes everyone into a potential killer.

The question of German guilt was raised already during the war by their opponents: Were all Germans guilty, or were they themselves victims of a criminal dictatorship? Conversely, while the Jews were acknowledged to have been (among) Germany's victims, the Allied war was not presented as being waged on their behalf, not least for fear of arousing antisemitic sentiments among the Allies' populations.[40] This created a great deal of ambiguity regarding the identities of both victims and perpetrators at the end of the war, much enhanced by the rapidly changing political and ideological circumstances after 1945.[41] The Cold War transformed old enemies into allies and former allies into sworn enemies; denazification applied a narrow definition of perpetrators, thereby making for a highly inclusive definition of victimhood. The perceived need of the democracies to unite against Communism meant that normalization in the West was accomplished by representing the war as a site of near universal victimhood.[42]

Germany's destruction was there for everyone to see; in the midst of this landscape of utter desolation, the concentration camps easily blended in. Although seen as examples of Nazi depravity and criminality, they did not readily divulge the identity of their victims. Moreover, the death camps were situated far from what had remained of the Old Reich. The town of Auschwitz, for instance, which nationalists had long claimed to be an important landmark of the medieval German eastern expansion, was now dissociated from German history and presented as a remote Polish locality by the name of Oświęcim.[43] At the same time, whereas the German and Austrian inhabitants of towns in the proximity of the camps had come to think of the inmates as "criminal elements,"[44] in subsequent postwar representations they often appeared as political prisoners who had fought against the Nazis. Thus, for instance, Alain Resnais's famous film

FIGURE 6. The competition of victims. Cross as monument to the victims of the
Little Fortress in Terezin (Theresienstadt), Czech Republic. Note the smaller Star
of David in the background (left). Jews were the majority of victims in this camp.

Night and Fog (1955), which powerfully evokes the reality and memory of the camps, neither distinguishes between the concentration
camps and the killing facilities, nor makes any mention of the fact that
the vast majority of the victims in the death camps were Jews.[45] This
supplied the enormity of the Nazi "concentrationary universe" with
a false logic, according to which the regime had simply, albeit ruth-
lessly, suppressed all opposition. It also implied that there had indeed
been a tremendous amount of resistance to Nazism. The far more
numerous victims who had been murdered in the name of racial ideology without ever presenting any objective danger to the regime were
at best relegated to a position of secondary importance, if not altogether ignored (fig. 6). In other words, the genocide of the Jews,
which defied the liberal logic by appearing wholly counterproductive to the German war effort, was left largely unexplained for many
years following the Holocaust, whether by historiography, legal discourse, documentaries, or other forms of representation.[46]

It has been noted that Germans experienced the last phases of World
War II and its immediate aftermath as a period of mass victimization.
Indeed, Germany's remarkable reconstruction was predicated both

on repressing the memory of the Nazi regime's victims and on the assumed existence of an array of new enemies, foreign and domestic, visible and elusive. Assertions of victimhood had the added benefit of suggesting parallels between the Germans and their own victims. Thus, if the Nazis strove to ensure the health and prosperity of the nation by eliminating the Jews, postwar Germany strove to neutralize the memory of the Jews' destruction, so as to ensure its physical and psychological restoration.[47]

To be sure, the crimes of the Nazi regime became a necessary component of both West and East German identity and self-perception, even if the meanings ascribed to them were very different.[48] But it must be stressed that Nazi criminality itself was persistently associated with the suffering of the *Germans*. Both the murder of the Jews and the victimization of the Germans were described as acts perpetrated by a third party; however, while Germans believed they had little in common with the Jews, they naturally felt their own suffering very keenly. Thus the Holocaust was an event carried out by one group of "others" on another such group, whereas the destruction of Germany was perpetrated by (possibly even the same) "them" directly on "us," the Germans. In this manner, the perpetrators of genocide were associated with the destroyers of Germany, and the Jewish victims were associated with German victims, without, however, creating the same kind of empathy.

Postwar German perceptions of victimhood entailed both inversion and continuity. In the Federal Republic the Third Reich's population was seen as the victim of both Hitler's terroristic regime and Joseph Stalin's no less criminal Communist order. This was reflected in the so-called *Berufsverbot* (employment ban), which barred German civil servants from membership in either Nazi or Communist organizations, thereby indicating that both ideologies were of an equally despicable nature. At the same time, however, the view persisted in some quarters that Germany had also been the victim of Western (and especially American) military might and imperialistic policies, now pursued by other means in a campaign of "cultural imperialism" that threatened the German way of life. A good example of this attitude was provided in the last part of Robert Busch and Edgar Reitz's TV saga *Heimat* (1984), which presents the final loss of the homeland as occurring after Nazism, with the infiltration of American norms and values. The same can be said of Rainer Werner Fassbinder's film *The Marriage of Maria Braun* (1979), where the "Americanization" of Germany during the "economic miracle" of the 1950s is shown as the moment in which the *Mutterland* lost its soul, and of Alexander Kluge's film *The Patriot* (1979), whose central motif is that the destruction of Germany in the war—not least through Allied bombing—had erased its cultural and historical memory and identity.[49] Instances of anti-Americanism were also strongly present during such events as the Vietnam and the Gulf Wars, accompanied by and associated with, growing anti-Israeli, and somewhat more couched antisemitic, sentiments particularly visible during the 1982 Lebanon War.[50] Conversely, in East Germany, the official view of fascism as the product of capitalism made it possible to deny all responsibility for the Nazi past and to retain pre-1945 prejudices against the West. In both Germanies, therefore, Americanization took on the appearance of an elusive enemy, not least because of its appeal for so many young Germans on both sides of the Iron Curtain, also making it thereby into the enemy within. Moreover, while East Germany presented Communism as the destroyer of the criminal Nazi clique and its capitalist supporters, deeply ingrained prejudices against Russians never quite disappeared there either, making them into yet another elusive enemy whose presence could not be openly criticized. All of these themes were, of course, reflected in the German historians' controversy, or *Historikerstreit,* of the mid-1980s, and, more recently, in the Goldhagen debate.[51]

West German representations of the past have often included the figure of "the Nazi," as can be found, for instance, in the early works of the writers Siegfried Lenz, Heinrich Böll, and Günter Grass.[52] This elusive type, rarely represented with any degree of sympathy, retains a complex relationship with its predecessor, "the Jew." Serving as a metaphor for "the Nazi in us," it inverts the discredited notion of "the Jew in us" (which postwar philosemitism in turn has inverted into a positive attribute).[53] Simultaneously, it presents "the Nazi" as the paradigmatic other, just as "the Jew" had been in the past (and in many senses remains despite "his" newly discovered moral qualities). If the 1935 Nuremberg Laws could define *Aryan* only negatively as having no Jewish ancestry, postwar representations defined *German* as not being (truly) Nazi. Both instances made for an array of "racial" or ideological *Mischlinge* (half-breeds). After all, just as in the Third Reich, there was always the fear or suspicion that everyone might have some Jewish ancestor in the remote past (quite apart from the fact that many "pure" Aryans, such as Hitler and Joseph Goebbels, did not display the physical attributes expected from Nordic types),[54] so, too, it was hard to find any Germans who had completely abstained from affiliation with the various agencies of the Nazi Party and its innumerable offshoots throughout the Third Reich's twelve years. Only the Jews were innocent on both counts, having been excluded from both the racial and the ideological community. But Jews rarely appear in German postwar representations of the past. Hence only those who had, by their actions or words, shown that they were "pure" Nazis were seen as such by postwar Germans, and even in that case they were rarely pursued and punished with much energy or severity. The innumerable others were said to have been affiliated with the regime unwillingly, unknowingly, naively, innocently, opportunistically, but in any case not out of true conviction. They were not, therefore, "really" Nazi, which left open the possibility that they were "good" Germans.[55]

The new enemy of postwar Germany, "the Nazi," is thus both everywhere and nowhere. On the one hand, "he" lurks in everyone and, in this sense, can never be ferreted out. On the other hand, "he" is essentially so different from "us" that he can be said never to have existed in the first place in any sense that would be historically meaningful or significant for "us," namely for contemporary Germany and especially for the vast majority of individual Germans, who were either not in positions of power in the Third Reich or belong to succeeding generations.[56] Hence "we" cannot be held responsible for "his" misdeeds. Just like the Devil, "the Nazi" penetrates the world from another sphere and must be exorcised; conversely, "he" is a metaphor of the satanic element in humanity. Both faces of "the Nazi" abound in German representations of the Third Reich, and both greatly facilitate identifying with its (German) victims. But the latter view, that of "the Nazi" as an inherent potential in humanity, while it can be construed as apologetic, also generates deep anxiety about the ubiquity of evil even in our own post-Nazi universe.

The public discourse on the Holocaust in postwar Germany has, until recently, largely concentrated either on the social marginality of the perpetrators or on the anonymous forces that made it into a reality. The Jewish victims have rarely featured as anything more than the by-products of this process. So-called ordinary Germans appear to have been either untouched by or irrelevant to genocide, and arguments to the contrary have been seen and condemned as attempts to assign collective national guilt. The largely defensive reaction to such arguments shows the difficulty many Germans still have in accepting that the Third Reich had perpetrated crimes on such a vast scale with the support and complicity of large sections of the population. Instead, it is *German* victimhood and, in some cases, martyrdom that tends to be stressed time and again.[57]

This can also be seen by reference to the debate over resistance to the Nazi regime. Notably, the conservative opposition, associated primarily with the bomb plot of July 20, 1944, has received much more attention in the Federal Republic than the resistance by the communists and socialists, especially during the early years of the regime. This is partly related to the available documentation, partly to the ideological inclinations of postwar historians, and partly to the circumstances of the Cold War. It should be pointed out, however, that the Nazi regime associated socialist and communist opponents, both domestic and foreign, with the Jews, and persecuted them from the very beginning. Indeed, the early concentration camps housed mainly members of the left-wing opposition, along with a variety of "asocials." Conversely, the conservative opposition came from the social and military elite and often had impeccable antisemitic credentials and a record of early support for the regime, which turned sour only when Hitler appeared to be taking Germany on a dangerous war course, or even later, after it became clear that, for all intents and purposes, the war was lost. This is not to cast doubt on the moral motivation of some conservative conspirators, or on the fact that they were appalled by the crimes of the regime. Yet it is just as true that they were potentially acceptable allies of Hitler, and for a long time they indeed served in that capacity, making possible the creation of the regime and the organization of the army that facilitated the disasters and crimes against which they ultimately rebelled. It should also be remembered that the conspirators were a very small minority, hardly representative of the milieu from which they stemmed. Nevertheless, during the Cold War it was as difficult for the Federal Republic to concede that resistance to Nazism had begun on the Left as it was for the German Democratic Republic to admit that the single most dangerous domestic challenge to Hitler had come from the old German elites. Moreover, the very notion of resistance to the regime during the war remained problematic, since it could be construed as another "stab in the back" along the model of 1918, a point of which the resisters themselves were well aware. Indeed, casting doubts on the legitimacy of the Nazi regime by praising the conspirators threatened the far more numerous officials who defended themselves from postwar accusations by asserting their legal and moral obligation to obey the regime, especially in wartime.[58]

The resisters have therefore retained a dual position long after 1945. Seen as both conspirators and heroes, they represent the ambivalent attitude toward resistance to the regime, so well reflected in the treatment by the Federal Republic of lesser acts of resistance or subversion by the lower ranks in the army, such as insubordination, desertion, and self-inflicted wounds. The Wehrmacht meted out severe punishments for such allegedly political offenses, including the loss of pensions, and the Federal Republic, until very recently, up-held these sentences without consideration for the circumstances of the time, yet it pays pensions to retired members of the Waffen-SS or their families. If the senior officers who rebelled in 1944 have been glorified, rebellious soldiers of the rank and file were for long seen as traitors and criminals.[59]

For historians, determining the identity of the Nazi regime's do-mestic opponents is also a matter of definition, not always corre-sponding to contemporary perceptions. While scholars engaged in reconstructing the history of everyday life (*Alltagsgeschichte*) in the Third Reich have noted resistance by the population to this or that governmental measure, this level of resistance was not always per-ceived by the regime as outright opposition, especially since it was often accompanied by conformity with or support for other aspects of Nazi rule: if everyone was a potential enemy, complicity was nevertheless pervasive.[60] Conversely, until recently, the everyday life of the regime's declared enemies received little attention, an implicit acceptance of Nazi distinctions, internalized by much of the popula-tion, between "Aryans" and Jews. This has been changing in recent years, but it should be noted that there is still a general tendency to write the history of the Germans and the Jews separately, even though many German Jews saw themselves first and foremost as Germans, at least as long as the Nazis did not force them to think otherwise, as eloquently expressed in Victor Klemperer's recently published diaries.[61] It could thus be argued that postwar scholarship has insti-tutionalized an ideologically imposed perception, with the result that the historiographies of perpetrators and victims rarely overlap. Al-though the lives of German Jews and gentiles were separated by the regime, it is the process of segregation that needs to be clarified rather than accepted as natural; and, although the categories of victims and perpetrators are distinct, it is the encounter between the two that fa-cilitates genocide, while keeping them strictly apart only blurs the fact that persecution, discrimination, and murder are actions in which one side does something to another side, that is, where there is an en-counter, physical and material, mental and imaginary, between the killer and victim.[62]

The Community of Martyrs

France emerged from World War II with a sketchy record. The de-bacle of 1940 was so astonishing that it left even the Germans gasping.

Perhaps its only redeeming feature was that it persuaded Hitler's skeptical generals of his military genius and their own invincibility, leading them to launch an attack against the Soviet Union where the Wehrmacht was eventually destroyed.[63] Pétain's regime, for all its promises of a New Order, quickly turned out to be corrupt, ineffective, blindly collaborationist, and increasingly criminal.[64] Even the purges that followed the Liberation turned sour; while thousands were executed without trial, many of the officials who played a key role in the deportations of Jews and resisters to Nazi camps escaped justice and went on to enjoy successful careers in postwar France.[65] The civil war during the last months of the Occupation left a bitter legacy that even the myth of the Resistance could not erase.[66] A few decades after the end of the war, even this myth, which had facilitated the reconstruction of the nation, came under increasing attack.[67]

The French have confronted the memory of "the somber years" by successively redefining and reconceptualizing the identity of the period's culprits, passive victims, and heroic martyrs.[68] The process, in turn, derived much of its own logic and terminology from the debate over the causes of the debacle in 1940 that began even before France signed an armistice with Germany.[69] While there were widespread anticipations of an apocalyptic war throughout the 1930s, and some on both the extreme Left and Right welcomed that prospect, hardly anyone expected defeat to be so rapid, overwhelming, and total. Nor was it anticipated the Germany would occupy most, and eventually all of France. It was the shock of defeat, as well as the disgust with the fallen republic and its leaders, that led to the initially massive support for Pétain.[70] Only this ancient "savior" of Verdun seemed to possess the gifts necessary to keep the nation together at a time of chaos and trauma. And he, as we know, readily made France the gift of his person.

Pétain also offered the nation clear-cut explanations for the defeat. These did not concern his own disastrous military leadership during much of the interwar period, nor did they refer much to the foreign foe on whose good will the Vichy regime depended. Rather, he focused on the nation's domestic enemies. For Pétain and his followers, the root of the debacle was to be found in republicanism itself and all that it stood for. France had been undermined from within by democracy and socialism, modernity and lax morals, the "new woman" and the abandonment of family values, refugees and immigrants, and, not least, the Jews. But since this long list encompassed a vast portion of the French people, Vichy had to articulate a worldview that contrasted such positive notions as patriotism, family values, and the Catholic faith, with a narrower category of domestic enemies, among whom the freemasons, the communists, and most important, the Jews, played a prominent role. Hence the alacrity with which Vichy passed its Jewish Statutes, not merely in anticipation of German pressure, but as an indication of the regime's need rapidly to identify an enemy who could be charged with all the evils that led to the defeat, and whose elimination from society would not undermine the unity of the nation, but rather symbolize Vichy's determination to rejuvenate it.[71]

This was, of course, a tactic used with considerable success by the Nazis. But unlike Germany, Vichy was ultimately a creature of Hitler's interests, and its popular support rapidly eroded. Indeed, the legitimacy of Pétain's regime was challenged from the very beginning by its opponents, among whom Charles de Gaulle gradually became the most prominent. Much as Vichy tried to discredit him as a traitor, de Gaulle ultimately succeeded in presenting himself as the very embodiment of France, whereas the progressive subservience of Pétain's regime to the Germans made it increasingly suspect as a true representative of French national interests, especially following the German occupation of the Free Zone in November 1942. To be sure, both Pétain and de Gaulle had grand notions of French fate and destiny, but there was much more grandeur in advocating resistance and sacrifice than in appealing for collaboration with the unloved *Boches*. Thus, almost by definition, the Resistance now became Vichy's primary elusive enemy, both because it vied with it over the role of the nation's legitimate leadership, and because while de Gaulle himself was out of reach, activists of the resistance could hypothetically be found anywhere, even among the regime's own officials. In this sense, as the movement expanded, the notion of an elusive enemy acquired an increasingly concrete form, since the very existence of resistance was predicated on demonstrating its presence through action while never being fully uncovered.[72]

Moreover, Vichy's anti-Jewish policies contrasted with those of the Third Reich in several important respects. Whereas the Germans began by trying to drive out their own Jewish citizens, Pétain's regime, despite its racist legislation, showed growing reluctance to act against Jews with French citizenship. This was in line with popular attitudes, which distinguished between recently arrived refugees and France's well-integrated Jewish community. The growing xenophobia and antisemitism of the 1930s, therefore, rooted as they were in economic crisis and anti-immigrant sentiments, did not have as deep an impact on the public in France as in Germany, not least because, until 1940, there was no openly antisemitic government to orchestrate them.

Hence, while in Germany the exclusion, isolation, and persecution of Jews made for widespread public indifference to their fate and growing complicity in mass murder, in France the realization that collaboration with the Nazis ultimately meant complicity in genocide, increasingly dampened both popular and official support for such actions.[73]

From this perspective we can say that just as was the case during the interwar period, in occupied France there was no unanimity regarding the identity of the nation's domestic enemies. Ultimately, a majority of the population came to reject the very legitimacy of Vichy and to view the collaborationists as traitors to the national cause. This profound transformation of perception, caused by Vichy's slavish subordination to Germany, the Reich's declining fortunes, and the ruthless exploitation of France's industrial, agricultural, and human resources, meant that by 1944 most of the French saw Vichy's representatives as almost synonymous with the foreign occupiers. And, as the Germans withdrew and the former collaborators tried to merge back into the population, they thereby made themselves into the nation's new elusive enemy who had to be ferreted out and punished for all the evils of the past, be they the debacle of 1940, the German occupation, or the crimes of Vichy. This redesignation of the enemy had the merit of endowing the past with logic and consistency, and because the definition of collaboration was swiftly narrowed down to include only the most obvious cases, it also legitimized the vast majority of the French as victims of foreign rule and domestic dictatorship, of whom many had become martyrs of a national struggle for liberation. Vichy's first and primary victims, however, were left out of this newly fabricated heroic narrative.[74]

Elusive enemies, therefore, never played the same unifying role in interwar and Vichy France as they had in Germany. Conversely, for several decades after 1945, conceptualizations of near-universal martyrdom enjoyed an even wider consensus in France than in Germany. Indeed, following the brief period of unofficial and legal purges, the French definition of victimhood made for a relatively smooth transition from the shame and humiliation of the Occupation to a view of the past as an imaginary site of common suffering and resistance to evil. This consensus facilitated the process of unifying the nation after a long period of domestic strife dating from the 1930s and continuing well beyond the Liberation to the end of the war in Algeria. But it was also predicated on suppressing the memory of both those who had quickly adapted themselves to German rule and those who were its most direct victims. Instead, the nation was presented as having shared, as a whole, the trauma of wartime pain, suffering, deprivation and loss. With the exception of a few collaborators who had allegedly been duly punished, postwar France therefore constructed its national identity on the myth of a solidarity of martyrdom. To be sure, within this community of victims there were some who deserved to be honored more than others, namely, the members of the Resistance, whose numbers had not unexpectedly swelled in the last period of the Occupation and especially immediately after the Liberation. And among the resisters, those who had been deported to concentration camps or were executed by the authorities were made into icons of national martyrdom. The Jews, however, whose proportionate losses far exceeded those of any other category in France's population, including the Resistance, were largely left unmentioned, while simultaneously being incorporated as a group into the national narrative of suffering and heroism. In this sense the Jews became the unifying elusive victims of the next few decades, since their fate symbolized the nation's martyrdom, yet could not be specified lest it open the way for distinctions that would threaten national unity. In other words, if the Nazis employed the notion of elusive enemies to create a solidarity of exclusion and fear, postwar France built its national identity on the concept of an inclusive community of martyrs, the identity of whose most distinct members was repeatedly evaded so as to ensure the consolidation of the nation and to cover up the complicity in genocide that cast doubt on the claim of universal solidarity.[75]

This manner of representing the past in the service of the present has been hotly contested in the last couple of decades. On the one hand, the reassertion of Jewish identity in France has increased the demand to recognize the specific fate of the victims of the Holocaust and the complicity of Vichy.[76] On the other hand, many people in France, including not a few Jews, fear that by focusing on the fate of one community during a period of national tragedy, and by charging elements in French society with participation in that group's exclusion and ultimate murder, the contemporary unity of the nation may be undermined, to the detriment of everyone, not least precisely those who had been victims of past conflicts over national identity.[77] And yet the process of rewriting the past was also the result of the belated exposure of centrally placed collaborators who rapidly transformed themselves into powerful and respectable civil servants in postwar France.[78] Thus public awareness of those long-forgotten, "elusive," yet highly visible former collaborators increased just as the memory of the "elusive," yet highly visible victims of those collaborators, began to emerge. Together, these two parallel and in many ways related currents revealed the extent to which the memory of Vichy as a whole had largely evaded critical scrutiny in the name of divergent postwar interests, even as its official narrative was gradually undermined by historians, filmmakers, testimonies and confessions throughout the intervening years.[79] That this was, and perhaps still is, a complex and at times even hazardous process, indicates that national identity is always based both on history and memory, and on erasure and repression. For both in Germany and in France, the price of postwar national unity was paid by the victims of those very forces that these resurrected nations claimed to have eliminated.

Distorting Mirrors

The memory of the Holocaust has been constructed as an elusive, unstable entity by both Germans and Jews. Shortly after the war, Hannah Arendt wrote that the past had become a matter of opinion, rather than fact, for many Germans.[80] Other observers were aware of the larger context of such views. It has been noted, for instance, that George Orwell

> regarded with alarm, even despair, the suggestion that we should accept the limits of our language as the limits of our world (hence the invention of Newspeak in *Nineteen Eighty-Four*); and so far from seeing anything "liberating" in the belief that all truths are "socially constructed," he regarded it as an inherently totalitarian notion. It was the Nazis, he pointed out, who spoke of "Jewish science" when confronted by facts they did not like; ditto, of course, the Stalinists, who damned any truth and value that stood in their way as "bourgeois."[81]

Ironically, an updated version of this view of the world has become common currency in some contemporary intellectual and scholarly circles. Most depressingly, perhaps, Holocaust deniers in several countries have adopted to their own purposes relativist and postmodern assertions regarding the instability or nonexistence of facts about the past, said to be as elusive as memory itself.[82] Interviewed by Claude Lanzmann in his film *Shoah* (1985), the former Nazi Party member and head of the Reich Railways Department 33, Walter Stier, admits that Hitler's dislike of the Jews "was well known. . . . But as to their extermination, that was news to us. I mean, even today some people deny it. They say there couldn't have been so many Jews. Is it true? I don't know. That's what they say."[83] Indeed, the very nature and unprecedented scale of the destruction has tended to put into question the capacity to remember, represent, and reconstruct it. Even while it was happening, many of the victims, the bystanders, the Allies, or potential victims in countries not yet occupied by the Germans, not least of which was the Jewish community in Palestine, found it impossible to believe and comprehend the evidence about the Holocaust.[84]

Atrocity thus becomes elusive precisely because it is ubiquitous, inconceivable because it is fantastic, faceless because it is protean. Jean-François Lyotard has written:

> Suppose that an earthquake destroys not only lives, buildings, and objects but also the instruments used to measure earthquakes directly and indirectly. The impossibility of quantitatively measuring it does not prohibit, but rather inspires in the minds of the survivors the idea of a very great seismic force. The scholar claims to know nothing about it, but the common person has a complex feeling, the one aroused by the negative presentation of the indeterminate.[85]

But devastation of such proportions not only destroys the very mechanisms capable of measuring its scale, it annihilates the ability to imagine it. It must therefore be reduced to a more manageable size and more conventional nature, so that the mind can take it in rather than totally blot it out. Paradoxically, those who want to keep the memory of atrocity and those who wish to deny it are both engaged in a similar attempt to force the event into an acceptable imaginary mold. If their goals are radically opposed to each other, their means are much less so: for both denial and remembrance begin by diminishing the event. Denial starts off by casting doubt on the minutiae of destruction, undermining thereby our acceptance of the whole; reconstruction similarly begins from the details, because the scale of the enormity is so vast that it denies its own existence and vanishes from the mind. Having created a reality beyond its wildest fantasies, humanity cannot imagine what it created. In this context human agency remains tenuous, the disaster being ascribed either to insane genius or to anonymous forces. Language, too, disintegrates; hence the resort, either to medieval imagery of hell and metaphysical speculation or to radical skepticism about reality and a perception of the world as text—complex and elusive but purged of the inarticulate screams of the millions, inscribed into every word pronounced since the Holocaust.[86]

For the Jewish survivors of the Holocaust, it would seem, there was nothing elusive about the identity of either the perpetrators or the victims. Yet both the event of the Holocaust itself and the identity of its human agents and victims have remained highly elusive in what has become by now a substantial body of Jewish ruminations on and representations of the event. By this I do not mean to accept the specious distinction between the so-called mythical memory of the Holocaust among the Jews and the scholarly (*wissenschaftlich*) analysis of the event by a less involved younger generation of German historians.[87] Rather, this has to do with the inherent nature of the event and the fact that its Jewish representation depends to a large extent on the ideological, national, and religious affiliations of the survivors, their offspring, and those who have been spared direct or family-related contact with the event. To be sure, the manner and extent of Jewish preoccupation with the Holocaust, more evident perhaps at present than at any other time in the past, seems tragically both to recapitulate and to invert the urging of the Haggadah (read during Passover) to tell the story of the liberation from slavery in Egypt as if they themselves had experienced it. For the Holocaust is not a story of liberation but of annihilation. In this sense, due to the scope of the destruction and the exterminationist aspirations of the Nazis, every Jew is a survivor by dint of having been a potential victim, including those born after the event, who would not have seen life had Hitler had his way. But precisely because the Holocaust poses the most profound existential questions to Jewish life since the Exile, any interpretation of it cannot be isolated from its implications for the present. And because the event as a whole defies the imaginative capacities of the human mind, it is open to an array of interpretations and ascribed meanings, whose single common element is that they all agree on their incapacity to "save" it completely from its inherently inexplicable nature. Hence the Holocaust can both serve to legitimize contradictory choices of various Jewish communities in the postwar era and simultaneously to cast doubt on each and every one of them, exposing them as precariously founded on a reading of an event that is perceived to be beyond comprehension. In this sense the Holocaust is both at the root of the extraordinary revival of Jewish life after the genocide and the cause of the deep anxiety and bewilderment that characterizes much of postwar Jewish thought and creativity.[88]

In the years immediately following the Holocaust, the two most influential and articulate Jewish communities left in the world, American Jewry and the State of Israel, largely kept silent about the event. While Soviet Jewry, the other major survivor of the Holocaust, found itself under political circumstances that made public, or even private, discussion of the Holocaust almost impossible, American Jews and Israelis, with some important exceptions, largely accepted the very different official state perception in their respective lands. To be sure, both narratives were constructed as a tale of ultimate triumph, either of American democracy and values or of Zionist ideology and Jewish statehood, and both claimed to have discovered the best remedy to the condition of Jewish Diaspora in Europe. Indeed, while American Jews were convinced that their country of choice had led the eventual victory over Nazism, Israelis believed that the very existence of their newly founded state constituted a defeat for Nazi aspirations to destroy the Jewish people. These narratives were not wholly consistent with historical reality. The United States did not fight Germany to save the Jews and could hardly be said to have pursued opportunities to hamper the killing process during the war with any conviction. Moreover, during the 1930s, the U.S. government permitted the entry into the United States of even fewer European refugees—the majority of whom would have been Jews escaping persecution—than the highly restrictive quotas it had already set actually allowed, a decision that proved to have had fatal consequences. Nevertheless, there was little doubt that the United States did play a major role in destroying the Third Reich, thereby putting an end to the extermination of the Jews (by which time, of course, the vast majority of European Jewry had already been murdered). What was just as important for Jewish perceptions of the United States was the fact that, following the war, many survivors were allowed to immigrate here and to begin a new and at least materially successful life.

The Zionist-Israeli narrative similarly contained some baffling contradictions. After all, the minuscule Yishuv, or pre-state Jewish community in Palestine, which numbered just over half a million people during the war, was hardly in a condition to fight Nazism. While the Zionist rhetoric subsequently claimed that unlike the Diaspora, the "new" Jews of Palestine would not have gone as "sheep to the slaughter," the fact of the matter is that had General Erwin Rommel broken through at El Alamein and reached Palestine, the Yishuv would have probably ended up just like any other major ghetto in Europe. What saved the Jews of Palestine was not Zionism but the same factor that saved British Jewry, namely, the British armed forces. No less disturbing for subsequent reconstructions of the period was the knowledge that, while the Holocaust was happening in Europe, the Yishuv was preoccupied mainly with ensuring its own survival and prosperity, building the economic and political infrastructure for the establishment of the future state, and preparing for the anticipated military confrontation with the Palestinian Arab population and the surrounding states. Similarly, American Jewry was extremely slow to acknowledge the reality of the genocide in Europe and was greatly troubled by the prospect that putting too much pressure on the American government to act on behalf of European Jews might have a detrimental effect on the still not fully established position of Jews in the United States. In this sense the same mechanism of repression functioned in the Yishuv and American Jewry during the Holocaust. Both communities found it difficult to believe the horror tales coming from Europe, and they blotted out for as long as they could the growing amount of information indicating that a whole Jewish world, including the families and towns from which so many American and Palestinian Jews had originated, was being systematically annihilated. Both communities also shared a certain level of complacency and self-satisfaction in view of the fact that their respective choices of residence had been justified by the plight of their brethren in Nazi-occupied Europe.[89]

At this point, of course, there was nothing particularly elusive about the self-declared enemy of the Jews. Yet, even while the Holocaust was still happening, the enemy was also being defined both more widely and more narrowly, closer to local concerns, on the one hand, and associated with traditional images, on the other. Moreover, the nature of the Holocaust itself made for a reluctance to concentrate on its details, producing instead an obsession with its implications and a preoccupation with the relationship between victim and perpetrator, complicity and resistance, individual and community, altruism and self-interest.

Many of these strands came together both in the United States and Israel during the trial in Jerusalem of Adolf Eichmann (1961), the first major public confrontation with the Holocaust in either country. Until that point the murder of the Jews was presented in the United States as part and parcel of World War II, specifically of the political persecution that had characterized the Nazi regime and had therefore made the struggle against it into a just war. The genocide of the Jews was still not referred to as the *Holocaust*, and the symbols of Nazi oppression were Bergen-Belsen, Dachau, and Buchenwald, namely those concentration camps—and not death camps—that had been liberated by the Western Allies and that had indeed served during much of their existence for the incarceration of the real and imaginary political enemies, rather than "biological" enemies, of the regime.[90] In Israel, the *Shoah,* or Catastrophe, as it was called there, was perceived as the most important event of the war, of course, as well as a major disaster for the Jewish people. But public discourse and education tended to emphasize such events as the Warsaw Ghetto uprising and other instances of Jewish resistance, on the one hand,

and the eventual illegal immigration (*Ha-apala*) of the survivors to British-occupied Palestine, on the other. The mass slaughter of the Jews was acknowledged but with a distinct measure of embarrassment and discomfort, since, while it could be used to justify the Zionist argument about the urgent need to create a new Jewish "type" in an independent Jewish state willing and able to fight for its existence, it was also perceived as a case of national humiliation and highlighted the Yishuv's own vulnerability as well as its inability to defend the vast majority of the Jewish people murdered in Europe by the Nazis. This combined sense of shame and anxiety made it appear all the more urgent during the early postwar years in Palestine and then Israel rapidly to convert the arriving survivors from Diaspora Jews into Zionist Israelis, that is, to erase those qualities in the new arrivals that had allegedly made the victims go "like sheep to the slaughter" and to remake them as patriotic citizens of the Jewish state, new types unburdened by the shadows and ghosts of the past, and capable of protecting the Jewish state from any more genocidal assaults. That the state was increasingly made up of survivors and that the Yishuv had been saved from the Holocaust due to circumstances wholly beyond its control was not, and perhaps could not, be acknowledged in those early and precarious years of Jewish statehood.[91]

The Eichmann trial redefined many of the categories hitherto employed by the two communities in representing the Holocaust. Receiving wide media exposure in Israel and the United States, the trial greatly complicated previous perceptions of the event, both by providing the public with masses of the information that until then had been the domain of only a few specialists and by casting doubt on conventional narratives and interpretations that had been employed in confronting, or avoiding, the reality and implications of the Holocaust. This was also the reason for the furor with which Arendt's controversial reports and subsequent book on the trial were greeted by both Jewish communities, posing (but also dodging) as she did some of the most crucial questions about the significance of the Holocaust for postwar society, issues that in large part have not been resolved to our own day. One major aspect of this controversy involved the nature and identity of both the enemy and the victim.

Jewish interpretations of the Holocaust conventionally assumed that the Nazi genocide was motivated mainly by a particularly virulent strain of antisemitism, perceived more generally as inherent to European Christian civilization. Arendt's argument—that the genocide of the Jews was carried out by loyal, law-abiding, and opportunistic bureaucrats, who cared little about ideology and a great deal about their own status and reputation as civil servants capable of executing their allotted tasks flawlessly and efficiently—introduced a highly disturbing element to the debate. Moreover, if previously the Jews had perceived themselves as the main victims of the war, Arendt claimed that Jewish traditions of compliance and accommodation in the face of adversity, and the inability of community leaders to recognize the true genocidal intent of the Nazis, led to fateful complicity of the victims in their own annihilation. While infuriating her critics, Arendt's assertion also indicated the need for more subtle analyses of victimhood and complicity. Conversely, while American public opinion had previously subsumed the murder of the Jews under the regime's persecution of its political enemies, the Eichmann trial heralded the emergence of the Holocaust in the United States and subsequently also in Western Europe as the paradigm of evil and the fate of the Jews as the epitome of victimhood.[92] We tend to forget that this was not always the case and may overlook the effects this had on the offspring of victims. For while the children of war veterans could say proudly that their father had been a soldier, those of Holocaust survivors tended to hide the fact that their own parents were victims; there was nothing heroic or satisfying about that status, quite apart from the fact of growing up in a traumatized family environment. Jeremy Adler recently wrote about his experience in Britain:

> In my childhood, there were no secrets at home about this period simply called "the wicked age" (*"die böse Zeit"*) or "the camp years" (*"die Lagerjahre"*) . . . ; yet outside the home a taboo occluded discussion of what, later, was debated as avidly as it had been repressed in terms of "Auschwitz," "the *Holocaust*" and "the *Shoah*." My friends could boast of how dad had fought with Monty in the desert. My own father's experiences were unmentionable. They had no place, until recently. The public cycle from repression to obsession in Britain took about fifty years.[93]

It should be noted that much of the historical evidence for Arendt's essay was taken from Raul Hilberg's magisterial study on the Holocaust.[94] Interestingly, Hilberg's own study was rejected by the Research Institute of Yad Vashem when he asked for assistance in publishing it, mainly because, in the view of the institute's staff, Hilberg had failed to pay due attention to Jewish fate and resistance and had instead focused primarily on the perpetrators. In a letter from Yad Vashem, dated August 24, 1958, he was told that since his "book rests almost entirely on the authority of German sources," and because of "reservations concerning" his "appraisal of the Jewish resistance (active and passive) during the Nazi occupation," the institute "cannot appear as one of the publishers."[95] Indeed, neither Hilberg's work nor Arendt's most important contributions to the debate, *The Origins of Totalitarianism* (1951) and *Eichmann in Jerusalem* (1963), have been translated into Hebrew (the latter is finally about to be published in Israel). However, Arendt's borrowing evidence from Hilberg should not create the impression that they were in agreement with each other. Not only has Hilberg voiced strong criticism of Arendt in his 1996 memoir and in a public lecture given at a conference on Arendt in Berlin during the summer of 1997, there is little doubt that these two scholars were of a very different cast of mind and were motivated by very different agendas.[96]

While Hilberg's focus on the perpetrators was based on his assumption that this was the only way to explain the genocide of the Jews, Arendt's intention was overtly to diminish the centrality of antisemitism in explaining the Holocaust and to show the inherent genocidal potential of the modern state. As other studies have since demonstrated,[97] her dismissal of antisemitism as a motivating factor among the perpetrators and within German society more generally can no longer be supported, but her insistence on the pernicious traits of the modern bureaucratic state greatly contributed to our understanding of the twentieth century and makes her work into a cardinal text of postwar scholarship. Conversely, Hilberg's analysis of the Third Reich has had a tremendous influence on all subsequent studies of the period, yet its limited focus has encouraged the views that the Holocaust can be explained with the victims more or less left out and that Nazi Germany can be analyzed in isolation from other totalitarian and genocidal systems. At the same time, while Arendt took a much wider and less precise view and Hilberg a narrower and more detailed one, both scholars have implied that the Jews were somehow complicit in their murder and did little to prevent it. They ignored, or did not know about, the numerous instances of Jewish resistance (fig. 7), on the one hand, and, on the other hand, failed to acknowledge the more or less unresisting annihilation by the Nazis and other regimes of many groups not normally charged with "having gone like sheep to the slaughter," such as, most prominently perhaps, the millions of Soviet prisoners of war murdered by the Nazi regime and its associates, but also the genocide of Armenians by Turks. (Today, we would add Cambodians by Cambodians, Tutsis by Hutus, and "ethnic cleansing" in the former Yugoslavia). Both Hilberg and Arendt tried to steer away from the monocausal interpretation of the

FIGURE 7. Victims' heroism. Statue commemorating the fighters of the Polish Bund (Jewish socialist party) killed in the Warsaw Ghetto uprising. Plaques only in Yiddish and Polish. Located in the vast and overgrown Jewish cemetery in Warsaw.

Holocaust as motivated only by antisemitism and, in the process, minimized its impact more than the evidence warrants. Yet Arendt was apologetic for German cultural traditions, Hilberg accusatory of German bureaucratic mentality. Both works threatened to replace one monocausality with another. But Hilberg was interested mainly in the mechanism of genocide, Arendt in its moral and philosophical implications.

Arendt's criticism of Eichmann's trial in Jerusalem and of Jewish behavior in the Holocaust, her unwillingness to condemn German culture as a whole, her impatience with the simplistic narrative of the Holocaust as the culmination of European antisemitism, and her association with and subsequent defense of Martin Heidegger cast her in the role of the proverbial self-hating Jew and critic of the newly established Jewish state. As the Hebrew University professor Shmuel Ettinger has written, Arendt

> charged the Jews, their conduct, their leadership, and their actions with much of the responsibility for the crime of antisemitism and even with the extermination of the Jews. . . . At the basis of such arguments are concepts prevalent in German society (and to a large extent even the effects of antisemitic and even Nazi views). In the past, Jews who have sought the roots of antisemitism occasionally came to accept the approaches and modes of thinking of their environment . . . and internalized the image of the Jew as seen by their environment. One might have expected that following the Holocaust this approach would change, but this did not happen to Hannah Arendt, and her attachment to the negative Jewish stereotype distinguishes her from other scholars.[98]

Such so-called self-hating Jews were a social and psychological phenomenon related to the secularization and often only partially successful assimilation of European Jews beginning in the nineteenth century and were anathema to the Zionist and Orthodox establishments alike. Often seen as the enemy within, they reflected the profound crisis in Jewish identity that Zionism, along with other political movements, had sought to rectify.

Especially in its early years, Israeli society found it much easier to deal with the image of the Jew as resister and fighter, even if he or she ended up as a victim, than with the Jew as the victim of another's perception, irrespective of his or her actions. In other words, while Jewish resisters were glorified, "passive" Jewish victims were treated with greater distance and discomfort. Conversely, the early tendency in the United States to view the Jews as a whole as political opponents of the Nazi regime, while it glorified them, did very little justice to their actual fate and arguably made for an integration into American society based on silence and repression. The Nazi regime, of course, ultimately differentiated only between part and full Jews, and occasionally (and temporarily) between Jews who could work and those who could not. Arendt, however, proposed yet another category of Jews, namely, those who in one way or another were complicit in their own genocide, whether (and most especially) as members of the Jewish councils (*Judenräte*) or as policemen and guards (*Kapos*) recruited to control the Jewish population in the ghettos and concentration camps. Unlike previous distinctions, then, between types of Jewish victimhood, Arendt's notion of Jewish complicity blurred the boundaries between victims and perpetrators. Indeed, it is likely that precisely because there was a tremendous amount of resentment toward such Jewish "collaborators" among both the survivors and the Jewish communities that received them (especially in Palestine), Arendt's emphasis on this phenomenon in a public (gentile) forum, well beyond the closed Jewish circles in which it was acknowledged, was perceived as a particularly pernicious type of treason.

In fact Israeli society was preoccupied with precisely these questions long before Eichmann was brought to justice there. During the 1950s, the country was shaken by the Kasztner Affair, in which Israel Kasztner, a Zionist activist in Hungary who tried to strike a deal with Eichmann to save the Jewish population there, was accused of collusion with the enemy and of saving only members of his own family.[99] Even earlier, the reactions of Zionist agents, sent to European "displaced persons" camps to encourage and organize their immigration to Palestine, revealed the contradictory attitude of young members of the Yishuv toward the survivors. One of them wrote, "I believe that those who survived lived because they were selfish, and cared first and foremost for themselves." Another insisted that "they became used to seeing death, they trampled on the living and on the dead and the will to help others was almost extinguished in them." Yet a third agent asserted that "among the survivors there are people, whose souls were cleansed even by the crematorium and who speak with such Zionist fervor, that I cannot imagine any circumstance, or any individual who could surpass them."[100] The painful encounter with the survivors was also the subject of a popular novel published in Israel in 1965 and has remained a controversial issue in Israel to this day.[101] Thus Idith Zertal's recent study *From Catastrophe to Power,* which argues that the Yishuv's political leadership organized illegal immigration primarily in order to enhance the demographic and military strength of the future state, has been the center of yet another public debate on the utilization and reception of the survivors in the aftermath of the Holocaust.[102]

Arendt's case is related in yet another way to more subtle, albeit not always cautious, distinctions between and within categories of victims and perpetrators. Educated in Germany and steeped in the German philosophical tradition, Arendt was unwilling to condemn German culture per se or to speak of German collective guilt for the Holocaust. However critical she might have been of early postwar Germany's failure to face up to its murderous past, its tendency to concentrate on its own victimhood and reconstruction, and its lack of empathy for the victims of the Nazi regime, she rejected interpretations that linked Hitler with earlier German history or assertions about the unique (or uniquely evil) German "character." The product of that remarkable, if also deeply troubled, Jewish-German (negative) symbiosis of Wilhelmine and Weimar Germany, Arendt was affiliated for a while with Zionism and retained a strong association for much of her adult life with Martin Heidegger, the great German philosopher who greeted the advent of the Nazi regime with so much enthusiasm. In this she had a great deal in common with many other German Jews in prestate Palestine and Israel, whose allegiance to and love for the culture from which they had been forced to flee was expressed in the libraries of German classics they had taken along with them on their way to exile in the Jewish homeland. These were not "self-hating Jews" but men and women who refused to condemn the world that had been part and parcel of their own identity and formation, even if they would never return to it. The survivors of German Jewry knew their enemies better than anyone else, since they had lived in their midst until they were finally driven out. Their ambivalence resulted from the fact that, while enemy and victim were so much alike, having largely shared the same educational and cultural background, they were also ultimately defined as stark opposites, so that their fellow citizens became their potential murderers, and they in turn were transformed from patriotic Germans into often ardent, even if at times somewhat schizophrenic, Zionists.[103]

This was only part of the troubled relationship between enemies and victims within the Israeli discourse on national identity. Zionism had formed in Europe as a reaction to political antisemitism, the view that "the Jew" was European society's most dangerous and yet elusive enemy. The Zionists, in turn, presented gentile European society as the greatest danger to Jewish existence and promoted the idea of a Jewish state, applying to it the very model of Central European nationalism that had increasingly viewed Jews as an alien race but combining it with traditional Jewish attitudes to their non-Jewish environment. Yet the new Jewish state was created in the Middle East, on the rim of an Arab and Islamic world, while the original vision of Zionism was to establish a political and social entity very much in line with liberal or socialist ideas brought over from Europe. This made for a great deal of ambivalence vis-à-vis Europe, seen as both the persecutor of the Jews and the model for an independent Jewish existence. Conversely, while Zionism aspired to create a "new Jew" closer to the ancient Israelites than to Diaspora ancestors, the only available example for this figure was the Arabs, who for their part increasingly resisted Jewish nationhood in Palestine. Hence the ambivalent attitude toward the Arab world, which was seen as both a model for a resurrected Hebrew culture and its worst enemy. Meanwhile, the arrival of large numbers of Sephardim from Arab countries to the newly established state was also greeted with mixed feelings. For while these "Orientals" appeared closer to the Hebraic precursors of the modern Jew, their traditional culture, social norms, and religious practices seemed positively alien and primitive to the largely secular Ashkenazim, even if it had the exotic appeal of Biblical times.[104]

All this made for a complex process of inversion and denial, whereby antisemitic stereotypes were employed by Zionism both in order to mold a new type of Israeli Jew and to forge a negative image of the Arab, while the virtues of that very European civilization from which the Zionists had emigrated were both appropriated by the state and set against the "oriental" nature of its Arab environment. At the same time, and in apparent contradiction to this first image, the Arabs were presented as the local manifestation of European antisemitism, and fighting them as a continuation of, and this time victory over, the genocidal aspirations of gentile Europe. Thus the Israelis could see themselves both as an outpost of European civilization on the fringe of barbarism and as winning the war against the collaborators of Nazism that their European ancestors had lost. Ironically, if the Arabs saw the Jewish state as a modern reenactment of the Crusades, to be ultimately destroyed by a latter-day Saladin, the Jewish memory of the Crusaders pictured them as the precursors of Europe's anti-Jewish pogroms, stretching from the Middle Ages all the way to Hitler; and if the Arabs saw the Jews as European colonizers, the Zionists claimed to have regained their ancestral homeland, whence they had been exiled into a two-thousand-year-long existence as the perennial victims of European civilization.[105]

Metaphors of Evil

The origins of modern genocide, as well as its long-term consequences, are thus deeply rooted in a history of metaphors of evil or, perhaps, of evil metaphors claiming to be history. The Israeli case presents only one important aspect of the discourse on persecution and victimhood that has become a central feature of our century. It is no coincidence that, while some Israelis have seen the Palestinians as the incarnation of Nazism, Palestinians have presented themselves as the Jews of the Middle East and some anti-Israeli speakers have compared the Israelis to the Nazis. Whatever the shortcomings of her thesis, Arendt's argument on the elusive nature of victimhood, complicity, and crime provides an important insight into the larger context of the Holocaust. For it is not only an event that defies conventional interpretations but one that has been appropriated by many groups yet ultimately belongs to us all.[106]

The Holocaust has been used to justify the unjustifiable; it has served as a measuring rod for every other atrocity, trivializing and relativizing what would otherwise be unacceptable; it has created an image of an enemy so monstrous that it can be employed to demonize all other enemies (as being the same) or to let them off the hook (as being not as bad); it has created an image of victimhood so horrific that all other suffering must be diminished in comparison or inflated to fit its standards. Itself the product of the idea of elusive enemies, the Holocaust has by now been repeatedly mobilized to perpetuate victimhood, even as attempts to save its memory from oblivion have been presented as providing an alibi for the avoidance, negation, and continuation of evil everywhere else in the world.[107]

What makes the event so maddening, so frustrating, so resistant to human understanding and to ordinary empathy and emotion is the elusiveness of its perpetrators and victims. The perpetrators are elusive because of the bureaucratic and detached manner in which they organized genocide (even if it was ultimately carried out by run-of-the-mill sadists or quickly brutalized "ordinary men"); the victims are elusive because the vast majority of them disappeared without a trace, and the few who survived for many years found it almost impossible to recount their experience, not only because humanity would not, and could not, accept the sheer horror of the event but also because they themselves were torn between the urgent need to recount the tale and the terror of plunging into infinite despair by evoking it once more. What is so devastating about the Holocaust is that there can never be any acceptable relationship between the crime and the punishment, between what humanity has been able to imagine and what it has wrought upon itself. This was already evident during the postwar trials, where the murderers of thousands, having been given a public hearing, were often let off with the lightest of punishments, while their victims had no voice at all. It was manifested by the necessary normalization of both the perpetrators' and the victims' existence, accomplished by repressing the memory and erasing the traces of a past that could not be assimilated into the present. It was, finally, established through the decision that life must continue after the apocalypse. And, as a result of this seemingly inevitable process, much that had been at the root of the original evil has persisted beyond its enactment and extended into the present. Hence the spectacle of victims being accused of complicity in their own destruction, of perpetrators enjoying a prosperous postwar respectability, of shattered, disjointed, and guilt-ridden memories of survivors, for whom the categories of victim and perpetrator as we understand them cannot have the same calming effect, cannot order the past into those convenient distinctions that we wish so much to draw in retrospect. For the final and most tragic legacy of the Holocaust is that even the few who survived know that they could have just as easily joined the endless rows of the "drowned," yet at the same time they are burdened by the sense that they owe a debt to the murdered they can never repay, the debt of their own lives. This is the atrocity after the event; for while so many perpetrators have neither paid for their crimes nor suffered from guilt, the "saved" are doomed to remain their own unrelenting enemies, struggling with the memory and vision of their death for the rest of their tortured lives.

In his last collection of essays, *The Drowned and the Saved,* published shortly before his apparent suicide, Primo Levi describes his reaction on hearing from a friend he met after being liberated from Auschwitz that his survival was the work of Providence:

> Such an opinion seemed monstrous to me. It pained me as when one touches an exposed nerve, and kindled the doubt I spoke of before: I might be alive in the place of another, at the expense of another; I might have usurped, that is, in fact, killed. The "saved" of the Lager were not the best, those predestined to do good, the bearers of a message: what I had seen and lived through proved the exact contrary. Preferably the worst survived, the selfish, the violent, the insensitive, the collaborators of the "gray zone," the spies. It was not a certain rule (there were none, nor are there certain rules in human matters), but it was nevertheless a rule. I felt innocent, yes, but enrolled among the saved and therefore in permanent search of a justification in my own eyes and those of others. The worst survived, that is, the fittest; the best all died.[108]

Defining Enemies, Making Victims

The victim trope is a central feature of our time. In a century that produced more victims of war, genocide, and massacre than all of previous recorded history put together, it is both a trope and a reflection of reality. Yet, at the same time, it is a dangerous prism through which to view the world, for victims are produced by enemies, and enemies eventually make for more victims. Traditional societies often create elaborate rites of vengeance and pacification; modern, industrial societies have the capacity to wreak destruction on such a vast scale that ultimately everyone becomes its victim. This chapter has examined German, French, and Jewish views of enemies and victims, and the extent to which the legacy of the Holocaust has molded the fate and identity of these peoples over the past fifty years. Although I have used the past tense, I believe that this legacy is still an inherent part of German, Jewish, and, to a lesser degree, French consciousness. Moreover this is merely a single, albeit especially pertinent, example of the pernicious effects of the discourse of victimhood in many other parts of the world. By way of conclusion, and without going into much detail, it may be instructive to point out a few more cases in which competing memories and representations of violence have embedded themselves in the historical consciousness and politics of identity of other twentieth-century nations.

The similarities and differences between German and Japanese "coming to terms" with the past have recently drawn the attention of several scholars and journalists. Most relevant to the present context is the tendency of the Japanese, throughout most of the postwar period, to portray their nation primarily as the victim of nuclear annihilation. The shrines erected in Hiroshima and Nagasaki are thus more than symbols of the destructive nature of modern war and cannot be seen as mere expressions of pacifist sentiments. Rather, by celebrating Japanese suffering, these sites have facilitated a process of long-term repression, if not denial, of Japan's own war of annihilation in China and other parts of Asia, as well as its criminal conduct toward prisoners of war. In a recent ironic twist, the German citizen and member of the Nazi Party who saved thousands of Chinese lives during the "Rape of Nanking" was described as the "Oskar Schindler of Nanjing." Thus another "good German" was discovered just as Japan's war of extermination was brought back to the public consciousness. At the same time, it should be stressed that the Chinese government has for long been reluctant to portray its own nation as the victim of Japanese atrocities, both for internal reasons and because of its relations with postwar Japan.[109]

Politics have played a major role also in the case of the Turkish genocide of the Armenians. While the Armenians have seen themselves not only as victims of Turkish extermination policies but also of many decades of concerted Turkish efforts to repress and deny their veracity, the Turks have asserted that claims about genocide were merely part of Armenian nationalism, which had allegedly sparked anti-Armenian policies during World War I in the first place. In this case, too, differing views of victimhood have been reflected in controversies over academic politics and educational policies. This was demonstrated, for instance, in the recent debate over the alleged intervention of the Turkish government in an appointment at an American university, as it was in the equally embarrassing dispute over teaching the Armenian genocide in Israeli schools. In yet another characteristic twist, recent revelations concerning the involvement of the German government in the Armenian genocide expose the highly complex links between instances of mass murder in the twentieth century, as well as their perception by groups of perpetrators, victims, and bystanders. Ironically, during the *Historikerstreit,* the German historians controversy of the mid-1980s, "revisionist" scholars used the Armenian genocide as an event that negated the "uniqueness" of the Holocaust, while millions of second and third generation Turks in Germany were being denied German citizenship, a situation that may be changing only now.[110]

Similarly, the Cambodian genocide ordered by the leader of the Khmer Rouge, Pol Pot, has been used and abused in political debates and ideological confrontations. Dating back to the American involvement in Cambodia during the Vietnam War, the genocide in Kampuchea has been presented by some as the consequence of Western imperialism, by others as one more instance of communism's destructive urge. It was used (along with the Armenian genocide) by German "revisionists" to relativize the Holocaust and has most recently become the focus of an attack on the director of the Cambodian Genocide Program at Yale University, a research project launched by a grant from the U.S. State Department.[111] Meanwhile, in one of the most grotesque, yet not untypical, statements by a modern genocidal dictator, Pol Pot was reported in October 1997 to have said to an interviewer what Hitler too might have said had he found refuge in some remote jungle: "I feel a little bit bored, but I have become used to that." And if Pol Pot has since died, two of his closest aides, former Khmer Rouge head of state, Khieu Samphan, and chief ideologue of the Khmer Rouge revolution, Nuon Chea, have now emerged from their holdouts with the plea to "let bygones be bygones," namely not to be prosecuted for the murder of an estimated 1.7 million people between 1975 and 1979. Days after their defection they were reported to have gone to the beach with their families.[112]

Finally, the three most glaring instances of genocide and "ethnic cleansing" in the 1990s are also deeply mired in a discourse on victimhood and enemies, traced by the protagonists many centuries back and showing few signs of being resolved any time soon. Thus the recent genocide in Rwanda was only the latest in a series of mass killings between Hutus and Tutsis. Moreover, new scholarship has demonstrated how the self-perception of the populations in Burundi and Rwanda has been molded by European ideas regarding the supposed "racial" differences between Hutus and Tutsis, very much in the service of colonial and postcolonial powers as well as of the Catholic church. That the media latched onto the stereotypes propagated by such interest groups, while failing to expose France's role in assisting the Hutu *génocidaires*, indicates that easy access to information in the electronic age by no means facilitates knowledge and understanding, let alone prevention of atrocity.[113] As for the genocide in Bosnia and "ethnic cleansing" in Kosovo, the long memories of southeastern Europe go much further back than the world wars and the horrendous massacres that have afflicted that region in the course of this century. As in the case of the Middle East, political discussions in the former Yugoslavia invariably begin and end by evoking the memory of ancient wars and animosities, deeply inscribed in popular lore, legend, and song. Chronological time and detached historiography play a minor role in people's perceptions of reality, especially at times of crisis (produced to some extent by precisely this hiatus of historical perspective). The heroes and martyrs of days gone by reappear on late twentieth-century battlefields, reenacting the sacrifices and atrocities of their forefathers. Thus the Croats describe the Serbs as "Chetniks," the Serbs call the Croats "Ustashe," and the Muslims are seen as "Turks." The horrors of the past are told, remembered, and repeated. The war, it has been said, was never over, "it was a question of waiting for the right moment to recommence it."[114]

All of this should amply demonstrate that perhaps more attention should be devoted to the process of defining enemies and making victims in future historical work. And yet, just as identifying the similarities between such cases is necessary, no less crucial is the need to make distinctions. Criticizing the recent revival of equating the Soviet and Nazi systems, Peter Holquist notes that "in contrast to the National Socialist regime's biological-racial standard, the Soviet regime employed a fundamentally sociological paradigm to key individual experience to its universal matrix."[115] Hence, he rightly argues, a comparison between Nazi and Soviet state violence indicates that "the Soviets did not see their task as intrinsically related to the total physical annihilation of a particular group," nor to the "outright physical elimination of every living being in that [sociological] category." The Soviets did not "engage in industrial killing" precisely because they viewed extermination a means to a goal, unlike the Nazis, for whom it was the goal itself.[116] Nevertheless, here, too, the Jews came to play a unique role. As Amir Weiner has shown, the post-1945 "twin institutions of hierarchical heroism and universal suffering," which constituted "the cornerstones of the Soviet ethnonational ethos of the war," both erased the Jewish participation in the Soviet struggle against the Germans from official commemoration and historiography and incorporated the Holocaust "into the epic suffering of the entire Soviet population." Indeed, while it practiced ethnic deportations already in the 1930s and continued them on a much greater scale after the war, following the defeat of Nazism, the Soviet leadership increasingly turned to a view "of the Jew as an undifferentiated biological entity," an image that combined traditional antisemitic features, racial criteria borrowed from the Nazis, and inherent socioeconomic, class, or "cosmopolitan" attributes that were allegedly impossible to correct. Consequently, despite the Soviet allegiance to sociological categories, "the postwar discourse on the Jewish question" became central to the "fight over the memory of the war and genocide," which "was rapidly turning into the dominant point of reference in the articulation of identities in the Soviet polity."[117]

The rapid realignment of forces and normalization of conditions after 1945, and the resulting tendency to blur the distinctions between the numerous victims of war and genocide, thus left Holocaust survivors as defenseless against the ravages of traumatic memory and mental devastation as they had been against the Nazi murder machine.[118] From this perspective one may view the fate of the Jews under Nazism as especially tragic; for while in the camps action was often either impossible or counterproductive, even those who survived were unable to act against the perpetrators, both in the context of post-Holocaust reality and in their fantasies. In this sense Holocaust survivors have remained eternal victims, devoid of any recourse to meaningful, even if ineffective and irrelevant, action, trapped within the very conditions of their original victimhood. Conversely, the far more numerous "Aryan" survivors of Hitler's Germany were also faced with the troubling fact that, while they perceived themselves as victims (and were therefore on the lookout for perpetrators), they were largely seen by their former enemies, who dominated much of the international discourse in the years immediately following the war, as perpetrators.[119]

As the protagonists of the Holocaust are slowly leaving the scene, it is the historians who are charged with the task of reconstructing the event and surmounting the barriers that have stood in the way of coming to terms with it. Yet historians, too, must not become so detached from the horror as to avoid perceiving some of those fundamental factors at its root that are still very much with us today. In a world obsessed with defining enemies and making victims, historians should remind those who would listen that there are other ways to view reality. And the first step in that direction is to study what this manner of perceiving the world had wrought on humanity in the past.

4

APOCALYPTIC
VISIONS

Carl Schmitt, the legal theorist and political philosopher, whose critique of liberalism in the last days of the Weimar Republic continues to draw the attention of neoconservatives and postmodernists alike, has been called "an apocalyptic of the Counter-revolution."[1] Schmitt's controversial essay *The Concept of the Political* (1932) presents the "political" as predicated on a friend-and-enemy relationship between and within states, the ultimate manifestation of which is the willingness to die and kill in a war against a recognized collective enemy. Without this relationship, argues Schmitt, politics, and therefore the state, will lose its meaning and wither away, thereby depriving human existence of the seriousness and commitment that ultimately makes it human.

Schmitt, of course, both reflected and influenced a general intellectual trend in Germany on the eve of Hitler's seizure of power. Other legal minds, such as future top SS official Werner Best, spoke at the time of the need to "exterminate the enemy without hating him."[2] For them the definition and eradication of an enemy was a crucial precondition for accomplishing the historical task of reasserting the nation's collective identity and purging it of everything that polluted and undermined it. Best and his comrades meant precisely what they said; they abhorred rhetoric and advocated ruthless action. Once in power they launched Germany on a campaign aimed at isolating and destroying its perceived enemies, both domestic and foreign. The Third Reich's politics were thus propelled by the very dynamic outlined by Schmitt, eventually hurling it into a moral and existential abyss. According to the logic of this argument, nations such as France, which had failed to agree on a collectivity of enemies (and friends), were doomed to degenerate to the status of a nonstate, since their inability to conduct adversarial politics deprived them of their viability as political entities. Similarly, the Jews' perceived inability to recognize the centrality of the enemy-and-friend relationship, prevented them from realizing the "political"; by the time they finally identified the enemy, they no longer existed as a people. Yet even as they were being destroyed, the Jews fulfilled an important task for the Germans, since by constituting the ideal domestic and foreign enemy, they enabled Germany to unite without actually posing any existential threat to it. Vis-à-vis the Jews, to use Schmitt's terminology, the Germans could embody all that was "dangerous" in man, that is, man's noble willingness to kill and die, without in fact putting their lives on the line. Indeed, although he does not mention them even once in this essay, one gets the distinct impression that, had the Jews not existed, Schmitt would have had to invent them.

As Leo Strauss pointed out in his brilliant critique of Schmitt's essay, the "political" is much more about enemies than friends, since the latter are primarily defined as those who do not belong to the former.[3] Thus while "Aryans" were defined as non-Jews, the numerous assimilated and converted Jews of Europe were forced by the Nazis to regain the Jewish identity they had relinquished, often just before being murdered for what they believed they no longer were (fig. 8). Bauchwitz, a labor camp inmate from Stettin, was baptized as a child. When the camp commandant decided to hang him, he requested to be executed by firing squad, in recognition of his service as a German officer in World War I, for which he received the Iron Cross, First Class. The commandant responded, "For me you are a stinking Jew and will be hanged as such." As Bauchwitz stood on the gallows, he called to the inmates, "Since I will die as a Jew, I ask you Jews to say Kaddish after me."[4] Marc Bloch, a wholly secular French patriot who served as an officer at the front in World War I and was executed by the Germans as a Resistance leader in June 1944, wrote in his testament:

> I have not asked to have read above my body those Jewish prayers to the cadence of which so many of my ancestors, including my father, were laid to rest. All my life I have striven to achieve complete sincerity in word and thought. . . . That is why I find it impossible, at this moment of my last farewell, when, if ever, a man should be true to himself, to authorize any use of those formulae of an orthodoxy to the beliefs of which I have ever refused to subscribe.
>
> But I should hate to think that anyone might read into this statement of personal integrity even the remotest approximation to a cow-

FIGURE 8. Fragments of identity. The secret synagogue in the ghetto of Terezin (Theresienstadt), Czech Republic. "Know before whom you stand." Other Hebrew inscriptions call upon God to "relent from Thy wrath" and declare that "He has not yet forgotten us."

ard's denial. I am prepared, therefore, if necessary, to affirm here, in the face of death, that I was born a Jew: that I have never denied it, nor ever been tempted to do so. In a world assailed by the most appalling barbarism, is not that generous tradition of the Hebrew prophets, which Christianity at its highest and noblest took over and expanded, one of the best justifications we have for living, believing, and fighting? A stranger to all credal dogmas, as to all pretended community of life and spirit based on race, I have, throughout my life, felt that I was above all, and quite simply, a Frenchman. . . . I have never found that the fact of being a Jew at all hindered these sentiments.[5]

Bloch was glorified in postwar France, which defined its identity in opposition to those it conceptualized as its domestic enemies, namely, Vichy and the collaborationists, who had previously claimed to rejuvenate the nation by identifying the Jews as the enemy in its midst.

If, drawing on Schmitt's concept of the "political," it was the Jews who made politics possible, then their extermination was the logical outcome of maintaining the "political." Neither Schmitt, nor his friend Ernst Jünger and the older Martin Heidegger—among the brightest minds to have remained in the Third Reich whose very (at least

initially strongly approving) presence greatly contributed to the legitimization of Nazism—ever broached the subject of the Holocaust after the war.[6] Yet Schmitt's theoretical construct can be seen not only
as a rejection of liberalism and as paving the way for an intellectual
adoption of the Nazi worldview but also as anchored in an unspoken
(in this essay) antisemitism, since it is precisely the Jews who must
"by definition" serve as the enemy in a politics based on an enemy-
and-friend relationship. Moreover, the Jews' lamentable—albeit, in
the context of the period, hardly surprising—tendency to support
liberalism, made it seem all the easier to identify them as the enemy.
As Strauss remarked, Schmitt's insistence on logic and on describing
"things as they really are," in fact conceals a concept of morality and
aesthetics that views war and destruction as an instance of glory and
heroism, and hence as a crucial component of human existence, a
necessary or even inevitable return to a state of nature that Schmitt
erroneously associates with Hobbes's view of humanity. In this sense
Schmitt's simple logic is akin to Hitler's, since it postulates that
might is right (and moral) and weakness must be uprooted (since it
is immoral). Yet unlike some of Nazism's less sophisticated adherents
(figs. 9 and 10), Schmitt's aesthetics is merely intellectual; he seems
uninterested in observing the reality of murder and destruction dic-

FIGURE 9. Mirrors of inhumanity. Bathtub of the commander of the Majdanek crematorium, facing the ovens.

FIGURE 10. Mirrors of inhumanity. The swimming pool of the German guards in the Little Fortress in Terezin (Theresienstadt), Czech Republic, located next to the path leading to the execution wall.

tated by his ideas. His is only the satisfaction of a logical argument brought to its ultimate conclusion: conflict and annihilation as an immanent and necessary element of politics.

Schmitt both anticipated and justified the reliance of politics in the modern state on an enemy-and-friend relationship. This was a view of human existence fed by apocalyptic visions and utopian schemes; it expected and called for conflict, but the destruction it brought about was more than it bargained for. Curiously, it is among the victims of the apocalypse—men and women who in some cases shared the utopian visions that facilitated it—that we occasionally find not only a rejection of the friend-and-enemy view of the world but even a capacity, born of suffering, to perceive the humanity of the murderers and to grasp the potential for evil even among the victims. Such perceptions were barred to Schmitt, as to many other Europeans, not because of any intellectual deficiency, but because his urge to bring matters to their most extreme conclusion was accompanied by a remarkable lack of imagination, or perhaps a remarkable facility to repress his imaginative faculties, so that, even when forced to confront the consequences of his ideas, he would look the other way and deny their reality. For his attack on humanism could only result in providing an intellectual validation for the dehumanization of others, a warrant for genocide. It is, perhaps, the cunning of history, that the rehumanization of the world, however limited in scope and duration, was taken up by some of the few who had escaped the exterminatory logic that consigned them to oblivion.

Utopia and Violence

> You cannot make an omelet without breaking eggs.
> Modern revolutionary motto

From the earliest records of human civilization to our own century, people have been fascinated by the notion of remaking humanity—molding individuals and societies in accordance with the laws of God or nature, history or science, into more perfect entities. But this quest for perfection has often been accompanied by an urge to unmake the present and erase the heritage of the past. Hence the path to utopia is strewn with shattered edifices and mounds of corpses. Because by definition it must always remain a goal, utopia engenders fantasies about a future whose imagined fabric draws heavily on myths about the past; fabricating a future earthly paradise is predicated on the imagery of a lost Garden of Eden. Such links between mythology and vision make for mechanisms of remembrance and prediction, fiction and representation, repression and categorization, which are at the core of humanity's self-perception and sense of identity. Materially nowhere, utopia fills the mind; a site of infinite fantasy, it can also trigger limitless destruction.

Boundaries and Transgressions

> Life as an idea is dead. This may be the beginning of a great new era, a redemption from suffering. . . . Only one crime remains: cursed be he who creates life. I cremate life. That is modern humanitarianism—the sole salvation from the future.
> Rolf Hochhuth, *The Deputy*

Utopia begins by setting up boundaries: between reality and vision, the desirable and the undesirable, the intimate and the alien. It banishes the disruptive in the name harmony, the eccentric in favor of the collective. Whether it is predicated on metaphysical dogmas, political principles, social ideals, or biological determinants, utopia cannot tolerate dissent. It is thus defined by what it excludes. Yet once the boundaries are set up, transgressions are bound to follow.[7]

Historically, we can speak of several types of boundaries, based on ethnic, religious, geographical, political, and social categories, as well as on gender and generational differences, although individual identity will normally be determined by belonging to more than one such category. Boundaries can produce a sense of security and stability but at same time may be the cause of tension and competition, oppression and submission. As long as they are accepted by the majority, boundaries can therefore make for an appearance of harmony; for this very reason, any transgression will be seen as posing a threat of disintegration and chaos. Conversely, transgression of established boundaries can also be presented as a step toward greater harmony. Indeed, perfect, universal utopia assumes the ultimate eradication of boundaries, between sexes or races, classes or faiths, the present and the future. Nevertheless, the idea of utopia is predicated on a fundamental rift between conventional, sordid reality and the ideal toward which one ought to strive. Hence it is a harmony based on difference.[8]

Antiquity recognized boundaries between civilization and barbarism. Barbarian conquest of Greek, Roman, or Chinese civilization led in turn to the emergence of new boundaries between an idyllic, remote past, and a more recent, decadent period, seen as the cause of destruction, occupation, and the erasure of previously established boundaries associated with cultural superiority and traditional privilege. But utopian visions were also informed by the image of a purer barbaric invader as yet uncorrupted by the social and moral ills of degenerate civilization, who could serve as a model of ancient ideals. Hence the boundaries between civilization and barbarism, reality and utopia, constantly shifted even as they asserted eternal immutability.[9]

In medieval and early modern Europe, the predominant utopia was heaven, whose essential attributes were similar across denominations and estates. But aside from this purely religious utopia, wherein the boundary between life and death had to be negotiated and traversed, other utopias focused on transforming the world of the living. Here one group's utopia was another's nightmare, whether it involved redeeming the Holy Land or unshackling the serfs, the "reconquest" of Spain or the Islamicization of Christendom, the rise of Protestantism or the Messianism of Shabbetai Zevi. If the gates of heaven could open only after the outrage of death, earthly paradise could be accomplished only by the violent overthrow of established regimes and religions, the massacre of dissidents, the conquest of land. Europe's emergence from the Middle Ages was followed by centuries of political and military expansion, invariably accompanied by the exclusion, expulsion, and murder of those perceived as obstructing the realization of religious and secular utopias and the redefinition of identity within newly drawn boundaries.[10]

This was especially noticeable in the course of European colonialism, which perforce made for encounters with hitherto unknown cultures and religions, customs and norms, races and ethnicities. Here the most fundamental boundary established was that between men and savages, or human and nonhuman. The European discourse on the humanity of colonized peoples largely determined both the fate of the indigenous populations in the colonies and the self-perception of Europeans and their increasing predilection to differentiate between, and rank, types and degrees of humanity according to physical, mental, and cultural criteria. Modern western utopias now included the same split we have noted in antiquity, between a romanticized view of nature and its "noble savages," on the one hand, and the dehumanization of other, "lower" races and cultures, on the other. But both the notion of "returning" to nature and Europe's "civilizing mission" involved a great deal of violence, exacerbated by rapidly improved technologies for killing. Thus utopian societies established far from civilization's corrupting reach could simultaneously assume the eradication or enslavement of indigenous populations, while schemes for social justice, liberty and equality, could at the same time be predicated on the exclusion or annihilation of those no longer recognized as members of humanity.[11]

Cultural differentiation extended also to distinctions between societies with and without history, increasingly seen as the basic criterion of civilization following the decline of religion and the concomitant recognition of non-Christian civilizations in Asia and Antiquity. If modern utopian visions aimed to reach a point where history would come to a standstill and humanity achieve a condition of perfect rest, this was a process to be accomplished *through* history rather than by avoiding it altogether, just as the true saint would emerge from the valley of sin, or classless society from a bitter struggle with an historically necessary phase of ruthless capitalism. The innocence of the original, pre-historical paradise was derived from an absence of history; this naiveté would now have to be replaced by an awareness of history as a precondition for the post-historical utopia. And while some sites of presumed innocence were still to be found in the shrinking white areas of European cartography, the utopias discovered there had to be unmade, and then remade again so as to fit the needs and dreams of modernity's refugees.[12]

Utopia was not perceived as a natural development, but as planned and controlled nature, whose boundaries were determined, set, and guarded by man, not by the whims of climate and biology. Nature was the site in which utopia would be built, but nature was also the ultimate transgressor and thus had to be kept under strict control and supervision. Utopia was a garden society, where chance and mutation, disorder and catastrophe could not to be allowed to disrupt the orderly development of man-made environment. This quest for domination over nature characterized most civilizations, both ancient and modern. Its most recent manifestations are related to the industrialization of the nineteenth century and can be found in fascist rhetoric and planning, liberal suburban schemes and garden cities, and postwar "Green" ideologies. The contemporary discourse on ecology, whose roots go back at least two centuries, is especially pertinent in this context, since it involves the relationship between categories of people and types of environment, nature preservation and human habitation, transgressing the laws of biology and setting limits to reproduction.[13]

Boundaries can also be set between species; nature prevents most interspecies procreation, civilization makes such transgressions strictly taboo. Yet modern science has been preoccupied with evolution, genetics, and cloning, while nineteenth- and early-twentieth-century ideologies have popularized the ideas of social Darwinism, eugenics, and scientific racism. If civilization has for millennia domesticated plants and bred animals, the modern utopia of a perfect humanity has included the idea of breeding pure races of human beings. This is the great temptation of purging physical deformities, mental handicaps, and foreign races, of manipulating nature to fit desirable aesthetic and intellectual criteria, and of eradicating so-called life unworthy of life or categories of people deemed detrimental to society's health and progress. Here conventional taboos against tampering with humanity are transgressed, while the boundaries between humans and animals tend to disappear: superhumans are put above the rest of humanity, subhumans are considered less worthy of life and often more pernicious than domestic animals. Nor should we think of this phenomenon as being limited to such extreme manifestations as Nazism, for the modern discourse on links between biology and society, science and ethics, nature and nurture is the necessary context for such radical policies as racial genocide.[14]

Plans and Inevitabilities

Man models himself on earth,
Earth on heaven,
Heaven on the way. And the way on that which is naturally so.
Lao Tzu

Utopias can be the products of ordering the past, planning the future, and controlling nature—both man's and his environment's. But they may also be perceived as the inevitable outcome of a divinely ordained apocalypse or of the immutable laws of nature and history. God or Hegel's *Weltgeist* (world spirit), evolution or the class struggle, racial war or genetic destiny may all be cited as potential agents in humanity's journey to utopia.

Apocalypse by divine decree and by human action are the two divergent paths to the end of history. The former entrusts the future to the metaphysical, the latter is determined to establish rational control over the universe. Both are at the very root of civilization across a vast array of cultures and societies, and both retain great relevance today, at a time of religious revival and a simultaneous faith in science. Whatever the specific path they have chosen, various religious and secular, ancient and modern, European and extra-European utopian notions have constructed a notion of inevitability. It is this idea that is the basis of both apocalyptic theology and planned society, geared as they are either to keep the anticipated catastrophe at bay or to exploit it for political purposes. It is thus also at the center of any discourse on the relationship between creativity and destruction, hope and despair, and is crucial to understanding how societies have come to terms with uncertainty and fear. At the same time, apocalypse is often seen as bearing utopian consequences; it is thus both an end and a beginning, feared and anticipated, accompanied by social violence and creative change. Precisely when secularized and incorporated into modern ideologies, apocalyptic reasoning and fantasies have fueled a paroxysm of unprecedented destruction.[15]

Human agency is of course a crucial feature both in planning utopia and in contemplating its place within God's scheme or the logic of history. The modern era has become especially preoccupied with the idea of remaking man and society, nature and the environment, according to precisely laid out plans that, at the same time, would remain in accordance with natural and inevitable progression. Hence, too, the perceived need to eradicate resistance to such plans, which by definition is regressive, reactionary, degenerate, or abnormal. For the link between healing and killing, creating and destroying life is derived from a modern utopianism that postulates the need to tamper with nature or change the course of history, while simultaneously asserting compliance with their laws. All that is called for is merely an acceleration of such inevitable natural processes as selection, evolution, and mutation, or of such inevitable social developments as the disappearance of one class and the hegemony of another. In other words, such utopias will either seek to ensure the survival of the fittest, or push toward the end of history, both of which are certain to happen yet also seem to be threatened by unnatural intervention or a lack of understanding. Those who do not fit into nature's plan, or the unfolding of history—as interpreted by man—must be eliminated as so much genetic waste, or will be discarded, thrown into the dustbin of history or ground to dust by the wheels of the revolution. In this context conventional moral arguments are seen as fundamentally immoral, for they obstruct the higher morality expressed in the course of nature or history and thus prevent humanity from reaching utopia by implementing plans based on objective biological determinants or the science of history. The destruction of those who stand in the way is therefore a moral imperative and individual existence must be subordinated to the good of humanity as a whole.[16]

It should be pointed out that notions of social engineering, economic planning, and inevitable historical processes have played some role in many parts of the world throughout the twentieth century. If communist regimes hoped to realize the proletarian paradise by means of planned economies and the destruction of feudal leftovers and capitalist ventures, liberal capitalism set out on a pursuit of universal happiness by combining trust in the "invisible hand" of market forces with state intervention at times of domestic social turmoil and international conflict. While imperialism legitimized itself by asserting both the West's "natural" superiority and its beneficial impact on indigenous populations, decolonization was also presented as a natural, inevitable process, yet one in which new nations were cast by persecuting minorities, suppressing public opinion, and seeking to reach a more "civilized" condition through molding and controlling social, political, and economic forces. Moreover, the clash between the defenders of natural procreation, whether religious or nationalist, and the promoters of family planning and demographic control, has been at the root of a variety of crucial discussions over the nature of and divisions within humanity. The utopian urge in human civilization can thus be seen in debates over the definition of life and the right to end or prevent it; in arguments for and against state intervention in the privacy of the individual; in struggles over relations between the genders and between poor and rich countries or classes; and in disputes on the role of religion or science in our perception of humanity and the option of remaking it in accordance with theological or ideological schemes. Indeed, assertions about the inevitable forces of nature or history, whose relentless logic induces either domination and submission or rebellion and planned intervention, combine with the modern predilection toward biological and psychological imperatives. Explaining individual and collective behavior by reference to innate or essential predispositions also leads to projects of genetic engineering that would remake humanity according to particular behavioral, moral, and aesthetic criteria, so as to better "fit" it into a predetermined plan or ideal. In this technological and moral utopia, humanity's environment must also be reordered, whether so as to return it to its perceived natural, primeval state, or to better serve the interests of civilization.[17]

Memory and Erasure

> However this war may end, we have won the war against you;
> none of you will be left to bear witness, but even if someone
> were to survive, the world will not believe him. . . . people will
> say that the events you describe are too monstrous to be believed.
> . . . We will be the ones to dictate the history of the Lagers.
>   SS man, cited by Simon Wiesenthal, in Primo Levi,
>   *The Drowned and the Saved*

Utopian visions combine hopes for an idyllic future with recollections of a mythical past; they are also about wiping out the reality and memory of the present in order to facilitate the creation of a new world no longer haunted by ancient nightmares and lingering nostalgia. The construction of utopia requires radical mental and physical measures, geared not only toward the future but also to a reorganization of the past. Holy war or social revolution, for instance, even while they strive to change present reality, derive their image of an ideal future from a selective representation of history, where both that which should be restored and that which must be destroyed are to be found. This in turn makes for the centrality of historical records, their keepers and interpreters. To be sure, memory and erasure are not only the outcome of conscious and willed acts of man but also of chance and nature. Yet the discourse of utopia often refers to precisely those past events whose disastrous consequences had ensured the destruction of their records, leaving behind only scattered remains and traumatic recollections. Thus if utopia is about radically changing the past, it does so both by material eradication and by erasure of memory; it therefore suffers from both chronic and self-induced amnesia, while legitimizing and sustaining itself by means of vivid, but highly selective memories.[18]

Such memories are contained not only in historical documents and personal recollections but also in collections of artifacts. For utopia's ambivalent relationship with the past concerns both a desire to overcome it and a need to retain a link to it, if only so as to manifest its own superiority. But this competition between past and future cannot avoid a measure of nostalgia, since the collected remnants of the past are by their very nature the last symbols of a lost world, acting as the agents provocateurs of a forbidden longing for preutopian existence. Yet utopias cannot desist from collecting and presenting such relics, even when they serve as evidence of the present's murderous roots. Thus the Nazis began collecting material for a museum of Judaica even as the Holocaust was in progress so as to document their triumph over Germany's most evil, repulsive enemy; precisely because the Jews were to be wiped off the face of the earth, the public had to be provided with the Nazi version of their past existence.[19] Similarly, Goebbels arranged for an exhibit of "degenerate art" before stowing away some of Germany's greatest modernist works. In this manner Germans were shown one last time what would never be seen again, that is, reminded of what must no longer be remembered: that so-called Nazi art was a cultural throwback made possible by massive erasure, just as Jewish life in Eastern Europe had been so thoroughly erased that its only surviving echo remains in Polish ethnic museums representing a long forgotten and exotic people that had once inhabited the land.[20]

Collections of remnants of the past have served many other regimes to glorify their own accomplishments and demonstrate their greater proximity to current ideals, while simultaneously provoking nostalgia for a mythical past. Communists often resorted to an arsenal of nationalist sentiments in periods of crisis. Thus Stalin encouraged references to Holy Russia's medieval wars against the Teutonic Order during the early phases of what was significantly called the Great Patriotic War of 1941–45, even if the Bolshevik revolution's main slogan had been "destroy the old world and build up the new." Nor could aesthetic sensibilities always entirely dismiss the great works of the past. The British and the French, for their part, filled vast museums with the riches of ancient empires looted from their colonies, even as they claimed to bring civilization to the "natives" and show them the path to Western utopia. The same Europeans who carried the "white man's burden" thus became fascinated with African "primitivism" and Japanese, Chinese, Indian, Near Eastern, and pre-Columbian art, and expressed a longing to a presumed state of primeval harmony that they were in the process of destroying.[21]

For utopia, the selective memory and erasure of past or competing utopias is crucial not least because attempts to create a perfect humanity often generate conflict, violence, and victims and therefore also potential counternarratives by witnesses and chroniclers. The memory of utopia is predicated on perspective, for in the process of carving out a place for itself in a world that denies it a site, utopia may resort to a violent overthrow of existing structures. Hence those who inhabit the newly created utopian space will necessarily perceive reality differently from those who had been bansished from it. In this sense one person's utopia is another person's hell. In our own century in particular, this mechanism has created a crisis of testimony and evidence, confronted as we are with a multiplicity of contradictory documents and memories all vying for attention with the kind of urgency and desperation characteristic of the extremity of the events they recall. Hence, too, the crisis experienced by historians, who find themselves torn between a hankering for the alleged objectivity of archival records and a sense that, however hard they toil, their reconstruction of the past will be dismissed or rejected by those whose perspective of the events cannot allow for the balanced narrative demanded by modern historiography. This, in turn, has led to the emergence of radical skepticism and historical relativity, for if the historian's utopia is to tell the past as it really happened, the reaction to this utopia's perceived failure is the assertion that the past can never be told, that it is, so to speak, not only a foreign country but a vast Tower of Babel in which each individual or group experiences the world through the prism of its own unique and untranslatable tongue.[22]

The historian is therefore actively, albeit not always consciously, engaged in the creation of utopia, for it is the historian's authority—dating back in some civilizations to early antiquity—that provides a picture of the past as a model for the future; it is the historian's selection of episodes and personages from both a documented and a mythical past that determines what will be remembered and what will recede forever into oblivion, erased without a trace from the written annals of historical time. And while this is surely the case when we ponder the remote past, our own time, too, contains gaping black holes, the consequence of material destruction, tormented and distorted memories, or events whose nature defies representation and comprehension by means of conventional scholarship and fiction, art and philosophy. Thus individual and often inarticulate, inexpressible, and unstable memories are ultimately erased through the biological extinction of their carriers, without ever having been molded into a transmittable, even if selective narrative. Paradoxically, it is precisely thanks to the haphazard but unrelenting erasure of these memories that future utopias can be woven, whose fundamental outlines do not differ in any essential sense from those that had produced the necessary space of material and mental erasure on which they are built. And yet, if our current civilization has recently become so concerned with memory, it is because the shattered utopias of the past have profoundly undermined hope; and in order to dream of the future, we need to remember the past.[23]

Final Solutions

> We have exterminated a bacterium because we do not want in the end to be infected by the bacterium and die of it. . . . All in all, we can say that we have fulfilled this most difficult duty for the love of our people. And our spirit, our soul, our character has not suffered from it.
>
> Heinrich Himmler, speaking to SS leaders in Posen, October 4, 1943, cited in Jeremy Noakes and Geoffrey Pridham, *Nazism, 1919–1945*

Utopias propose final solutions to perennial questions of human existence and social organization. Utopian society permanently eliminates irking problems that had never been resolved before. Such attempts to eradicate the inherent ills of civilization or human biology, often generate violence, whose perceived legitimacy in view of the noble goal it serves greatly enhances its ferocity.

Both the nature of utopia, and the type and scope of its violence, reflect the societies and cultures that produce it. Religious utopias must be understood within the context of the established religious doctrine, social organization, and power structure they hope to reform or overthrow. Here the first step to utopia is made by adopting a new or reformed faith, even if eventually the inevitable institutional, hierarchical, and social organization of this new creed tends to divert its followers from the path on which it had originally set out. Moreover, since numerous religions associate utopia with death, the afterlife, or reincarnation, earthly existence maintains an ambivalent relationship with its final destination, goal, and purpose.[24]

Modern utopias reflect the growing predominance of science and technology, mass politics and state control, secularization and alienation. Hence the longing to achieve greater proximity to nature and thereby also social harmony in an increasingly industrialized and atomized environment, while harnessing modern science and techniques of social organization for that purpose. If the vast expanses of colonial empires seemed to offer the best opportunity to realize such schemes, it soon transpired that modern utopias of this genre create a relationship of subjugation and control vis-à-vis their human environment, even as they brought the newcomers closer to the natural setting. Indeed, the evident links between utopia and violence in the European colonies demonstrate that imperialism is one crucial root of modern utopian thinking, whose most distinct and devastating outcome in our own century has been the totalitarian state.[25]

The nineteenth century produced an array of utopian visions. Some, such as the Hegelian *Weltgeist*'s curious culmination in Prussia and Giuseppe Mazzini's optimistic fraternity of national liberation movements, were directly related to the emerging nation-state. Others, such as the British trust in improvement and the French enchantment with positivism, as well as Henri de Saint-Simon's republic of technocrats, were rooted in the new religion of scientific discovery and progress. Conversely, such grand utopian schemes as Charles Fourier's "phalanx" and Karl Marx's classless society, expressed a reaction to the impoverishment and alienation that came in the wake of industrialization, urbanization, and secularization. But totalitarian utopia was finally propelled into existence by the event of total, industrial war, which combined modern science and technology, universal mobilization of soldiers and workers, and an elaborate surveillance apparatus geared to control and mold the conduct and mind of the public. Totalitarianism evolved from the crises it claimed to resolve, offering a final solution to humanity's ills predicated on the proven ability to eradicate everything that could not or would not be suppressed, healed or transformed. For here the goal was not mere control, but rather making control altogether unnecessary by recreating humanity in a manner that would ensure its acceptance of and active participation in the new society. Totalitarianism is modern utopia brought to its ultimate concrete conclusion; obsessed with mobilizing mass society and employing the most sophisticated technological means and administrative practices to establish its rule, it simultaneously strives to put an end to history and to prevent any movement beyond what it perceives as the utopian phase. Once the ideal has been achieved, nothing should be allowed to undermine it; once the undesirable classes have been eliminated, the polluting races exterminated, the old elites smashed, the history and memory of past events erased or rewritten, time must come to a standstill. From this point on, change can only spell subversion.[26]

But just as in Aristotelian physics, this ideal point of absolute rest can never be reached, its closest approximation being a circle, which in the case of modern utopia is a vicious cycle of constant striving toward perfection in a violent process of remaking and unmaking humanity. The totalitarian state insists on being defined as such precisely because it can recognize no limits to its unrelenting march toward utopia. But totalitarianism is only the most extreme expression of a widespread, if at times more benign urge, whose roots stretch back to the beginning of civilization and whose modern manifestations are distinguished by unprecedented technological and organizational capacities unaccompanied by a matching expansion of either wisdom or moral sensibilities. This is the urge to seize control over time, matter, and mind, to gain the power to make and unmake, to arrest or accelerate the drift of history and to challenge whichever natural or divine laws may rule it. Since the utopia of controlling the universe is both the consequence and the cause of domestic and international conflict, its wars are all the more absolutist in their goals and execution, geared as they are toward final solutions to problems and final removal of obstacles by means of total annihilation. For while war is always about destruction, the most destructive armies are those motivated by utopian theologies or ideologies. And the vast conscript armies of total war—raised and supported by mass modern societies—have released unparalleled annihilatory energies, not least because the tremendous exertion and suffering that modern warfare demands of citizen soldiers can only be justified by reference to abstract utopian goals, be they eternal peace or social justice, freedom from hunger or universal liberation from oppression, world empire and endless living spaces or total eradication of racial and ideological foes.[27]

Modern war and totalitarianism therefore necessitate and devise final solutions in which humanity is perceived as a mass of matter to be molded, controlled, moved, purged, and annihilated. This conceptualization of the world "biologizes" society and "sociologizes" biology; humanity becomes an organism in need of radical surgery, or a social construct in need of extreme sociological reordering. Hence the vast population transfers, brutal operations of ethnic cleansing, eradication of whole social classes, and ultimately outright genocide, the most final solution of all. For while the modern world has learned how to extend life, it has also come to think of death as the absolute end of existence. Once the afterworld has been discarded and both paradise and hell have become mere metaphors to describe (or serve as a model for creating) conditions in our own world, death has assumed a more important function than ever before, and mass murder can be seen as both an achievable goal (figs. 11–13) and a perfect means for resolving previously insoluble problems.[28]

Final solutions are of an inherent interest to historians, not only because of their potential to transform them into antiquarians by putting a stop to history but because in the process of working toward utopia they mobilize the past and exploit the tools and sources of the historian, albeit with the goal of ultimately undermining the raison d'être of the historical profession. In the modern era, final solutions are predicated on bureaucratic structures that in turn depend on archives, documentation, and experts in all areas relevant to organizing society and ordering the past. Moreover, final solutions require techniques that will facilitate their task of identifying the enemy, mobilizing perpetrators, and ensuring the collaboration or passivity of bystanders, all within the context of mass society. Identity, whether

FIGURE 11. Industry of destruction. Gas chamber and crematorium in Majdanek concentration camp, near Lublin, Poland.

FIGURE 12. Industry of salvation. Oskar Schindler's factory in Kraków, Poland.

biologically, sociologically, or historically constructed, is a crucial component in motivating genocide and defining its parameters, just as it is a requisite element in delineating the future utopia whose creation will have been made possible by mass murder. Here, of course, not only the social sciences are involved, but also the medical and legal professions, whose role in legitimizing and organizing genocide as a necessary step on the path to utopia is obviously indispensable. Hence utopian violence in the twentieth century reflects the complexity of modern identity, the ambiguities of its historical and institutional roots, and the perilous potentials of its future aspirations.[29]

Scholarly rumination and scientific innovation, studies of the past and investigations of nature have all played a role in planning,

FIGURE 13. The factory of death. Crematorium II complex (undressing room, gas chamber, and crematorium), Auschwitz-Birkenau, Poland.

legitimizing, and enacting violent final solutions to the contradictions of human existence.[30] And yet, despite some important but ultimately marginal exceptions—mostly incorporated into the conventional disciplinary and intellectual discourse—the prestige and status of the social and natural sciences has, by and large, not diminished, and their basic assumptions have escaped fundamental critique and revision in view of their impact on society in the context of modern war and genocide.[31] In all major cases of state-organized murder in this century, the rhetoric of the past has legitimized the horror of the present, technology has facilitated mass killing, war has provided a convenient psychological and organizational context. Moreover, in all these instances either religion or science (and at times a mix thereof) claimed a monopoly over truth, knowledge, and visions of a utopian future: by asserting divine sanction to purge the infidel, linking ethnicity to faith, or mobilizing the moral authority of religious leaders—as in the Armenian, Rwandan, and Bosnian genocides; by claiming to obey the allegedly immutable, if also ruthless, laws of history—as in the "scientific" Marxism of the Soviet Union, China, and Cambodia; or by making biology into destiny and asserting the need for eugenic policies of breeding, selection, and eradication—as in the case of Nazi "scientific" racism, "racial hygiene," "euthanasia," and racial genocide.[32]

At the end of the second millennium, modernism, nationalism, and indeed history itself are again being questioned even as they serve to fan new utopias and further violence. The fall of the Berlin Wall, the disintegration of Communism, the "victory" of capitalism, the exile of war to parts of the world that rarely concern the West, and the ongoing project of genetic mapping, to name just some of the most important recent developments, have induced some to argue that we are either at the end of history or on the threshold of a utopian future. Yet growing poverty, economic exploitation, raging new viruses, global warming and, not least, the threat of biological, chemical, and nuclear terrorism may similarly indicate that our world is about to plunge into another apocalypse. It is thus more than likely that the twenty-first century will be no less afflicted by utopian and apocalyptic visions, and by attempts to reshape humanity in their image, than the century of violence that is finally coming to a close.

Remaking and Unmaking Humanity

The subterranean stream of Western history has finally come to the surface and usurped the dignity of our tradition. . . . And this is why all efforts to escape from the grimness of the present into nostalgia for a still intact past, or into the anticipated oblivion of a better future, are vain.

Hannah Arendt, *The Origins of Totalitarianism*

Exposed and vulnerable, humanity itself can die. It is at the mercy of men, and most especially of those who consider themselves as its emissaries or as the executors of its great designs. The notion of crimes against humanity is the legal evidence of this realization.

Alain Finkielkraut, *Remembering in Vain: The Klaus Barbie Trial and Crimes against Humanity*

Humanity has always been haunted by the idea of its own making and unmaking. This is both an exhilarating and a frightening notion; it encompasses creation and destruction, social organization and religious doctrine, cultural upheaval and biological determinants. It has generated visions of universal happiness and of apocalyptic annihilation. Hence the optimism of progress and evolution is often accompanied by fear of the unknown, resentment of the unfit, and an impatient urge to wipe the slate clean once and for all.

The modern era has been especially plagued by tension between social improvement, scientific discovery, and technological innovation, on the one hand, and social disintegration, abuse of nature, and technological devastation, on the other. And while the notion of the end of an era has often been associated both with nostalgia for the vanishing past and with hopes for a better future, what the modern age has added to this is the capacity to bring about far more radical and rapid change. Time, space, and human sentiment have been revolutionized; within the span of a single individual's lifetime the world has changed several times over, destroyed and rebuilt and destroyed again with such thoroughness and speed that the meaning of nostalgia and the vision of the future have been transformed almost beyond recognition.

The twentieth century has, moreover, cast doubt on the very definition of the "human."[33] The mortality of humanity has been posited as being situated in the definitive historical legacies of our time: genocide and the Holocaust, imperialism and postcolonialism, Enlightenment traditions leading to both industrial capitalism and industrial killing.[34] Hence the creation, extinction, erasure, and remaking of the "human" must be understood within the context of this century's tremendous efforts to remold humanity through indoctrination and education, population transfers and resettlement, ethnic cleansing and urban planning, policies of natalism, eugenics, and genetics, the redrawing of maps and frontiers, redefinitions of individual and collective identities and, not least, mass murder. Both universalist and particularistic utopian ideologies, allied with the administrative, technological, and bureaucratic powers of the modern state, have wrought vast changes on the human condition in a continuing process of annihilation and reconstruction, demographic restructuring and exterminatory outbursts. Hence the predilection of some to abandon claims to universality altogether and thus to defy the very possibility of a history and a reality of "humanity," all-encompassing theories about which have caused so much suffering and bloodshed. Hence, too, however, the insistence of others to retain the Enlightenment conceptualization of humanity as a conglomerate of individuals endowed with inalienable rights to life and justice, as the only bulwark against the genocidal tendencies and capacities of our time.[35]

Such transformations in our perception of humanity may be cited as evidence of fragmentation, dissolution, and anarchy, or, conversely, as the beginning of a liberatory narrative and the emergence of new, hitherto neglected or ignored "humanities." Similarly, the public and scholarly fascination with genocide and destruction, erasure and commemoration can be viewed as indicating a deep cultural pessimism at the end of the millennium, or as sign of a new willingness to face up to and confront the devastating legacy of the past. Current struggles over the historical agents of humanity are also deeply implicated in questions of inclusion and exclusion, identity and enemies, utopian dreams of rebirth and renewal, and apocalyptic visions of war and extermination. At the end of the millennium, civilization seems to be both exhausted by, and yet endlessly obsessed with, its bloody chronicles of happy futures.[36] We know the history of those "republics of virtue" and "brave new worlds," the "workers' paradise" and the "racial community"; what we fear is their future. For while the history of remaking and unmaking of humanity is about the actions and perceptions of individuals and collectives in search of the "human," it is just as much about the maginalization, confinement, or destruction of the "un" or "subhuman," the socially, physically, or culturally "unfit." The "human" has been variously defined as that which was created in the image of God or as that which has self-consciousness; it has been identified as possessing the ability to distinguish good from evil, and as such has been endowed with the inalienable right to life and happiness. But since we know that civilization has often divided humanity into categories and degrees, we should beware of toying with the notion of social, cultural, and genetic engineering, whether its goal is to make for greater uniformity or to produce controlled diversity.[37]

Lessons of the Holocaust

Recognized today as an event of momentous scale and implications, the Nazi-attempted genocide of the Jews has elicited a wide range of responses and interpretations. Having traumatized a vast number of individuals, the Holocaust was also the occasion of a collective historical trauma. Hence, while coming to terms with its reality and ramifications was initially delayed, it can now be said to have projected its impact both forward *and backward* in time, an explosion of destructive energy at the heart of Western civilization that compels us to rethink our assumptions about the nature of humanity and culture, history and progress, politics and morality.

Accepting the centrality of atrocity for our time, however, does not mean unanimity about its implications for our view of the world. Indeed, the urge to discover the lessons of the event is often accompanied by a desire to relegate it to a no-longer-relevant past. Both the insistence on applicable lessons and the refusal to integrate genocide into our self-perception derive from and serve to legitimize a variety of contending ideological, philosophical, and political stances. Yet neither the Final Solution, nor its subsequent analysis, can be understood without taking into account the wider historical framework, in which reactions to the first collective trauma of the century, World War I, are of paramount importance. In trying to make sense of that initial instance of mass industrial killing in Europe, some viewed it, during the interwar period, as a mere aberration and hoped against hope to return to what Stefan Zweig called the "world of yesterday." Among those who recognized immediately after the war that it embodied the terrifying destructive potential of modern society, some sought shelter in militant pacifism, others rushed to endorse a utopian (and increasingly violent) revolutionary communism, and others still embraced the nihilistic rhetoric of fascism or Nazism, which glorified and aestheticized war, death, and destruction. The origins of the Holocaust cannot be grasped without understanding Europe's first attempts to draw lessons from the butchery of 1914–18.

Launched with the technological violence of World War I, the twentieth century has come to a close filled with echoes of the Holocaust, reverberating with seemingly growing intensity in museums and lecture halls, cinemas and television documentaries, scholarly works and fiction. In part this has to do with the urgency felt by the witnesses of the event to establish the Holocaust's veracity before they finally leave the scene and can no longer transmit the unmediated memory of an atrocity all too often described as unimaginable. But repeated cases of genocide and atrocity since 1945—even if Western observers are reluctant to associate them with our own civilization—have also intensified public interest in the causes and nature of that undeniably Western product, the Nazi death factories. Indeed, the Holocaust increasingly appears as the core event of a century whose promise of moral and material progress so often ended up in carnage, disillusionment, and despair. What Eric Hobsbawm has called "the age of extremes" combined improvements in living standards and concentration camps, mass production and industrialized murder, totalitarianism and moral relativism, boundless optimism and radical evil.

Some might argue that all we can learn from Auschwitz is that it was and remains possible to annihilate millions of people rapidly and efficiently, with little protest and resistance. Others would counter that in the end, Nazism was crushed, Communism collapsed, and a relatively humane democracy has emerged as an ideal—if not a reality—in much of the world. One could also claim that rather than evaluating the lessons of the Holocaust, what deserves scrutiny is the very need for such lessons, and especially the urge to derive a message of hope and affirmation, courage and dignity, from one of history's darkest periods. But whatever is one's position, the Holocaust has come to play an important role in people's views of the past, understanding of the present, and expectations of the future. This can be seen by examining some attempts to draw lessons from the Holocaust, in the areas of politics and ideology, religion and morality, psychology and sociology, history and education. If there is room to criticize the use of atrocity to justify ideological agendas, it is nevertheless true that studying the Holocaust is the best means to prevent its mystification. At the same time, while those who study the past hope to learn from it, history has taught us that its lessons are precariously tenuous guides for the future. Hence the central tension in this undertaking is between the historical decontextualization of the Holocaust, on the one hand, and the ideological and self-serving biases that may inform its study, on the other.

Politics and Ideology

Since the Holocaust was perpetrated by a totalitarian regime, whose distinguishing feature was a murderous racist ideology, it has been assumed that the enemies of Nazism were committed to eradicating genocide. The democracies, however, did not wage war against Germany because it was a genocidal dictatorship but to protect their own political and strategic interests. Had Hitler killed Jews within internationally sanctioned borders, they would have not tried to thwart him; had he promised to stop killing the Jews late in the war, they would not have made peace. Indeed, one reason for the Western Allies' reluctance to use the Holocaust for propagandistic purposes was their fear that Hitler would suggest that they accept "his" Jews in response to their accusations of genocide.[38] Moreover, the destruction of the Third Reich could not have been accomplished without the massive efforts of the Soviet Union, whose own record as a brutal totalitarian regime may lead us to conclude that it took one evil system to put an end to another.[39]

The tendency to exaggerate the differences between Germany and the West has also contributed to some false lessons. The "Final Solution" was organized and implemented in a manner quite consistent with the industrial and bureaucratic structures of contemporary modern states. The current notion that the best guarantee against a recurrence of genocide is a firm belief in progress, science, and the rule of law can hardly be maintained considering the rhetoric of improving the lot of (part of) humanity, the ostensibly rational scientific assertions, and the seemingly reasonable legal arguments, that were crucial to the legitimization, organization, and implementation of the Holocaust. Indeed, numerous members of these professions actively collaborated in perpetrating murder.[40] To be sure, saying that the Holocaust was a modern undertaking should not obscure its particular origins and characteristics. But what made the Final Solution unique was precisely its heavy reliance on the structures and mentalities typical of modern industrial societies of the kind that we still inhabit today.

Interpretations of Nazism and the Holocaust have, of course, served very different national and ideological agendas. Thus the German Democratic Republic (GDR) never accepted responsibility, or felt a need for its government and citizenry to atone, for the Holocaust. Following Marxist theory, the GDR presented fascism as the last phase of a degenerate capitalism from which the Communist Party had liberated the German "masses," who were now engaged in building a socialist society with a perfectly clear conscience. Conversely, the Federal Republic of Germany (FRG) claimed to be the only legitimate successor German state, which in turn implied at least a qualified acceptance of responsibility for Nazi crimes. But by adopting the Cold War rhetoric of identifying between Nazi and Soviet totalitarianism, the FRG presented its anti-Soviet policies as a valuable lesson of the Nazi past—even though the Soviet Union (allegedly led by the Jews) had also been the Third Reich's greatest enemy. This political rhetoric had the added benefit of facilitating the integration of the German conservative elites into the FRG in the 1950s. The numerous generals, top civil servants, leaders of industry and scholars, who had given their support to Hitler because of his anti-Bolshevik crusade, could now feel both vindicated and more comfortable with a democratic Germany that was part of an anti-Soviet alliance.[41]

Turning to the Holocaust's victims, we should note that since Zionism was largely predicated on the assumption of an approaching catastrophe for European Jewry long before the rise of Nazism, after the war it tended to present the mass murder of the Jews as the final—if, for millions, belated—proof of the need for a Jewish national home. The notion that the victims had mostly gone "like sheep to the slaughter" was interpreted by Zionist leaders as having taught postwar Jews another lesson, namely, that only as citizens of their own state could they ensure their survival and, by implication, even rectify the "shame" of the ghettos and the gas chambers. Yet behind this confident rhetoric there were profound anxieties and uncertainties. Israeli Zionists in particular were haunted by the loss of the Jewish state's potential "manpower reserves" in Eastern Europe incurred during the Holocaust and even more so by their own failure to rescue more victims of Nazism. The sense of anguish and frustration at having been too weak to matter, and the partially repressed sense of guilt for having led a relatively normal existence during the Holocaust while refusing to believe the ominous news from Europe until late in the war, have cast a shadow over the ostensibly positive lessons of Zionism.[42]

Nevertheless, the Zionist interpretation of the Holocaust constitutes a major component of Israeli national identity, encapsulated in the (traditionally Jewish) exhortation "Remember!" and its modern, future-oriented response "Never Again!" The state, in fact, is founded on the undiminished memory of past national disasters—the destruction of both Temples, catastrophic rebellions against foreign rule, pogroms and expulsions in the Diaspora, and the Holocaust—while at the same time it claims to be the embodiment of the promise that cataclysms of that nature and magnitude will never happen to the Jewish people again. In other words Israel legitimizes its existence by apocalyptic visions of the past and the promise to thwart apocalypse in the future.

The slogan "Never again," inscribed in many languages on camp memorials in Europe (fig. 14), refers primarily to the determination never to allow such inhumanity as displayed by the Nazis to recur in the world (a vow mocked, of course, by the innumerable massacres and genocides since 1945). It also reflects the early postwar tendency to see all camp inmates as political resisters rather than helpless "racial" victims. The Israeli interpretation of this slogan indicates the diametrically opposed lessons derived from the event by Zionism, which provides an ethnocentric reading with a powerfully nationalist and militant message: Israel is presented as the sole repository of the Holocaust's memory and as the official representative of its Jewish victims. It was on the basis of such assertions that Israel negotiated the restitution agreement with the FRG, built Yad Vashem, a national memorial to the Holocaust to which visiting foreign dignitaries are taken (fig. 15), and linked its foreign policies to fears of another genocide.[43] Hence that unique mélange of realpolitik, deep-seated anxieties, manipulation, determination, and outbursts of excessive violence and aggression, which have come to characterize Israeli policy and public sentiment since the establishment of the state.

FIGURE 14. Mass death as universal redemption. Monument at
Treblinka, Poland. Plaque carries the words "never again" in
Yiddish, Russian, English, French, German, and Polish.

Religion and Morality

The cataclysmic nature of the Holocaust has prompted profound
disagreements over its theological and moral lessons. Having occa-
sioned a final break with God by some Jews, the Holocaust has im-
pelled others to seek religious comfort in the face of man-made
atrocity and to reassert Jewish survival and continuity by adhering
to Judaic tradition.[44] The complicity in, or indifference to, Nazi policies of many established Christian churches has led to both denial by
those religious bodies of their role in the Holocaust and, often rather
belatedly, to admissions of guilt and revisions of dogma. Conversely,

FIGURE 15. Appropriated martyrdom. A section of the commemoration complex "Valley of the Communities" (Bik-at
ha-kehilot), next to Yad Vashem, Jerusalem. The names of all
major European Jewish communities destroyed by the Nazis
are inscribed on the steep walls of tunnels dug into the mountain.
This section commemorates Warsaw and other Polish towns.

it is also true that individual Christians were at times motivated by
their faith to resist Nazism and rescue victims and that some of the
Christian clergy attempted to set moral limits to inhumanity in the
Third Reich, Nazi-occupied Europe, and among Germany's allies
and satellites.[45] Against those who see Auschwitz as the *anus mundi*
of humanity, others assert that the extraordinary individual acts of
heroism and sacrifice in the camps redeemed the human race by

demonstrating the ability of men and women to produce a moral life even in the heart of evil.

West Germany demonstrates some of the ambiguities of seeking religious and moral lessons in atrocity. Dominated for the first two decades of its existence by the old conservative elites, politics in the FRG was guided by the premise that Nazism had exemplified a pagan, anti-Christian, and immoral ideology, whose worst aspects were a lack of respect for traditional authority, religion, gender roles, and the family.[46] In fact, of course, Hitler could not have consolidated his power without the support, or at least the acquiescence, of the traditional elites and the churches, whose prejudices against Jews, the Left, and modern society made them susceptible to Nazi rhetoric. Indicatively, in the 1930s both the Lutheran and the Catholic Churches tended to accuse the Jews of precisely the same kind of godlessness with which they charged the Nazis after the collapse of the Third Reich. It was only when Hitler failed to deliver the goods, bringing chaos and destruction instead of social order and tranquillity, that the church stepped in once more, this time as the postwar and allegedly anti-Nazi enforcer of order, tradition, and family values. The silence of the evangelical leaders and the Vatican during and after the Holocaust thus greatly facilitated the remarkably smooth transition of the church from the Third Reich to the Federal Republic.[47]

For the ultra-Orthodox Jewish enclaves in the United States and Israel, the wartime destruction of their great counterpart communities in Eastern Europe underlined the urgent necessity to sustain a traditional Jewish way of life elsewhere.[48] Conversely, secular and in large part socialist Israeli Zionists perceived the Holocaust as the final proof of the need to do away with the Diaspora altogether. Yet among the Israeli extreme right wing, whose numbers include many immigrants from the United States, the recent revival of religion has been accompanied by apocalyptic visions informed by vicarious memories of the Holocaust, or what has come to be called Holocaust consciousness. Complicating the picture even further, radical Sephardi activists in the 1970s claimed that the Holocaust was being instrumentalized by the Ashkenazi elite as a means to downplay Sephardi suffering. Paradoxically, one sign of Sephardi integration into Israeli society in the intervening years is that this community has by now come to see the Holocaust as part of a collective Jewish trauma, rather than an experience that "belongs" only to Jews who came from Europe. At the same time, the new Shas party, which now serves as the political representative of many Sephardim in Israel, has reinterpreted Zionism as a return to tradition and religion, and presents secular Zionists as

Westernized, hedonistic Ashkenazim. From this perspective we can say that drawing political borders in Israel—a process that overlaps with attempts to define national identity—is closely linked to the religious and moral lessons that various sectors of the population claim to derive from the Holocaust.[49]

A different but related set of questions concerns the moral lessons of the Holocaust. The German sociologist Wolfgang Sofsky has recently argued that the exercise of absolute power in the Nazi concentration camps caused the total disintegration of morality among the inmates, since the struggle for physical survival overwhelmed any considerations of moral conduct.[50] This position has been rejected by the Bulgarian-born French critic Tzvetan Todorov, whose own recent work on this issue constitutes a passionate plea to recognize what he calls moral life in the concentration camps as a guide for posterity.[51] These polar positions represent, of course, a larger trend of reevaluating the lessons of this century, in which we can also often recognize an explicit or implicit tendency to compare the Soviet and Nazi systems. Interestingly, Todorov identifies moral life in the camps by considering the wider societal context in which the "concentrationary universe"[52] was established, whereas Sofsky's rejection of the possibility of morality in the camps relies heavily on viewing them in isolation from the rest of society and on his consequent insistence on the irrelevance of ideology.

Thus the different lessons Todorov and Sofsky draw from their analyses of life in the camps depend largely on their differing perspectives. Conversely, their agreement on the—to my mind, false— equivalence of the Soviet Gulags and the Nazi concentration camps results from a similar failure to distinguish between racial genocide and political persecution. It should be noted that while many Soviet prisoners actually shared the ideology of the regime, the victims of the Nazis were either ideologically opposed to Nazism or were considered to be "biologically" barred from belonging to the "racial community." But this distinction must be maintained even if we focus only on the Nazi camps. There was a crucial difference between the Nazis' political prisoners, men and women who were often bound together by ideological commitment and the mass of Jewish inmates—including numerous children—whose only link to each other was often merely the racial label attached to them by the regime. These objective realities could not but produce a very different moral existence, quite apart from the fact that "racial" victims suffered a far higher death rate than the "politicals." Moreover, political prisoners could hope that if they survived, their families would be waiting for them, their countries and towns would give them a hero's welcome; the Jewish inmates understood that even if they survived, there would be nothing to return to, neither family nor community. The "politicals" believed that if they, as individuals, perished, their cause would eventually win; the Jews often felt that they were the last Jews in the world and that their individual deaths could quite possibly spell the end of Jewish existence. Simha Rottem, one of a handful of survivors of the Warsaw Ghetto uprising, returned from a mission on the "Aryan" side on the night of May 8–9, 1943. As he told Claude Lanzmann many years later, on climbing out of the sewer "I didn't meet a living soul. At one point I recall feeling a kind of peace, of serenity. I said to myself: 'I'm the last Jew. I'll wait for morning, and for the Germans.'"[53]

Todorov concedes that there is "a threshold of suffering beyond which an individual's actions teach us nothing more about the individual but only about the reactions that unbearable suffering elicits from the human mechanism" and explains that he does not "dwell at length on situations where that threshold has been crossed."[54] But by saying this, Todorov in fact implies his inability to face the extremes of the mussulmen, Primo Levi's "drowned," in other words, the mass of the totally emaciated and dehumanized Jewish victims and the vast majority of the inmate population in the Nazi camps who were mentally dead even before they expired. In seeking the moral essence of humanity even under the most inhuman conditions devised by man, Todorov underlines the wholly unselfish acts of caring for others, as well as the continuation of what he calls the life of the mind. Even if they were anything but numerous, he argues, such acts constituted vital proof of the inability of the Nazis to reduce the camps' populations to utter bestiality and worthlessness. But the moral problem we are faced with is that such laudable conduct was more prevalent among inmates treated less severely by the Nazis— that is, the non-Jewish political prisoners—and was ruled out in most cases for the mass of Jewish victims who were either murdered outright or rapidly debilitated by physical violence and hunger. Moreover, as Sofsky shows, such moral life among the primarily communist "politicals" was predicated on their ability to maintain a privileged position in the camps by lording it over the less fortunate "racial" victims and on sustaining a system of ideological solidarity that excluded everyone else. Altruism within the group thus often depended on sacrificing those who did not belong to it:

> This was not a *Leidensgemeinschaft*—there was no community of suffering here. The laws of the jungle prevailed in the daily struggle for survival. . . . Frequently, the only way to survive was at the expense

of others. One prisoner's death was another's bread. . . . Solidarity is based on the principle of mutual aid and sharing. But where there is nothing to share, except at the cost of common destruction and doom, solidarity lacks a material basis. . . . Absolute power is based on a cleverly devised system of classification and collaboration, gradation of power and privilege. . . . [It] thrusts individuals into a condition where what is ultimately decisive is the right of the stronger.[55]

The difference in the moral lives of "politicals" and Jews in the camps was therefore an outcome of the crucial distinctions made between them by the Nazis. This is reflected in Todorov's own examples of moral conduct, such as the case of a young Jewish woman who voluntarily joined her mother on a transport to Treblinka.[56] While this was indeed an act of caring, valued most highly by Todorov on his scale of morally motivated actions, it was also an instance of fully conscious suicide. As Primo Levi noted, a Jewish working inmate who cared for another was likely to waste away himself and die within a few days or weeks. Survival depended on gaining some privilege through luck, coincidence, and skill, as happened to Levi himself. Only a position of privilege made it possible to act humanely without risking rapid deterioration and annihilation.[57] Similarly, when speaking, as Todorov does, of the "life of the mind,"[58] we must note the vast difference between Levi, who desperately, and not very successfully, tried to recall a few lines from Dante while in a state of near physical and mental collapse in Auschwitz, and such political prisoners as the writer Jorge Semprun, who recounts in a recently published memoir how his privileged position in Buchenwald actually allowed him to borrow books in the camp's modest library.[59] Indeed, when the young Jewish Hungarian protagonist of Imre Kertész's quasi-autobiographical novel *Fateless* is saved and sheltered by the Communists, their part of Buchenwald appears to him as paradise, compared to the Jewish compound where the vast majority of the inmates died. No wonder that the Communists, among whom was the young Semprun, had the physical and mental strength to take over the camp shortly before it was liberated.[60]

In 1976 the American scholar Terrence Des Pres argued in his book *The Survivor* that survival in the camps depended on the ability to preserve *one's humanity* even in the face of the most terrible horror.[61] But beyond the question of moral life in the camps as a *means* for survival, what Des Pres and Todorov assert with great urgency is that humanity did not die in the camps, indeed, that while people were murdered en masse, *humanity as a moral concept* survived. Others, including camp survivors such as Levi, Tadeusz Borowski,

Jean Améry, and Ka-Tzetnik (Yehiel Dinur), have—each in his own way—pointed to what the younger philosopher Alain Finkielkraut has described as the realization after the Holocaust that *humanity as an idea* is mortal, that it is, in fact, possible to assassinate the very concept of moral existence along with millions of individual human beings.[62] The fragility and precariousness of the *idea of humanity* and the need to preserve it with utmost care is the lesson that these writers see as the enduring legacy of the Holocaust. Where they differ from Des Pres and Todorov is in their lack of confidence about humanity's ability to refrain from self-annihilation. Todorov's and Des Pres's view is one with which most people can live more comfortably. Levi's belief that the Holocaust destroyed the best while the worst were saved, is a notion that makes post-Holocaust existence almost unbearable. Indeed, one of the most frightening consequences of the Holocaust may well be that rather than serving as a warning to preserve humanity at all cost, it has provided a license to privilege physical survival over moral existence. This may be one reason, along with the realization that mass murder has continued unabated since 1945, that such men as Borowski, Améry, Paul Celan, and Levi finally decided to put an end to their own lives.

Psychology and Sociology

Psychological factors played a role in the daily routine of genocide. One reason that the SS constructed death camps was its concern about reports indicating the adverse psychological effects of face-to-face killing on its murder squads. The killing facilities minimized contact between killers and victims, were far more "efficient," and had the added benefit of preventing panic among the victims by deceiving them about their purpose until the last moment (see, however, figs. 9 and 10).[63] Jewish resisters, for their part, strove to transform the perceived predilection of their communities passively to accept their fate. On the first day of 1942, the Jewish Pioneer Youth Group in the Vilna Ghetto issued a proclamation calling for resistance against the Germans.[64] Culminating with the plea, "Let us not go as sheep to the slaughter!" this was one of the earliest and most forceful calls for armed Jewish resistance to Nazi genocidal policies; it also exemplified the difference between Jewish and gentile opposition to the Germans.

Setting out from the assumption that the Jews were already doomed, these young men and women insisted on choosing the manner of their death; they believed in the historical significance of going down fighting rather than being passively led to the killing sites. As their manifesto proclaimed, "It is better to fall as free fighters than to live by the grace of the murderers."[65] That this was a minority opinion, held mainly by young Zionists, had to do, of course, with the objective limits on resistance: numerical inferiority, isolation within a largely hostile gentile society, and lack of arms and training. More important, however, was the fact that the decision to leave the ghetto and form fighting units in the forests meant abandoning parents, siblings, children, and spouses to be murdered by the Nazis.[66] Here there were no easy moral choices, even if the expectation was that ultimately all would die. This is why the Warsaw Ghetto rebellion occurred only after the bulk of the Jewish population—including most of the old, the sick, and the very young—had already been sent to the gas chambers, and the remaining Jews knew that the final elimination of the ghetto was imminent.[67] Paradoxically, then, the choice to fight was an admission of the inevitability of destruction, while the choice to struggle for survival represented hope, however slim, for the future. If gentile resistance was motivated by the prospect of liberation and national resurrection, Jewish resistance was an expression of despair, a final gesture by a slaughtered people. Especially in those parts of Eastern Europe and western Russia where the vast majority of the Jews lived, fighting meant choosing how to die, not how to live (fig. 16).

FIGURE 16. Contested martyrdom. Memorial to the Polish uprising of summer 1944, built after the fall of Communism in central Warsaw, Poland, and shunned by the population.

Outside observers were quick to reach conclusions about the psychological makeup of both camp inmates and their guards. Such theories may have facilitated coming to terms with unprecedented inhumanity, but they distorted reality. Defining the Holocaust as a case of unique extremity made it possible to repress its implications for subsequent "normality."

Bruno Bettelheim's early attempt to analyze camp inmates' psychology focused on what he saw as their regression into childhood behavior, manifested in a tendency to soil themselves, an inability to act as mature adults, and an internalization of the values of the SS.[68] Having experienced only the relatively benign camps of the 1930s, Bettelheim had little knowledge of the vastly different concentration, labor, and death camps of the war years. He also tended to confuse patterns of behavior imposed on the inmates by the camp system (such as restricted access to latrines, rampant diseases, and intentional humiliation) with actual changes in their personalities, which often ended up in total disintegration and transformation into musselmen. Yet Bettelheim did qualify the widespread view that political prisoners were invariably heroic adversaries of the Nazis, and seems to have been right about the tendency of some inmates to emulate their tormentors, if mostly as a survival technique. Subsequent conceptualizations of the Jewish victims' psychology reflected prejudices about so-called Diaspora mentality. Here the argument was made that the Jews became complicit in their own destruction at the hands of the Nazis by reverting to "traditional" strategies of accommodation with their persecutors. Paradoxically, while Raul Hilberg and Hannah Arendt, for instance, were attacked by the Zionist establishment for stressing Jewish complicity—and hence for being the proverbial self-hating Jews— Zionist rhetoric itself maintained that, with a few heroic exceptions (greatly highlighted in Israeli Holocaust remembrance), the Jews went like sheep to the slaughter precisely because of that very Diaspora mentality that Zionism was striving mightily to transform.[69]

Recent studies of survivors, as well as of their (and the perpetrators') children, often reveal the impact of the Holocaust on individual and collective psychology.[70] This belated recognition of the Holocaust's long-term effects has been accompanied by a growing scholarly preoccupation with trauma in a variety of disciplines, ranging from psychology to history, from literary criticism to law and philosophy.[71] In the early years after the event, however, survivors who wished to talk about their experiences rarely found anyone prepared to listen. This imposed silence added to the survivors' mental turmoil. Even psychologists were often unwilling to confront this phenomenon of mass trauma at the time, preferring to integrate it into existing and not necessarily relevant theories. This contrasted sharply with the far more efficacious reaction of psychologists to the massive incidence of "shell shock" during World War I and to its World War II equivalent, renamed "combat fatigue" (and later still "combat stress" or "combat syndrome"), not least because armies and states had a much greater interest in returning mentally disabled troops to battle than in focusing on the shattered minds of the survivors of genocide.[72] Fifty years after the Holocaust, it is, naturally, less difficult to deal with its traumatic consequences: by now the Holocaust *seems* to lack any immediate implications and no longer appears to threaten conventional views of civilization. This perhaps guarantees the return of the repressed in the form of yet more atrocity.

As for the psychology of the killers, two polar arguments have recently been debated. In his 1992 study, *Ordinary Men,* historian Christopher Browning refers to the psychologist Stanley Milgram's behavioral experiments—conducted a generation earlier—to suggest that peer group pressure was the main reason why men participated in the Third Reich's genocidal campaigns.[73] He thus implies that under similar circumstances all people could become mass murderers. Daniel Jonah Goldhagen in his book *Hitler's Willing Executioners* (1996) traces the main motivation for the Holocaust to German antisemitism. To his mind it was not so much the Holocaust that was unique, but rather the German hatred of Jews, whose cultural and historical roots stretch all the way back to Martin Luther.[74] Of the two views, Goldhagen's is the less threatening, since it comes with the qualification that "the Germans" have changed since 1945 and hence that what they did or were capable of doing is of mere historical interest with little relevance for the present. Indeed, his thesis adds little to our understanding of the numerous postwar genocides and atrocities. Conversely, Browning's assertion that humanity will *always* contain within itself the potential to perpetrate mass murder is far more disturbing. Yet while it provides insight into genocide as a universal phenomenon, his thesis does not explain why in certain situations where genocide might have been expected to manifest itself it did not take place. By overemphasizing the influence of behavioral patterns on participation in mass murder, Browning minimizes the often crucial role of ideological motivation, and ends up with a generalization that obscures some aspects of the specific circumstances he is simultaneously at such pains to reconstruct.

This brings us to a very different approach to understanding modern genocide, whose focus is more on the general socioeconomic context than the psychological makeup of particular actors or collectives. The late German historian Detlev J. K. Peukert made the argument that the collapse of the Weimar Republic and the subsequent establishment of the Nazi regime must be understood within the context of German society's failure to adjust to a rapid process of modernization, which produced what he called a crisis of classical modernity.[75] The tremendous material and psychological pressures experienced by large sectors of society undergoing rapid economic and social transformation made them increasingly susceptible to radical political movements and tenets. Moreover, the promises made by the allegedly objective modern science of eugenics about its capacity to improve society by means of biological manipulation were especially welcomed by a public pervaded by phobias about degeneration and pollution. For Peukert, Germany at the end of the Weimar Republic represented the European malaise in extremis, a disease whose symptoms were deep anxiety, paranoia, growing aggression—and violence.

The sociologist Zygmunt Bauman pushes this conclusion even further.[76] Blaming his colleagues for having failed to integrate the Holocaust into the general stream of European history since the Enlightenment, Bauman demonstrates that precisely because sociology was founded on assumptions of rationality and improvement, it has not been able to come to terms with an event that refuted the notion of humanity's inevitable progress, the assumed interdependence of humanism and technological and scientific development, and the proposition that in modern society people's actions are susceptible to rational explanation. According to Bauman, rather than being a throwback to a premodern era, or a phenomenon that embodies atavistic impulses, the Holocaust was, in fact, facilitated by modern modes of thinking and organization. The Enlightenment notion of the "gardening society," whereby man must learn to order and control both his natural environment and his own nature, rather than creating a "crisis of modernity," set the stage for operations of radical social surgery, whose scale and efficiency were tremendously enhanced by the advances made in science and technology. Progress, therefore, could mean widespread destruction in the name of improving the lot of humanity as such.

What we have here, then, is an attempt to read back the lessons of the Holocaust all the way to the Enlightenment, the source of everything we normally associate with progress, democracy, and morality, that is, the values and forces that are thought to have opposed Nazism. Such a radical critique was proposed thirty years earlier by Jacob Talmon, who claimed to identify the roots of both liberal democracy and totalitarianism in the ideas of the Enlightenment and their implementation in the French Revolution;[77] it is also indebted, of course, to Hannah Arendt's better known and pioneering study of totalitarianism.[78] For Bauman, the belief that man can take his destiny into his own hands and mold his species' future combined with the nineteenth century's faith in the positive and creative powers of science to make possible mass democracy and unparalleled material progress. But, at the same time, this combination also fueled the nihilistic energies of those who wished to attain total control over the life and fate of humanity, to weed out whoever appeared to them unworthy of life, to crush all opponents, misfits, inferior races, and anachronistic classes and to decide what was to be thrown into the dustbin of history, what the future would look like, and what were the best ways and means to get there. In other words, Bauman sees the main lesson of the Holocaust as the realization that the values we trust in and the institutions we have created, perceived by us as bulwarks of liberty, justice, and humanism, contain within them seeds of totalitarianism, nihilism, and genocide.

History and Education

The historiography of the Holocaust has both reflected and influenced popular views about the event; it also bears a relationship to national, ideological, and generational perceptions. During the two postwar decades only a few comprehensive monographs were produced, indicating that in those years the Holocaust had not touched the cultural nerve that it did subsequently.[79] Western historians often saw it as of secondary importance to the war's military history;[80] Communist historiography integrated it into its story of resistance to Nazism;[81] Zionist historians mainly saw it as the culmination of a long tradition of antisemitic persecution.[82] Little was said about the particularity of Jewish fate under Nazi rule or the singularity of the Holocaust.

The main interpretive schools of Holocaust historiography that eventually emerged after those years also drew very different lessons from the event. The "intentionalists" propounded a view that stressed the role of Hitler and Nazi ideology in preparing for the Holocaust well before it was launched, and underlined the uniqueness of German antisemitism and the German public's susceptibility to exterminationist rhetoric. The Holocaust, according to the intentionalists, could only be understood within the context of the peculiarities of

German history and the German "mentality." It is interesting to note that the *Sonderweg,* or "special path" theory of German history—which, strictly speaking, did not concern the Holocaust—was also predicated on the notion of a unique historical development in Germany that made it susceptible to Nazism. But while the supporters of the *Sonderweg* interpretation focused on social, political, and economic structures, intentionalism was much more interested in personality and ideology. Nevertheless, both schools assumed that the *Stunde Null* (zero hour) of 1945 was the point at which German history began to follow a new and "normal," that is, Western, path. Conversely, the "functionalists" shared with the *Sonderweg* theory an interest in structures but saw nothing peculiar or anomalous in German history. Indeed, for them the Holocaust was the outcome of unique *circumstances,* rather than a uniquely German *history* or *mentality.* Genocide was thus seen by the functionalists not as the anticipated result of policies and actions taken before its perpetration but as their unintentional byproduct. Hence the stress on a dynamic of "cumulative radicalization" within a "polycratic" system of agencies competing with each other over the favors of a weak but extremist Führer, whose continued rule depended precisely on this power struggle between his underlings. The Holocaust, according to this model, was, in effect, the product of a modern, bureaucratic, industrialized state—placed in an extraordinary set of circumstances, ruled by a racist dictatorship, and embroiled in a vicious, expansionist war. Since the political and administrative structures that characterized Germany have much in common with those of contemporary modern states, the functionalists concluded that it is imperative for other nations to avoid the kind of circumstances that may weaken democracy, lead to war, and thereby produce a recurrence of genocidal urges.[83]

These schools of interpretation are primarily concerned with the perpetrators. Indeed, the historiography of the Holocaust largely reflects the strict separation between killers and victims imposed by the Nazis, despite the recognized fact that the event cannot be fully understood without considering the interaction between both groups, as well as the no less crucial role played by numerous types of bystanders in the vast "gray zone" between collaboration and resistance. The historiography of the victims, for its part, has reconstructed their political, social, and cultural organization; their reactions to Nazi policies, techniques of survival, incidents of complicity, and resistance and rescue attempts; and the effects of the Holocaust on postwar Jewish life and identity. In this context, two debates have been especially painful and acrimonious. The first concerns the role of the Jewish councils (*Judenräte*), with some scholars stressing their collaboration with the Nazis and others noting that they strove, under the most difficult of circumstances, to "save what could be saved."[84] The second concentrates on the reactions of Jewish communities outside the Nazi sphere of influence—especially in the United States and Palestine—to news of the Holocaust, and what some commentators view as their failure to do all they could to save European Jewry. A related controversial issue has to do with the political motivation of the Yishuv leadership in bringing masses of survivors to Palestine and with the flaws and errors of their subsequent absorption into Israeli society.[85]

One important lesson for Holocaust historians is to remember that the victims of genocide led a normal existence before they were targeted for destruction and that their lives deserve as much attention as the manner in which they were extinguished. Indeed, we need to ask: What is the intrinsic educational value of teaching the details of the Holocaust? What are the risks involved in focusing on atrocity and inhumanity? Is it possible that an excessive stress on Holocaust education might be detrimental, perhaps even pernicious, for students and the general public, because it creates a perception of Jews as perpetual victims and can all too easily encourage or reinforce a voyeuristic fascination with violence?

A strongly worded expression of concern by the Israeli historian Yehuda Elkana, himself a child survivor, shows what might be at stake. In 1988 Elkana published a short and controversial article in the Israeli daily *Ha-aretz*, entitled "In Praise of Forgetting." Writing in reaction to reported acts of brutality by Israeli troops against Palestinian civilians, Elkana insisted on the links between such incidents and the policy of exposing children repeatedly to images of the Holocaust. He asked: "What did we expect these children to do with this experience? We chanted thoughtlessly, heartlessly, without explanation—'Remember!' To what end? What was a child supposed to do with these memories? . . . 'Remember' could be interpreted as a call for perpetual and blind hatred." Hence Elkana's belief that "any lesson or view about life whose origin is the Holocaust is disastrous." According to Elkana, "The very existence of democracy is threatened when the memory of the victims of the past takes an active part in the democratic process. . . . Democracy is about cultivating the present and the future; cultivation of the 'remembered' and addiction to the past undermine the foundations of democracy." He therefore urged Israelis to put an end to the constant preoccupation with

"symbols, ceremonies, and lessons of the Holocaust. We must eradicate the dominion of the historical 'remembered' over our lives."[86]

One need not agree wholeheartedly with Elkana to grasp the deeply
disquieting significance of his observations. It could also be noted
that overexposure in schools and media representations to the Holocaust and a preoccupation with more immediate concerns about survival may have rather unforeseen consequences; thus, ironically, one
sees today far fewer youngsters in lectures on the Holocaust in Israel
than in Germany. What should be clear, however, is that teaching the
Holocaust does not necessarily make for better politics, more toler-
ance, or deeper humanism and compassion; it can also create hatred,
frustration, anger, and aggression. As Elkana quite rightly noted,
this is not merely a matter of employing the Holocaust to justify the
occupation or expulsion of another people; it is just as much about
the danger that children and youths might be brutalized by excessive
exposure to scenes and tales of atrocity, that a numbing of the senses
would be accompanied by seething rage, that moral outrage would
motivate misdirected action, and that the vicarious experience of the
camps would unleash a yearning for vengeance. Teaching inhumanity, in other words, even with the declared intention of preventing its
recurrence, may imbue young minds with images of barbarism that
will seek aggressive and violent expression.

There is yet another side to all this. Those who teach the Holocaust are often seen as moral guides for the young. There is, however, a bitter irony in this assertion. For one of the most depressing
and troubling lessons of the Holocaust is that the German intelligentsia and academic elite played a major role in the electoral successes of the Nazi party and in the establishment of a rule of terror,
violence, and finally mass murder. The legal profession was deeply
complicit in passing and enforcing racial legislation that facilitated
the Holocaust. The medical profession organized and legitimized the
murder of the mentally and physically handicapped, the horrifying
medical "experiments" in the concentration camps, the selections
at the killing centers. The leaders of the notorious Einsatzgruppen,
the murder squads of the SS, as well as many of the most active and
extreme members of the Reich Main Security Office—charged with
organizing the Final Solution—were holders of doctorates from
Germany's most prestigious universities. The Third Reich's school
system was filled with Nazi teachers who taught eugenics, racism, and
antisemitism to millions of children. Anthropologists, geographers,
historians, biologists, as well as professors of literature, writers, journalists, artists, filmmakers, radio announcers, actors, and so forth were

all involved in this venture of transforming Germany into a genocidal society.[87] The issue is not whether all Germans ultimately acquired an "exterminationist" mentality (which cannot be proven in any case), nor deciding how many of these professionals, intellectuals, academics, and media people actually believed in Nazi ideology and how many were merely looking out for their own interests by supporting Hitler. The question is, rather, how do we as educators and scholars confront the fact that education and knowledge have been shown, in the Germany of 1933–45, to be anything but morally elevating, indeed, were easily transformed into ready tools in the service of evil? How do we come to terms with the realization that it is often people like us who are the first to join the ranks of those whom we now describe as the scourges of humanity?

Having said this, I do not believe that ignorance about the past is a solution. And, once we study and teach an historical event, we cannot help but try and derive lessons from it. To be sure, we should beware of being contaminated by the evil we study and should be even more sensitive to its effects on our audience. But the Holocaust was a crucial event in the history of this century and leaving it out or relegating it to a marginal status would create a vast void in the center of Western civilization whose effect would be to distort our understanding of the world we live in. Indeed, it is ignorance that has made it possible to use the Holocaust as a legitimation for indefensible policies and pernicious ideologies, to promote prejudice, xenophobia, and intolerance. Precisely because of its extremity, the Holocaust has been used all too often as the testing ground for theories on human nature, politics, and representation. While it has been the site of a great deal of morbid fascination, in other contexts it has been wholly sanitized of its horrors and held up as nothing more than an interesting interpretive issue. If there is a pedagogical lesson here, it is that the Holocaust should be taught as any other major historical event, but with full awareness both of its potentially disturbing impact on students and of its capacity to undermine the intellectual and cultural traditions that constitute the moral basis of those who teach it. As long as we keep this in mind, and transmit these worries and fears to our audience, perhaps we will be able to say that we have learned some lessons from the Holocaust.

The Other Planet

It has recently been suggested that the historiography of the Holocaust lacks a "thick description" of the event.[88] This desire to complement, if not replace, the more complex but seemingly detached interpretations of the Nazi genocide of the Jews with the gory details of the horror per se may itself be motivated by a variety of conscious or unconscious urges and intentions. Indeed, there is a great deal to be said on the prevalence of such "thick descriptions" in the scholarly literature and their potential effect on the historical reconstruction of the Holocaust. But for those on the lookout for evidence of sadism and brutality, degradation and inhumanity there is no dearth of documentary, biographical, and literary sources.[89] One of the most extraordinary examples of this kind of representation can be found in the writings of Yehiel Dinur, formerly Feiner, an author who has remained relatively unknown outside of Israel despite translations of his books into numerous languages, but whose impact, under the pen name Ka-Tzetnik, on several generations of young Israelis has been enormous. By analyzing some of the most pertinent themes in Ka-Tzetnik's oeuvre, we may gain some insight into the merits and perils of plunging directly into the man-made *anus mundi* of Auschwitz—for the writer as individual, for his literary representation of the event, and for his readership.

Yehiel Feiner was born in Poland in 1917, studied in a yeshiva in Lublin, and published a volume of poetry in Yiddish with the Warsaw publishing house Kultur Liga in 1931.[90] During the German occupation of Poland he was first in a ghetto and then in Auschwitz, where, according to his own account, he escaped from a selection despite the fact that he had already been reduced to the level of a mussulman. He once more escaped from a death march only moments before the prisoners were executed by their SS guards (who then proceeded to put on the prison uniforms of the dead so as to avoid punishment by the Red Army). Feiner came to Palestine as part of the *Brihah* (illegal immigration) operation organized by the Jewish Brigade and the Haganah (the defense organization of the Yishuv)[91] and changed his name to Dinur, or *of fire* in Aramaic (the name may also be associated with the Hebrew word *din,* which can mean trial, justice, and punishment, and especially with the Di-nur River mentioned in the Book of Daniel and interpreted by the Kabbalah as "a river of fire in the upper reaches of hell that descends upon the evil after their death to purify them"). For the next four decades he devoted himself to writing on his own experience in the camps, on the fate of his parents, siblings, and wife, who all died in the Holocaust, and on his post-Auschwitz life in Israel and his struggle to build a new identity, while remaining totally obsessed with the genocide he had survived.

Until the early 1960s Dinur retained his anonymity. His books were all published under the pseudonym Ka-Tzetnik, which is derived from the German acronym for concentration camp (*KZ*, for *Konzentrationslager*) and was a commonly used term among the inmates (but may also be associated with Franz Kafka's character K). His identity was revealed during the Eichmann trial, where his testimony, which was cut short when he collapsed in the courtroom and was ushered to a hospital, made public his assertion that Auschwitz was "another planet," that is, a universe in which the conventional rules and customs of human civilization did not apply.[92] This concept, which has since been repeatedly employed, often without reference to its originator, constituted the central theme of Ka-Tzetnik's literary production, although, as we shall see and contrary to what most critics have claimed, in his later writings he completely reversed its meaning.

At the heart of Ka-Tzetnik's oeuvre is the sextet *Salamandra,* subtitled *A Chronicle of a Jewish Family in the Twentieth Century.*[93] This subtitle is somewhat misleading, since only some of these semiautobiographical volumes are concerned with Dinur's family, and especially the latter books can be read more as ruminations on the personal, metaphysical, and mystical meanings of the Holocaust. The first volume, titled also *Salamandra,* opens with a citation from an ancient Hebrew source: "When fire burns in one place for seven years without pause, a creature emerges from it called Salamandra." The word *salamandra*, or *salamander* in English, which came into these languages from Greek, denotes both a lizard-like animal and a mythical creature supposed to live in fire. Another Hebrew source describes it as "being born of fire; he who is covered by its blood will not burn." Hence the whole sextet, totaling over a thousand pages in its latest edition, is dominated by the notion of being (re-)created by or forged from fire, living through annihilation, and emerging as a different being, whose bridges to the past have been burned and whose present existence is made meaningful only through that essential link to total destruction. There is here both a sense of profound vulnerability and insecurity, derived from long exposure to imminent death, and a sense of tremendous strength, almost invincibility, by one who survived the fire and lived to tell the tale, even if he is no longer the same person who had originally been thrown into the flames. This heroic mode, reminiscent of the *Nibelungenlied,* where Siegfried became invincible by bathing in the dragon's blood, is of course also deeply ironic, since it is Siegfried's descendants, so to speak, who are out to cremate Ka-Tzetnik and indeed destroy his world. And yet, while Siegfried is eventually slain by Hagen's spear, aimed at the only vulnerable spot in his body where the dragon's blood had been obstructed by a leaf fallen from the mythical Germanic linden tree, Ka-Tzetnik's initiation to the rite of blood and fire is so thorough that he can no longer succumb even to his own raging psyche.

The sextet, written between the late 1940s and the late 1980s, is constructed as follows. Volume 1, *Salamandra,* tells the story of Harry Preleshnik, a thinly veiled Yehiel Feiner, his fiancée and future wife Sonia Schmidt, and some members of his family. It begins just before the war and ends with Harry's final escape from the Germans at the very last phases of the war. Volume 2, *House of Dolls (Bet ha-bubot),* focuses on Harry's sister Daniela, who is made into a so-called *Feld-Hure,* a prostitute for German soldiers, and dies by exposing herself to gun fire by the camp guards. Volume 3, *Piepel,* is the story of Harry's young brother Moni, who is made into the servant and sexual slave of various barracks commanders (*Blockleiter*) in Auschwitz until he too is finally killed (such child prostitutes were called *Piepel* in the jargon of the camps, a term apparently derived from the German provincial word for *lad* and *penis*).[94] Volume 4, *The Clock (Ha-shaon),* is a kind of summary of and initial rumination on the central themes and events of the first three volumes. Volume 5, *The Confrontation (Ha-imut),* which continues Harry's life after his survival and describes his arrival in Palestine, the beginning of his literary career, and his encounter and later marriage with Galiliya, culminates with his wife's mental crisis provoked by both his persistent obsession with the Holocaust and the confrontation between the Jewish and Arab populations in Israel. Finally, volume 6, *Shivitti (Ha-tsofen,* literally *The Code*), is apparently a purely autobiographical account of the author's treatment for depression by a Dutch psychiatrist using controlled doses of LSD, and it ends in a mystical kabbalistic vision whereby Ka-Tzetnik's initial perception of Auschwitz as "another planet" is radically reversed and his mind is liberated from its haunting memory by accepting that Auschwitz was and remains an integral part of the human experience.[95]

Explicit Sincerity

In the present context it is especially interesting to consider the relationship between two central aspects of Ka-Tzetnik's writing. The first has to do with the bizarre and startling mixture of kitsch, sadism, and what initially appears as outright pornography, with remarkable and at times quite devastating insights into the reality of Auschwitz, the fantasies it both engendered and was ruled by, and the human condition under the most extreme circumstances imaginable. While this mélange often seems contradictory and baffling, as if written by two different personae (which, as we shall see, to some extent it was), it also constitutes the basis of the tremendous tension with which these volumes are charged and can be said to be the source of their occasionally uncontrolled energy and nihilistic impulse. The second aspect concerns the impact that Ka-Tzetnik's work, and especially the earlier volumes of this sextet, has had on several generations of Israelis; the reasons for its appeal and ultimate adoption by the Israeli ministry of education (at a time when its popularity among the young was actually waning); and, conversely, its relative obscurity outside of Israel and the tendency of most writers on Holocaust literature to ignore it.[96] In other words I propose to discuss some of the central motifs in Ka-Tzetnik's writing, its reception by the public, and the extent to which it may inform us on the links between representing depravity and comprehending horror.

I should say at the outset that my own second encounter with Ka-Tzetnik, and this time with his complete works rather than the fragments I read in my youth, revealed that my memory—and, I suspect, that of other members of my generation—of what he was all about, indeed, my internalized understanding of his representation of the Holocaust, was largely false. And yet what I found just as troubling was that those elements of the work that had fascinated so many youths born in Israel between the late 1940s and early 1960s have retained that quality that makes it impossible to put down these volumes even as I now realize, and rebel against, what it is about them that makes them so gripping: namely, their obsession with violence and perversity. For Ka-Tzetnik is the kind of writer who under different circumstances would have appealed mainly to a juvenile readership; his prose is mediocre, and his ability to reconstruct human relations, to infiltrate the minds of his protagonists, and to enter the sphere of the emotions with any degree of subtlety is at best limited. Love, loyalty, tragedy, and even loss are all treated with dramatic brush strokes, often accompanied by bombastic exclamations; sexual relations between lovers are described in an almost embarrassingly adolescent manner. In short, parts of this sextet, when read in isolation from the rest, would have earned this writer a not particularly prominent place on the shelves of an average teenager's library and would have been forgotten immediately after they were read. But these books treat the sphere not of the normal but of the depraved. And it is precisely because they are written by an author who lacks the gifts of a great writer (and who claims not to be a writer at all, but merely a chronicler) yet is determined to apply his limited literary abilities to an experience that lacks any precedent either in history or in representation, that the result is so striking, baffling, outrageous, and yet devastating.[97] For how does one write a juvenile novel on the Holocaust? And how can this be done by a writer who himself seems never to have completely emerged from adolescence and yet has been through, and survived, all chambers of hell?

Being explicit about what one sees, feels, or does may emanate from an adolescent urge for honesty and sincerity, and an impatience with perceived or real (adult) subterfuge and deception, hypocrisy and cynicism. It can also be expressed or interpreted as pornography, providing the details of human anatomy or sexual activity generally considered too intimate or crass for public exposure, or lingering on instances of physical and mental abuse and torture, or any other form of inflicting bodily and psychological pain. Normally we would distinguish between sincere exposure of hidden truths and pornography by both the intentions of the representation and its potential effects on the public. Pornography would therefore be defined as a voyeuristic activity whereby the viewer is titillated by watching the (often perverse) sexual activities and pain of others.[98] But it is clearly very difficult to determine how a given public will react to either form of representation; intentions and consequences do not always follow predictable paths. Thus, for instance, "thick descriptions" need to be explicit so as to be true to their goal of representing past or present reality as it "actually happened." And while they would assert a high degree of truthfulness and honesty, they might also have the unintended result of attracting a public more interested in vicariously participating in breaking sexual taboos and committing atrocity than in any search for the causes and meanings of violence and murder.

From this perspective we might note that there are some not altogether obvious links between juvenile and popular (pulp) prose or cinematic fiction, on the one hand, and explicitly honest or explicitly pornographic representation, on the other. Sincerity is of course never merely about telling all the facts, and pornography is never merely an explicit portrayal of sex or violence. Self-perceived honesty may be based in error, and the most honestly reported facts can lie; conversely, representations of perversity and sadism can expose falsehood. But the urge of youth to be told the truth about facts of life that adults seem to be hiding from them, and their simultaneous curiosity about and fascination with matters of sex and violence, make them into a particularly receptive audience for representations of what could be called "explicit sincerity," namely the conscious or unconscious manipulation of readers' and viewers' articulated or unspoken fears, urges, and obsessions.

Illicit Fantasies

During the first two decades following World War II, Israeli youths were exposed to a highly charged discourse on the Holocaust in which the encounter with the survivors and ideological biases, selective information and widespread ignorance, repressed shame and denial of guilt, prejudice and embarrassment all combined to make it exceedingly difficult for young men and women to make any sense of the event. That the Holocaust had been an unprecedented disaster for the Jewish people was generally accepted; that it was also perceived as an instance of national humiliation, whereby millions of Jews were said to have gone "like sheep to the slaughter," made coming to terms with it an almost unbearable burden and a seemingly insurmountable challenge. Because the state of Israel was presented as the definitive and only possible answer to the (destruction of the) Jewish Diaspora and because the new Israeli Jews—armed, aggressive, and victorious—were depicted as the polar opposite of the defenseless, weak, and submissive Jewish victims of European persecution, identifying with one's ancestors in the Exile was ideologically a contradiction in terms, especially as far as young Sabras (Jews born in Israel) were concerned. The inhabitants of ghettos and the inmates of concentration camps could hardly serve as a model for youths raised on the myth of Masada and Tel Hai, according to which dying for one's country and sacrificing oneself for the national cause was the greatest achievement a person could strive for. Indeed, it might be said that, during those early years of statehood, Israeli identity was largely based on a negative model, whereby "we," the Sabras, were defined as being the opposite of "them," the Jews of the *Galut* (exile), and the new national entity was constructed as the extreme negation of the discredited Diaspora.[99]

There were of course positive models—historical, mythical, and fictional—ranging from the biblical Israelites, the Maccabees, and the Zealots' anti-Roman rebellion to the early Zionist defense organizations, such as Ha-shomer, and, to be sure, the fighters of the Warsaw Ghetto uprising and other instances of Jewish resistance to the Nazis. But because the Holocaust (along with, though also in contradiction to, the wars with the Arabs) was so central to the minds of young Israelis, yet furnished the most distinct negative example of Jewish helplessness and victimhood, and because the Nazis were perceived as strong, relentless, and victorious (in that they had achieved their goal of annihilating Jewish existence in much of Europe), it was difficult to avoid a complex, bizarre, and highly disturbing attitude toward the persecutor. For the Nazi manifest will to sacrifice, devotion to a cause, urge to take revenge on real and imagined enemies, and unbound ruthlessness and cruelty were constructed as an ambiguous example to the future generation of Israeli warriors. Thus, if from one perspective the Nazi perpetrators were the epitome of evil and the Jewish victims the fundamental legitimation of Israeli statehood, then at the same time the notion arose that one had to be just like one's enemies so as to avoid the fate of one's ancestors.[100]

In pre-1967 Israel, two types of literature about the Holocaust were available to young Israelis.[101] The first could be called "legitimate" literature. Strongly didactic, imbued with Zionist ideological biases, and often employed as teaching material in the appropriate grades, much of this literature consisted of quasi-fictionalized accounts of resistance to the Nazis, whereby the heroic youths of the ghettos rise against their elders, rebel against the age-old Jewish tradition of compliance and compromise with the enemy, and react to adversity just as their brethren in Palestine would have by taking up arms and dying as warriors rather than victims. Alongside these tales, which appropriated the rebels of the ghettos into the Zionist pantheon, were also stories about heroic children who smuggled food (as well as guns and ammunition) into the ghettos and of some adults, such as Janusz Korczak, who sacrificed themselves for the children. Hence the focus of these stories was on action, sacrifice, and meaningful death. The vast majority of the Jews in the ghettos and camps were ignored, and by implication were treated as having lacked the qualities necessary to give their existence a meaningful content of struggle and resistance; surrounded by an embarrassed silence rooted in an unwillingness to understand how they had allowed themselves to be murdered without fighting, the millions of victims were hidden in the shadow cast by the heroic few. While the rebels were presented as the link between the Diaspora and the "new" Jews in Israel, the rest were portrayed as almost inevitably doomed precisely because they had not learned how to adapt to a new environment, that is, to fight rather than hide, to be like their enemies rather than like their fathers.[102]

The second type of literature, which might be called "illegitimate," was passed secretly from one youth to another, read at night under a street lamp far from the eyes of adults, hidden under stones in the backyards of tenements, never brought home, hardly ever discussed, a source of illicit excitement and shameful pleasure. These were the so-called Stalags, a type of pornographic literature that circulated in Israel of the time, written by anonymous (but most probably Israeli) writers, replete with perverse sex and sadistic violence.[103] The excitement evoked in young readers by such pulp fiction stemmed both from the encounter with forms of human activity kept tightly sealed from them by the puritanical nature of pre-1967 Israeli society and from the fact that the central sites for these actions were the concentration camps. Nothing could be a greater taboo than deriving sexual pleasure from pornography in the context of the Holocaust; hence nothing could be as exciting. That Israeli youth learned about sex and perversity, and derived sexual gratification, from books describing the manner in which Nazis tortured Jews, is all the more disturbing, considering that we are speaking about a society whose population consisted of a large proportion of Holocaust survivors and their offspring. What effects such extracurricular sexual "education," combined with the elevating and generally optimistic "legitimate" literature on the Holocaust, may have had on the evolving psychology of young Israelis and eventually on society as a whole can only be guessed; generalizing would hardly do justice to this underresearched phenomenon. But there is little doubt that subsequent generations, although exposed to a much more elaborate and sophisticated discourse on the Holocaust (and far more explicit pornography), have not been wholly liberated from this pernicious trap, whereby they must have more of the violent and ruthless attributes associated with the perpetrators so as not to become their victims (whom on some level of consciousness they are still defending). Simultaneously, in the course of this liberating transformation of roles, they may also discover a whole range of illicit fantasies and secret pleasures.

God's Mussulman

In an addendum to the newly reissued volume *House of Dolls,* the publisher has included a letter written by a young Israeli soldier to his girlfriend shortly before he was killed in the 1967 war: "I have just finished reading the book *House of Dolls* by Ka-Tzetnik," he writes,

> and I feel that from all the horror and helplessness a tremendous ability to be strong is growing and flourishing in me; so strong that one could weep; as sharp as a knife; both silent and terrible. This how I want to be now! I want to know that never again will bottomless eyes stare from behind electrified fences! They will not stare this way only if I am strong! If all of us are strong! Strong and proud Jews! We will

never be led again to the slaughter! In the commando unit we were like that, we were swift, strong, and silent as devils . . . and we felt that we could overcome them. We did everything they had refused to believe we could do, we were sure of our strength. Can a soldier feel anything better than being silent, alert, and dangerous? We passed by settlements, mountains, fields, like shadows, and no one knew that we had been there.[104]

More than any other of his volumes, Ka-Tzetnik's *House of Dolls* is related to both, and yet belongs to neither, the "legitimate" nor the "illegitimate" literature on the Holocaust. Indeed, throughout his writings, Ka-Tzetnik may be said to maintain an ambivalent position between these two categories. Here we find no glorification of resistance, in fact hardly any armed resistance at all. If Sonia eventually joins the partisans, that episode remains marginal to the account, and she ultimately dies in the gas chamber rather than in a gun fight with the Nazis. If Harry does carry a gun at the end of the war, the only episode in which he is shown to be at the point of killing an SS man ends up with him hesitating so long that the German is finally shot quite casually by a Soviet soldier.[105] Nor does he become an effective resistance fighter against the British in Palestine, and later on he reverses his initial position of equating the Arabs with the Nazis by promoting understanding with the former. To be sure, Harry is ultimately cast in a somewhat heroic mold but never one rooted in physical, armed action. Similarly, Ka-Tzetnik's books cannot be said to be pornographic in the sense of consciously trying to manipulate their readers and merely excite their senses, even if in parts, and especially in *House of Dolls,* they share some characteristics with the Stalag pulp fiction, which also employed women's camps and prostitute inmates as the "historical" context for their plots. Nevertheless, it is in the sheer violence and explicit physical and mental atrocity of the *Salamandra* sextet that we must begin to explore the reasons for Ka-Tzetnik's popularity among Israeli youth long before he was officially adopted by the state's political establishment.

What is most striking and baffling about Ka-Tzetnik is the unexpected manner in which the content and the form of his writing interact. Almost up to the end of his sextet, Ka-Tzetnik's prose resembles the writing common to the youth literature on the Holocaust that was circulating in pre-1967 Israel. This does not seem to be a deliberate technique but merely reflects the author's mind cast and literary ability. And yet precisely because he fails to adapt the form of his writing to its content, that is, the banalities of juvenile literature to the context of the Holocaust as he experienced it, an infernal region in which humanity was reduced to its most base instincts even before it was destroyed, his writing becomes more brutally explicit and free of all euphemism and distance than almost any other such text on the Holocaust.[106] At the same time it reflects the writer's complete inability to take delight in the pain and perversion he so meticulously describes (although it has the potential of evoking such a voyeuristic urge in its readers). Hence also the paradoxical outcome that whenever Ka-Tzetnik writes about "our" planet, namely, describes "normal" events and relationships, his prose is so replete with kitsch and clichés that it can only appeal to a juvenile audience. However, once he plunges into that "other" planet, that very predilection toward the banal makes possible a remarkable transformation whereby the author achieves devastating insights into the human condition that have been barred to far more sophisticated writers—not least, perhaps, due to their greater concern for the aesthetic aspects and moral effect of their work.

In this context it might be useful to refer to Primo Levi, probably the most articulate and significant writer on Auschwitz, who, interestingly, became known in Israel to a larger public only after the translation of his *Survival in Auschwitz* appeared in Hebrew in 1988, forty years after its original publication.[107] To be sure, Levi also delves deeply into the horror of Auschwitz, but his profound commitment to humanity and his keen awareness of both the moral issues at stake and the aesthetic rules of prose writing prevent him from lingering on the horror to the same extent as Ka-Tzetnik, and they compel him to try and view events from a certain distance and perspective, even in his earliest writing on the Holocaust, composed shortly after his return from the camps. Thus while Ka-Tzetnik is almost never able to distance himself from the experience of the camps up to the last volume of his sextet, Levi moves in the opposite direction, becoming inextricably enmeshed in the past and the paradoxes of its representation, as is so painfully revealed in his own last essays.[108] Reading Ka-Tzetnik, we are in the midst of the horror; there is no control here, no embarrassment, no qualifications. Indeed, Ka-Tzetnik does what Levi ultimately reproaches himself for having been unable to accomplish, namely, he writes from the point of view of the drowned, the mussulman. Nor is his writing on horror in any way contrived (in stark contrast to his attempts to describe "normality"), and precisely because of its wholly uninhibited, raw nature, his representation of evil is not only disturbing but in many ways annihilating of the manner in which we all desire to see and understand the interaction between humanity and the Holocaust.

The paradoxical consequences of the tension between aesthetic control and devastating experience, bewilderment and insight, chaos and articulation may also be demonstrated by contrasting the writings of the highly assimilated Primo Levi and Jean Améry, whose world of associations was an integral part of the European Renaissance and Enlightenment, with those of Elie Wiesel and Ka-Tzetnik, both of whom were raised in a traditional East European Jewish environment, studied Talmud and the Kabbalah, and perforce were compelled to relate the Holocaust to their increasingly shaken belief in God and his Covenant with the Chosen People.[109] While Levi and Améry view the Holocaust as a manifestation of the crisis of European civilization and try to sustain their hope in humanism and humanity, Wiesel and Ka-Tzetnik are constantly struggling with their religious belief and their understanding of Jewish fate and faith. Levi is of course the strongest defender of humanism, as is so powerfully demonstrated in the key episode of *Survival in Auschwitz* when he attempts to reconstruct in memory the essence of Dante's humanistic vision, those crucial lines in which Ulysses distinguishes man from beast by his eternal quest for a higher meaning:

> Think of your breed; for brutish ignorance
> Your mettle was not made; you were made men,
> To follow after knowledge and excellence.[110]

Améry, for his part, ends up as the disillusioned and betrayed believer in the Enlightenment who can no longer live with the unacceptable realization that the Holocaust continues to happen under different guises in a post-Auschwitz world indifferent to the destruction it inflicts on itself. Ultimately, Levi too seems to be overtaken by a sense of depression and hopelessness, both about his ability truthfully to reconstruct the experience of the Holocaust and about transmitting it to others in any meaningful way. Since he counts himself among the saved, while the true representatives of Auschwitz are the drowned, the mussulmen who had died even before they were finally gassed, and because he senses that the lesson of the Holocaust has been unlearned by subsequent generations, he eventually appears to succumb to that very urge to put an end to his life that he had earlier condemned so strongly in Améry.[111]

Wiesel and Ka-Tzetnik, who have gone through the same hell of Auschwitz, offer a wholly different perspective on their experience. While Wiesel is the more sophisticated and controlled of the two, he is consequently also far more contrived, and his account bears the characteristics of well-crafted, skillful, didactic rhetoric, which may also partly explain his successes among the French- and English-reading public. Wiesel's kitsch, his bombastic utterances and exclamations about the human condition in the mode of French Existentialism that was fashionable when he wrote much of his *Night* trilogy, has appealed both to youthful readers and to a more adult public searching for a palatable representation of the Holocaust and its implications for humanity.[112] Conversely, Ka-Tzetnik's anguished, at times almost insane, obsession with depravity, his wild fantasies, and his anarchic refusal to conform to any rules of the genre have barred him from gaining attention in cultures that prefer a well-told story, insist on close attention to matters aesthetic, require some moral lesson, and instinctively reject such baffling, messy, and often repelling accounts. At his best, his kitsch is of such an extraordinary nature that it penetrates the most hidden, darkest, and most repulsive recesses of the human psyche. Yet the very core of these two writers' literary works is almost uncannily alike, to the extent that they seem to present two versions of the same experience: a young traditional Jew's encounter with limitless evil. Both set out from their own very personal, Jewish experience. In Wiesel's writing this hearkens back to his quasi-mythical Jewish town of Sighet in Hungary; in Ka-Tzetnik's writing this is associated with the wealthy Jewish-Polish bourgeoisie and the protagonist's Zionist aspirations. Ironically, it is Wiesel who universalizes his experience from the very beginning, not least by implicit references to Fyodor Dostoevsky and Jean-Paul Sartre just as much as to Jewish tradition.[113] Ka-Tzetnik, on the other hand, begins by focusing almost exclusively on himself and all other Jewish victims, and subsequently on the Zionist experience in Israel. It is only in the last sections of his sextet that he attempts a universalization of the Holocaust. Yet it is Wiesel who is thought of by now (at least in France, Britain, and especially the United States, but not in Israel, possibly because of his having left the country) as the public representative par excellence of both Jewish fate and its universal meaning, while Ka-Tzetnik has been assigned almost everywhere (with the partial exception of Israel, and even there for the wrong reasons) to the lunatic fringe. Interestingly, despite their doubtless torment and pain throughout the post-Auschwitz era, which spans the main bulk of their lives, neither Wiesel nor Ka-Tzetnik have reached the radical conclusion of Levi and Améry. They struggle with God and fate, belief and identity, but precisely because their point of departure is the role of providence in human evil, by the time they come to ruminate on the inherent evil in man and human society they are no longer prepared to give up all hope. Instead, they take up the traditional role of the ancient Hebrew prophets, decrying evil, fighting with God, yet never relenting in their struggle to reintroduce the divine sparks back into the world of men, just as the Kabbalah spoke of the *tikkun* (restoration) of the spiritual lights by liberating them from the domination of the *kelippot* (forces of evil).

Contaminating Survivors

Yehiel Dinur collapsed in the courtroom during the Eichmann trial shortly after he revealed that he was indeed the writer Ka-Tzetnik, the man without a name who had written those harrowing tales from the "other" planet of Auschwitz. Hence he seems to have been overcome by his inability to link his two personae, rigidly kept apart all those years precisely because bringing them together again might have precipitated a mental crisis and thereby prevented him from continuing his life's work. In the trial Dinur was asked by the judge: "Why did you hide behind the pen-name Ka-Tzetnik?" To which he replied: "This is not a pen-name. I do not see myself as an author who writes literature. This is a chronicle from the planet of Auschwitz, whose inhabitants had no names, they were neither born nor bore any children; they were neither alive nor dead. They breathed according to different laws of nature. Every fraction of a minute there revolved on a different time scale. They were called Ka-Tzetnik, they were skeletons with numbers."[114]

The Eichmann trial was the first occasion in which large sectors of the Israeli public, who had until then had only a rudimentary knowledge of the Holocaust, were exposed to its details. This did not, however, bring greater understanding but rather served precisely the purpose for which it was intended by David Ben-Gurion, prime minister and towering political figure at the time.[115] It fortified the sense of Israeli identity, at least overtly (on a deeper level the trial may have also shaken Israeli self-assurance), and set it against that other identity, on that other planet, which came to symbolize the Diaspora as a whole as well as its alleged culmination in Auschwitz. The witnesses were recruited from among both victims and resisters. Young Israelis could feel distant from and uncomprehending of the victims, and they could strongly identify with the resisters, who had acted according to the logic inculcated in the youth raised in Palestine and Israel at a time of foreign war and domestic conflict. In this context it was unlikely that Ka-Tzetnik's perspective would be understood, namely, that he was reporting directly from that other planet, that he not only identified with but was indeed a living remnant of those lowliest of the low, the mussulmen of the camps, the Jews who had been transformed into nonhuman beings. It was therefore all the easier to understand Ka-Tzetnik in a wholly different manner, as asserting that Auschwitz was another planet in precisely the sense that the discourse in Israel of the period would have it, symbolizing everything that Zionism was created to undo, and serving as the ultimate and absolute justification and legitimation for the foundation of the Jewish state.

This is not to say that on another level Ka-Tzetnik himself did not share this vision. Indeed, the blurb printed on the cover of every volume of the sextet, which includes portions of Ka-Tzetnik's above-cited statement in the trial, goes on to describe these books in the following manner: "*Salamandra*—the apocalyptic vision of that period reflected in today's mirror. The confrontation, the bare chest of an orphaned generation fighting for its survival in the midst of the battle cry. *Salamandra*—the song of songs to love that overcomes evil and death." This is of course everything that Ka-Tzetnik's writing is not. But there is no reason to think that the author did not approve the blurb, nor that he disagreed with it as a precise summary of his work. For Ka-Tzetnik seems only rarely to grasp the full meaning of his writing and begins to realize the inherent contradiction that runs through the first five volumes only as he writes the sixth, forty years after he began this mammoth undertaking. And, not untypical for this remarkable writer, he appears to finally find peace only by resolving this contradiction in a manner that is devastating for the present, that is, by extending the planet of Auschwitz to include our own world and time.

In another addendum to the 1994 reissue of *House of Dolls*, a special edition supported by the Israeli ministry of education, we find an article by Yitzhak Sadeh (commander of the Haganah), published originally in 1946. Although it was obviously meant to change (and therefore also reflects) the attitudes of his subordinates toward the Jewish refugees from Europe, whom they were smuggling into British-ruled Palestine in the *Brihah,* it is in fact a disturbing document on the reception and perception of Holocaust survivors by young men and women (but in this case especially men) raised in what was soon to become the state of Israel. It is just as interesting that the officials of the ministry of education and the editors and publishers of this volume appear to have been wholly unaware of the extent to which this essay reflected the ambivalence of young Sabras on encountering the remnants of the Diaspora, their sense of pity and revulsion, their urge to cleanse the survivors of the evil they had been exposed to and their fear of pollution by it, their uncertainty as to the true status of these representatives of "another planet": Were they sanctified by going through all chambers of hell, or was their very survival, so unlikely considering the millions who had perished, an indication of some complicity with the perpetrators? It is with this context in mind that we should read Sadeh's short essay, on the opposite page of which the publisher has reproduced what is said to be "an authentic photograph of Paela, heroine of the book *House of Dolls,*" portraying a woman whose bare chest carries the tattoo: FELD-HURE.

> Night. On the wet sand my sister stands before me: filthy, her clothes in disarray, her hair disheveled, barefoot, her head bowed—she stands and weeps.
> I know: Her flesh is stamped with the tattoo: "for officers only."
> And my sister weeps and says:
> Comrade, why am I here? Why was I brought here? Am I worthy of the young and healthy lads who risk their lives for me? No, I have no place in the world. I should not go on living.
> I hug my sister . . . and say to her: You have a place in the world, my sister, a special and unique place. Here, in this our land you should live, my sister. Here we will give you our love. You are dark and beautiful, my sister. You are dark, for the suffering has scorched you, but you are beautiful, as beautiful to me as beauty itself, as sanctified to me as sanctity itself. . . .
> I know: The villains have tortured her and made her barren. . . .
> I say to her: . . . We love you my sister; you carry all the glow of motherhood within you, all the beauty of womanhood is in you. To you our love is given, you will be a sister to us, you will be a bride to us, you will be a mother to us.
> Before these sisters of mine I kneel, I cover myself with the dust of their feet. And when I rise to my feet, I stand erect, I hold my head high and I feel and know: For these sisters of mine—I am strong.
> For these sisters of mine—I am brave.
> For these sisters of mine—I will also be cruel.
> For you [I will do] anything—anything.[116]

And this is how Ka-Tzetnik was read, indeed, this is in some respects a gist of the manner in which the Holocaust itself was read as a crucial, formative event for *Israeli* history. The survivors arrived, contaminated by the evil from which they had barely escaped, barren and defiled. And yet they were accepted by those who wished to see themselves as their saviors, accepted not only (or even primarily) as individuals but as the irrefutable legitimization of the struggle, as the fundamental sanction to be strong, courageous, and cruel, to fight one's enemies as if they were the Nazis, to fear defeat as if it could only spell another Auschwitz, to repress any sense of pity and compassion for anyone but one's own kind. For weakness was the chief characteristic of those very same Jews whose genocide had made survival into the highest moral imperative and any action ensuring it not only permissible but noble.

Yet on a more profound level, Ka-Tzetnik took a wholly different path, one much harder to follow at the time and even to this day, precisely because it contradicts so much of what many of us would like to believe when we think of the Holocaust. For if Ka-Tzetnik set out by seeing Auschwitz as another planet and Israel as his (and the Jewish people's) only salvation, during the subsequent decades he came to realize that salvation was not at hand, and he found himself torn between that self which had entered the Holocaust and that other self that was born again, out of the fire, when he escaped the transport to the gas chambers by hiding in the coal box on the truck that took him and his fellow mussulmen to their death. There, curled inside that coal box as a baby in the womb, he was reborn, as a Salamandra, from the flames of hell, invincible and yet a monster, a creature protected from annihilation by having bathed in the blood of the doomed. Initially, upon arriving in Palestine, he still shares Sadeh's vision; he perceives the Arabs as Nazis, the Jews as warding off extermination. He refuses to feel pity, compassion, even fear. But for him the essential confrontation always remains more than the struggle between the past and the present, or the Jews and their enemies. The remarkable fifth volume, *The Confrontation (Ha-imut)*, is ultimately about the polluting effects of the Holocaust survivor on those who love him, whose urge to identify with his suffering leads them to torture their own body and soul, and it is just as much about the tragic reversal of roles in Israel (as he perceives it), where the Jews treat the Arabs the way the gentiles treated the Jews. It is, then, about the implantation of evil in the very fabric of that new, cleansed, and optimistic Jewish existence in an independent state—that is, about the contaminating effects of the Salamandra, whose invincibility is derived from blood and hate, revenge and brutality. To be sure, this extraordinary volume is rarely cited in the various official ceremonies and celebrations surrounding Ka-Tzetnik in Israel (which he never attends). It was probably not even read by those who appended to it the above-cited documents. Yet it is an early and strikingly powerful rumination on the long-term effects of evil and destruction. And while it is not free from the kitsch of a cheap romance that mars this writer's prose (precisely because much of this volume is devoted to post-Auschwitz "normality"), it carries a dark and forbidding vision, not at all one of love surpassing evil and death, but rather of evil overcoming hope and compassion.

The notion of the survivors as polluted by evil and thereby threatening to contaminate their post-Holocaust environment was prevalent both among those who had received them into their midst and among the survivors themselves.[117] Feelings of guilt were never far from the surface on both sides—guilt for having survived while others perished, guilt for having not done enough to help the victims, and shame for having led a more or less normal existence while the crematoria worked day and night.[118] Some have argued that this deep sense of guilt was at the root of the numerous cases of suicide among survivors (and their children), often many years after the event. But Ka-Tzetnik's case is once more different, since his mythical vision of himself as having been born again from the flames of Auschwitz made for a radical break into two personae; his new, fire-proof self is immune even to his most pernicious enemy, his inability to find the link between present reality and the tormenting memories (and torments) of the past.[119] Yet this invincibility is achieved at a price, that of remaining a monster, a Salamandra, a creature dipped in the blood of that other planet's victims. And whenever his other persona attempts, or is compelled, to emerge, the conflict inevitably leads to mental collapse, an escape perhaps into a state of semi-insanity in which the inability to fuse the splinters of his personality is no longer registered in the mind.[120]

Universal Auschwitz

A few years ago the Israeli ministry of education, then headed by Zevulun Hammer, chair of the National Religious Party, a Zionist and in recent years increasingly right-wing party, decided to collaborate in a reissue of Ka-Tzetnik's sextet and to deliver thousands of these volumes to Israeli high schools as recommended reading on the Holocaust. It seems unlikely that these officials had an intimate knowledge of Dinur's writings; rather, they most probably either retained a faint memory of reading the earlier volumes in their own youth, or simply accepted the common view in Israel of Ka-Tzetnik as an icon of Hebrew-language representation of the Holocaust. Consequently, these officials in fact provided the final sanction to a writer as widely known in Israel as he has been almost universally misread and misunderstood, whose views on Israeli society, Jewish identity and faith, indeed the human condition as such, challenge much of mainstream thinking in current Israel and starkly contradict the conventional interpretation of the Holocaust by the political right and the religious community. Thus we might say that Ka-Tzetnik was never read for what he said but for what his readers imagined (or expected) him to be saying, that is, he was read as a confirmation of prevailing views and prejudices on the Holocaust and as one who could legitimately express (since he was the survivor par excellence) what others dared not utter. In the 1950s and 1960s Israeli youngsters often read Ka-Tzetnik because he was the only legitimate source of sexually titillating and sadistic literature in a still puritanical and closed society, with the result that the Holocaust somehow became enmeshed in their minds with both repelling and fascinating pornographic images.[121] Similarly, by now the complete sextet may well have the opposite effect from that expected by the Israeli educational establishment. For ultimately, when read from beginning to end, Ka-Tzetnik casts doubt both on the Zionist venture and on the possibility of dividing humanity and history into different planets. His "recovery" from schizophrenia and depression is not achieved by "coming to terms" with the past, but by accepting that the past and the present are one and the same, and that the victim of yesterday may turn out to be today's executioner. Most radically, he concludes that yesterday's victim was potentially also the killer and that the killer could have easily been the victim. In a mystical scene pregnant with kabbalistic symbolism, Dinur finally "resolves" the mystery and unites with his other self by bringing the evil of Auschwitz into our own world:

> I raise my eyes to the heavens of Auschwitz. On the horizon is a picture of "Shivitti" such as those found normally over the prayer-column before the cantor in every synagogue. Only here, this "Shivitti" . . . looks different. . . . it is burning like a torch, glittering with the colors of the rainbow. But —and this is what is strange about it—all its light is shining inward and upward. . . .
>
> I am struck with terror. Cramped by the skeletons I stand on the truck and stare at the letters JEHOVAH shining out of the "Shivitti" with a light not of this world; and at the pair of lions, to the right and left, which guard between them the secret of the combination: "I imagine [shivitti] God [Jehovah] always before me." . . . And the letters JEHOVAH mix and stir one in each other, one on top of the other. And I call out:
>
> "God! God! Who decreed this?!
>
> God! God! Auschwitz—to whom does it belong?!"
>
> With trembling I raise my eyes to see God's face in His characters, and see in front of me the face of an SS man standing by the front of the truck. His eyes still show the signs of sleep. The dawn is cold, and

his hands are in the pockets of his black military coat. Before his eyes—
a stream of skeletons silently flowing from the gate of the barracks
to the opening of the truck. And then his mouth opens with a long
yawn. . . .

And I am inside the rolling truck, a naked skeleton among naked
skeletons, being sent now by the yawning German to the crematorium. I look at him and his yawn, and suddenly I ask myself: Does he
hate me? After all, he does not even know me. Not even my name.
I continue to look at him and I ask myself: Do I hate him? After all,
I do not even know his name. . . .

At that very moment I am struck with a horror such as I have never
known before: If so, then he could have been here instead of me, a
naked skeleton in the truck, and I, I could have been there instead of
him, on this cold morning, making sure that I send him, and millions
like him, to the crematorium—and just like him I would have yawned,
because I would have preferred, just like him, to stay in bed on such
a cold morning. . . .

Oh, God, merciful and compassionate, is it I, is it I who created
Auschwitz? . . .

Ah, God, Great God of the heavens of Auschwitz! Show Your face
to Your creature so that I know who is it who dwells inside me and
is being sent now to the crematorium—and why? And who is it who
dwells inside him and sends me to the crematorium—and why? You
Who know that at this moment the two of us, the sender and the sent,
are equal as men! Your own creatures, in Your very image.

The truck passes the gate of Auschwitz and over it the German
words:

ARBEIT MACHT FREI

And they change into the Hebrew words:

"And He made him in the image of God."[122]

It is at this point, as he relives he moment of his near destruction
and rebirth under the influence of LSD, viewing himself not only
from the perspectives of "then" and "now" but also through the eyes
of his own yawning perpetrator, that Ka-Tzetnik begins the process
of coming to terms not with the event but with the Salamandra he
believes he had become. Made in fire, of fire, both victim and killer,
he is one and the same, a man. Immediately after the event, in his first
book, Primo Levi had asked, *Ecce homo*? Forty years later he could
neither refute that assumption nor live with it any longer. Ka-Tzetnik
had set out by dividing humanity into monsters and men, time into
"then" and "now," the world into "there" and "here." Forty years later
he finally fuses them all together into one continuous apocalyptic vision encompassing our own present reality. A world, that is, in which
Salamandras can feel at home:

I look at the number written at the top of the page on which I am writing these lines, and I cannot believe my eyes: I have already covered scores of pages with tiny letters and have not noted the innovation in them. I have never written on this subject in the first person. In all my books I wrote in the third person, although that form of writing was difficult for me, since all I wrote was a kind of personal diary, a testimony: I saw these things, I experienced these experiences, I lived through the events, I, I, I, and yet while writing I had to transformed the "I" into "he." I felt a splitting, a discomfort, a strangeness, and worst of all—I felt myself, God forbid, as if I were preoccupied with literature. Yet I knew that if I did not write in the third person I might have not been able to write at all. And all of a sudden, without even noticing it, for the very first time, and already in the first line: "I, I, I . . . "[123]

Up to this point Ka-Tzetnik/Dinur has used the metaphor of the Salamandra, a foreign import into Jewish mysticism. Now as he prepares himself to go to another LSD-induced psychiatric session, he recalls the words of the psychiatrist: "Through this opening you must enter in order to find the answer."[124] On the opposite page we find a citation from the Hebrew sources, invoking the ancient equivalent of the Salamandra, the Phoenix, or, as it is called in the Hebrew source (*Bereshit Raba,* 19:5), the Bird of Hol, which no longer bears the same monstrous characteristics of the Salamandra, even though it is still a creature of fire: "There is a bird whose name is Hol—it lives a thousand years and at the end of a thousand years a fire comes out of its nest and burns it and what remains of it is like an egg that grows limbs again and lives."[125]

On returning to Israel from the psychiatric ward in Leiden, Dinur gradually realizes the transformation that has occurred: "Before Leiden, the splitting was—*I:* A nightmare from within myself that seizes me under the cover of darkness. But now, after Leiden, the nightmare of splitting stands before me in the light of day, and it is of all humanity, even cosmic."[126] He concludes:

> In the past I sought solitude, far from human habitation, for I wanted to be alone with Auschwitz. Now Auschwitz threatens all men. Wherever man is, there is Auschwitz, because it is not Satan who created Auschwitz, but I and you, just as it is not Satan who creates the [nuclear] mushroom but I and you.
> Man!
> I am no longer haunted by the monstrous nightmare at night; it appears before my eyes in the light of day.[127]

And thus, finally, after hundreds of pages filled with the most explicit descriptions of that "other planet," of sadism and cannibalism, sexual perversity and torture, endless suffering and hopelessness, and an unfathomable degradation of humanity, he ends his sextet with these words:

> In the past I used to say: Auschwitz is another planet! It can not be explained and it can not be described. Auschwitz is a cosmic Holocaust! Its nightmare attacks me at night. As if Auschwitz has no rule in the daytime when men are awake and alert. Auschwitz is of hell, of the night, on the other side of man-in-the-image-of-God. . . .
> Auschwitz and the splitting? God and Satan? The other planet and man? Questions, questions. And the answer? End![128]

For Ka-Tzetnik, it seems, relief has at last come from the realization that the whole world is inhabited by Salamandras.

No Other Planet

Reading Ka-Tzetnik is an unsettling, disturbing experience. Just as he employs a multitude of clichés and banalities when writing on normality, so, too, he shatters all the clichés and banalities about atrocity that we hold dear; just as he maintains the tone of a wide-eyed adolescent when describing love and friendship in conventional times, so, too, he uncovers with almost unequaled power and deeply troubling relish the seemingly unlimited human capacity, among victims and perpetrators alike, for betrayal and sadism, hate and perversity in the infernal regions of the Auschwitz. If the Nazis are always in the background of the evil he portrays, his attention is focused much more on the disintegration of even the most basic human relationships and moral codes among the inmates, the cruelty of the *Kapos*, the murderous instincts to which hunger, deprivation, and humiliation give rise, the fall of those who under other circumstances would have been the most admired members of a community. Few figures retain their humanity for long in his version of the camps, and the isolated figures that do so are quickly destroyed precisely because of their failure to adapt to that new and for them unacceptable world. Underlying his representation of the Holocaust, even if rarely asserted, is the assumption that only those who adapted by shedding their humanity, forsaking their loved ones, their faith, indeed leaving their old selves behind in the crematoria, had even the faintest chance of surviving. If in some of his writing he may be said to abuse the memory of the Holocaust by applying it to contemporary politics, and if his volumes have indeed been employed for that purpose by readers, critics, religious leaders, and politicians, the most crucial portions of the sextet constitute a complete rejection of this tendency to invoke the camps whenever their memory seems to serve present needs.[129] If the Germans are for Ka-Tzetnik the personification of evil, they are also and simultaneously men just like ourselves; if the victims are for him the embodiment of suffering, they are also and at the same time (with few exceptions) the incarnation of human brutality and savagery; if love for him can surmount evil, it is also polluted by it and turns against itself. If revenge is a necessary condition to survive survival, then revenge means to him also playing into the hands of the Devil. If God had hidden his face from the Jews and can no longer be trusted, then God is also suffering the betrayal of man by man. And finally, if Auschwitz is another planet, then we are still living on that planet today, as Ka-Tzetnik ultimately argues after forty years of writing that culminate in a decade of slowly internalizing and unraveling the mystical visions he had experienced in the psychiatric lab in Leiden.

The Ka-Tzetnik that Israeli youth read in the first two decades of the state is very different from the Ka-Tzetnik/Dinur of the last two of decades. His is a slow and in many ways fascinating transformation, a voyage of revelation and understanding, an internal quest not wholly divorced (despite his personal abhorrence of public life) from contemporary affairs. To some extent, perhaps precisely because of his quasi-adolescent mind, his evolution is closely related to the changing images of the Holocaust among Israeli youth during the past fifty years. In the 1950s and 1960s the Holocaust was fascinating by its very destructiveness and cruelty, perversion and sadism; it had a powerfully liberating effect in that it allowed its (potential) victims to act in the world as if all their actions were a vicarious vendetta against the assassins of their people; it also made for some bizarre and disturbing tendencies toward identifying with the killers, wanting to be as cruel and efficient and even as dashing as they appeared to be in some youngsters' imagination.[130] In the last two decades, however, the Holocaust has been the site of an increasingly mythical and mystical view of Jewish history and faith. For some twenty years God seemed to have been banished from the world of Auschwitz, but then he began coming back, step by step, filling the voids that rational explanation and historical reconstruction had left behind. Contemporary extremists in Israel, some of whom come from the United States, were raised on a memory of the Holocaust that combines terror of destruction with an urge for revenge, mystical visions with a willingness for ruthless political and military action. This is a new type of instrumentalization of the Holocaust, whose roots can be traced in part to an eschatological frame of mind that was wholly foreign to the youth of pre-1967 Israel. It is, perhaps, the nemesis of God's exile from the landscape of his people's destruction for so many years. Ka-Tzetnik's mysticism reflects this tendency, this search for answers that secular thinking failed to provide. But while his underlying political stance has been in favor of reconciliation, perhaps precisely because of his recognition of every man's potential brutality, these young fanatics have retreated again into a narrow world of "us" against "them," and a willingness to wreak destruction not only because of past crimes against their people but also because of God's perceived sanction for such actions in the present. Yet for now such newly sanctified politicization of the Holocaust is a minority view among Israeli youths.

When Menachem Begin said in 1982 that, by fighting Yasir Arafat in Beirut, he was actually fighting Hitler in Berlin, what was most striking about that proclamation was not the fact that it was made but the rejection with which it was met by large sectors of Israeli society.[131] This kind of politicization of the Holocaust was no longer universally acceptable, whereas in the 1950s there was no need for such pronouncements, since for most people it was self-evident that Israel's enemies were Hitler's allies and that the Jews in Israel were all potential victims of gas chambers. Moreover, as Israeli society opened up to the West and became exposed to increasingly graphic representations of sex and violence in the media, there was no longer a need to look for titillating scenes in Stalag pulp fiction or the explicit fantasies of a writer such as Ka-Tzetnik. By now *Playboy* magazine and pornographic videotapes could replace *House of Dolls* as the source of information for youths on matters their parents would not discuss with them and as a forbidden kind of entertainment.[132]

This does not mean that the Holocaust has ceased to serve as a site for sexual titillation and pornographic representation, often clad in the respectable garment of historical novels or films and asserting special importance (while arousing greater interest) by dint of dealing with a "serious" topic. But this is a different matter that goes well beyond this discussion.[133] Indeed, by now many Israelis watching such films or reading such novels will react in a not wholly dissimilar manner from, say, Americans or Germans, while very few readers would find Ka-Tzetnik particularly pornographic. At the same time, since we have recently been urged to consider the need for a more explicit language in historical writing on the Holocaust, we must note that such representations may well attract readers more interested in detailed descriptions of sadism and murder than in understanding their causes and motivations.

It is for this reason that the recent debate over Daniel J. Goldhagen's book *Hitler's Willing Executioners* should have paid more attention to his assertion that he had provided the kind of "thick description" of the killers' actions missing from previous historical monographs.[134] Leaving aside the question of whether this was indeed such a scholarly innovation,[135] and keeping in mind Ka-Tzetnik's vivid accounts of his own experiences in Auschwitz, one might have asked to what extent the historian can faithfully provide such a description without filling the gaps in the available documentation by exercising his imagination beyond the bounds of scholarly writing. Put differently, might the historian be in danger of fantasizing about the events and protagonists he writes on and thereby distort the historical record in a manner that is acceptable perhaps for survivor-chroniclers such as Dinur but is far more perilous for those displaying scholarly credentials? What, for instance, are we to do with a scholarly work that not only vividly describes the horrible deaths of children but also speculates on what the perpetrators were thinking while they were doing the killing, neither of which can possibly be found in any documents nor, in this case, can be based on the writer's personal experience, but must rather stem from his own (morbid) fantasies, which in turn would be at least partly influenced by televised, cinematic, and literary representations?[136] And since fantasies of horror tend to find an audience, it is reasonable to assume that some of those who rushed to buy the book were curious to read precisely those "thick" descriptions of atrocities that, they had been told, were so much more "powerful" and "gripping" than the laborious interpretations of conventional historians. *This* is a disturbing thought, because it implies that what is most marketable about the Holocaust is its horror, and hence that the more one concentrates on horror the more one is likely to appear to be engaged in a sincere attempt to expose "what actually happened," and at the same time to achieve commercial success. This of course should not come as a great surprise to any Hollywood producer who has made his millions through blockbuster horror films.

Moreover, anyone who has followed the flood of reviews of Goldhagen's book, especially but not exclusively in Germany, might have noticed that they were often accompanied by photographic evidence from the Holocaust.[137] And although there are thousands upon thousands of available photographs, only a few of them tend to appear over and over again: a child with raised hands threatened by an armed German soldier, naked women running to their deaths, a Jew having his beard shorn by laughing soldiers, a mound of skeletal corpses. These are the most common images of the Holocaust, and one must stop and wonder how these images are interpreted by those who see them repeatedly reprinted in newspapers and magazines, no matter what the text actually argues. These photographs are a celebration of inhumanity, degradation, horror, and pornography. Repeated exposure to them in the mass media may have consequences well beyond this or that thesis on the causes and course of the Holocaust, for what remains in the mind are images, and those images are the ones that the Nazis had wished us to have.

This brings me back to Ka-Tzetnik. If explicit, quasi-pornographic representations of brutality and sadism in the Holocaust do indeed attract readers, how is it that Ka-Tzetnik never even came close to the kind of sale figures reached almost overnight by Goldhagen? To my mind, the answer lies in the final lines cited above from *The Code,* which, although they contradict his earlier description of Auschwitz as another planet (akin to Goldhagen's argument of Germany as a "radically different culture" to be approached "with the critical eye of an anthropologist disembarking on unknown shores"),[138] were in fact all along the crucial subtext of his representation of the concentrationary universe. For from the very first volume, Ka-Tzetnik insists that under such conditions all human beings become savages and yet that all savages are human. That the Germans are out to kill the Jews is of course a given; but that the Jews and other non-Jewish inmates incessantly brutalize each other, that all members of that universe—with very few exceptions—are ultimately reduced to the level of potential murderers, is an insight that is difficult to bear. Pornography may be attractive, violence may be fascinating, but lack of boundaries and loss of control is dangerous and threatening. No one wants to think of himself or herself as an SS guard sending people to the gas chambers with an early morning yawn. It is much easier, indeed, almost comforting, to read about brutalities with the certainty that those who inflict them are essentially different from us (and that we are also no longer in danger of being brutalized by "such" types). Even young contemporary Germans, the so-called third generation, who are reported to have received Goldhagen's book with particular enthusiasm,[139] can read about what other Germans perpetrated fifty years ago and feel personally safe from similar murderous urges and fantasies thanks to their chronological distance from these events (as well as to the fact that Goldhagen himself had absolved postwar

Germans of antisemitism, to his mind the primary motivation of the Holocaust).[140]

Curiously, it was only in pre-1967 Israel that Ka-Tzetnik was widely read, and then, as I have noted, mostly for the wrong reasons. This is a sad statement on the ability to represent the Holocaust in historiography, fiction, or personal memoirs. Nevertheless, in the long run one must credit Ka-Tzetnik/Dinur with a tremendous achievement, whose ultimate peak was reached in the last volume of the sextet, after forty years of solitary struggle. To have transcended his own vision of another planet and applied it to our own could have only been possible after an inner conflict of indescribable pain and suffering. But for us its importance lies in the fact that it casts a different light on his whole oeuvre by making us read this final conclusion back all the way into his first lines. Those who wish, and are able, to read hundreds of pages of thick descriptions on the *anus mundi* that was Auschwitz must add this sextet to their lists, perhaps even put it on top of everything else. And those who are unhappy with simplistic and banal interpretations of the Holocaust must make the effort to plunge into these harrowing, uneven, at times frustrating, even outrageous, but ultimately extraordinary volumes.

In late 1993 the seventy-six-year-old Yehiel Dinur surreptitiously took a rare copy of his first published work, his 1931 volume of poetry, from the National Library in Jerusalem, and a few days later he sent its burned remains back to the director of the library with the request to complete the task of burning all the "remnants" of the book "just as all that was dear to me and my world was burned in the crematoria of Auschwitz."[141] By this act Dinur seems to have expressed the wish to reverse Adorno's dictum, itself by now a cliché, that to write poetry after Auschwitz is barbarism. For Dinur, it was poetry written *before* Auschwitz that was barbarism (and it was *his* poetry that he had a right, indeed a duty, to burn). The world that had existed before the great conflagration had no right of expression any longer, and whatever remnants of it were still scattered in the world must be destroyed.

This is a dark, almost nihilistic vision of our time. But there is a truth in it that we ignore at our peril. For Auschwitz is a mirror in which the history of our century is reflected. It is by no means the only mirror, and we may well prefer other, more elevating sights. Not all that had existed before Auschwitz was leading to the crematoria, nor everything created after Auschwitz is polluted by it. But in this post-Auschwitz world we can no longer view the civilization that produced the Holocaust in the same manner: we cannot and must not consign Auschwitz to another planet, nor perceive the perpetrators as a different species. If Dinur's act was characteristically juvenile and bombastic, it just as typically implied a profound insight that most of us would like to avoid: that when we look in the mirror of the Holocaust, we see our own reflection.

Conclusion

This book has attempted to sketch out some of the complex links between war, genocide, and modern identity. While this is a historical issue with numerous collective ramifications, it is also very much a contemporary problem with profound personal, as well as public, implications. In thinking about how to conclude this book, I decided to avoid a recapitulation of its main arguments, which would have merely entailed both repetition and simplification. Instead, these concluding pages will discuss three recent examples of highly publicized and, in very different ways, troubling attempts to come to terms with the devastating legacy of our century.

As I write these lines, Germany has just emerged from one controversy and is already being rocked by yet another in a series of public debates concerning the Holocaust. There is something almost obscene about this constant rehashing of old arguments by all sides involved over the burden of the past and the need both to remember and to put it aside once and for all. The controversies over the screening of the TV miniseries *Holocaust* in the late 1970s, President Reagan's visit to the military cemetery in Bitburg and the German historians' debate of the mid-1980s, the screening of Steven Spielberg's *Schindler's List,* and the publication of Goldhagen's book have all generated almost the same arguments, recriminations, apologetics, moral outrage, pity, shame, and sorrow. They have provided an array of figures, politicians, historians, media people, with an opportunity to gain a fair amount of publicity and notoriety, to establish themselves as the conscience of the nation, or at least as the spokespersons for this or that group. What makes this phenomenon morally dubious is, of course, the fact that all these figures are performing a sort of *Totentanz* over the graves—or rather ashes—of millions of victims. What makes it depressing is that it tends to be most of the time circular, intellectually arid, and almost entirely devoid of either scholarly or political insights. Nevertheless, it may be useful to make a few comments on the recent so-called Walser-debate, while keeping in mind its implications and relevance for the most current storm over the exhibition on the crimes of the Wehrmacht that cannot be discussed here.

The controversy was unleashed by Martin Walser, a well-known novelist, in a speech he made on being awarded the German publishers Peace Prize in October 1988. Walser expressed growing impatience with what he called the "intrumentalization of the Holocaust" as "a routine threat, a tool of intimidation, a moral cudgel or just a compulsory exercise." For this he was accused by the leader of the Jewish community in Germany, Ignatz Bubis, a Holocaust survivor, of "mental arson." The quarrel between these two men became associated with a wider ongoing public controversy over the then still undecided status of the planned Holocaust memorial in Berlin. This project, initiated by former chancellor Helmut Kohl, is seen far less enthusiastically by the present social democratic government and many left-liberal intellectuals. Indeed, the editor of the mass-circulation liberal magazine *Der Spiegel*, Rudolf Augstein, has dismissed the plan submitted by the (Jewish) American architect Peter Eisenman with the argument that foreigners should not be allowed to "dictate how we deal with memories of the past in our new capital."[1]

Two issues need to be briefly touched on in this context. First, it has been said that this debate is merely a last ditch effort by the older generation that had still experienced the Third Reich in its youth to have its say on national identity. Indeed, the major voices in the debate, both Walser and Bubis, are past seventy (and Bubis has meanwhile died). Yet it would be naive to think that once the older generation vanishes German preoccupation with the past will simply disappear. German politicians, intellectuals, and scholars who belong to the generation of 1968 and have now reached positions of prominence are no less concerned with the past, even if in different ways. Indeed, what is striking about the new German elite is that it feels much more comfortable in expressing its loyalty to German culture, history, and political interests than its predecessors. The former rebels of the students' revolt, who demanded to eradicate the remnants of fascism in German society now move in the halls of power, wear fashionable Italian suits, and insist on the need to be liberated from the burden of the past in words that sound remarkably similar to, if not more strident than, those used by their predecessors of the previous generation, of whom Ernst Nolte was the extreme representative in the 1980s and Walser is the more suave representative in the 1990s. Nothing demonstrates the presence of the past more clearly than the persistent calls to do away with it. Hence we should not expect it to disappear from the public agenda any time soon.

Second, the argument regarding the instrumentalization of the Holocaust, which I myself have applied especially regarding the case of Israel, has an entirely different import when it is made in Germany. For the question in this case obviously is, Who are instrumentalizing the Holocaust "against" the Germans, and what price has Germany paid for this alleged instrumentalization of its past crimes? Put in this way, rather than in Walser's obfuscating manner, one perforce comes up with rather embarrassing answers. Those who instrumentalize the Holocaust in Germany can only be "the Jews," even if the present political climate does not allow to say this outright. Instead, one speaks of foreigners, the (American) media, greedy (American) lawyers, all of which is (and of course was very much in the past) a veiled reference to Jews. And if it is indeed the Jews who instrumentalize the Holocaust, one must ask what profit do they derive from this exercise and what price are the Germans forced to pay? Here, of course, one thinks first and foremost in monetary terms, and notes the vast amounts of money paid by German governments over the years as restitution payment to the Jewish victims of the Holocaust. Thus the instrumentalization of the Holocaust is a process whereby Jews are getting German money. To be sure, these funds are intended to compensate Jewish victims for the genocide perpetrated by the Nazis regime. But all this happened half a century ago and hardly any of the Germans living today had anything to do with these crimes. Hence the feeling of being exploited (by the Jews) for acts one cannot be held responsible for. But beyond such mundane monetary issues, there is a sense that the Holocaust is still putting limits on the exercise of German politics, in other words, that by constantly reminding the world of the Nazi period the Jews are preventing the normalization of German existence. That Germany is the most powerful country in Europe, that its flourishing economy still contains numerous firms whose fortunes were greatly expanded through the use of slave labor during the war, for which they never paid any compensation, does not seem to prevent speakers of Walser's ilk from viewing their nation as a victim of persecution and victimization.

What makes this argument so bizarre is that it expresses a desire both to appropriate the Holocaust and to erase it. Thus Augstein rejects the option of a (Jewish American) foreigner "telling" the Germans how to deal with *their* past—that is, with *their* Holocaust—and, at the same time, he rejects the very idea, rather than any specific plan, of a Holocaust memorial. Similarly, Walser criticizes the instrumental-ization of the Holocaust and at the same time—just like Gerhard Schröder, the new chancellor and former participant in the 1968 protests—says that it is time for the Germans to put all that behind them and look to the future. In other words, the Holocaust belongs to the Germans so that they can finally do away with it. What Walser finds most objectionable is the attempt to "monumentalize our shame" on the best piece of real estate in the world, a football field–sized plot smack in the center of Berlin. The term Walser used was *Schande* (disgrace), rather than *Scham* (shame). Whereas *shame* is what one feels, *disgrace* is the act or condition that ought to bring about this feeling. Primo Levi felt shame for the acts of the Germans, for they disgraced the whole of humanity.[2] Walser rejects the notion that foreigners should dictate to the Germans how to feel about the disgrace of their past. It is, to his mind, up to them to decide whether to feel shame and how to express it, and there is no reason why such shame, if they indeed feel it, should be so prominently displayed, right in the center of the new, or rather newly regained, capital.

Walser may not be representative of intellectual opinion in Ger-many but neither is he a marginal figure. He has been attacked by many in the media and has also found many defenders—especially those who lamented the formulation rather than the content of his argument. But while he might have chosen his words badly, funda-mentally, he is not far from Schröder, who for his part is representa-tive of much of the new political, economic, and academic elite in Ger-many. These middle-aged baby boomers, members of the 1968 protest movement, are no less patriotic than Walser and his generation, and see no reason to be apologetic about it. Patriotism means owning up to your past; it also means forging your past in a manner that would make it possible to be proud of, or at least to be comfortable with, your na-tional identity. The Holocaust stands in the way of this process. And since the Holocaust was about killing Jews and the Jews have not all been done away with, the Jews may appear to some as an obstacle to normalization. Thus the genocide of the Jews remains at the center of German identity whether it is recognized as part of an "unmasterable past" or it is wished away. It is there in the public domain; it is also in the most private. This is where I would like to turn now.

In 1995 two small books were published in German that quickly became international best-sellers, were hailed by critics and scholars as works of unparalleled moral and historical significance, and entered the canon of Holocaust literature from its two polar perspectives: that of the perpetrators and that of the victims. Both books had an obviously autobiographical element that, in the case of one, became the focus of a major scandal whose final outcome is still in doubt. Both books were written by men in their fifties and thus straddle the fine line between personal experience and the second-generation's often traumatized consciousness. Indeed, the degree of the authors' personal engagement in the events they describe is both inherent to their books' impact and reception, and raises questions regarding their authenticity and moral candor. They come at a time when the direct witnesses of Nazism and the Holocaust are quietly leaving the stage, yet also when public fascination, not to say obsession, with this period has reached unprecedented proportions, as evidenced by the tremendous commercial success of these books and the intellectual debate they have triggered. Hence we may examine these texts as indicators of a legacy whose destructive realities are as horrifying as its implications for individual and collective identity are troubling and contentious.

Bernhard Schlink's *The Reader,* originally published in German and the recipient of several important literary prizes in a number of countries, is the story of a relationship between a "second generation" German man and an older woman who, as it later transpires, was an SS guard in Auschwitz and another camp "near Cracow."[3] Told in the first person by the man, the story appears to have many autobiographical aspects, although Schlink does not indicate this directly anywhere. Born in Germany in 1944, Schlink is now a professor of law, a practicing judge, and the author of several other novels. His protagonist, Michael Berg, meets Hanna Schmitz when he is fifteen years old and she is thirty-six, and various comments in the book indicate that the meeting takes place in 1959, that is, that Michael was also born in 1944. Moreover, Michael also studies law, and although he refuses to become either a lawyer or a judge and prefers to do research on the history of law, he, too, becomes a published author.

The core of *The Reader* is an inversion of conventional roles, moral assumptions, and categories. The powerful link between Michael and Hanna is his immense physical attraction to her, since she initiates him into sex as a teenager, and her dependence on him as a reader. For as it turns out later in the novel, Hanna is illiterate. Rather than escaping her past as a perpetrator, the reason she both becomes an SS guard and keeps moving from place to place in postwar Germany is her desperate effort to hide that shameful disability. Her sensuality, as described by Schlink, reminds one of Hanna Schygulla in Rainer

Werner Fassbinder's *The Marriage of Maria Braun* (1979); she is tall, blond, physically strong, and disdainful of sentimentality. But her sexual appeal is also related to her dark, criminal, brutal past. Such links between atrocity and eroticism remind one of Lina Wertmuller's *Seven Beauties* (1975) and Liliana Cavani's *The Night Porter* (1973). It is no wonder that all these films were made in the 1970s, when the new German and Italian cinema was engaged in both coming to terms with the past and in exploring its subversive meanings for the present, often by focusing on the aestheticization of violence and the sexual attraction of perversity and sadism. Unlike the case of Ka-Tzetnik, however, what we have here is a view from the outside, by members of a different generation and of a group that belonged to the victimizers or the bystanders, never the victims.

And yet, as *The Reader* unfolds, we realize that both Hanna and Michael are victims; she of her handicap, he of the helpless shame of belonging to the second generation of the perpetrators. Following a seven-year separation, Michael recognizes Hanna at a trial of SS perpetrators he visits as a law student in 1966. She is then forty-three and he is twenty-two. Now we realize that Hanna has become victim of both postwar German justice and of the other Nazi defendants and their lawyers. Her refusal to concede her illiteracy, along with her relative youth, beauty, and charisma, make her appear as the main culprit. She is thus given a life sentence and spends the next eighteen years in jail. About to be released in 1984, we encounter her as a prematurely aged sixty-one year old, while Michael, despite his professional successes, is a psychologically deeply scarred forty year old. For he, too, is a victim not merely of the fate of his whole generation, but of his inability to emerge from the emotional cul-de-sac of his passion for Hanna and the knowledge of her crime. He is thus the victim of a victim and can only confront this condition by becoming emotionally paralyzed, escaping his feelings for Hanna by escaping from his own self and leading a sterile, empty existence. In this sense both he and she are "inner emigrants," refugees of their respective handicaps in the midst of an uncomprehending and uncaring society. At the same time, they may represent Schlink's view of postwar German society as a whole: a sterile, emotionally dead victim of its own crimes. When Michael meets Hanna a few days before her release, her physical deterioration and his emotional paralysis prevent him from showing her any sincere warmth. Not having seen him even once during those eighteen years, but having learned to read and write by listening to readings of literary works he records and sends to her (and apparently by reading on her own memoirs of Holocaust survivors), Hanna hangs herself during her last night in prison.

Schlink's novel is a tale of emotional numbness and sexual passion. The emotional numbness is associated not only with Michael but also with everyone else—except Hanna, who is the most natural, physical, and emotionally "healthy" character in the novel—and becomes the main trademark of the trial. The barrage of horrors makes all those present at the trial increasingly numb, a numbness which Michael believes was just as characteristic of the reality of atrocity itself. But for Michael there is another emotion during the trial, for as he watches Hanna after a seven-year separation, he cannot help being aroused by her: as the crimes of the SS women are described, he recalls making love to her, she being in physical control, he providing intellectual nourishment by reading her novels. Only now he realizes that in the camp she also had inmates read her stories just before they were sent to be gassed. Did she take them to her to prolong their lives and give them a measure of comfort, or did she send them to be gassed to prevent them from revealing her handicap? Michael prefers to believe the former, yet perceives himself now as one more of Hanna's victims, whom she might have also sent to die had she not been able to leave him when she sensed that her secret might be revealed. Thus the "now" and "then" become inextricably linked in his mind: as he associates the numbness that engulfs the courtroom with the numbness of both perpetrators and victims in the camps, the courtroom becomes a replica of a concentration camp, in the midst of which his only emotion is a tremendous sexual longing for a woman accused of murder by a man who sees himself as her victim.

Michael's only encounter with a real victim, one of the only two survivors of the camp in which Hanna "worked," seems to confirm his assertion that the victims became as numb as the perpetrators. To be sure, as we know—and as Hanna might have also known had she in fact read the survivors' memoirs he finds in her prison cell after her suicide—his emotional block and their traumatized state are so far apart that the very idea of associating them with each other reflects Michael's, or Schlink's, incapacity to envisage the fate of the victims. Indeed, Michael's view of himself and of Hanna as victims is predicated on entirely excluding Hanna's victims as complete human beings beyond their role as targets of their victimizers or witnesses of atrocity. It also makes for a confusion of categories, whereby the author links between social or ideological handicaps and victimhood. But while Hanna's illiteracy makes her first into a perpetrator and then into a victim of justice (as Michael ultimately believes), the handicap of the Nazis' victims, their Jewishness, spelled an immediate or eventual death sentence. Hanna's illiteracy makes her into a murderer; her victims' Jewishness makes them the target of murder.

Michael raises a question about second-generation Germans that was asked—from a polar perspective—by Yehuda Elkana about second-generation Israelis, as we have seen in chapter 4:

> What should our generation have done, what should it do with the knowledge of the horrors of the extermination of the Jews? We should not believe we can comprehend the incomprehensible, we may not compare the incomparable, we may not inquire because to inquire is to make the horrors an object of discussion, even if the horrors themselves are not questioned, instead of accepting them as something in the face of which we can only fall silent in revulsion, shame, and guilt. Should we fall silent in revulsion, shame, and guilt? To what purpose?

Sitting through the trial, he asks himself, "that some few would be convicted and punished while we of the second generation were silenced by revulsion, shame, and guilt—was that all there was to it now?"[4]

The crime of which Hanna is accused is indeed not comparable to what we know of the Holocaust. She and her comrades failed to unlock the doors of the church in which the inmates of a camp, sent on a death march to Germany, had been put up for the night, even as the church was set on fire by Allied bombers. Of course, SS guards had in fact frequently locked Jews in buildings (usually synagogues) and set them on fire themselves, without the assistance of enemy bombers, but not in Schlink's book. Moreover, we are never certain whether the SS women had the key, were frightened and confused because their own comrades were also killed or wounded in the bombing raid, or acted out of pure murderous malice. Hanna is obviously (to the reader) no more guilty than anyone else. But since she will not admit her illiteracy, she refuses to submit a writing sample and falsely admits to having written the damning report on the incident that she could not have possibly written. She is thus convicted for the wrong reason. Nor is her sentence—life imprisonment—typical of such trials in 1960s Germany, in which perpetrators with far greater responsibility for far worse crimes, if convicted at all, were regularly given ridiculously light sentences, as Schlink, a judge, clearly knows. And yet she is a perpetrator, and Michael, as her former lover, is a victim of the handicap that made her, too, into a victim, since she joined the SS only to avoid exposure as an illiterate in her work place at Siemens (a German firm that, incidentally, employed slave labor during the war). Indeed, Hanna's relative innocence is revealed to Michael during the trial. Initially, she exhibits "confusion and help-lessness," and while she wants "to do the right thing," she has "no sense of the context, of the rules of the game." But then, when she fi-nally naively asks the judge, "What would you have done?" she reveals the truth, namely, that there was no choice, that anyone in that situ-ation would have done the same, even those who accuse her now.[5] She is a perpetrator, but so would everyone else have been.

Hanna's specific guilt is thus qualified by the claim of universal potential guilt (guilt in the subjunctive mode), and her helplessness in the camp and in the courtroom shows her as an innocent victim of circumstances. Conversely, the status of the witnesses is made dubi-ous by the fact that their testimony, according to Michael, "was not precise, nor could it be."[6] To be sure, there is no doubt as to their sta-tus as victims, but it is clear that they are in no position to ascertain the identity and guilt of the perpetrators; indeed, they may victimize the innocent, or at least, those who, like Hanna, are "guilty, but not as guilty as it appeared."[7] Hence, too, the memoir by a survivor and witness of the event, as Michael claims, "exudes the very numbness I have tried to describe,"[8] namely, that of the perpetrators, the lawyers, the judge, the audience. It evokes in him none of the compassion or passion he feels toward Hanna. And because of his love for her and his inability to feel the pain of her victims, he prefers to think of her crime as akin to "a car accident on a lonely road on a cold winter night, with injuries and totaled vehicles, and no one knowing what to do," or as "a conflict between two equally compelling duties that required action." But, he says, "nobody was willing to look at it in such terms."[9] And so, Michael is caught between believing Hanna innocent and knowing she is guilty, while seeing himself as "not guilty because one cannot be guilty of betraying a criminal," and yet also as "guilty of having loved a criminal."[10]

But Michael's awareness of Hanna's crimes only increases his passion for her: "The worst were the dreams in which a hard, impe-rious, cruel Hanna aroused me sexually; I woke from them full of longing and shame and rage. And full of fear about who I really was." He resolves his dilemma by asserting that his dreams "were unfair to the Hanna I had known and still knew." In retrospect he realizes "how little observation there actually was" of the Holocaust, so that "the imagination was almost static: the shattering fact of the world of the camps seemed properly beyond its operations." Conversely, he writes, now, after "the television series *Holocaust* and movies like

Schindler's List," the imagination "actually moves in it," "it" being presumably the Holocaust.[11] Hence hearing evidence in the courtroom about Hanna's crime was numbing intellectually and arousing sexually; seeing "it," the Holocaust, in Hollywood productions, made it come alive.

Michael wants "simultaneously to understand Hanna's crime and to condemn it," but he finds it "impossible to do both."[12] Eventually, he seems to condemn without understanding and to understand without condemning. What he condemns most strongly is what it did to him: "Would she have sent me to the gas chamber if she hadn't been able to leave me, but wanted to get rid of me?" And yet he finds her sentence "a miscarriage of justice."[13] But he fails to tell the judge about Hanna's secret and instead watches her when the sentence is read: "A proud, wounded, lost, and infinitely tired look. A look that wished to see nothing and no one."[14]

Soon after Hanna's imprisonment the 1968 students' revolt takes place. Although he does not participate, Michael sees it as the expression of a sense of collective guilt:

> Pointing at the guilty parties did not free us of shame, but at least it overcame the suffering we went through on account of it. It converted the passive suffering of shame into energy, activity, aggression. And coming to grips with our parents' guilt took a great deal of energy.

Here, then, is another core theme of the book: Those young Germans who "dissociated themselves from their parents and thus from an entire generation of perpetrators, voyeurs, and the willfully blind, accommodators and accepters, thereby overcoming their suffering because of the shame" and preferring to "parade" their "self-righteousness," in truth made all this noise merely "to drown the fact that their love for their parents made them irrevocably complicit in their crimes." Yet Michael's situation is far worse, for while, as he says, "The pain I went through because of my love for Hanna was, in a way, the fate of my generation, a German fate," unlike other members of his generation he *chose* Hanna, indeed, was infatuated with her sexuality, while they had no choice in determining the identity of their parents.[15]

Unlike Schlink, Michael does not become a judge, since "judging was the most grotesque oversimplification of all."[16] This leads us to assume that the author's views are more complex than his protagonist's, or more ready to compromise, come to terms, relent. Michael becomes as stunted as Hanna. He works, publishes books, lectures, has lovers, but his emotional life is dead, his marriage breaks down, his daughter wanders from parent to parent. The only thing that gives meaning to his life is the memory of his relationship with Hanna and the tapes he sends her of himself reading novels. Now both he and Hanna are stunted, handicapped, victims of forces outside their control, somewhat reminiscent of Günter Grass's Oskar, the dwarf, in his novel *The Tin Drum*. And when she dies, the victim of his emotional impotence, he too seems to die, a victim of her handicap, which had in turn made her a victim (and a perpetrator).

This is a remarkable novel, and it cannot be interpreted in a single fashion. Possibly, one reason for its success is that it can be read differently by different people. It is both a kind of coming to terms with the past and an apology, depending on where our sympathies lie, and whether we see Michael as expressing Schlink's views or as the author's attempt to create a figure that would manifest how the second generation in Germany became warped by the crimes and complicity of their parents. In this sense it has something in common with Jean-Paul Sartre's *Childhood of a Leader,* which reconstructs the making of a fascist youth in 1930s France, or with Louis Malle's *Lacombe Lucien* (1974). Yet there are elements in this novel that, precisely because of its effectiveness as a work of literature, are highly disturbing. For this is a book in which the true victims of the period, those who died and those who survived, have no face; their suffering, though conceded, remains abstract and evokes no emotion in the reader. The victims we encounter, and the suffering with which we empathize as readers, belong to the second generation as well as to the innocent, illiterate, choiceless perpetrators, caught in a historical fate they cannot evade. As Schlink (or Michael) puts it unambiguously, second-generation Germans are victims of their shame for the perpetrators and suffer for their love to them, indeed, for their illicit, painful, yet intense passion for them. For true, passionate, authentic sexual pleasure can be derived only from the perpetrators; everything else is numb, lifeless, meaningless. Even the attempt to come to terms with the past, to research it, to try the perpetrators and punish, hate, and disown them is useless. Germany, here, is emasculated, emotionally dead, an automaton making the motions of a living organism without heart or soul. As Michael says at the end of Hanna's trial: "I felt the numbness with which I had followed the horrors of the trial settling over the emotions and thoughts of the past few weeks. It would be too much to say that I was happy about this. But I felt it was right. It allowed me to return to and continue to live my everyday life."[17]

The Reader, then, is about Germany as victim. It is a victim of its history of murder, to be sure, but then, even the murderers themselves are victims, and those they ultimately victimize are the next generation of Germans. It is a German fate. Hanna may be reading the memoirs of Primo Levi, Jean Améry, and Tadeusz Borowski, but Michael is suffering his own pain. He cannot comprehend, much as he may try, the pain of those whom Hanna and her likes had tortured, or rather, he can understand only in so far as their fate resembles his own, since, from his perspective, he is ultimately the most comprehensible victim. Indeed, metaphorically, Michael *becomes* the Jewish victim, both by virtue of his association with Hanna as the reader and thanks to the grace of his late birth, which prevented him from becoming a perpetrator. Yet even as he tilts toward the category of victim, Schlink contextualizes his tale within a framework of emotional numbness and sexual obsession, both of which are above or below morality, since the former is a blank and a void, and the latter is involuntary and uncontrollable. Thus numbness and obsession are a means to avoid responsibility and reject all ethical categories.

This latent self-transformation into a Jewish victim seems to become manifest in Binjamin Wilkomirski's *Fragments.* As I write these lines, the scandal that erupted around his book, published originally in German and translated into twelve languages to tremendous critical acclaim and commercial success, has subsided somewhat, but the questions it raised have not been resolved.[18] Indeed, it is possible that we will never know whether the accusations recently leveled at Wilkomirski are true and may even have to accept that there is no truth here in the sense that we would—quite rightly, in this specific case—want to have it. But the debate itself is ultimately of much greater importance than its resolution, if one is ever reached, since it demonstrates the extent to which the mass crimes and profound trauma of this century have undermined our ability to determine the nature of truth, to establish identity, to distinguish between fact and fiction, and to make moral judgments of universal applicability.

Fragments is a devastating memoir by a man in his fifties who was born into the Holocaust. It is unlike any other memoir of the Holocaust because it describes events from the perspective of a very young child, who cannot remember and did not know, the historical events, the names of places, the identities of the protagonists, the realities and fantasies of the period, but who has retained, inscribed in his mind, certain fragments, largely of the most terrifying brutality, of utter inhumanity, of hopelessness, of pain and suffering. In some ways *Fragments* is reminiscent of Jerzy Kosinski's *The Painted Bird,* which also describes the fate of a child during the Holocaust, although Kosinski's protagonist evades the camps and is subject to the brutality of the peasant population.[19] Indeed, the similarity with *The Painted Bird* does not end with the narrative and the perspective. Kosinski had been accused of having presented a work of fiction as autobiography, since, it was claimed, various indications made it appear that he could not have possibly been the child depicted in his novel. Precisely because of the nature of his book and its commercial success, the possibility that it was fiction (which was never openly denied by Kosinski) created a major stir and ultimately tarnished his name.[20] This is what seems to be happening now with Wilkomirski's memoir as well.

In August 1998 the popular Swiss weekly *Weltwoche* published an article by the writer Daniel Ganzfried that accused Wilkomirski of having invented his identity out of thin air. Ganzfried, who was born in 1958 and lives in Zurich, is himself the child of Holocaust survivors and the author of a novel on the difficulties of remembering from the perspective of the second generation.[21] His own background may explain his reluctance to believe Wilkomirski's version, according to which he was born to a Jewish family in Riga in 1939, spent the first years of his life in the camps, and came to Switzerland only after the war, living first in an orphanage and subsequently being adopted by a childless couple. Ganzfried's evidence indicated that in fact Wilkomirski was born in Switzerland in 1941 as Bruno Grosjean, the illegitimate (Protestant) son of Yvonne Berthe Grosjean, was adopted in 1945 by a Swiss family, and was registered officially as Bruno Doessekker in 1947 after the name of his adoptive parents. Hence, while the memoir is supposed to tell the true story of a child who lived through the Holocaust, according the Ganzfried, Wilkomirski had been to the camps "only as a tourist."[22]

There are many possible explanations for this case. The most obvious is that Wilkomirski/Doessekker wrote a work of fiction in which he imagined himself as a child in the Holocaust. What makes this option especially troubling is that, since the publication of his book, Wilkomirski has spoken at numerous public forums as the true embodiment of his protagonist. In this sense he has gone significantly beyond Schlink, since rather than presenting a second-generation German as a victim, he transformed a second-generation Swiss into a Jewish victim. Identification with the victims of genocide, therefore, shattered the limits of identity and truth. But this brings us to a second possible explanation, namely, that Wilkomirski/Doessekker quite candidly believed himself to be that child, creating for himself a fictitious—but for him entirely real—world of memories, culled from Holocaust memoirs, scholarship, documentaries, fiction, film, a world in which he now lives *as if* it were his own past. Finally, however, it is still possible (though quite unlikely) that Wilkomirski is indeed that child, but that the Swiss authorities who arranged for his adoption provided him with a false identity and erased any record, if any remained, of his previous life. After all, official documents tell only the truth of the officials who issued them and the system they represent.

We are now at a point in time where unmediated memories of the Holocaust are becoming increasingly rare. Within a decade or so, there will be hardly anyone left who experienced the Holocaust as a person old enough to have distinct, more or less articulate memories of the event. Alongside a recent spate of memoirs by survivors—testifying to their sense of urgency about the need to transmit recollections of their experiences to posterity—we are also witnessing an increasing number of works by writers of the second generation, who either imagine themselves into the Holocaust or recount their fate as children of survivors. French Jewish writer Henri Raczymow's *Writing the Book of Esther,* Israeli writer David Grossman's *See Under—Love,* and Polish (non-Jewish) writer Jaroslaw Rymkiewicz's *The Final Station: Umschlagplatz* are but a few examples of this genre.[23] Yet Wilkomirski's case is far more disturbing and must indeed raise alarm signals as to the uses and abuses of the Holocaust in the late twentieth century's quest for identity, recognition, fame, even fortune. To be sure, the twists and turns of this affair surely indicate the difficulty—by writers and readers alike—of distinguishing between fact and fiction, reality and fantasy. But while arguments regarding the tenuous nature of such distinctions are part and parcel of the emergence of modern literature and representation, in the case of the Holocaust they may appear facile considering the extremity of the event and the profound moral questions it raises for humanity.

Within a few years, Wilkomirski's book has become a prominent member in the canon of Holocaust memoirs: Schlink would have added it to Hanna's bookshelf in her prison cell had she remained there for another decade. What, then, are we to do now with the realization that it may have been a work of fiction? There are various reactions to this revelation. Some historians, such as Raul Hilberg, have argued that they were suspicious from the start, since there were various inconsistencies in the account, and especially errors in the identification of places, dates, and actions.[24] But this kind of criticism is hardly relevant. If *Fragments* is a true memoir, we could scarcely

expect a small child undergoing the most traumatic experiences conceivable to remember the kind of details favored by historians. Indeed, had he got all the facts right, we would have been all the more
skeptical of his memoir's authenticity. In other words, errors of fact
may reflect either lapses of memory or a skilled writer's attempt to
make fiction appear authentic.

Another complaint has come from literary critics and writers. Even
before the book's authenticity as a memoir was challenged, some
commentators were critical of its prose, finding it an unsuccessful
work of literature. But, of course, this did little to diminish its quality as a memoir, as long as one believed it to be one. Ganzfried is
much harsher in his literary critique of the book, which he considers
to be of inferior quality. He argues that the main, if not the only reason, for the book's success was that it masqueraded itself as a memoir and that had it been overtly a work of fiction it would have been a
commercial failure. This is probably an exaggeration. As publishers
know, in recent years books on the Holocaust—whether fiction,
memoirs, or scholarship—tend to find a ready market even if their
quality is mediocre. For my part, I found Wilkomirski's text, fiction
or not, quite devastating. Nor was I alone in finding it one of the most
harrowing memoirs I had ever read. It is true, however, that I would
have read it differently, if at all, had I believed it to be fiction.[25]

Scholars are faced now with a painful dilemma. I have cited Wilkomirski's text in this book and elsewhere, and many other scholars
have read, cited, and taught it as a memoir, as the purest form of testimony, that given by the most innocent conceivable victim, a young
child.[26] We may have done so even had we thought it to be fiction;
after all, there are important works of fiction on the Holocaust that
are studied with great profit. Yet we would have made very different
use of the book, since it would have been an example of Holocaust
fiction, not testimony. Scholars, various media outlets, conference
conveners, professional organizations, educational institutions, and
so forth, must, as Ganzfried rightly points out, be more careful in the
future in accepting texts as testimony that may be fiction. This is all
the more important in view of the delight with which those who
deny the Holocaust have greeted this scandal as an opportunity to
argue that all other Holocaust memoirs are also mere figments of
their writers' imagination. In the case of the Holocaust, then, the
danger of presenting fiction as fact is that it legitimizes those who
present fact as fiction.

But the main problem lies elsewhere. The question is: Can we
say that the Holocaust is a case in which the rules of representation

operate differently, in which what is allowed, indeed, what has been almost taken for granted in recent times, should be forbidden? And if the Holocaust *is* placed beyond the rules and conventions of representation, does this also imply that it is beyond history? Would this not lead us down the perilous path of dehistoricizing the Holocaust and thereby transforming it from a concrete past event into an increasingly malleable myth? Is this not the surest way of ultimately detaching the Holocaust from human experience and morality by making it disappear into the mists of mythology, incomprehension, and ineffability?

If at times we feel betrayed by those who claim to be writing about themselves and are then shown to have written "only" fiction, we often also admire their creative powers all the more. After all, the annals of literature are filled with such cases. The role of the artist, as defined at least since the romantic period, is, precisely, to imagine himself or herself into another life, as another person, and as another identity. Our quest for truth and facts is thus matched by our urge for imagination and fantasy, since it is there that an even higher truth may be found. And yet the phenomenon of a writer who imagines himself into the role of, and who claims publicly to have been, a victim of the Holocaust, yet was never there, fills us with outrage: we feel cheated, morally disarmed, our sensibilities and compassion mocked and violated. For there is a difference between our pain on reading about the suffering of another human being, and our pain on reading about the suffering of a literary character. In the former case, we empathize with the writer; in the latter, with his creatures. Hence a lying writer cheats us of our feelings and abuses our sorrow.

Wilkomirski is not the only one to have—perhaps—written fiction that was read as fact about the Holocaust. Tadeusz Borowski, whose place in the canon of Holocaust memoirs is assured, also wrote fiction. He was not the brutal, cynical *Kapo* who narrates the horrifying tales of Auschwitz in the first person.[27] Had he been that *Kapo*, he would not have committed suicide in 1951 but would have continued to grow fat from the suffering of others as his *Kapo* does in the camp. But, of course, Borowski was in Auschwitz, and Wilkomirski, it is claimed, was not. Hence the point is not merely fiction or truth, but presence or absence. Ida Fink is also a survivor, and yet her stories are fiction, even if obviously influenced by her experience. So is the case of Imre Kertész, Aharon Appelfeld, and other writers.[28] But we distinguish between fiction by those who were there and fiction by those who were not, just as we distinguish between authentic and assumed identity. And there is an even more disturbing distinction.

For as Primo Levi wrote in his last essays, although he had always striven to provide a truthful report of life in Auschwitz, he ultimately came to view his account as largely false, since he had written it from the perspective of the saved, not of the drowned, who were, after all, the majority, and thus the only true witnesses.[29]

Louis Begley's *Wartime Lies* is about falsifying the truth and dissimulating identity as a precondition for survival during the Holocaust.[30] While he calls it a novel, the book has all the marks of a memoir, and yet it cannot be a memoir precisely because it denies the very possibility of truth and authenticity. The child, who along with his aunt survives throughout the war in Poland under an assumed identity, can no longer recover his own self. He has to pick one of several possible identities and hold on to it after the war, make it his own in order to survive survival. From this perspective the issue is not whether Wilkomirski wrote a memoir or "mere" fiction. For while we agree that the Holocaust is unimaginable, we rebel against the thought that it has been imagined, and while we insist on the truthfulness of direct witnesses, we cannot imagine ourselves sharing their experiences. Hence we cannot empathize with them, much as we are horrified by the horrors they recount. And without empathy, the truth they transmit to us cannot become our own but remains a foreign, distant, and yet disturbing, destabilizing, threatening presence.

This is all to say that the Holocaust is at the center of a crisis of identity, whose ramifications range far beyond its chronological boundaries and the life span of its survivors. This crisis has in many ways become the characteristic feature of the twentieth century, originating in World War I and felt with even greater urgency today. It is the crisis of encountering—by way of perpetrating, observing, and being a target of—the annihilatory force of modern violence: massive, all-encompassing, unrelenting, and faceless. It is a crisis that casts doubt on the very definition of identity, on what it means to know who you are, where you come from, what you are capable or incapable of doing, experiencing, imagining. It is a very personal crisis for those of us who would reflect on the implications of the century's events for our own lives, and it is a collective crisis for those of us aware of our responsibility for humanity. For while we seek the truth about ourselves, our past, the meaning of our identity, we are afraid of what we may discover. We search for the inner core of human existence in an age of mass murder, but we have to turn our gaze away from the spectacle, lest we turn into stone.

I do not know whether Wilkomirski was that child. But the thousands of "children without identity" who came out of the Holocaust are the most extreme manifestation of a period in which humanity itself had lost its identity and, just like those children, was "furnished with false names and often with false papers too," as he writes.[31] Begley concludes his novel about the child Maciek with the following lines:

> And where is Maciek now? He became an embarrassment and slowly died. A man who bears one of the names Maciek used has replaced him. Is there much of Maciek in that man? No: Maciek was a child, and our man has no childhood that he can bear to remember; he has had to invent one.[32]

Should we invent a childhood in the camps where we have never been, or should we invent a bearable childhood, far from the camps, to erase forever the memory of having been there? Should we face up to the truth? Can we know it? Can we bear it? If the truth of atrocity is borne by its witnesses, we must remember Primo Levi's assertion that the survivors "are not the true witnesses," since "those who saw the Gorgon, have not returned to tell about it or have returned mute."[33] If we are willing to face the truth, then we would do well to heed Levi's words that "what had happened . . . was irrevocable. Never again could it be cleansed; it would prove that man, the human species—we, in short—had the potential to construct an infinite enormity of pain and that pain is the only force created from nothing, without cost and without effort. It is enough not to see, not to listen, not to act."[34]

Notes

Abbreviations

MES	Middle East Studies
MGM	Militärgeschichtliche Mitteilungen
NGC	New German Critique
NYRB	New York Review of Books
NYT	New York Times
NZZ	Neue Zürcher Zeitung
PP	Planning Perspectives
SZ	Süddeutsche Zeitung
T&B	Teorya ve-Bikoret
TAJB	Tel Aviver Jahrbuch für deutsche Geschichte
TLS	Times Literary Supplement
TNR	The New Republic
TNY	The New Yorker
TP	T'oung Pao
VfZ	Vierteljahrshefte für Zeitgeschichte
W&S	War and Society
WG	Werkstattgeschichte
YJLH	Yale Journal of Law and the Humanities
YLJ	Yale Law Journal
ZfG	Zeitschrift für Geschichte
ZfS	Zeitschrift für Sozialgeschichte des 20. und 21. Jahrhunderts

Introduction

1. *Ha-tsofen* (*The Code*, or *Shivitti*) (Tel Aviv, 1994), pp. 22–24. See further below, chapter 4, last section: "The Other Planet." Jorge Semprun's rumination on Buchenwald opens with the writer's realization of the condition to which he has been reduced as he sees his image reflected in the horrified eyes of his liberators, an experience shared by numerous survivors of this century's atrocities. Semprun, *Literature or Life* (New York, 1998), chapter 1, "The Gaze." Primo Levi grasps the essence of Auschwitz when his eyes meet the gaze of Doktor Pannwitz, commander of the Chemical Kommando, and fail to identify even a hint of mutual human recognition. Levi, *Survival in Auschwitz* (New York, 1961), pp. 96–97. It was the gaze of the jailers that deprived prisoners of their humanity; it was the gaze of the inmates that made the difference between life and death. For while survival depended on retaining a flicker of humanity, an eye that betrayed human intelligence and sensibilities could bring instant annihilation. Franz Kafka's *Metamorphosis* (1916) heralded an understanding of our century's predilection for dehumanization: Gregor Samsa "realizes" his monstrosity only when he sees it reflected in the eyes of his family.

2. *The Night Trilogy* (New York, 1988), p. 119.

3. *The Human Species* (Marlboro, Vt., 1992), pp. 51–53.

4. *Forever in the Shadow of Hitler? Original Documents of the* Historikerstreit, *the Controversy Concerning the Singularity of the Holocaust* (Atlantic Highlands, N.J., 1993); C. S. Maier, *The Unmasterable Past: History, Holocaust, and German Nationalism* (Cambridge, Mass., 1988); R. Evans, *In Hitler's Shadow: West German Historians and the Attempt to Escape from the Nazi Past* (New York, 1989).

5. A. Brossat, *L'épreuve du désastre: Le XXe siècle et les camps* (Paris, 1996); S. Courtois (ed.), *Le livre noir du communisme: Crimes, terreur, répression* (Paris, 1997);

T. Todorov, *Les abus de la mémoire* (Paris, 1995); J.-M. Chaumont, *La concurrence des victimes: Génocide, identité, reconnaissance* (Paris, 1997); Y. Ternon, *L'État criminel: Les Génocides au XXᵉ siècle* (Paris, 1995); A. Finkielkraut, *Remembering in Vain: The Klaus Barbie Trial and Crimes against Humanity* (New York, 1992).

Chapter 1

1. W. J. Mommsen, *Imperial Germany, 1867–1918: Politics, Culture, and Society in an Authoritarian State* (London, 1995), pp. 205–16; J.-J. Becker, *1914: Comment les Français sont entrés dans la guerre* (Paris, 1977), pp. 269–363; P. Fussell, *The Great War and Modern Memory* (New York, 1975), pp. 18–29; R. Wohl, *The Generation of 1914* (Cambridge, Mass., 1979). For representations of modern war, see T. F. Schneider (ed.), *The Experience of War and the Creation of Myths: The Image of "Modern" War in Theatre, Photography, and Film*, 2 vols. (Osnabrück, 1999).

2. M. Eksteins, *Rites of Spring: The Great War and the Birth of the Modern Age* (New York, 1989), pp. 300–331; J.-J. Becker, *The Great War and the French People* (Leamington Spa, 1985), pp. 29–63; S. Hynes, *A War Imagined: The First World War and English Culture* (New York, 1991), pp. 3–56. For pre-1914 visions of destruction, see D. Pick, *War Machine: The Rationalisation of Slaughter in the Modern Age* (New Haven, Conn., 1993).

3. J.-J. Becker et al. (eds.), *Guerre et cultures, 1914–1918* (Paris, 1994), pp. 133–91; G. Hirschfeld et al. (eds.), *Keiner fühlt sich hier mehr als Mensch . . . : Erlebnis und Wirkung des Ersten Weltkriegs* (Essen, 1993); A. Becker, *Oubliés de la grande guerre. Humanitaire et culture de guerre, 1914–1918: Populations occupées, déportés civils, prisonniers de guerre* (Paris, 1998).

4. S. Audoin-Rouzeau, *Men at War, 1914–1918: National Sentiment and Trench Journalism in France during the First World War* (Providence, R.I., 1992); F. Coetzee and M. Shevin-Coetzee (eds.), *Authority, Identity, and the Social History of the Great War* (Providence, R. I., 1995), part III. A good example of the British view is R. Graves's autobiography, *Good-bye to All That* (1929).

5. R. W. Whalen, *Bitter Wounds: German Victims of the Great War, 1914–1939* (Ithaca, N.Y., 1984); A. Prost, *In the Wake of War: "Les Anciens Combattants" and French Society, 1914–1939* (Providence, R.I., 1992).

6. R. Bessel, *Germany after the First World War* (Oxford, 1993), pp. 254–84; N. Ingram, *The Politics of Dissent: Pacifism in France, 1919–1939* (Oxford, 1991).

7. G. L. Mosse, *Fallen Soldiers: Reshaping the Memory of the World Wars* (New York, 1990); A. King, *Memorials of the Great War in Britain: The Symbolism and Politics of Remembrance* (Oxford, 1998); A. Becker (ed.), *Les monuments aux morts: Mémoire de la Grande Guerre* (Errance, 1988).

8. J. Winter, *Sites of Memory, Sites of Mourning: The Great War in European Cultural History* (Cambridge, 1995); D. W. Lloyd, *Battlefield Tourism: Pilgrimage and the Commemoration of the Great War in Britain, Australia and Canada, 1919–1939* (Oxford, 1998); A. Becker, "From Death to Memory: The National Ossuaries in France after the Great War," *H&M* 5/2 (fall/winter 1993): 32–49.

9. K. S. Inglis, "Entombing Unknown Soldiers: From London to Paris to Baghdad," *H&M* 5/2 (fall/winter 1993): 7–31.

10. V. Ackermann, "La vision allemande du Soldat inconnu: Débats politiques, réflexion philosophique et artistique," in Becker, *Guerre et cultures*, pp. 385–96, and more generally, part IV of that book.

11. For two very different reactions, see A. Becker, *La Guerre et la foi: De la mort à la mémoire, 1914–1930* (Paris, 1994); K. Theweleit, *Männerphantasien,* 2 vols. (Basel, 1977).

12. On how the war reshaped views on education, rape, gender, women's consciousness, violence, and the enemy, see S. Audoin-Rouzeau, *La guerre des enfants, 1914–1918: Essai d'histoire culturelle* (Paris, 1993), and his *L'enfant de l'ennemi, 1914–1918: Viol, avortement, infanticide pendant la Grande Guerre* (Paris, 1995); M. R. Higonnet et al. (eds.), *Behind the Lines: Gender and the Two World Wars* (New Haven, Conn., 1987), chapters 4–5, 7–9, 14; M. L. Roberts, *Civilization without Sexes: Reconstructing Gender in Postwar France, 1917–1927* (Chicago, 1994); C. M. Tylee, *The Great War and Women's Consciousness: Images of Militarism and Womanhood in Women's Writings, 1914–64* (Iowa City, Iowa, 1990); T. Nevin, *Ernst Jünger and Germany: Into the Abyss, 1914–1945* (Durham, N.C., 1996), chapter 2; M. Jeismann, *Das Vaterland der Feinde: Studien zum nationalen Feindbegriff und Selbstverständnis in Deutschland und Frankreich, 1872–1918* (Stuttgart, 1992), part III.

13. G. Caplan of Georgetown University and B. Crim of Rutgers University are now in the process of rewriting the history of the German veterans associations, which has been neglected since such works as V. R. Berghahn, *Der Stahlhelm, Bund der Frontsoldaten, 1918–1935* (Düsseldorf, 1966), and J. M. Diehl, *Paramilitary Politics in Weimar Germany* (Bloomington, Ind., 1977), and is almost nonexistent regarding Jewish veterans. For France the major work is A. Prost, *Les Anciens Combattants et la société française, 1914–1939,* 3 vols. (Paris, 1977).

14. G. Pedroncini, *Les mutineries de 1917* (Paris, 1967); L. V. Smith, *Between Mutiny and Obedience: The Case of the French Fifth Infantry Division during World War I* (Princeton, N.J., 1994), pp. 175–214.

15. D. Carrol, *French Literary Fascism: Nationalism, Anti-Semitism, and the Ideology of Culture* (Princeton, N.J., 1995), part II.

16. P. Burrin, *France under the Germans: Collaboration and Compromise* (New York, 1996).

17. R. Bessel, "Militarismus im innenpolitischen Leben der Weimarer Republik: Von den Freikorps zur SA," in *Militär und Militarismus in der Weimarer Republik,* ed. K.-J. Müller and E. Opitz (Düsseldorf, 1978), pp. 193–222; H. J. Gordon, Jr., *The Reichswehr and the German Republic, 1919–1926* (Princeton, N.J., 1957); R. G. L. Waite, *Vanguard of Nazism: The Free Corps Movement in Postwar Germany, 1918–1923* (Cambridge, Mass., 1952); H. Schulze, *Freikorps und Republik, 1918–1920* (Boppard am Rhine, 1969).

18. B. Hüppauf, "Langemarck, Verdun and the Myth of a New Man in Germany after the First World War," *W&S* 6/2 (1988): 70–103.

19. M. Kitchen, *The Silent Dictatorship: The Politics of the German High Command under Hindenburg and Ludendorff, 1916–1918* (New York, 1976)

20. G. D. Feldman, *Army, Industry and Labor in Germany, 1914–1918,* 2nd ed. (Providence, R.I., 1992). On the origins of total war, see S. Förster and J. Nagler (eds.), *On the Road to Total War: The American Civil War and the German Wars of Unification, 1861–1871* (Cambridge, 1997); M. F. Boemeke et al. (eds.), *Anticipating Total War: The German and American Experience, 1871–1914* (Cambridge, 1999).

21. A. Bullock, *Hitler: A Study in Tyranny,* rev. ed. (New York, 1964), p. 112.

22. W. Deist, *Militär, Staat und Gesellschaft: Studien zur preussisch-deutschen Militärgeschichte* (Munich, 1991), pp. 83–163, 293–338, 385–429, and his *The Wehrmacht and German Rearmament* (London, 1981); K.-J. Müller, *The Army, Politics and Soci-*

ety in Germany, 1933–45: Studies in the Army's Relation to Nazism (New York, 1987); M. Geyer, "Professionals and Junkers: German Rearmament and Politics in the Weimar Republic," in *Social Change and Political Development in the Weimar Republic,* ed. R. Bessel and E. J. Feuchtwanger (London, 1981), pp. 77–133, and his "The Militarization of Europe, 1914–1945," in *The Militarization of the Western World,* ed. J. R. Gillis (New Brunswick, N.J., 1989), pp. 65–102.

23. U. Herbert, *Best: Biographische Studien über Radikalismus, Weltanschauung und Vernunft, 1903–1989* (Bonn, 1996), parts I–II; L. Hachmeister, *Der Gegnerforscher: Die Karriere des SS-Führers Franz Alfred Six* (Munich, 1998), chapters 1–7; M. Wildt, *Das Führungskorps des Reichssicherheitshauptamtes: Versuch einer Kollektivbiographie* (Hamburg, 1996).

24. P. Paret (ed.), *Makers of Modern Strategy: From Machiavelli to the Nuclear Age* (Princeton, N.J., 1986), part IV; J. L. Wallach, *Das Dogma der Vernichtungsschlacht* (Frankfurt am Main, 1967), and his *Kriegstheorien, ihre Entwicklung im 19. und 20. Jahrhundert* (Frankfurt am Main, 1972).

25. On the controversies surrounding the German concept of Blitzkrieg and the transition to total war, see T. Mason, *Nazism, Fascism and the Working Class,* ed. J. Caplan (Cambridge, 1995), chapters 1, 4, 9; R. J. Overy, *War and the Economy in the Third Reich* (Oxford, 1994), chapters 6–8, 9; O. Bartov, "From *Blitzkrieg* to Total War: Controversial Links between Image and Reality," in *Stalinism and Nazism: Dictatorships in Comparison,* ed. I. Kershaw and M. Lewin (Cambridge, 1997), pp. 158–84. See also W. Deist et al. (eds.), *Das Deutsche Reich und der Zweite Weltkrieg,* vol. 1 (Stuttgart, 1979), parts II–III.

26. For Hitler's popular appeal, see I. Kershaw, *The "Hitler Myth": Image and Reality in the Third Reich* (Oxford, 1987); for his image among the Wehrmacht's soldiers and their internalization of Nazi ideas, see O. Bartov, *Hitler's Army: Soldiers, Nazis, and War in the Third Reich* (New York, 1991), chapter 4.

27. F. L. Carsten, *The Reichswehr in Politics, 1918–1933,* 2nd ed. (Berkeley, Calif., 1973); J. Wheeler-Bennett, *The Nemesis of Power: The German Army in Politics, 1918–1945,* 2nd ed. (London, 1980), part I.

28. J. Förster, "The German Army and the Ideological War against the Soviet Union," in *The Policies of Genocide: Jews and Soviet Prisoners of War in Nazi Germany,* ed. G. Hirschfeld (London, 1986), pp. 15–29, and his "Das Unternehmen 'Barbarossa' als Eroberungs- und Vernichtungskrieg," in *Das Deutsche Reich und der Zweite Weltkrieg,* vol. 4 (Stuttgart, 1983), pp. 440–47; M. Messerschmidt, *Die Wehrmacht im NS-Staat: Zeit der Indoktrination* (Hamburg, 1969); O. Bartov, *The Eastern Front, 1941–45: German Troops and the Barbarisation of Warfare* (London, 1985), pp. 68–105; K.-J. Müller, *General Ludwig Beck: Studien und Dokumente zur politisch-militärischen Vorstellungswelt und Tätigkeit des Generalstabschefs des deutschen Heeres, 1933–1938* (Boppard am Rhein, 1980).

29. J. M. Hughes, *To the Maginot Line: The Politics of French Military Preparation in the 1920's* (Cambridge, Mass., 1971).

30. Apart from Bartov, *Hitler's Army,* see T. Schulte, *The German Army and Nazi Policies in Occupied Russia* (Oxford, 1989), pp. 1–27, 211–76; S. G. Fritz, *Frontsoldaten: The German Soldier in World War II* (Lexington, Ky., 1995); H. Heer and K. Naumann (eds.), *War of Extermination: Crimes of the Wermacht, 1941–1945* (New York, 2000).

31. "Schnappschüsse," *Mittelweg 36* 5 (February/March 1996): 1–10, for examples of cover illustrations. U. G. Poiger, "Rock 'n' Roll, Female Sexuality, and the Cold

War Battle over German Identities," in *West Germany under Construction: Politics, Society, and Culture in the Adenauer Era,* ed. R. G. Moeller (Ann Arbor, Mich., 1997), pp. 373–41.

32. For a summary of the historiography, see O. Bartov, "German Soldiers and the Holocaust: Historiography, Research and Implications," *H&M* 9/1–2 (fall 1997): 162–88.

33. See, e.g., such collections of letters as O. Buchbender and R. Sterz (eds.), *Das andere Gesicht des Krieges: Deutsche Feldpostbriefe, 1919–1945* (Munich, 1982); *Sieg Heil! War Letters of Tank Gunner Karl Fuchs, 1937–1941,* ed. H. Fuchs Richardson (Hamden, Conn., 1987).

34. On the integration of veterans into West German society, see J. M. Diehl, *The Thanks of the Fatherland: German Veterans after the Second World War* (Chapel Hill, N.C., 1993); on the memory of the war and the return of prisoners of war, see R. Moeller, *War Stories: The Search for a Usable Past in the Federal Republic of Germany* (Berkeley, Calif., 2000), and his "War Stories: The Search for a Usable Past in the Federal Republic of Germany," *AHR* 101 (1996): 1000–48; and F. Biess, "The Protracted War: Returning POWs and the Making of East and West German Citizens, 1945–1955" (Brown University, Ph.D. dissertation, 2000), his "'Pioneers of a New Germany': Returning POWs from the Soviet Union and the Making of East German Citizens, 1945–1950," CEH 32 (1999): 143–80, and his "Survivors of Totalitarianism: Returning POWs and the Reconstruction of Masculine Citizenship in West Germany, 1945–1955," in *The Miracle Years Revisited: A Cultural History of West Germany,* ed. H. Schissler (Princeton, N.J., forthcoming).

35. K. Naumann, *Der Krieg als Text: Das Jahr 1945 im Kulturellen Gedächtnis der Presse* (Hamburg, 1998).

36. C. Streit, *Keine Kameraden: Die Wehrmacht und die sowjetischen Kriegsgefangenen, 1941–1945,* 2nd ed. (Bonn, 1991).

37. Bartov, *Hitler's Army,* chapter 4, and *Eastern Front,* chapter 3. On collaboration with the SS, see H. Krausnick and H.-H. Wilhelm, *Die Truppe des Weltanschauungskrieges: Die Einsatzgruppen der Sicherheitspolizei und des SD, 1938–1942* (Stuttgart, 1981). See also O. Bartov, "Savage War," in *Confronting the Nazi Past: New Debates on Modern German History,* ed. M. Burleigh (London, 1996), pp. 125–39, and Bartov, "The Missing Years: German Workers, German Soldiers," in *Nazism and German Society, 1933–1945,* ed. D. F. Crew (London, 1994), pp. 41–66. And see the important new contribution to this debate, T. Kühne, "Kameradschaft—'das Beste im Leben des Mannes': Die deutschen Soldaten des Zweiten Weltkriegs in erfahrungs- und geschlechtergeschichtlicher Perspektive," *G&G* 22/4 (1996): 504–29.

38. Extracts from Himmler's Posen speeches to SS leaders on October 4, 1943, and to a meeting of generals in Sonthofen, on May 5, 1944, can be found in J. Noakes and G. Pridham (eds.), *Nazism, 1919–1945: A Documentary Reader,* vol. 3 (Exeter, 1988), pp. 1199–200.

39. For one of numerous examples of anticipation of revenge for atrocity, see E. Klee et al. (eds.), *"The Good Old Days": The Holocaust as Seen by Its Perpetrators and Bystanders* (New York, 1991), pp. 38–43. A soldier from a motorized column, who watched a massacre of Jews in Lithuania, wrote: "I can only say that the mass shootings in Paneriai were quite horrific. At the time I said: 'May God grant us victory because if they get their revenge, we're in for a hard time.'" Ibid., p. 43. And see a reproduction of Hitler's political testament in G. Fleming, *Hitler and the Final Solution* (Berkeley, Calif., 1984), between pp. 92–93; the English translation is in

R. Hilberg, *The Destruction of the European Jews,* rev. ed. (New York, 1985), vol. 3, p. 989.

40. *A French Tragedy: Scenes of Civil War, Summer 1944* (Hanover, N.H., 1996). See also M. de Keiser, "The Skeleton in the Closet: The Memory of Putten, 1/2 October 1944," *H&M* 7/2 (fall/winter 1996): 70–99.

41. On the 1944 Oradour massacre, the 1953 trial of the perpetrators in Bordeaux, and the role of the event in France's politics of memory, see P. Beck, *Oradour: Village of the Dead* (London, 1979); S. Farmer, *Martyred Village: Commemorating the 1944 Massacre at Oradour-Sur-Glune* (Berkely, Calif., 1999). On the SS division Das Reich in Oradour, see M. Hastings, *Das Reich: Resistance and the March of the 2nd SS Panzer Division through France, June 1944* (London, 1981), chapter 9.

42. For a general background, see A. Clayton, *The Wars of French Decolonization* (London, 1994).

43. A. Horne, *A Savage War of Peace: Algeria, 1954–1962* (London, 1977); J.-P. Rioux (ed.), *La Guerre d'Algerie et les Français* (Paris, 1990); J.-F. Sirinelli, *Intellectuels et passion françaises: Manifestes et pétitions au XXe Siècle* (Paris, 1990), chapter 9.

44. Curiously, the mammoth project edited by P. Nora, *Les Lieux de mémoire,* 2nd (paperback) ed., 3 vols. (Paris, 1997), does not contain a single chapter heading on the colonies. Conversely, in the part entitled *La Nation,* under category 3, "L'idéel," vol. 2, pp. 1673–918, we find the main chapter "La gloire," with the following entries: "Mourir pour la patrie" (P. Contamine), "Le soldat Chauvin" (G. de Puymège), "Le retour des Cendres" (J. Tulard), "Verdun" (A. Prost), "Le musée historique de Versailles" (T. W. Gaehtgens), "Le Louvre" (J.-P. Babelon), "Les morts illustres" (J.-C. Bonnet), "Les statues de Paris" (J. Hargrove), and "Le nom des rues" (D. Milo). While in "Divisions politiques," vol. 2, pp. 2467–87, there is an entry on Vichy by P. Burrin, this 4,751-page enterprise does not include the category "shame" or "ignominy," although one can think of various sites of memory in France that would fit such terms.

45. See A. Prost, "The Algerian War in French Collective Memory," in *War and Remembrance in the Twentieth Century,* ed. J. Winter and E. Sivan (Cambridge, 1999), pp. 161–76.

46. One indication of the preoccupation with national identity—defined in a manner that greatly diminishes such minor events as, for instance, Vichy and the Collaboration—is another mammoth work, F. Braudel, *The Identity of France,* 2 vols. (New York, 1991).

47. See, e.g., A. Prost (ed.), *14–18: Mourir pour la patrie* (Paris, 1992).

48. See, e.g., the controversy over F. Fischer's *Griff nach der Weltmacht. Die Kriegszielpolitik des kaiserlichen Deutschland, 1914/18* (Düsseldorf, 1961) and *Krieg der Illusionen: Die deutsche Politik von 1911 bis 1914* (Düsseldorf, 1969), translated in abbreviated form as *Germany's Aims in the First World War* (New York, 1967) and *War of Illusions: German Policies from 1911 to 1914* (New York, 1975). For the debate, see H. W. Koch, *The Origins of the First World War: Great Power Rivalry and German War Aims,* 2nd ed. (London, 1977), chapters 3–7, and H. H. Herwig, *The Outbreak of World War I,* 6th ed. (Boston, 1997), parts III–IV.

49. See above, Introduction, n. 4. See also P. Baldwin (ed.), *Reworking the Past: Hitler, the Holocaust, and the Historians' Debate* (Boston, 1990), especially M. Broszat, "A Plea for the Historicization of National Socialism," pp. 77–87.

50. See, e.g., U. Herbert (ed.), *National Socialist Extermination Policies: Contemporary German Perspectives and Controversies* (New York, 1999).

51. See above, n. 39. German propaganda made much of this theme, first to justify launching the war as aimed at thwarting an expected enemy attack and then as justifying continued resistance by threats of anticipated enemy revenge. See Bartov, *Hitler's Army,* pp. 106, 126, 129–31, 135, 137, 139, 155–56, 163, 168, and following. A Wehrmacht captain wrote in February 1943: "May God allow the German people to find now the peace of mind and strength which would make it into the instrument needed by the Führer to protect the West from ruin, for what the Asiatic hordes will not destroy, will be annihilated by Jewish hatred and revenge." Ibid., p. 169.

52. S. Friedländer, *Nazi Germany and the Jews,* vol. 1: *The Years of Persecution, 1933–1939* (New York, 1997); J. Weiss, *Ideology of Death: Why the Holocaust Happened in Germany* (Chicago, 1996); and, most controversially, D. J. Goldhagen, *Hitler's Willing Executioners: Ordinary Germans and the Holocaust* (New York, 1996), chapter 2.

53. D. Bankier, *The Germans and the Final Solution: Public Opinion under Nazism,* 2nd ed. (Oxford, 1996).

54. The most remarkable example for this line of argumentation among German scholars of an earlier generation was A. Hillgruber, *Zweierlei Untergang: Die Zerschlagung des Deutschen Reiches und das Ende des europäischen Judentums* (Berlin, 1986).

55. H. Arendt, "The Aftermath of Nazi Rule: Report from Germany," *Commentary* 10 (October 1950): 342–53. In this context see also A. Grossmann, "Trauma, Memory, and Motherhood: Germans and Jewish Displaced Persons in Post-Nazi Germany, 1945–1949," *AfS* 38 (1998): 230–54; Y. M. Bodemann, "Gedächtnisnegativ: Genealogie und Strategien deutscher Erinnerung an Auschwitz," in *Soziologie der Gewalt,* ed. T. von Trotha (Opladen/Wiesbaden, 1997), pp. 357–79; F. Stern, "The Historic Triangle: Occupiers, Germans and Jews in Postwar Germany," *TAJB* 19 (1990): 47–76.

56. See, e.g., the biographies analyzed in R. Schörken, "Jugendalltag im Dritten Reich," in *Geschichte im Alltag—Alltag in der Geschichte,* ed. K. Bergmann and R. Schörken (Düsseldorf, 1982), pp. 238–44. See also A. Heck, *A Child of Hitler,* 3rd ed. (Toronto, 1986); W. Schumann, *Being Present: Growing Up in Hitler's Germany* (Kent, Ohio, 1991).

57. For how Germans remembered the Third Reich several decades after its fall, see, e.g., B. Engelmann, *In Hitler's Germany: Everyday Life in the Third Reich* (New York, 1986); L. Niethammer (ed.), *"Die Jahre weiss man nicht, wo man die heute hinsetzen soll": Faschismus im Ruhrgebiet* (Berlin, 1983).

58. T. W. Ryback, "Stalingrad: Letters from the Dead," *TNY* (February 1, 1993): 58–71.

59. Hilberg, *Destruction,* vol. 3, pp. 976–79.

60. H. Graml et al., *The German Resistance to Hitler* (London, 1970), pp. 195–97, 232–33; M. G. Steinert, *Hitler's War and the Germans* (Athens, Ohio, 1977), p. 267; J. Von Herwarth, *Against Two Evils: Memoirs of a Diplomat-Soldier during the Third Reich* (London, 1981), pp. 203–205, 254–55.

61. For recent works on the resistance, see P. Hoffmann, *The History of the German Resistance 1933–1945,* 3rd rev. ed. (Montreal, 1996); J. Fest, *Plotting Hitler's Death: The Story of the German Resistance* (New York, 1996); T. S. Hamerow, *On the Road to Wolf's Lair: German Resistance to Hilter* (Cambridge, Mass., 1997).

62. K. Naumann, "Wenn ein Tabu bricht: Die Wehrmachts-Ausstellung in der Bundesrepublik"; W. Manoschek, "Die Wehrmachtsausstellung in Österreich: Ein Bericht," both in *Mittelweg 36* 5/1 (1996): 11–24 and 25–32. Hamburger Institut für Sozialforschung (ed.), *Besucher einer Ausstellung: Die Ausstellung "Vernichtungskrieg. Verbrechen der Wehrmacht 1941 bis 1944" in Interview und Gespräch* (Hamburg, 1998).

63. O. Bartov, "'Seit die Juden weg sind . . . ': Germany, History, and Representations of Absence," in *A User's Guide to German Cultural Studies,* ed. S. Denham et al. (Ann Arbor, Mich., 1997), pp. 209–26. For a comparison between West and East Germany, see J. Herf, *Divided Memory: The Nazi Past in the Two Germanys* (Cambridge, Mass., 1997).

64. The best and most updated discussion of this whole issue is in Naumann, *Krieg als Text.*

65. G. Hartman (ed.), *Bitburg in Moral and Political Perspective* (Bloomington, Ind., 1986).

66. D. C. Large, *Germans to the Front: West German Rearmament in the Adenauer Era* (Chapel Hill, N.C., 1996).

67. D. Abenheim, *Reforging the Iron Cross: The Search for Tradition in the West German Armed Forces* (Princeton, N.J., 1988).

68. See, e.g., *Zeit-Punkte: Gehorsam bis zum Mord? Der verschwiegene Krieg der deutschen Wehrmacht—Fakten, Analysen, Debatte* (Hamburg, n.d.); "Wehrmachtsverbrechen," *Mittelweg 36* 3 (June/July 1994): 41–50 (discussion with J. Förster, M. Messerschmidt, and C. Streit, moderated by H. Heer and T. Neumann).

69. F. Stern, *The Whitewashing of the Yellow Badge: Antisemitism and Philosemitism in Postwar Germany* (Oxford, 1992), esp. chapter 7; T. Segev, *The Seventh Million: The Israelis and the Holocaust* (New York, 1993), part IV. On continuity in the German legal profession, see I. Müller, *Hitler's Justice: The Courts of the Third Reich* (Cambridge, Mass., 1991), part III.

70. K. H. Jarausch and Volker Gransow (eds.), *Uniting Germany: Documents and Debates, 1944–1993* (Providence, R.I., 1994), chapter 7, documents 7, 13, 18, 23; K. H. Jarausch, *The Rush to German Unity* (New York, 1994), pp. 197–210; S. Parkes, *Understanding Contemporary Germany* (London, 1997), chapter 9. See also C. S. Maier, *Dissolution: The Crisis of Communism and the End of East Germany* (Princeton, N.J. 1997); J. C. Torpey, *Intellectuals, Socialism, and Dissent: The East German Opposition and Its Legacy* (Minneapolis, Minn., 1995).

71. J. H. Schoeps (ed.), *Ein Volk von Mördern? Die Dokumentation zur Goldhagen-Kontroverse um die Rolle der Deutschen im Holocaust* (Hamburg, 1996); R. R. Shandley (ed.), *Unwilling Germans? The Goldhagen Debate* (Minneapolis, Minn., 1998); N. G. Finkelstein and R. B. Birn, *A Nation on Trial: The Goldhagen Thesis and Historical Truth* (New York, 1998).

72. J. Habermas, "Über den öffentlichen Gebrauch der Historie: Warum ein 'Demokratiepreis' für Daniel J. Goldhagen? Eine Laudatio," *Die Zeit* 12 (March 14, 1997): 13–14.

73. *Ich will Zeugnis ablegen bis zum letzten: Tagebücher, 1933–1945,* ed. W. Nowojski with H. Klemperer, 2 vols. (Berlin, 1995). Now available in English: *I Will Bear Witness: A Diary of the Nazi Years,* vol. 1, 1933–1941 (New York, 1998); vol. 2, 1941–1945 (New York, 2000). See my review essay on the diary, "The Last German," *TNR* (December 28, 1998): 34–42.

Chapter 2

1. This account is taken from reports in *Journal,* 14 December 1927, *Avenir,* 15 December 1927, and *Volonté,* 15 December 1927, all to be found in AN, F7 13021. In some of the reports Mme Murati appears as Veuve Delord or Delort.

2. A. Williams, *Republic of Images: A History of French Filmmaking* (Cambridge, Mass., 1992), pp. 86–88. For a still picture from the film *Napoléon,* see D. and M. Johnson, *The Age of Illusion: Art and Politics in France, 1918–1940* (New York, 1987), p. 71; for scenes from *J'accuse* and *Les Croix de bois,* see A. Prost, *Les Anciens combattants, 1914–1940* (Paris, 1977), between pages 96–97.

3. For photographic evidence of the horrors of the "Great War," see, e.g., the following: dead soldiers hanging from a treetop (censured by the military during the war); soldiers recovering from the first shock of battle; and the effects of a delayed-action shell that exploded on the liaison bunker of the Twenty-third Infantry Regiment on November 18, 1918, all in Prost, *Anciens combattants,* between pages 96–97. Photograph of the delegation of French *Mutilés de Guerre* to the Congress of the Versailles Treaty, 28 June 1919, in K. E. Silver, *Esprit de Corps: The Art of the Parisian Avant-Garde and the First World War, 1914–1925* (Princeton, N.J., 1989), p. 188. See further in J. Winter and B. Bagget, *The Great War and the Shaping of the Twentieth Century* (New York, 1996); J. M. Winter, *The Experience of World War I* (New York, 1989). Thoughtful comments on rehabilitation and interesting photographs in R. Panchasi, "Reconstructions: Prosthetics and the Rehabilitation of the Male Body in World War I France," *Differences* 7/3 (1995): 109–39.

4. For a well-illustrated account of the period, see C. Rearick, *The French in Love and War: Popular Culture in the Era of the World Wars* (New Haven, Conn., 1997).

5. *Strange Defeat: A Statement of Evidence Written in 1940* (New York, 1968). See also M. Hanna, *The Mobilization of Intellect: French Scholars and Writers during the Great War* (Cambridge, Mass., 1996).

6. For a detailed account of France's belated preparations for war, see J.-L Crémieux-Brilhac, *Les Français de l'an 40,* 2 vols. (Paris 1990). See also J. Blatt (ed.), *The French Defeat of 1940: Reassessments* (Providence, R.I., 1998); J.-P. Azéma, *1940 l'année terrible* (Paris, 1990); P. Richer, *La drôle de guerre des Français: 2 septembre 1939—10 mai 1940* (Paris, 1990).

7. *Prison Journal, 1940–1945,* trans. A. D. Greenspan (Boulder, Colo., 1995), pp. 7, 13, 28–29, 91. Citations are from the translated version.

8. For photographs, see Johnson, *The Age of Illusion,* p. 21.

9. O. Bartov, "Martyrs' Vengeance: Memory, Trauma, and Fear of War in France, 1918–1940," in Blatt, *The French Defeat,* pp. 71–73, for photographs and sources.

10. *Prison Journal,* pp. 109–10.

11. *France under the Germans: Collaboration and Compromise,* trans. J. Lloyd (New York, 1996), pp. 37–39. Citations are from the translated version.

12. *The Hollow Years: France in the 1930s* (New York, 1994), p. 22. Citations are from E. Weber's translations of the original French texts.

13. Ibid., p. 103.

14. V. Caron, "The Antisemitic Revival in France in the 1930s: The Socioeconomic Dimension Reconsidered," *JMH* 70/1 (March 1998): 24–73, and literature cited therein; Caron, *Uneasy Asylum: France and the Jewish Refugee Crisis, 1933–1942*

(Stanford, Calif., 1999). Further new works on French antisemitism in the 1930s and under Vichy include R. Schor, *L'Antisémitisme en France pendant les années 30: Prélude à Vichy* (Brussels, 1992); P. Birnbaum, *Un mythe politique: la "République juive". De Léon Blum à Mendès France* (Paris, 1995); P.-A. Taguieff (ed.), *L'Antisémitisme de Plume: 1940–1944. Études et documents* (Paris, 1999).

15. Weber, *The Hollow Years,* pp. 238–46, 257 (title of chapter 10).

16. J. Renoir, *La grande illusion: Découpage intégral* (Paris, 1971); L. Braudy, *Jean Renoir: The World of His Films* (New York, 1972); C. Bertin, *Jean Renoir: A Life in Pictures* (Baltimore, Md., 1991); A. Sesonske, *Jean Renoir: The French Films, 1924–1939* (Cambridge, Mass., 1980); J. Buchsbaum, *Cinema Engagé: Film in the Popular Front* (Urbana, Ill., 1988). More generally, see D. Andrew, *Mists of Regret: Culture and Sensibility in Classic French Film* (Princeton, N.J., 1995).

17. See, e.g., N. Ingram, *The Politics of Dissent: Pacifism in France, 1919–1939* (Oxford, 1991); C. Jelen, *Hitler ou Staline: Le prix de la paix* (Paris, 1988); C. Prochasson, *Les Intellectuels, le socialisme et la guerre, 1900–1938* (Paris, 1993); J.-L. Loubet del Bayle, *Les non-conformistes des années 30: Une tentative de la renouvellement de la pensée politique française* (Paris, 1969); P. Burrin, *La dérive fasciste: Doriot, Déat, Bergery, 1933–1945* (Paris, 1986); Z. Sternhell, *Neither Right nor Left: Fascist Ideology in France,* 2nd ed. (Princeton, N.J., 1996); P.-M. Dioudonnat, *Je suis partout, 1930–1944: Les maurassiens devant la tentation fasciste* (Paris, 1973); R. Soucy, *French Fascism: The First Wave, 1924–1933* (New Haven, Conn., 1986), and his *French Fascism: The Second Wave, 1933–1939* (New Haven, Conn. 1995).

18. Photographs in Bartov, *Martyrs' Vengeance,* pp. 75, 77, 78.

19. For photograph, see ibid., p. 78.

20. For photographs, see ibid., pp. 79–80.

21. Photograph in Johnson, *The Age of Illusion,* p. 147.

22. Ibid.

23. Ingram, *Politics of Dissent,* pp. 192–93, 318–19.

24. See leaflets in AN, F7 13233, 13235, 13239.

25. H. Rousso, *The Vichy Syndrome: History and Memory in France since 1944* (Cambridge, Mass., 1991). See also contributions by J. Hellman, P. Nora, B. M. Gordon, and H. Rousso, in "Forum: The Vichy Syndrome," *FHS* 19/2 (fall 1995): 461–526.

26. Note the following passage in Daladier, *Prison Journal,* p. 280, written on June 25, 1944: "Bernanos has addressed a message to the 'people of France,' just a simple little message to the entire nation. Is there anyone these days who isn't addressing messages to 'the people of France'? This one is solemn and as vague as they come: spiritual values . . . economic injustice . . . noble Normandy. A slew of stock images squeezed into a few lines. The unbelievable conceit of all these expatriates in America and elsewhere."

27. See especially R. O. Paxton, *Vichy France: Old Guard and New Order, 1940–1944* (New York, 1972). Also J.-P. Azéma and F. Bédarida (eds.), *Le régime de Vichy et les Français* (Paris, 1992).

28. R. J. Golsan (ed.), *Memory, the Holocaust, and French Justice: The Bousquet and Touvier Affairs* (Hanover, N.H., 1996); E. Paris, *Unhealed Wounds: France and the Klaus Barbie Affair* (New York, 1985); A. Finkielkraut, *Remembering in Vain: The Klaus Barbie Trial and Crimes against Humanity* (New York, 1992); P. Péan, *Une Jeunesse française: François Mitterrand, 1934–1947* (Paris, 1994).

29. *Prison Journal,* p. 90.

30. Ibid., pp. 211, 275, 284.

31. Ibid., p. 34.

32. Ibid., p. 73.

33. Ibid., p. 88.

34. Ibid., pp. 138–39.

35. Ibid., pp. 141, 151.

36. Ibid., pp. 280, 299.

37. Ibid., pp. 315–16.

38. Ibid., p. 333.

39. M. R. Marrus and R. O. Paxton, *Vichy France and the Jews* (New York, 1983); S. Zucotti, *The Holocaust, the French, and the Jews* (New York, 1993); R. H. Weisberg, *Vichy Law and the Holocaust in France* (New York, 1996); M. O. Baruch, *Servir l'État français: L'administration en France de 1940 à 1944* (Paris, 1997); D. F. Ryan, *The Holocaust and the Jews of Marseille: The Enforcement of Anti-Semitic Policies in Vichy France* (Urbana, Ill., 1996); A. Cohen et. al., *History of the Holocaust: France* (Jerusalem, 1996, in Hebrew). On the memory of the Holocaust in France and the problem of distinctions between Jewish and political deportees, see A. Wieviorka, *Déportation et génocide: Entre la mémoire et l'oubli* (Paris, 1992). For criticism of the growing preoccupation with the memory of Vichy's crimes against the Jews, see E. Conan and H. Rousso, *Vichy: An Ever-Present Past* (Hanover, N.H., 1998).

40. *Choices in Vichy France: The French under Nazi Occupation*, 2nd ed. (New York, 1994), pp. 83, 94–95, 130.

41. Ibid., p. 93. See also T. Todorov, *A French Tragedy: Scenes of Civil War, Summer 1944* (Hanover, N.H., 1996), p. 94.

42. For Germany, see U. Herbert, *Best: Biographische Studien über Radikalismus, Weltanschauung, und Vernunft, 1903–1989* (Bonn, 1996); for France, see Baruch, *Servir l'État français*.

43. Sweets, *Choices in Vichy France*, p. 120.

44. Ibid., p. 131. On perpetrators as dutiful professionals, see R. Hilberg, *The Destruction of the European Jews*, 3 vols., rev. ed. (New York, 1985); Z. Bauman, *Modernity and the Holocaust*, 2nd ed. (Ithaca, N.Y., 1991). On Hitler's popularity in Germany, see I. Kershaw, *The "Hitler Myth": Image and Reality in the Third Reich* (Oxford, 1987); and on French public opinion during the Occupation, P. Laborie, *L'Opinion française sous Vichy* (Paris, 1990).

45. Cited in Sweets, *Choices in Vichy France*, pp. 146–47.

46. Ibid., pp. 149–50.

47. Ibid., p. 163.

48. Ibid., pp. 168–69, 187, 192, 224.

49. W. D. Halls, *Politics, Society and Christianity in Vichy France* (Oxford, 1995), pp. 37–40 (Citations are from Hall's translations of the original French). Another important recent study on this issue is E. Fouilloux, *Les chrétiens français entre crise et libération, 1937–1947* (Paris, 1997). On the German side, Count von Galen, bishop of Münster, who has become an icon of Catholic resistance to the Nazis thanks to his public condemnation of the "euthanasia" campaign, never spoke openly against the "Final Solution." See B. A. Griech-Polelle, "A Pure Soul Is Good Enough: Bishop von Galen, Resistance to Nazism, and the Catholic Community of Münster" (Rutgers University, Ph.D. dissertation, 1999).

50. Halls, *Politics, Society and Christianity*, p. 48.

51. Ibid., pp. 61–62.

52. Ibid., pp. 70–82.

53. Ibid., pp. 99–109, 119–21.

54. Ibid., p. 132.

55. Ibid., p. 137. See also P. Hallie, *Lest Innocent Blood Be Shed: The Story of the Village of Le Chambon and How Goodness Happened There*, 2nd ed. (New York, 1994). Also fascinating is the documentary film on the Le Chambon by Pierre Sauvage, who was saved there as a baby.

56. Halls, *Politics, Society and Christianity*, p. 219.

57. Ibid., p. 143.

58. Ibid., pp. 165–71.

59. Ibid., pp. 184–86.

60. Ibid., pp. 346–48.

61. Ibid., p. 355.

62. Ibid., pp. 367–68, 378–79.

63. *France under the Germans*, p. viii.

64. Ibid., pp. 2–4.

65. Ibid., p. 17.

66. Ibid., p. 31.

67. Ibid., p. 109.

68. Ibid., pp. 128–32.

69. Ibid., pp. 133–34, 140–41, 157–59.

70. Ibid., pp. 185–87.

71. Ibid., p. 207. On the flood of denunciations in France, see also Sweets, *Choices in Vichy France*, pp. 99–101. On German denunciations, see R. Gellately, *The Gestapo and German Society: Enforcing Racial Policy, 1933–1945* (Oxford, 1990); G. Diewald-Kerkmann, *Politische Denunziation im NS-Regime, oder Die kleine Macht der "Volksgenossen"* (Bonn, 1995).

72. Burrin, *France under the Germans*, p. 245.

73. Ibid., p. 277.

74. Ibid., pp. 282–90.

75. Ibid., pp. 299–305.

76. Ibid., pp. 308–9.

77. Ibid., pp. 317–23. Burrin's section on Febvre was greeted with some resentment by French scholars. A slightly less damning version of the Febvre/Bloch affair can be found in C. Fink, *Marc Bloch: A Life in History* (Cambridge, 1989), pp. 261–63. The recent revelations regarding the complicity of *German* historians in the Third Reich—some of whom were the academic "grandfathers" of today's scholars—were debated in the Forty-second German Historians' Meeting in Frankfurt in September 1998. This was the first time that this forum came to grips with its own historical legacy. See, e.g., W. Behringer, "Schuldige Väter, milde Söhne, strenge Enkel: Der 42. Deutsche Historikertag in Frankfurt am Main stellt sich der Vegangenheit der Zukunft," *BeZ* (September 1998); "Die unfrohe Wissenschaft: Der 42. Deutsche Historikertag in Frankfurt fragte vor allem nach der Geschichte der eigenen Zunft," *SZ* (September 1998). For earlier media reports, see B. Mrozek, "Hitlers willige Wissenschaftler," *Die Weltwoche* (July 3, 1997), and articles in *Tagesspiegel* (June 17, 1997) and *FR* (July 1, 1997). For scholarship on this issue, see M. Burleigh, *Germany Turns Eastwards: A Study of "Ostforschung" in the Third Reich* (Cambridge, 1988), and his *Ethics and Extermination: Reflections on Nazi Genocide* (Cambridge, 1997), chapters 1–2; G. Aly and S. Heim, *Vordenker der Vernichtung:*

Auschwitz und die deutschen Pläne für eine neue europäische Ordnung (Hamburg, 1991).

78. Burrin, *France under the Germans,* pp. 324–51. See also D. Carroll, *French Literary Fascism: Nationalism, Anti-Semitism, and the Ideology of Culture* (Princeton, N.J., 1995); P. Assouline, *L'épuration des intellectuels* (Brussels, 1990); N. Oxenhandler, *Looking for Heroes in Postwar France: Albert Camus, Max Jacob, Simone Weil* (Hanover, N.H., 1996).

79. Burrin, *France under the Germans* p. 360.

80. Ibid., pp. 459, 463. See also P. Novick, *The Resistance versus Vichy: The Purge of Collaborators in Liberated France* (London, 1968).

81. *The Drowned and the Saved*, trans. R. Rosenthal (New York, 1988), pp. 70–71. Citations are from the translated version.

82. P. Levi, *Survival in Auschwitz* (New York, 1961), pp. 153–57, and his *The Reawakening* (New York, 1987), pp. 1–7.

83. *Fragments: Memories of a Wartime Childhood*, trans. C. B. Janeway (New York, 1996), pp. 148–49. Citations are from the translated verions. On the recent debate over the authenticity of Wilkomirski's memoir, see the conclusion to this book.

84. *The Liberation of France: Image and Event* (Oxford, 1995), p. 9.

85. On this and other French films on war and the Resistance, see S. Lindeperg, *Les écrans de l'ombre: La Seconde Guerre mondiale dans le cinéma français (1944–1969)* (Paris, 1997). And see M. O'Shaughnessy, *"La Bataille du rail:* Unconventional Form, Conventional Image?" in Kedward and Wood, *The Liberation of France,* pp. 15–27.

86. J. C. Simmonds, "Immigrant Fighters for the Liberation of France: A Local Profile of Carmagnole-Liberté in Lyon"; K. Adler, "No Words to Say It? Women and the Expectation of Liberation"; H. Diamond, "Women's Aspirations, 1943–47: An Oral Inquiry in Toulouse," in Kedward and Wood, *The Liberation of France,* pp. 29–41, 77–89, 91–101. On the issue of gender in interwar France, see M. L. Roberts, *Civilization without Sexes: Reconstructing Gender in Postwar France, 1917–1927* (Chicago, 1994); S. Reynolds, *France between the Wars: Gender and Politics* (London, 1996).

87. S. Kitson, "The Police in the Liberation of Paris," in Kedward and Wood, *The Liberation of France*, pp. 51–52.

88. J. Proud, "Plus ça change . . . ? Propaganda Fiction for Children, 1940–1945," in Kedward and Wood, *The Liberation of France,* pp. 57–74.

89. Diamond, "Women's Aspirations," in Kedward and Wood, *The Liberation of France,* p. 98.

90. M. Kelly, "The Reconstruction of Masculinity at the Liberation," in Kedward and Wood, *The Liberation of France*, pp. 117–128.

91. C. Laurens, "'La Femme au Turban': Les Femmes tondues," in Kedward and Wood, *The Liberation of France*, pp. 176–77. This chapter contains a brief history of shearings in France from as early as the fourteenth century (pp. 156–57) and a series of remarkable photographs of shearings after the Liberation (pp. 159–73). See also Burrin, *France under the Germans,* p. 205, for shearings of German women during the French occupation of the Rhineland in the 1920s.

92. M. Cornick, "From Resister to Knight of the Round Table: Jean Paulhan and the Liberation," in Kedward and Wood, *The Liberation of France,* pp. 183–96.

93. N. Atkin, "France's Little Nuremberg: The Trial of Otto Abetz," in Kedward and Wood, *The Liberation of France,* pp. 197–208.

94. N. Ingram, "Pacifism and the Liberation," in Kedward and Wood, *The Liberation of France*, pp. 209–23. On interwar pacifism, see N. Ingram, *The Politics of Dissent: Pacifism in France, 1919–1939* (Oxford, 1991).

95. *Les Tondues, Un carnaval moche* (Paris, 1992), pp. 62–63.

96. "Memory by Analogy: *Hiroshima, mon amour,*" in Kedward and Wood, *The Liberation of France,* p. 318.

97. Ibid., p. 316.

98. See also S. Willis, *Marguerite Duras: Writing on the Body* (Urbana, Ill., 1987), pp. 33–62.

99. The proceedings of this conference are now available as C. Coquio (ed.), *Parler des camps, penser les génocides* (Paris, 1999). The term *camps* can, of course, refer to anything ranging from extermination and concentration camps to prisoner of war (POW), displaced persons (DP), and refugee camps. All are typical of this century and related to each other, but the distinctions between them are just as crucial. For an interesting view of French POWs, see M. Thomas, "Captives of Their Countrymen: Free French and Vichy French POWs in Africa and the Middle East, 1940–3," in *Prisoners of War and Their Captors in World War II,* ed. B. Moore and K. Fedorowich (Oxford, 1996), pp. 87–118. On Jewish survivors of the Holocaust in DP camps in Germany and Austria and their subsequent attempts to rebuild their lives, see M. Brenner, *After the Holocaust: Building Jewish Lives in Postwar Germany* (Princeton, N.J., 1997); H. Embacher, *Neubeginn ohne Illusionen: Juden in Österreich nach 1945* (Vienna, 1995).

100. According to Wieviorka, *Déportation et génocide,* pp. 20–21, of 63,085 people deported from France to concentration camps as resisters, hostages, persons captured in raids, and political and criminal prisoners, 59 percent, or 37,025, returned. Conversely, of at least 75,721 Jews deported from France to death camps in the East, only 3 percent, or 2,500, returned. Seen differently, while Jews constituted 54 percent of those deported from France, 95 percent of the survivors were non-Jews.

101. *L'épreuve du désastre: Le XXe siècle et les camps* (Paris, 1996).

102. Ibid., pp. 20, 23.

103. "D'un 'détail' qui masque le tableau," *Le Monde* (January 21, 1998).

104. S. Courtois et al., *Le livre noir du communisme: Crimes, terreur, répression* (Paris, 1997), p. 19.

105. "'Valeur' des vies, 'valeur' des mots," *Le Monde* (January 27, 1998).

106. *Les Abus de la mémoire* (Paris, 1998).

107. "Je conspire, Hannah Arendt conspirait, Raymond Aron aussi . . . ," *Le Monde* (January 21, 1998). The original *Black Book* appeared in a definitive French edition as I. Ehrenbourg and V. Grossman, *Le Livre noir: Textes et témoignages* (Paris, 1995).

108. *La Concurrence des victimes* (Paris, 1997).

109. *Facing the Extreme: Moral Life in the Concentration Camps* (New York, 1996).

110. "Ukraina bez evreev," in S. Markish, *Vasilii Grossman: Na evreiskie temy* (Jerusalem, 1985), vol. 2, pp. 333–40. Cited in A. Weiner, "Nurture, Nature and Memory in a Socialist Utopia: Delineating the Soviet Socio-Ethnic Body in the Age of Socialism," *AHR* 104/4 (October 1999): 1150–51.

111. *The Passing of an Illusion: The Idea of Communism in the Twentieth Century* (Chicago, 1999. Orig. pub. in French in 1995). See also the response by I. Kershaw, "Nazisme et stalinisme: Limites d'une comparaison," *Le Débat* 89 (March–April

1996): 177–89. A proposal to return to the terminology of totalitarianism was also made by K. Pomian, "Totalitarisme," *Vingtième Siècle* 47 (July–September 1995): 4–23. For an analysis of Arendt's conceptualization of this term and its reception, see S. E. Aschheim, "Nazism, Culture and *The Origins of Totalitarianism:* Hannah Arendt and the Discourse of Evil," *New German Critique* 70 (winter 1997): 117–39. A comparison between systems and leaders can be found in A. Bullock, *Hitler and Stalin: Parallel Lives* (New York, 1992); I. Kershaw and M. Lewin (eds.), *Stalinism and Nazism: Dictatorships in Comparison* (Cambridge, 1997). See also H. Maier and M. Schäfer (eds.), *Totalitarismus und Politische Religionen: Konzepte des Diktaturvergleichs,* 2 vols. (Paderborn, 1996–97).

112. *L'État criminel: Les Génocides au XXe siècle* (Paris, 1995).

113. *Vichy: An Ever-Present Past,* trans. N. Bracher (Hanover, N.H., 1998). The authors open their book with the sentence: "Our nation's conscience is obsessed with memories of the Occupation." They see this as "a warning signal for the future of French identity and the strength of its universalist values." They end their introduction by stating that they "felt it was urgent to get away from the sanctification of the memory of World War II that we have been seeing recently: in our opinion, it is the biggest favor we could do for it." Ibid., pp. 1, 15 (Citations are from the English translation).

114. The best survey of this phenomenon is in P. Vidal-Naquet, *Assassins of Memory: Essays on the Denial of the Holocaust* (New York, 1992). See also D. Lipstadt, *Denying the Holocaust: The Growing Assault on Truth and Memory* (New York, 1993).

115. *Les Champs d'honneur* (Paris, 1990). Translated as *Fields of Glory* (New York, 1992).

116. *Le roi des Aulnes* (Paris, 1970). Translated as *The Ogre* (New York, 1972).

117. M. Halbwachs, *On Collective Memory* (Chicago, 1992), and his *The Collective Memory* (New York, 1950); M. Bloch, *The Historian's Craft* (New York, 1953). On Halbwachs's death in Buchenwald, see J. Semprun, *Literature or Life* (New York, 1997), pp. 16–24. On Bloch and fraud, see C. Fink's introduction to his *Memoirs of War, 1914–15,* 2nd ed. (Cambridge, 1988), pp. 64–67.

118. Letter to P. Souday, reproduced in M. Proust, *A la recherche du temps perdu* (Paris, 1954), vol. 1, p. xxiii. German and Austrian novels that come to mind in this context include T. Mann's *The Magic Mountain,* begun before the Great War but published in 1924, and R. Musil's *The Man Without Qualities,* written during the entire interwar period (vol. 1 published in 1930, vol. 2 in 1932, vol. 3 only after Musil's death in 1942). Both works are about pre-1914 Europe from the perspective of its aftermath.

119. Cited in L. A. Coser's introduction to Halbwachs, *Collective Memory,* p. 22.

120. Ibid., p. 34. Coser also cites B. Schwartz's statement that "the collective memory comes into view as both a cumulative and an episodic construction of the past." Ibid., p. 30.

121. On the most obvious case, see A. Grossmann, "A Question of Silence: The Rape of German Women by Occupation Soldiers," *October* 72 (spring 1995): 43–63.

122. O. Bartov, "War, Memory, and Repression: Alexander Kluge and the Politics of Representation in Postwar Germany," in Bartov, *Murder in Our Midst: The Holocaust, Industrial Killing, and Representation* (New York, 1996), chapter 7, and Bartov, "'Seit die Juden weg sind . . . ': Germany, History, and Representations of

Absence," in *A User's Guide to German Cultural Studies*, ed. S. Denham et al. (Ann Arbor, Mich., 1997), pp. 209–26.

123. Compare, e.g., S. Fishman, "The Power of Myth: Five Recent Works on Vichy France," *JMH* 67 (1995): 666–73, with the introduction by A. Prost to the volume *14–18: Mourir pour la patrie* (Paris, 1992), p. 8: "What has changed is not so much reality, but the discourse of legitimation. The heroic bombast, the moralizing tone sound false now, and we have little patience with collective ceremonies. This does not mean that our national identity is less solid, nor that the French are less capable of defending it if need be. Let us not regret that we have not had the opportunity to do so: The trouble with patriotism, just as with courage, is that its depth is revealed only at time of war."

124. On the normalization of the memory of the war and the attempt to associate the victims of the bombing with those of the Holocaust by way of official commemoration, see K. Naumann, "Dresdener Pietà: Eine Fallstudie zum 'Gedenkjahr 1995,'" *Mittelweg 36* 4 (1995): 67–81. On the penetration of Nazi terminology into the language of both left and right wing activists, see U. Linke, "Murderous Fantasies: Violence, Memory, and Selfhood in Germany," *NGC* 64 (winter 1995): 37–59.

125. *The First Man* (New York, 1995), trans. D. Hapgood. Orig. pub. as *Le premier homme* (Paris, 1994). Citations are from the English translation.

126. Ibid., p. 80.

127. Ibid., 147–49.

128. *W or The Memory of Childhood* (Boston, 1988), trans. D. Belles. Orig. pub. as *W, ou le souvenir d'enfance* (Paris, 1975). Citations are from the English translation.

129. Ibid., p. 6.

130. Ibid., p. 42.

131. Ibid., p. 6.

132. For a recent example, see D. Lorch, "Frantic, Bittersweet Reunion for Rwandan Exile Children," *NYT* (September 18, 1995): A1, A3.

133. See, e.g., R. Evans, *In Hitler's Shadow: West German Historians and the Attempt to Escape from the Nazi Past* (New York, 1989); C. S. Maier, *The Unmasterable Past: History, Holocaust, and German Nationalism* (Cambridge, Mass., 1988); J. E. Young, *The Texture of Memory: Holocaust Memorials and Meaning* (New Haven, Conn., 1993); T. Des Pres, *The Survivor: An Anatomy of Life in the Death Camps* (New York, 1976); G. H. Hartman (ed.), *Holocaust Remembrance: The Shapes of Memory* (Oxford, 1994).

134. S. Paskuly (ed.), *Death Dealer* (New York, 1996), which contains the memoirs of Höss, commander of Auschwitz, written on the eve of his execution in 1947. G. Sereny, *Into That Darkness: An Examination of Conscience* (New York, 1983), where she records her conversations with Stangl, former commander of Treblinka.

135. H. Gouri, *The Glass Cage: The Jerusalem Trial* (Tel Aviv, 1962 [in Hebrew]). See also J. von Lang and C. Sibyll (eds.), *Eichmann Interrogated: Transcripts from the Archives of the Israeli Police* (New York, 1984).

136. See, e.g., I. Buruma, *The Wages of Guilt: Memories of War in Germany and Japan* (New York, 1994); G. J. Horwitz, *In the Shadow of Death: Living outside the Gates of Mauthausen* (New York, 1990); L. Langer, *Holocaust Testimonies: The Ruins of Memory* (New Haven, Conn., 1991); T. Segev, *The Seventh Million: The Israelis and the Holocaust* (New York, 1993).

137. For a variety of views on trauma and memory, see C. Caruth (ed.), *Trauma: Explorations in Memory* (Baltimore, Md., 1995).

138. *What's to Become of the Boy? Or Something to Do with Books* (New York, 1985). Orig. pub. as *Was soll aus dem Jungen bloss werden? Oder, Irgendwas mit Büchern* (Bornheim, 1981).

139. *The Train Was on Time* (London, 1973). Translation of *Der Zug war pünktlich* (Munich, 1972), orig. pub. in 1949. *A Soldier's Legacy* (New York, 1985). Translation of *Das Vermächtnis* (Bornheim, 1982), orig. pub. in 1947.

140. Back cover of *Der Zug war pünktlich*.

141. See more on this in O. Bartov, "The Conduct of War: Soldiers and the Barbarization of Warfare," in *Resistance against the Third Reich: 1933–1990,* ed. M. Geyer and J. W. Boyer (Chicago, 1994), pp. 39–52. See also H. Peitsch, "Toward a History of *Vergangenheitsbewältigung:* East and West German War Novels of the 1950s," *Monatshefte* 87/3 (fall 1995): 287–308; Peitsch, "Von Böll bis Buchheim: Deutsche Kriegsprosa nach 1945," *ABG* 42 (1997): 63–90; Peitsch, "Discovering a Taboo: The Nazi Past in Literary-Political Discourse, 1958–67," in *Taboos in German Literature,* ed. D. Jackson (Providence, R.I., 1996).

142. *Innenseiten des Krieges* (Frankfurt am Main, 1985).

143. On this issue see further in O. Bartov, *The Eastern Front, 1941–45: German Troops and the Barbarisation of Warfare* (London, 1985), chapter 2.

144. *When Memory Comes,* 2nd ed., trans. H. R. Lane (New York, 1991), pp. 70–78. Orig. pub. as *Quand vient le souvenir . . .* (Paris, 1978). Citations are from the English translation.

145. Ibid., pp. 87–88.

146. S. Breznitz, *Sedot ha-zikaron* (Tel Aviv, 1993), pp. 35–36. The book also appeared in English as *Memory fields* (New York, 1993). Citations are from the Hebrew edition.

147. *When Memory Comes,* pp. 137–38

148. *The Imaginary Jew* (Lincoln, Neb., 1994). Translation of *Le Juif imaginaire* (Paris, 1980).

149. *Sedot ha-zikaron,* p. 11.

150. *When Memory Comes,* p. 3.

151. *Sedot ha-zikaron,* p. 11.

152. *When Memory Comes,* pp. 134–35.

153. In a private communication with my father.

154. *Wartime Lies* (New York, 1991).

Chapter 3

1. For some works on nationalism, see B. Anderson, *Imagined Communities: Reflections on the Origin and Spread of Nationalism,* rev. ed. (London, 1991); R. Brubaker, *Citizenship and Nationhood in France and Germany* (Cambridge, Mass., 1992); L. Greenfeld, *Nationalism: Five Roads to Modernity* (Cambridge, Mass., 1992); E. J. Hobsbawm, *Nations and Nationalism since 1780: Programme, Myth, Reality,* 2nd ed. (Cambridge, 1992).

2. P. Sahlins, *Boundaries: The Making of France and Spain in the Pyrenees* (Berkeley, Calif., 1989); V. Caron, *Between France and Germany: The Jews of Alsace-Lorraine, 1871–1918* (Stanford, Calif., 1988); M. Burleigh, *Germany Turns Eastwards: A Study of "Ostforschung" in the Third Reich* (Cambridge, 1988); E. Weber, *Peasants into Frenchmen: The Modernization of Rural France, 1870–1914* (Stanford, 1976); H. Lebovics, *True France: The Wars over Cultural Identity, 1900–1945* (Ithaca, N.Y.,

1992); C. Applegate, *A Nation of Provincials: The German Idea of Heimat* (Berkeley, Calif., 1990); A. Confino, *The Nation as a Local Metaphor: Württemberg, Imperial Germany, and National Memory, 1871–1918* (Chapel Hill, N.C., 1997).

3. On the origins of German anti-Gypsyism, its impact on Nazi genocidal policies, and its post-1945 perpetuation, see S. Tebbutt (ed.), *Sinti and Roma: Gypsies in German-Speaking Society and Literature* (New York, 1998); M. Zimmermann, *Rassenutopie und Genozid: Die nationalsozialistische "Lösung der Zigeunerfrage"* (Hamburg, 1996); G. Margalit, "Die deutsche Zigeunerpolitik nach 1945" *VfZ* 45/4 (1997): 557–88; and his *Postwar Germany and the Gypsies: The Treatment of Sinte and Roma in the Aftermath of the Third Reich* (Jerusalem, 1998 [in Hebrew]); *Revue d'Histoire de la Shoah: Le monde juif* (September–December 1999): 8–52, "Le Tsiganes dans l'Europe allemande."

4. For documentation on early French discussions about Jewish citizenship, see L. Hunt (ed.), *The French Revolution and Human Rights: A Brief Documentary History* (Boston, 1996); S. Glotzer, "Napoleon, the Jews and the Construction of Modern Citizenship in Early Nineteenth Century France" (Rutgers University, Ph.D. dissertation, 1997). Further in A. Hertzberg, *The French Enlightenment and the Jews: The Origins of Modern Anti-Semitism* (New York, 1968); J.-D. Bredin, *The Affair: The Case of Alfred Dreyfus* (New York, 1986). For Germany, see, e.g., G. L. Mosse, *The Nationalization of the Masses: Political Symbolism and Mass Movements in Germany from the Napoleonic Wars through the Third Reich*, 2nd ed. (Ithaca, N.Y., 1991); D. Sorkin, *The Transformation of German Jewry, 1780–1840* (New York, 1987); J. Reinharz and W. Schatzberg (eds.), *The Jewish Response to German Culture: From the Enlightenment to the Second World War* (Hanover, N.H., 1985). On coming out of the ghetto and confronting European civilization, see J. Katz, *Out of the Ghetto: The Social Background of the Emancipation of the Jews, 1770–1870* (New York, 1978); G. L. Mosse, *Confronting the Nation: Jewish and Western Nationalism* (Hanover, N.H., 1993); G. Scholem, *On Jews and Judaism in Crisis: Selected Essays*, ed. W. J. Dannhauser (New York, 1976). On Jews and antisemitism in Eastern Europe, see D. D. Moore (ed.), *East European Jews in Two Worlds: Studies from the YIVO Annual* (Evanston, Ill., 1990); E. Mendelsohn, *The Jews of East Central Europe between the World Wars* (Bloomington, Ind., 1983); M. Opalski and I. Bartal, *Poles and Jews: A Failed Brotherhood* (Hanover, N.H., 1992); I. Gutman et al. (eds.), *The Jews of Poland between Two World Wars* (Hanover, N.H., 1989); M. C. Steinlauf, *Bondage to the Dead: Poland and the Memory of the Holocaust* (Syracuse, N.Y., 1997). See also W. W. Hagen, "Before the 'Final Solution': Toward a Comparative Analysis of Political Anti-Semitism in Interwar Germany and Poland," *JMH* 68 (June 1996), and sources cited therein.

5. See, e.g., M. Adas, *Machines as the Measure of Men: Science, Technology, and Ideologies of Western Dominance* (Ithaca, N.Y., 1989); M. Eksteins, *Rites of Spring: The Great War and the Birth of the Modern Age* (New York, 1989); S. Kern, *The Culture of Time and Space, 1880–1918* (Cambridge, Mass., 1983); D. Pick, *War Machine: The Rationalisation of Slaughter in the Modern Age* (New Haven, Conn., 1993), and his *Faces of Degeneration: A European Disorder, c. 1848–c. 1918* (Cambridge, 1989); A. Rabinbach, *The Human Motor: Energy, Fatigue, and the Origins of Modernity* (Berkeley, Calif., 1992). A key and pioneering text for understanding the relationship between antisemitism, imperialism, and totalitarianism is still H. Arendt's *The Origins of Totalitarianism* (New York, 1951).

6. F. Fischer, *Germany's War Aims in the First World War* (London, 1967); H.-U. Wehler, *The German Empire, 1871–1918* (Leamington Spa, 1985), chapter 8; V. R.

Berghahn, *Germany and the Approach of War in 1914,* 2nd ed. (New York, 1993); J.-J. Becker, *1914: Comment les Français sont entrés dans la guerre* (Paris, 1977), part IV; E. J. Weber, *The Nationalist Revival in France, 1905–1914* (Berkeley, Calif., 1959).

7. See, e.g., F. Coetzee and M. Shevin-Coetzee (eds.), *Authority, Identity, and the Social History of the Great War* (Providence, 1995); P. Fussell, *The Great War and Modern Memory* (New York, 1975); G. Hirschfeld et al. (eds.), *Keiner fühlt sich hier mehr als mensch . . . : Erlebnis und Wirkung des Ersten Weltkriegs* (Essen, 1993).

8. On instances of frustration, rage, mutiny, and violence during and after the war, see, e.g., G. Dallas and D. Gill, *The Unknown Army: Mutinies in the British Army in World War I* (London, 1985); A. Prost, *In the Wake of War: "Les Anciens Combattants" and French Society, 1914–1939* (Providence, R.I., 1992); D. E. Showalter, *Little Man, What Now? Der Stürmer in the Weimar Republic* (Hamden, Conn., 1982); K. Theweleit, *Männerphantasien,* 2 vols., 2nd ed. (Reinbeck bei Hamburg, 1987); R. W. Whalen, *Bitter Wounds: German Victims of the Great War, 1914–1939* (Ithaca, N.Y., 1984). Further on the veterans and the *Freikorps* of 1920s Germany in J. M. Diehl, *Paramilitary Politics in Weimar Germany* (Bloomington, Ind., 1977); R. G. L. Waite, *Vanguard of Nazism: The Free Corps Movement in Postwar Germany, 1918–1923,* 2nd ed. (Cambridge, Mass., 1970); V. R. Berghahn, *Der Stahlhelm, Bund der Frontsoldaten, 1918–1935* (Düsseldorf, 1966).

9. On the "Jew count," the Jewish veterans association Reichsbund jüdischer Frontsoldaten (RjF), and the struggle against antisemitism during and after World War I in Germany, see especially E. Zechlin, *Die Deutsche Politik und die Juden im Ersten Weltkrieg* (Göttingen, 1969); R. Pierson, "Embattled Veterans: The *Reichsbund jüdischer Frontsoldaten,*" *LBIY* 19 (London, 1974); W. T. Angress, "Das deutsche Militär und die Juden im Ersten Weltkrieg," *MGM* 1 (1976): 77–146; U. Dunker, *Der Reichsbund jüdischer Frontsoldaten, 1919–1938: Geschichte eines jüdischen Abwehrvereins* (Düsseldorf, 1977); M. Brenner, *The Renaissance of Jewish Culture in Weimar Germany* (New Haven, Conn., 1996), pp. 31–35. For contemporary texts, see L. Geiger, *Die Deutsche Juden und der Krieg* (Berlin, 1915); J. Segall, *Die Deutsche Juden als Soldaten im Kriege, 1914–1918* (Berlin, 1922); Reichsbund jüdischer Frontsoldaten, *Die Jüdischen Gefallenen des Deutschen Heeres, der Deutschen Marine, und der Deutschen Schutztruppen, 1914–1918* (Berlin, 1932); Reichsbund jüdischer Frontsoldaten, *Kriegsbriefe Gefallener Deutscher Juden* (Stuttgart, 1961 [orig. pub. in 1935]). For a discussion of this issue, using sources from the publication of the RjF, *Der Schild,* see B. Crim, "War alles nur ein Traum? German Jewish Veterans and the Confrontation with völkisch Nationalism in the Interwar Period" (unpublished paper, 1998). On antisemitism in the officer corps, see, e.g., the private letter written by Colonel-General von Fritsch in 1939, that is, *after* he was dismissed by Hitler as commander in chief of the army on the fabricated accusation of homosexual relations, in which he states that soon after the Great War he had concluded that for Germany to be powerful again, it would have to win the battle against the Jews. Cited in J. Wheeler-Bennett, *The Nemesis of Power,* 2nd ed. (London, 1980), p. 380. Ludwig Beck, who was later the architect of Hitler's army as its chief of staff, only to become a major figure in the resistance after 1938, wrote in a private letter on November 28, 1918, as a young staff officer: "At the most difficult moment in the war we were attacked in the back by the revolution, which I now do not doubt for an instant had been prepared long before." Cited in K.-J. Müller, *General Ludwig Beck* (Boppard am Rhein, 1980), p. 323. See further in W. Deist, *Militär, Staat, und Gesellschaft* (Munich, 1991), pp. 83–233. For a re-

markable account by a Jewish officer in the Austro-Hungarian army that illustrates the extent of antisemitism in its ranks, see Avigdor Hameiri, *The Great Madness* (New York, 1952 [orig. pub. in Hebrew in 1929]).

10. On popular pre-1914 nationalism and antisemitism see, e.g., M. S. Coetzee, *The German Army League: Popular Nationalism in Wilhelmine Germany* (New York, 1990); G. Eley, *Reshaping the German Right: Radical Nationalism and Political Change after Bismarck,* 2nd ed. (Ann Arbor, Mich., 1991); W. Angress, "Prussia's Army and the Jewish Reserve Officer Controversy before World War I," in *Imperial Germany,* ed. J. J. Sheehan (New York, 1978); S. Volkov, *The Rise of Popular Antimodernism in Germany: The Urban Master Artisans, 1873–1896* (Princeton, N.J., 1978). Further on Jewish wartime reactions in D. J. Engel, *Organized Jewish Responses to German Antisemitism during the First World War* (Ph.D. dissertation, University of California at Los Angeles, 1979). Further on the war's aftermath in R. Bessel, *Germany after the First World War* (Oxford, 1993), and his "The 'Front Generation' and the Politics of Weimar Germany," in *Generations in Conflict: Youth Revolt and Generation Formation in Germany, 1770–1968,* ed. M. Roseman (New York, 1995). See also suggestive essays in W. J. Mommsen, *Imperial Germany, 1867–1918: Politics, Culture, and Society in an Authoritarian State* (London, 1995); G. Eley, *From Unification to Nazism: Reinterpreting the German Past* (London, 1986).

11. On the growth of an antisemitic ideology among the young academic elites of the period, see U. Herbert, *Best: Biographische Studien über Radikalismus, Weltanschauung und Venunft, 1903–1989* (Bonn, 1996), part I, and the literature cited therein; see also his 1996 unpublished paper, "Den Gegner vernichten, ohne ihn zu hassen: Loathing the Jews in the World View of the Intellectual Leadership of the SS in the 1920s and 1930s." Further in S. M. Bolkosky, *The Distorted Image: German Jewish Perceptions of Germans and Germany, 1918–1935* (New York, 1975); D. L. Niewyk, *The Jews in Weimar Germany* (Baton Rouge, La., 1980); G. Iggers, "Academic Anti-Semitism in Germany, 1870–1933—A Comparative Perspective," *TAJB* 27 (1998): 473–89. For the most recent study of antisemitism in the Weimar Republic, see D. Walter, *Antisemitische Kriminalität und Gewalt: Judenfeindschaft in der Weimarer Rupublik* (Bonn, 1999). On Weimar culture and the role of the Jews in it, see W. Laqueur, *Weimar: A Cultural History, 1918–1933* (New York, 1974), and P. Gay, *Weimar Culture: The Outsider as Insider* (New York, 1968). A recent work on Jewish emigration in Weimar and the Third Reich is Doron Niederland, *German Jews: Emigrants or Refugees? Patterns between the Two World Wars* (Jerusalem, 1996 [in Hebrew]); Niederland, "Leaving Germany—Emigration Patterns of Jews and Non-Jews during the Weimar Period," *TAJB* 27 (1998): 169–94. See also the works cited above, especially Brenner, *Renaissance of Jewish Culture;* Mosse, *Confronting the Nation;* Reinharz and Schatzberg, *Jewish Response;* and Scholem, *Jews and Judaism.* For interpretations of Weimar as the site of a crisis of modernity or of a new type of reactionary modernism, see D. J. K. Peukert, *The Weimar Republic: The Crisis of Classical Modernity* (New York, 1992); J. Herf, *Reactionary Modernism: Technology, Culture, and Politics in Weimar and the Third Reich,* 2nd ed. (Cambridge, 1984). Further in M. Brio, "The New Man as Cyborg: Figures of Technology in Weimar Visual Culture," *NGC* 62/2 (1994): 71–110; M. Nolan, *Visions of Modernity: American Business and the Modernization of Germany* (New York, 1994).

12. See further suggestive comments in M. Hughes, *Nationalism and Society: Germany, 1800–1945* (London, 1988); W. D. Smith, *The Ideological Origins of Nazi*

Imperialism (New York, 1986); and S. E. Aschheim, *Culture and Catastrophe: German and Jewish Confrontations with National Socialism and Other Crises* (New York, 1996).

13. G. Pedroncini, *Les mutineries de 1917* (Paris, 1967); S. Audoin-Rouzeau, *Men at War, 1914–1918: National Sentiment and Trench Journalism in France during the First World War* (Providence, R.I., 1992); L. V. Smith, *Between Mutiny and Obedience: The Case of the French Fifth Infantry Division during World War I* (Princeton, N.J., 1994); J. Snyder, *The Ideology of the Offensive: Military Decision Making and the Disasters of 1914* (Ithaca, N.Y., 1984).

14. J.-J. Becker, *The Great War and the French People* (Leamington Spa, 1985).

15. For the domestic crisis in interwar France and French attitudes toward war, see, e.g., E. Weber, *The Hollow Years: France in the 1930s* (New York, 1994); S. Berstein, *La France des années 30* (Paris, 1988); J.-L. Loubet del Bayle, *Les nonconformistes des années 30: Une tentative de renouvellement de la pensée politique française* (Paris, 1969); P. Andreu, *Révoltes de l'esprit: Les revues des années 30* (Paris, 1991); J.-F. Sirinelli, *Génération intelectuelle: Khâgneux et Normaliens dans l'entre-deux-guerres* (Paris, 1994).

16. P. Burrin, *La dérive fasciste: Doriot, Déat, Bergery, 1933–1945* (Paris, 1986); Z. Sternhell, *Neither Right nor Left: Fascist Ideology in France,* 2nd ed. (Princeton, N.J., 1996); P.-M. Dioudonnat, *Je suis partout, 1930–1944: Les maurassiens devant la tentation fasciste* (Paris, 1973); R. Soucy, *French Fascism: The First Wave, 1924–1933* (New Haven, Conn., 1986), and his *French Fascism: The Second Wave, 1933–1939* (New Haven, Conn., 1995).

17. N. Ingram, *The Politics of Dissent: Pacifism in France, 1919–1939* (Oxford, 1991); C. Jelen, *Hitler ou Staline: Le prix de la paix* (Paris, 1988).

18. C. Prochasson, *Les Intellectuels, le socialisme et la guerre, 1900–1938* (Paris, 1993); J. Jackson, *The Popular Front: Defending Democracy, 1934–38* (Cambridge, 1988); M. Chavardès, *Le 6 février 1934: La République en danger* (Paris, 1966).

19. V. Caron, "The Antisemitic Revival in France in the 1930s: The Socioeconomic Dimension Reconsidered," *JMH* 70/1 (March 1998): 24–73; R. Schor, *L'Antisémitisme en France pendant les années trente: Prélude à Vichy* (Brussels, 1992); M. Winock, *Nationalisme, antisémitisme et fascisme en France* (Paris, 1982, 1990); P. Birnbaum, *Un mythe politique: la "république juive." De Léon Blum à Pierre Mendès France* (Paris, 1995).

20. P. Burrin, *France under the Germans: Collaboration and Compromise* (New York, 1996); H. R. Kedward, *In Search of the Maquis: Rural Resistance in Southern France, 1942–1944* (Oxford, 1993).

21. An interesting comparison can be made here between Marc Bloch and Victor Klemperer, whose respective accounts of the period reflect both the similarities in their patriotism and the radical distinctions between their condition. See V. Klemperer, *I Will Bear Witness: A Diary of the Nazi Years, 1933–1945,* 2 vols.(New York, 1998, 2000); M. Bloch, *Strange Defeat: A Statement of Evidence Written in 1940* (New York, 1968).

22. On France just before and during the debacle, see, e.g., R. Rémond and J. Bourdin (eds.), *La France et les Français: 1938 en 1939* (Paris, 1978); P. Richer, *La drôle de guerre des Français, 2 septembre 1939–10 mai 1940* (Paris, 1990); J.-L Crémieux-Brilhac, *Les Français de l'an 40,* 2 vols. (Paris 1990); J.-P. Azéma, *1940 l'année terrible* (Paris, 1990); J. Blatt (ed.), *The French Defeat of 1940: Reassessments* (Providence, R.I., 1998).

23. On the liberation and the purges, see H. R. Kedward and N. Wood (eds.), *The Liberation of France: Image and Event* (Oxford, 1995); P. Novick, *The Resistance versus Vichy: The Purge of Collaborators in Liberated France* (London, 1968). On the memory of Vichy and the genocide of the Jews, see H. Rousso, *The Vichy Syndrome: History and Memory in France since 1944* (Cambridge, Mass., 1991); E. Conan and H. Rousso, *Vichy: An Ever-Present Past* (Hanover, N.H., 1998); A. Wieviorka, *Déportation et génocide: Entre la mémoire et l'oubli* (Paris, 1992). On decolonization and national identity, see A. Clayton, *The Wars of French Decolonization* (London, 1994); J.-P. Rioux (ed.), *La Guerre d'Algerie et les Français* (Paris, 1990); J.-F. Sirinelli, *Intellectuels et passion françaises: Manifestes et pétitions au XXᵉ Siècle* (Paris, 1990). On the politics of victimhood, see A. Brossat, *L'épreuve du désastre: Le XXᵉ siècle et les camps* (Paris, 1996); T. Todorov, *Les abus de la mémoire* (Paris, 1998); J.-M. Chaumont, *La concurrence de victimes: Génocide, identité, reconnaissance* (Paris, 1997).

24. For conflicting views on this issue, see I. Kershaw, *Popular Opinion and Political Dissent in the Third Reich: Bavaria, 1933–1945* (Oxford, 1983); D. Bankier, *The Germans and the Final Solution: Public Opinion under Nazism* (Oxford, 1992).

25. On the manner in which this was reflected in German attitudes toward foreign enemies, see J. Förster, "The German Army and the Ideological War against the Soviet Union," in *The Policies of Genocide: Jews and Soviet Prisoners of War in Nazi Germany*, ed. G. Hirschfeld (London, 1986); O. Bartov, *Hitler's Army: Soldiers, Nazis, and War in the Third Reich* (New York, 1991).

26. For an account of the origins of antisemitic thinking within German liberalism and its links to the politics of gender, see D. Herzog, *Intimacy and Exclusion: Religious Politics in Pre-Revolutionary Baden* (Princeton, N.J., 1996).

27. See esp. R. Rürup, *Emanzipation und Antisemitismus* (Göttingen, 1975); J. Katz, *From Prejudice to Destruction: Anti-Semitism, 1700–1933* (Cambridge, Mass., 1980); P. Pulzer, *The Rise of Political Anti-Semitism in Germany and Austria*, rev. ed. (Cambridge, Mass., 1988); S. Volkov, *Jüdisches Leben und Antisemitismus im 19. und 20. Jahrhundert* (Munich, 1990). See also N. Cohn, *Warrant for Genocide: The Myth of the Jewish World-Conspiracy and the Protocols of the Elders of Zion* (Harmondsworth, U.K., 1970); B. W. Segel, *A Lie and a Libel: The History of the "Protocols of the Elders of Zion,"* ed. Richard S. Levy (Lincoln, Neb., 1995).

28. See esp. R. N. Proctor, *Racial Hygiene: Medicine under the Nazis* (Cambridge, Mass., 1988); P. Weindling, *Health, Race and German Politics between National Unification and Nazism, 1870–1945* (Cambridge, 1989); M. Burleigh, *Death and Deliverance: "Euthanasia" in Germany, 1900–1945* (Cambridge, 1994); H. Friedlander, *The Origins of Nazi Genocide: From Euthanasia to the Final Solution* (Chapel Hill, N.C., 1995). See also G. L. Mosse, *The Image of Man: The Creation of Modern Masculinity* (New York, 1996).

29. See the important article by P. Holquist, "'Information is the Alpha and Omega of Our Work': Bolshevik Surveillance in Its Pan-European Context," *JMH* 69 (September 1997): 415–50, and the literature cited therein. See also M. B. Miller, *Shanghai on the Métro: Spies, Intrigue, and the French between the Wars* (Berkeley, Calif., 1994). Some of Alfred Hitchcock's 1930s films reflected (and at the time also enhanced) the period's obsession with espionage, intrigue, and conspiracy. See, e.g., *The Man Who Knew Too Much* (1934), *The Secret Agent* (1936), *Sabotage* (1936; title in the United States: *The Woman Alone*), *The Lady Vanishes* (1938). For a discussion of French interwar apocalyptic films and novels, see also Burrin, *France under the Germans,* pp. 43–46; and for views about foreigners and fear of war, see Weber, *The*

Hollow Years, pp. 87–110, 237–56, respectively. I refer here, of course, to Robert Louis Stevenson's *Strange Case of Dr. Jekyll and Mr. Hyde* (1886) and Franz Kafka's *Die Verwandlung* (1916), translated as *Metamorphosis.*

30. Otto Weininger, *Geschlecht und Charakter* (Vienna, 1903), translated as *Sex and Character* (New York, 1908, 1975). Another twist in this history is the play by Yehoshua Sobol, *Otto Weininger's Last Night* (Tel Aviv, 1982 [in Hebrew]), whose 1982 performance in Israel, under the name *Nefesh yehudi* (*The Soul of a Jew*), created a stir on the intellectual scene. On Jewish, and especially Zionist, preoccupation with degeneration around the turn of the century, see, e.g., J. M. Effron, *Defenders of the Race: Jewish Doctors and Race Science in Fin-de-Siècle Europe* (New Haven, Conn., 1994); D. Bechtel et al. (eds.), *Max Nordau, 1849–1923: Critique de la dégénérescence, médiateur franco-allemand, père fondateur du sionisme* (Paris, 1996); S. Gilman, *Jewish Self-Hatred: Anti-Semitism and the Hidden Language of the Jews* (Baltimore, Md., 1986).

31. Apart from the literature cited above, see also U. Tal, *Christians and Jews in Germany: Religion, Politics, and Ideology in the Second Reich, 1870–1914* (Ithaca, N.Y., 1975); G. L. Mosse, *Germans and Jews: The Right, the Left, and the Search for a "Third Force" in Pre-Nazi Germany* (New York, 1970); J. Kornberg, *Theodor Herzl: From Assimilation to Zionism* (Bloomington, Ind., 1993); P. Mendes-Flohr and J. Reinharz (eds.), *The Jew in the Modern World: A Documentary History,* 2nd ed. (New York 1995); P. Birnbaum and I. Katznelson (eds.), *Paths of Assimilation: Jews, States, and Citizenship* (Princeton, N.J., 1995); B. F. Pauley, *From Prejudice to Persecution: A History of Austrian Anti-Semitism* (Chapel Hill, N.C., 1992); S. Beller, *Vienna and the Jews, 1867–1938: A Cultural History* (Cambridge, 1989).

32. For an excellent discussion of the importance of the myth of the *Volksgemeinschaft* in prewar Nazi Germany, which revises the previous tendency to dismiss it altogether, see G. Diewald-Kerkmann, *Politische Denunziation im NS-Regime, oder Die kleine Macht der "Volksgenossen"* (Bonn, 1995), pp. 33–50. The most extreme position on the role of antisemitism was recently taken by D. J. Goldhagen, *Hitler's Willing Executioners: Ordinary Germans and the Holocaust* (New York, 1996); my own criticism of it, arguing that antisemitism is insufficient in explaining the Holocaust, can be found in O. Bartov, "Ordinary Monsters," *TNR* (April 29, 1996): 32–38. Another argument for the importance of antisemitism in Germany and Austria is presented in J. Weiss, *Ideology of Death: Why the Holocaust Happened in Germany* (Chicago, 1996). A more subtle interpretation, which highlights what the author calls "redemptive antisemitism," can be found in S. Friedländer, *Nazi Germany and the Jews,* vol. 1: *The Years of Persecution, 1933–1939* (New York, 1997). The previous position, which asserted the relative unpopularity of antisemitism within the German population, is well argued in S. Gordon, *Hitler, Germans, and the "Jewish Question"* (Princeton, N.J., 1984); it is criticized in turn by R. Gellately, *The Gestapo and German Society: Enforcing Racial Policy, 1933–1945* (Oxford, 1990). The classic argument for the evolution of Nazi anti-Jewish policies with antisemitism largely left out is in K. A. Schleunes, *The Twisted Road to Auschwitz: Nazi Policy toward German Jews, 1933–1939,* 2nd ed. (Urbana, Ill., 1990). The most important arguments for the resistance of the working class to Nazi ideology are to be found in T. W. Mason, *Social Policy in the Third Reich: The Working Class and the "National Community",* ed. Jane Caplan (Providence, R.I., 1993), orig. pub. as *Sozialpolitik im Dritten Reich: Arbeiterklasse und Volksgemeinschaft* (Opladen, 1975).

33. Hitler's speech on January 30, 1939, cited in J. Noakes and G. Pridham (eds.), *Nazism, 1919–1945: A Documentary Reader,* vol. 3: *Foreign Policy, War and Racial Extermination* (Exeter, 1988), p. 1049. The most recent biography of Hitler is I. Kershaw, *Hitler, 1889–1936: Hubris* (New York, 1999), but it covers only his early years as Führer of Germany. For his "making," see B. Hamann, *Hitler's Vienna: A Dictator's Apprenticeship* (New York, 1999); for attempts to explain him, see R. Rosenbaum, *Explaining Hitler: The Search for the Origins of His Evil* (New York, 1998). On references to the Jews in his political testament, see A. Bullock, *Hitler: A Study in Tyranny,* rev. ed. (New York, 1962), p. 794; J. C. Fest, *Hitler,* 2nd ed. (New York, 1982), p. 746; G. Fleming, *Hitler and the Final Solution* (Berkeley, Calif., 1984), pp. 186–89, and reproduction of the original document between pages 92–93. On his foreign policy "program," see Noakes and Pridham, *Nazism,* pp. 609–23; E. Jäckel, *Hitler's World View: A Blueprint for Power* (Cambridge, Mass., 1981). A recent interpretation gives this speech special prominence as Hitler's commitment to annihilate the Jews in case of a *world* war (*Weltkrieg*). Thus, it is argued, Hitler ordered the "Final Solution" only after the Soviet counteroffensive and the German declaration of war on the United States, both in December 1941, which transformed the war into a prolonged universal confrontation. Hitler's (still elusive) order therefore came just in time to change the original agenda of the postponed Wannsee Conference, ostensibly intended to discuss only the status of the *Mischlinge* (half-breeds). See C. Gerlach, "The Wannsee Conference, the Fate of German Jews, and Hitler's Decision in Principle to Exterminate All European Jews," *JMH* 70/4 (December 1998): 759–812.

34. O. Bartov, *The Eastern Front, 1941–1945: German Troops and the Barbarisation of Warfare* (London, 1985); Bartov, *Hitler's Army.* See also I. Kershaw, *The "Hitler Myth": Image and Reality in the Third Reich* (Oxford, 1987); M. Steinert, *Hitler's War and the Germans: Public Mood and Attitude during the Second World War* (Athens, Ohio, 1977). For more on soldiers' attitudes, see S. G. Fritz, *Frontsoldaten: The German Soldier in World War II* (Lexington, Ky., 1995); T. Schulte, *The German Army and Nazi Policies in Occupied Russia* (Oxford, 1989).

35. Cited in Bartov, *Hitler's Army,* 129–30.

36. Both citations in Noakes and Pridham, *Nazism,* pp. 1199–200. I have used the editors' translation of the original German text. Further examples in E. Klee et al. (eds.), *"The Good Old Days": The Holocaust as Seen by Its Perpetrators and Bystanders* (New York, 1988).

37. See esp. D. Pohl, *Nationalsozialistische Judenverfolgung in Ostgalizien, 1941–1944: Organisation und Durchführung eines staatlichen Massenverbrechens* (Munich, 1996). See also T. Sandkühler, *"Endlösung" in Galizien: Der Judenmord in Ostpolen und die Rettungsinitiativen von Berthold Beitz, 1941–1955* (Bonn, 1996); W. Manoschek, *"Serbien ist judenfrei": Militärische Besatzungspolitik und Judenvernichtung in Serbien, 1941/42* (Munich, 1995); U. Herbert (ed.), *National Socialist Extermination Policies: Contemporary German Perspectives and Controversies* (New York, 1999).

38. G. Sereny, *Into That Darkness: An Examination of Conscience* (1974; rpt. ed., New York, 1983), pp. 201, 233. To my mind, this is also the manner in which one should read the evidence presented in C. R. Browning, *Ordinary Men: Reserve Police Battalion 101 and the Final Solution in Poland* (New York, 1992). Shortly after the war, a Jewish journalist described the entry of the German army into Warsaw in 1939 in the following words: "The young soldiers, who had never seen such Jews

at home, cheered with joy. There they are before their eyes, Germany's and the world's haters. Now they will make them pay for all the suffering brought about by the Versailles Treaty, for a Germany deprived of its 'Lebensraum,'—just as they had been taught in the Nazi schools." C. Shashkes, *A Velt vos is forbei* (Buenos Aires, 1949), p. 276, cited in D. Michman, *The Holocaust and Holocaust Research: Conceptualization, Terminology and Basic Issues* (Tel Aviv, 1998 [in Hebrew]), p. 201.

39. Apart from the works by Burleigh, Friedlander, Proctor, and Weindling cited above, see also R. J. Lifton, *The Nazi Doctors: Medical Killing and the Psychology of Genocide* (New York, 1986); M. H. Kater, *Doctors under Hitler* (Chapel Hill, N.C., 1989); E. Klee, *"Euthanasie" im NS Staat: Die "Vernichtung lebensunwerten Lebens"* (Frankfurt am Main, 1983); Klee (ed.), *Dokumente zur "Euthanasie"* (Frankfurt am Main, 1985); and Klee, *Was sie taten—was sie wurden: Ärzte, Juristen und andere Beteiligte am Kranken- oder Judenmord* (Frankfurt am Main, 1986).

40. For the best and most balanced assessment of the liberal states' attitudes toward the Holocaust, see T. Kushner, *The Holocaust and the Liberal Imagination: A Social and Cultural History* (Oxford, 1994). The earlier literature on this issue is cited and analyzed in Kushner's introduction, esp. pp. 1–18.

41. See examples in S. E. Aschheim, "The German-Jewish Dialogue and Its Limits: The Case of Hermann Broch and Volkmar von Zuehlsdorff" and "Hannah Arendt and Karl Jaspers: Friendship, Catastrophe and the Possibilities of German-Jewish Dialogue," both in Aschheim, *Culture and Catastrophe*, pp. 85–114; H. Arendt, "The Aftermath of Nazi Rule," *Commentary* 10 (October 1950): 342–53; D. Diner, "Negative Symbiosis: Germans and Jews after Auschwitz," in *Reworking the Past: Hitler, the Holocaust, and the Historians' Debate*, ed. P. Baldwin (Boston, 1990), pp. 251–61; A. Rabinbach, *In the Shadow of Catastrophe: German Intellectuals between Apocalypse and Enlightenment* (Berkeley, Calif., 1997), part II.

42. For a recent attempt to associate the Holocaust with other war-related atrocities and instances of mass killing of civilian populations, see E. Markusen and D. Kopf, *The Holocaust and Strategic Bombing: Genocide and Total War in the Twentieth Century* (Boulder, Colo., 1995).

43. On the long prewar history of Auschwitz, its impact on Nazi plans in the area, and subsequent postwar attempts to detach it from German history, see D. Dwork and R. Jan van Pelt, *Auschwitz: 1270 to the Present* (New York, 1996).

44. See, especially, G. J. Horwitz, *In the Shadow of Death: Living outside the Gates of Mauthausen* (New York, 1990).

45. For the most recent and comprehensive collection on the Nazi camps, see U. Herbert et al. (eds.), *Die nationalsozialistischen Konzentrationslager: Entwicklung und Struktur*, 2 vols. (Göttingen, 1998).

46. An excellent recent summary and analysis of Holocaust historiography can be found in D. Pohl, "Die Holocaust Forschung und Goldhagens Thesen," *VfZ* 45/1 (1997): 1–48.

47. For a recent important analysis, see R. G. Moeller, *War Stories: The Search for a Usable Past in the Federal Republic of Germany,* (Berkely, Calif., 2000); more specifically for the 1950s, Moeller (ed.), *West Germany under Construction: Politics, Society, and Culture in the Adenauer Era* (Ann Arbor, Mich., 1997). For recent examples, see K. Naumann, *Der Krieg als Text: Das Jahr 1945 im Kulturellen Gedächtnis der Presse* (Hamburg, 1998). For an argument on the centrality of the politics of collective memory for German postwar politics, see A. S. Markovits and S. Reich, *The German Predicament: Memory and Power in the New Europe* (Ithaca, N.Y., 1997).

48. See esp. J. Herf, *Divided Memory: The Nazi Past in the Two Germanys* (Cambridge, Mass., 1997). For an incisive analysis of the role of the Holocaust in German sexual politics, see D. Herzog, "'Pleasure, Sex, and Politics Belong Together': Post-Holocaust Memory and the Sexual Revolution in West Germany" *CI* 24 (winter 1988): 393–444.

49. For a more extended discussion of Kluge, see O. Bartov, "War, Memory, and Repression: Alexander Kluge and the Politics of Representation in Postwar Germany," in Bartov, *Murder in Our Midst: The Holocaust, Industrial Killing, and Representation* (New York, 1996). See also G. Koch, *Die Einstellung ist die Einstellung: Visuelle Konstruktionen des Judentums* (Frankfurt am Main, 1992); A. Kaes, *From Hitler to Heimat: The Return of History as Film* (Cambridge, Mass., 1989); E. L. Santner, *Stranded Objects: Mourning, Memory, and Film in Postwar Germany,* 2nd ed. (Ithaca, N.Y., 1993); S. Sontag, "Fascinating Fascism" and "Syberberg's Hitler," in Sontag, *Under the Sign of Saturn,* 7th ed. (New York, 1981), pp. 73–105, 137–65; S. Friedländer, *Reflections of Nazism: An Essay on Kitsch and Death,* 2nd ed. (Bloomington, Ind., 1993).

50. See. e.g., D. Diner, *America in the Eyes of the Germans: An Essay on Anti-Americanism* (Princeton, N.J., 1996).

51. On the German historians' controversy, see *Forever in the Shadow of Hitler? Original Documents of the "Historikerstreit," the Controversy Concerning the Singularity of the Holocaust,* trans. J. Knowlton and T. Cates (Atlantic Highlands, N.J., 1993); C. S. Maier, *The Unmasterable Past: History, Holocaust, and German Nationalism* (Cambridge, Mass., 1988); R. Evans, *In Hitler's Shadow: West German Historians and the Attempt to Escape from the Nazi Past* (New York, 1989). On the Goldhagen debate, see J. H. Schoeps (ed.), *Ein Volk von Mördern? Die Dokumentation zur Goldhagen-Kontroverse um die Rolle der Deutschen in Holocaust* (Hamburg, 1996); R. R. Shandley (ed.), *Unwilling Germans? The Goldhagen Debate* (Minneapolis, Minn., 1998); N. G. Finkelstein and R. B. Birn, *A Nation on Trial: The Goldhagen Thesis and Historical Truth* (New York, 1998). A balanced review of the historiography is I. Kershaw, *The Nazi Dictatorship: Problems and Perspectives of Interpretation,* 3rd ed. (London, 1993).

52. For a more detailed analysis, see O. Bartov, "'. . . seit die Juden weg sind': Germany, History, and Representations of Absence," in *A User's Guide to German Cultural Studies,* ed. S. Denham et al. (Ann Arbor, Mich., 1987), and "Trauma and Absence," in *European Memories of the Second World War,* ed. H. Peitsch, et al. (New York, 1999), pp. 258–71.

53. F. Stern, *The Whitewashing of the Yellow Badge: Antisemitism and Philosemitism in Postwar Germany* (Oxford, 1992). On Jewish life in postwar Germany, see M. Brenner, *After the Holocaust: Rebuilding Jewish Lives in Postwar Germany* (Princeton, N.J., 1997); J. Borneman and J. M. Peck, *Sojourners: The Return of German Jews and the Question of Identity* (Lincoln, Neb., 1995); S. L. Gilman, *Jews in Today's German Culture* (Bloomington, Ind., 1995); Y. M. Bodemann, *Gedechtnistheater: Die jüdische Gemeinschaft und ihre deutsche Erfindung* (Hamburg, 1996); L. Rapaport, *Jews in Germany after the Holocaust: Memory, Identity, and Jewish-German Relations* (Cambridge, 1997); H. C. Bala and C. Scholz (eds.), *"Deutsch-Jüdisches Verhältnis"? Fragen, Betrachtungen, Analysen* (Essen, 1997).

54. The category of *Mischlinge* was the focus of a debate during the Wannsee Conference, where Reinhard Heydrich coordinated the participation of state and party agencies in the "Final Solution" and asserted his overall responsibility for this

undertaking. Several other meetings took place in order to decide on the question of whether murdering Germans of mixed "Aryan" and Jewish ancestry would ensure the total elimination of the Jewish peril, or rather destroy the good "Aryan" blood that might otherwise be saved in such *Mischlinge*. See K. Pätzold and E. Schwarz, *Tagesordnung: Judenmord. Die Wannsee-Konferenz am 20. Januar 1942. Eine Dokumentation zur Organisation der "Endlösung,"* 3rd ed. (Berlin, 1992).

55. The cover page of the widely read weekly magazine *Der Spiegel* greeted the screening of Steven Spielberg's film *Schindler's List* (1993) with a photograph of Liam Neeson, the actor who played Oskar Schindler in the film (rather than the man himself), accompanied by the possibly ironic caption: "The good German" (*Der gute Deutsche*). See further, including a reproduction of the magazine's cover, in Liliane Weissberg, "The Tale of a Good German: Reflections on the German Reception of *Schindler's List*," in *Spielberg's Holocaust: Critical Perspectives on* Schindler's List, ed. Yosefa Loshitzky (Bloomington, Ind., 1997). There are several other interesting articles in this collection.

56. It has been argued that the enthusiastic reception by third-generation Germans of Goldhagen's book, which argued that in the Third Reich Nazis and Germans were synonymous, was related to this sense of the past being "another country," or rather the grandparents' Fatherland. See, for example, E. Roll, "Goldhagens Diskussionsreise: Der schwierige Streit um die Deutschen und den Holocaust. Eine These und drei gebrochene Tabus," *SZ* (September 9, 1996); V. Ullrich, "Daniel J. Goldhagen in Deutschland: Die Buchtournee wurde zum Triumphzug," *Die Zeit* 38 (September 13, 1996); J. Joffe, "Goldhagen in Germany," *NYRB* (November 28, 1996): 18–21. Conversely, recent outbreaks of neo-Nazism in Germany, especially after reunification, also very much among the young and far more prevalent in the former GDR, are attributed both to economic hardship and widespread unemployment and to the communist rejection of any responsibility for Nazism and hence the lack of anti-Nazi education. See, e.g., A. Cowell, "Neo-Nazis Carving Out Fiefs in Eastern Germany," *NYT* (February 8, 1998). More generally, see H. Kurthen et al. (eds.), *Antisemitism and Xenophobia in Germany after Unification* (New York, 1997).

57. Apart from the literature cited above, see also the excellent analysis in E. Domansky, "'Kristallnacht,' the Holocaust and German Unity: The Meaning of November 9 as an Anniversary in Germany," *H&M* 4 (spring/summer 1992): 60–94.

58. Early histories of the resistance by non-German scholars were critical of the army's involvement in politics and collaboration with Hitler's regime. See Wheeler-Bennett, *Nemesis of Power;* F. L. Carsten, *The Reichswehr and Politics, 1918–33* (1966; Berkeley, Calif., 1973); and G. A. Craig, *The Politics of the Prussian Army, 1640–1945* (London, 1964). Less negative views of the generals are to be found in H. C. Deutsch, *The Conspiracy against Hitler in the Twilight War* (Minneapolis, 1968); and Deutsch, *Hitler and His Generals: The Hidden Crisis, January–June 1938* (Minneapolis, 1974). Early German scholarship tended to glorify the resisters. See, e.g., G. Ritter, *Carl Goerdeler und die deutsche Widerstands-Bewegung* (Stuttgart, 1954); J. Kramarz, *Stauffenberg: The Architect of the Famous July Twentieth Conspiracy to Assassinate Hitler* (New York, 1967); H. Graml et al., *The German Resistance to Hitler* (London, 1970). However, see also the far more critical position taken in K.-J. Müller, *The Army, Politics and Society in Germany, 1933–45* (New York, 1987).

59. For more recent works on the resistance, see P. Hoffmann, *German Resistance to Hitler* (Cambridge, Mass., 1988), which is relatively apologetic; and J. Fest,

Plotting Hitler's Death: The Story of the German Resistance (New York, 1996), which is somewhat less so. See also P. Hoffmann, *Stauffenberg: A Family History, 1905–1944* (Cambridge, 1995). For a useful survey of the literature, see M. Housden, *Resistance and Conformity in the Third Reich* (London, 1997). On the treatment of soldiers tried by the Wehrmacht in postwar Germany, see W. Wette (ed.), *Deserteure der Wehrmacht: Feiglinge—Opfer—Hoffnungsträger? Dokumentation eines Meinungswandels* (Essen, 1995); N. Haase and G. Paul (eds.), *Die anderen Soldaten: Wehrkraftzersetzung, Gehorsamsverweigerung und Fahnenflucht im Zweiten Weltkrieg* (Frankfurt am Main, 1995). See also contributions to "Gehorsam bis zum Mord? Der verschwiegene Krieg der deutschen Wehrmacht—Fakten, Analysen, Debatte," in *Zeit-Punkte,* special issue of *Die Zeit* (n.d.); H. Heer and K. Naumann (eds.), *War of the Extermination: Crimes of the Wehrmacht, 1941–1945* (New York, 2000); and W. Wette, "Bilder der Wehrmacht in der Bundeswehr," *BdIP* (February 1998): 186–96.

60. An excellent analysis of this problem is M. Nolan, "The *Historikerstreit* and Social History," in Baldwin, *Reworking the Past.* For a more general discussion of *Alltagsgeschichte,* see A. Lüdtke (ed.), *The History of Everyday Life: Reconstructing Historical Experience and Ways of Life* (Princeton, N.J., 1995).

61. Klemperer, *I Will Bear Witness.* See also O. Bartov, "The Last German," *TNR* (December 28, 1998): 34–42, and P. Gay, *My German Question: Growing Up in Nazi Berlin* (New Haven, Conn., 1998). Fischer Verlag has been publishing a series of studies on Jews in Germany under the title *Jüdische Lebensbilder,* which is now being issued in an English translation by Northwestern University Press. There are, of course, important studies of German Jewry in English. In addition to works cited above, see, e.g., for the Nazi period, A. Barkai, *From Boycott to Annihilation: The Economic Struggle of German Jews, 1933–1943* (Hanover, N.H., 1989); S. Friedländer, *Nazi Germany and the Jews;* M. A. Kaplan, *Between Dignity and Despair: Jewish Life in Nazi Germany* (New York, 1998). For earlier periods, see R. Gay, *The Jews of Germany* (New Haven, Conn., 1992); M. A. Kaplan, *The Making of the Jewish Middle Class: Women, Family, and Identity in Imperial Germany* (New York, 1991); J. Wertheimer, *Unwelcome Strangers: East European Jews in Imperial Germany* (New York, 1987); S. E. Aschheim, *Brothers and Strangers: The East European Jew in German and German Jewish Consciousness, 1800–1923* (Madison Wisc., 1982); P. E. Hyman, *Gender and Assimilation in Modern Jewish History: The Roles and Representation of Women* (Seattle, Wash., 1995). For a new history of modern European Jewry—translated from the French original—see V. Karady, *Gewalterfahrung und Utopie: Juden in der europäischen Moderne* (Frankfurt am Main, 1999).

62. See more on this in the last section of O. Bartov, "German Soldiers and the Holocaust: Historiography, Research and Implications," *H&M* 9 (fall 1997): 162–88. Conversely, for a recent example of confusing between the political and "racial" victims of the regime, see the otherwise excellent study by W. Sofsky, *The Order of Terror: The Concentration Camp* (Princeton, N.J., 1997); and my review essay on this work, "The Penultimate Horror," *TNR* (October 13, 1997): 48–53.

63. O. Bartov, "From *Blitzkrieg* to Total War: Controversial Links between Image and Reality," in *Stalinism and Nazism: Dictatorships in Comparison,* ed. I. Kershaw and M. Lewin (Cambridge, 1997).

64. See esp. R. O. Paxton, *Vichy France: Old Guard and New Order, 1940–1944* (New York, 1972).

65. Novick, *Resistance versus Vichy;* R. J. Golsan (ed.), *Memory, the Holocaust, and French Justice: The Bousquet and Touvier Affairs* (Hanover, N.H., 1996).

66. See, e.g., T. Todorov, *A French Tragedy: Scenes of Civil War, Summer 1944* (Hanover, N.H., 1996).

67. See esp. Rousso, *Vichy Syndrome.*

68. See esp. Wieviorka, *Déportation et génocide.*

69. Bloch, *Strange Defeat;* Blatt, *The French Defeat.*

70. H. Amouroux, *Quarante millions de pétainistes, Juin 1940–Juin 1941* (Paris, 1977); Burrin, *France under the Germans.*

71. On Vichy's Jewish policies, see esp. M. R. Marrus and R. O. Paxton, *Vichy France and the Jews* (New York, 1983); S. Zucotti, *The Holocaust, the French, and the Jews* (New York, 1993); R. H. Weisberg, *Vichy Law and the Holocaust in France* (New York, 1996). On French intellectuals and fascism, see D. Carroll, *French Literary Fascism: Nationalism, Anti-Semitism, and the Ideology of Culture* (Princeton, N.J., 1995), part II; R. J. Golsan (ed.), *Fascism, Aesthetics, and Culture* (Hanover, N.H., 1992), chapters by R. J. Golsan, M. J. Green, R. Scullion. See also J.-P. Rioux (ed.), *La vie culturelle sous Vichy* (Brussels, 1990); P. Ory, *Les collaborateurs, 1940–1945* (Paris, 1976). On bureaucratic collaboration, see M. O. Baruch, *Servir l'État français: L'administration en France de 1940 à 1944* (Paris, 1997). On rural fascism, see R. O. Paxton, *French Peasant Fascism: Henry Dorgères's Greenshirts and the Crises of French Agriculture, 1929–1939* (New York, 1997).

72. On the vicissitudes and ambiguities of French resistance, see, e.g., J. Bruller (Vercors), *The Silence of the Sea* (New York, 1991); A. J. Liebling (ed.), *The Republic of Silence* (New York, 1947); J.-P. Azéma et al. (eds.), *Le parti communiste français des années sombres, 1938–1941* (Paris, 1986); F. Couderc, *Les R.G. sous l'occupation: Quand la police française traquait les résistants* (Paris, 1992); P. Assouline, *L'épuration des intellectuels* (Brussels, 1990); T. Judt, *Past Imperfect: French Intellectuals, 1944–1956* (Berkeley, Calif., 1992).

73. See, e.g., P. Laborie, *L'Opinion française sous Vichy* (Paris, 1990); J. F. Sweets, *Choices in Vichy France: The French under Nazi Occupation,* 2nd ed. (New York, 1994); R. Zaretsky, *Nîmes at War: Religion, Politics, and Public Opinion in the Gard, 1938–1944* (University Park, Penn., 1995).

74. A good example is the commemoration of the massacre at Oradour as the paradigmatic event of French martyrdom. See S. Farmer, *Martyred Village: Commemorating the 1944 Massacure at Oradour-sur-Glane* (Berkeley, Calif., 1999).

75. The best works on this are Rousso, *Vichy Syndrome,* and Wieviorka, *Déportation et génocide.*

76. A. Finkielkraut, *The Imaginary Jew* (Lincoln, Neb., 1994); L. D. Kritzman (ed.), *Auschwitz and After: Race, Culture, and the "Jewish Question" in France* (New York, 1995).

77. See esp. Conan and Rousso, *Vichy;* Todorov, *Les abus de la mémoire;* Chaumont, *La concurrence de victimes.* See also A. Wieriorka, *L'Ère du témoin* (Paris, 1998); N. Wood, *Vectors of Memory: Legacies of Trauma in Postwar Europe* (Oxford, 1999).

78. Golsan, *Memory;* E. Paris, *Unhealed Wounds: France and the Klaus Barbie Affair* (New York, 1985); A. Finkielkraut, *Remembering in Vain: The Klaus Barbie Trial and Crimes against Humanity* (New York, 1992); P. Péan, *Une Jeunesse française: François Mitterrand, 1934–1947* (Paris, 1994).

79. D. Nicolaïdis (ed.), *Oublier nos crimes: L'amnésie nationale, une spécificité française?* (Paris, 1994); J. Miller, *One, by One, by One: Facing the Holocaust* (New

York, 1990), pp. 13–60 on Germany, pp. 61–92 on Austria, pp. 112–57 on France. See also G. H. Hartman (ed.), *Holocaust Remembrance: The Shapes of Memory* (Oxford, 1994); and S. Felman and D. Laub, *Testimony: Crises of Witnessing in Literature, Psychoanalysis, and History* (New York, 1992), which, however, also includes Felman's tortuous justification of Paul de Man's silence about his past. On another infamous silence, see B. Lang, *Heidegger's Silence* (Ithaca, N.Y., 1996).

80. *Aftermath.*

81. D. Jacobson, "The Invention of Orwell: Plainness, Swagger and Delicacy in Twenty Volumes," *TLS* (August 21, 1998): 3–4.

82. P. Vidal-Naquet, *Assassins of Memory: Essays on the Denial of the Holocaust* (New York, 1992); D. Lipstadt, *Denying the Holocaust: The Growing Assault on Truth and Memory* (New York, 1993); H. White, "Historical Emplotment and the Problem of Truth," in *Probing the Limits of Representation: Nazism and the "Final Solution,"* ed. S. Friedländer (Cambridge, Mass., 1992); O. Bartov, "Intellectuals on Auschwitz: Memory, History, and Truth," in Bartov, *Murder in Our Midst.*

83. C. Lanzmann, *Shoah: An Oral History of the Holocaust: The Complete Text of the Film* (New York, 1985), p. 138.

84. See, e.g., A. D. Morse, *While Six Million Died: A Chronicle of American Apathy* (New York, 1967); W. Laqueur, *The Terrible Secret: Suppression of the Truth about Hitler's "Final Solution"* (London, 1980); D. S. Wyman, *The Abandonment of the Jews: America and the Holocaust, 1941–1945* (New York, 1984); H. L. Feingold, *Bearing Witness: How America and Its Jews Responded to the Holocaust* (Syracuse, N.Y., 1995); and W. D. Rubinstein, *The Myth of Rescue: Why the Democracies Could Not Have Saved More Jews from the Nazis* (London, 1997), who rejects all earlier scholarship. See also D. Porat, *The Blue and the Yellow Stars of David: The Zionist Leadership in Palestine and the Holocaust, 1939–1945* (Cambridge, Mass., 1990).

85. *The Differend: Phrases in Dispute* (Minneapolis, 1988), p. 56. See also M. Blanchot, *The Writing of the Disaster* (Lincoln, Neb., 1986). Two insightful recent discussions on the difficulties of representing Auschwitz both in legal discourse and in academic and intellectual writings, are L. Douglas, "The Memory of Judgment: The Law, the Holocaust, and Denial," and S. DeKoven Ezrahi, "Representing Auschwitz," both in *H&M* 7 (fall/winter 1996): 100–120 and 121–54.

86. Recent works on the links between genocide and modernity have both the potential of distancing us from the horror (by sanitizing it) and of making us all complicit in it (since we belong to an age that perpetrates horror). See, e.g., D. J. K. Peukert, *Inside Nazi Germany: Conformity, Opposition, and Racism in Everyday Life* (New Haven, Conn., 1982); Peukert, *The Weimar Republic;* and D. Peukert, "The Genesis of the 'Final Solution' from the Spirit of Science," in *Reevaluating the Third Reich,* ed. T. Childers and J. Caplan (New York, 1993). See also Z. Bauman, *Modernity and the Holocaust* (Ithaca, N.Y., 1989).

87. Such an argument was made by Martin Broszat in his correspondence with Saul Friedländer, now included in Baldwin, *Reworking the Past,* p. 106. See also Kershaw, *Nazi Dictatorship,* pp. 80–81.

88. See, most recently, Y. Gutman (ed.), *Major Changes within the Jewish People in the Wake of the Holocaust* (Jerusalem, 1995 [in Hebrew]); Y. Kashti et al. (eds.), *A Quest for Identity: Post War Jewish Biographies* (Tel Aviv, 1996); R. Moses (ed.), *Persistent Shadows of the Holocaust: The Meaning to Those Not Directly Affected* (Madison, Conn., 1993). On Jewish theology after the Holocaust, see, e.g., R. L. Rubenstein, *After Auschwitz: History, Theology, and Contemporary Judaism,* 2nd ed.

(Baltimore, Md., 1992); Z. Braiterman, *(God) After Auschwitz: Tradition and Change in Post-Holocaust Jewish Thought* (Princeton, N.J., 1998). On the links between religion and modern genocide, see O. Bartov and P. Mack (eds.), *In God's Name: Genocide and Religion in the Twentieth Century* (New York, 2000).

89. For some recent literature on the United States, see R. H. Abzug, *America Views the Holocaust: A Brief Documentary History* (Boston, 1999); R. Breitman and A. M. Kraut, *American Refugee Policy and European Jewry, 1933–1945* (Bloomington, Ind., 1987); Feingold, *Bearing Witness;* A. H. Rosenfeld (ed.), *Thinking about the Holocaust: After Half a Century* (Bloomington, Ind., 1997), part III; G. N. Arad, "American Jewish Leadership and the Nazi Menace," (Ph.D. dissertation, Tel Aviv University, 1994), forthcoming in book form from Indiana University Press; P. Novick, *The Holocaust in American Life* (Boston, 1999). On the *Yishuv* and Israel, see T. Segev, *The Seventh Million: The Israelis and the Holocaust* (New York, 1993); Porat, *Blue and Yellow Stars;* D. Ofer, *Escaping the Holocaust: Illegal Immigration to the Land of Israel, 1939–1944* (New York, 1990); Y. Bauer, *Jews for Sale? Nazi-Jewish Negotiations, 1933–1945* (New Haven, Conn., 1994); Rosenfeld, *Thinking about the Holocaust,* part II.

90. See, e.g., J. Shandler, *While America Watches: Televising the Holocaust* (New York, 1999); J. Reilly, *Belsen: The Liberation of a Concentration Camp* (London, 1998).

91. For greater detail, see the last section of chapter 4, "The Other Planet," and references cited therein.

92. H. Arendt, *Eichmann in Jerusalem: A Report on the Banality of Evil,* rev. ed. (New York, 1977). A typical attack on her book can be found in the introduction to S. Ettinger, *Modern Anti-Semitism: Studies and Essays* (Tel Aviv, 1978 [in Hebrew]), pp. x–xi. See also Segev, *Seventh Million,* pp. 357–60, 465; *Hannah Arendt and Eichmann in Jerusalem,* special issue of *H&M* 8 (fall/winter 1996); and S. E. Aschheim, "Nazism, Culture and the *Origins of Totalitarianism:* Hannah Arendt and the Discourse of Evil," *NGC* 70 (winter 1997): 117–39.

93. J. Adler, "The One Who Got Away: H. G. Adler and Theodor Adorno: Two Approaches to Culture after Auschwitz," *TLS* (October 4, 1996): 18–19. See also H. Epstein, *Children of the Holocaust: Conversations with Sons and Daughters of Survivors* (New York, 1979). On children of the perpetrators, see D. Bar-On, *Legacy of Silence: Encounters with Children of the Third Reich* (Cambridge, Mass., 1989). On children in the Holocaust, see N. Tec, *Dry Tears: The Story of a Lost Childhood* (New York, 1984); D. Dwork, *Children with a Star: Jewish Youth in Nazi Europe* (New Haven, Conn., 1991); L. Holliday, *Children in the Holocaust and World War II: Their Secret Diaries* (New York, 1995); J. Marks, *The Hidden Children: The Secret Survivors of the Holocaust* (New York, 1993).

94. *The Destruction of the European Jews,* 3 vols., rev. ed. (1961; New York, 1985).

95. R. Hilberg, *The Politics of Memory: The Journey of a Holocaust Historian* (Chicago, 1996), pp. 110–11.

96. See esp. ibid., pp. 147–57.

97. See, e.g., Herbert, *Best;* Goldhagen, *Hitler's Willing Executioners;* Weiss, *Ideology of Death;* S. Friedländer, *Nazi Germany;* Bartov, *Hitler's Army;* Pohl, *Nationalsozialistische Judenverfolgung.*

98. Ettinger, *Modern Anti-Semitism,* pp. x–xi. See also S. Almog (ed.), *Antisemitism through the Ages: A Collection of Essays* (Oxford, 1988), esp. the essays by Almog, Ettinger, Gutman, and Bauer. These writers refer also with a great deal of criticism to Arendt's earlier massive study, *The Origins of Totalitarianism.*

99. Segev, *Seventh Million,* pp. 255–320.

100. I. Keynan, "Between Hope and Anxiety: The Image of the Survivors among the Emissaries from Palestine to the DP Camps in Germany, 1945," in *Haapala: Studies in the History of Illegal Immigration into Palestine, 1934–1948,* ed. A. Shapira (Tel Aviv, 1990 [in Hebrew]), p. 222. See also Keynan, *Holocaust Survivors and the Emissaries from Eretz-Israel: Germany, 1945–1948* (Tel Aviv, 1996 [in Hebrew]); and the controversial study, Y. Grodzinsky, *Good Human Material: Jews Facing Zionists, 1945–1951* (Jerusalem, 1998 [in Hebrew]).

101. H. Bartov, *The Brigade* (New York, 1968). This writer, journalist, and veteran of the Second World War and the 1948 war was born in Palestine in 1926. Yet his essay collection, *I Am Not the Mythological Sabra* (Tel Aviv, 1995 [in Hebrew]), rejects the notion that the Sabras (Jews born in Palestine or Israel) were alienated from their European roots. For a very different sociological interpretation, see O. Almog, *The Sabra—A Profile* (Tel Aviv, 1997 [in Hebrew]).

102. *From Catastrophe to Power: Holocaust Survivors and the Emergence of Israel* (Berkeley, Calif., 1998), orig. pub. as *Zehavam shel ha'yehudim,* or *The Jews' Gold* (Tel Aviv, 1996). Among the most interesting reactions is an essay by the poet, writer, and veteran of the 1948 war, H. Gouri, "On Books and What Is between Them," *Alpayim* 14 (1997 [in Hebrew]): 9–30. Apart from the literature cited above on the reception of survivors in Israel, see H. Yablonka, *Foreign Brethren: Holocaust Survivors in the State of Israel, 1948–1952* (Jerusalem, 1994 [in Hebrew]).

103. On the so-called *Yekes,* or German Jews, in Palestine, see Segev, *Seventh Million,* pp. 15–64. See also N. Sheffi, "Rejecting the Other's Culture—Hebrew and German in Israel, 1933–1965," *TAJB* 27 (1998): 301–19.

104. See, e.g., A. Shapira, *Land and Power: The Zionist Resort to Force, 1881–1948* (New York, 1992); Y. Zerubavel, *Recovered Roots: Collective Memory and the Making of Israeli National Tradition* (Chicago, 1995); Y. Gorny, *The Quest for Collective Identity: The Place of Israel in Jewish Public Thinking, 1945–1987* (Tel Aviv, 1990 [in Hebrew]); N. Gertz, *Captive of a Dream: National Myths in Israeli Culture* (Tel Aviv, 1995 [in Hebrew]).

105. See Z. Sternhell, *The Founding Myths of Israel: Nationalism, Socialism, and the Making of the Jewish State* (Princeton, N.J., 1998); A. Shapira, *New Jews, Old Jews* (Tel Aviv, 1997 [in Hebrew]); and Shapira, *Visions in Conflict* (Tel Aviv, 1997 [in Hebrew]); E. Sivan, *The 1948 Generation: Myth, Profile, and Memory* (Tel Aviv, 1991 [in Hebrew]); M. Tessler, *A History of the Israeli-Palestinian Conflict* (Bloomington, Ind., 1994); B. Kimmerling and J. S. Migdal, *Palestinians: The Making of a People* (Cambridge, Mass., 1994); M. Litvak, "A Palestinian Past: National Construction and Reconstruction," *H&M* 6 (fall/winter 1994): 24–56. On the "new historians" and the so-called *Historikerstreit* in Israel, see J. Mahler, "Uprooting the Past: Israel's New Historians Take a Hard Look at Their Nation's Origins," *LF* 7 (August 1997): 24–32; G. N. Arad (ed.), *Israeli Historiography Revisited,* special issue of *H&M* 7 (spring/summer 1995); A. Elon, "Israel and the End of Zionism," *NYRB* (December 19, 1996): 22–30. For a savage attack on the critics of traditional Zionist historiography, see E. Karsh, *Fabricating Israeli History: The "New Historians"* (London, 1997). For an illuminating comparison between the German and Israeli historical controversies, see J. Brunner, "Pride and Memory: Nationalism, Narcissism and the Historians' Debates in Germany and Israel," *H&M* 9 (fall 1997): 256–300.

106. In this context, see also D. Diner, "Historical Experience and Cognition: Perspectives on National Socialism," *H&M* 2 (1990): 84–110.

107. This is by no means to say that I accept such relativizing arguments as those recently propounded in A. Brossat, *L'épreuve du désastre: Le XXᵉ siècle et les camps* (Paris, 1996), pp. 20, 23 (cited and rejected above, in chapter 2 of this book).

108. *The Drowned and the Saved* (New York, 1988), p. 82. These essays are not only about coming to terms with the memory of the Holocaust but also with life after the event. See also F. Camon, *Conversations with Primo Levi* (Marlboro, Vt., 1989). The same problem is confronted in a very different manner by J. Améry, *At the Mind's Limits: Contemplations by a Survivor on Auschwitz and Its Realities,* 2nd ed. (New York, 1986), and in much of the poetry of Paul Celan. Both Améry and Celan committed suicide. On the latter, see J. Felstiner, *Paul Celan: Poet, Survivor, Jew* (New Haven, Conn., 1995); I. Chalfen, *Paul Celan: A Biography of His Youth* (New York, 1991). The question of life after death in the camps is addressed in a very different manner by the Israeli writer Ka-Tzetnik, *Shivitti: A Vision* (San Francisco, 1989), who came from a religious background and underwent psychiatric treatment many years after Auschwitz. See further on this issue in my above-cited essay "Intellectuals on Auschwitz," and in chapter 4, "The Other Planet," of this book; E. Traverso, *L'Histoire déchirée: Essai sur Auschwitz et les intellectuels* (Paris, 1997); and D. L. Niewyk (ed.), *Fresh Wounds: Early Narratives of Holocaust Survival* (Chapel Hill, N.C., 1998). On the reluctance of the FRG to pay restitution to the victims of the Nazis and the traumatizing effects of this process on the survivors, see C. Pross, *Paying for the Past: The Struggle over Reparations for Surviving Victims of the Nazi Terror* (Baltimore, Md., 1998). On legal and political reactions to genocide, see A. J. Kochavi, *Prelude to Nuremberg: Allied War Crimes Policy and the Question of Punishment* (Chapel Hill, N.C., 1998); M. R. Marrus, *The Nuremberg War Crimes Trial, 1945–46: A Documentary History* (Boston, 1997).

109. I. Buruma, *The Wages of Guilt: Memories of War in Germany and Japan* (New York, 1995); C. Gluck, "The Rape of Nanking: How 'The Nazi Buddha' Resisted the Japanese," *TLS* (June 27, 1997): 9–10; I. Chang, *The Rape of Nanking: The Forgotten Holocaust of World War II* (New York, 1997). In this context see also the discussions of Alain Resnais's film in N. Wood, "Memory by Analogy: *Hiroshima, mon amour,*" in *The Liberation of France: Image and Event,* ed. H. R. Kedward and N. Wood (Oxford, 1995); C. Caruth, *Unclaimed Experience: Trauma, Narrative, and History* (Baltimore, Md., 1996), pp. 25–56; M. Roth, "*Hiroshima Mon Amour:* You Must Remember This," in *Revisioning History: Film and the Construction of a New Past,* ed. R. A. Rosenstone (Princeton, N.J., 1995), pp. 91–101. For the most recent discussion, see J. A. Fogel (ed.), *The Nanjing Massacre in History and Historiography* (Berkeley, Calif., 2000).

110. V. N. Dadrian, *The History of the Armenian Genocide: Ethnic Conflict from the Balkans to Anatolia to the Caucasus* (Providence, R.I., 1995) and *German Responsibility in the Armenian Genocide: A Review of the Historical Evidence of German Complicity* (Watertown, Mass., 1996); R. G. Hovannisian (ed.), *The Armenian Genocide in Perspective* (New Brunswick, N.J., 1986); R. W. Smith et al., "Professional Ethics and the Denial of the Armenian Genocide," *HGS* 9 (spring 1995): 1–22; and Y. Auron, *The Banality of Indifference: The Attitude of the Jewish Yishuv in Palestine and the Zionist Movement to the Armenian Genocide* (Tel Aviv, 1995 [in Hebrew]), his "Again Musa Dagh? And Again the World is Silent?" *Ha'aretz* (April 18, 1997 [in Hebrew]), and his "Zionist and Israeli Attitudes toward the Armenian Genocide," in Bartov and Mack, *In God's Name.*

111. B. Kiernan (ed.), *Genocide and Democracy in Cambodia: The Khmer Rouge, the United Nations and the International Community* (New Haven, Conn., 1993); and Kiernan, "Genocidal Targeting: The Two Groups of Victims in Pol Pot's Cambodia," in *State Organized Violence: The Case of Violent Internal Repression,* ed. P. T. Bushnell et al. (Boulder, Colo., 1991); E. Press, "Unforgiven: The Director of the Cambodian Genocide Program Rekindles Cold War Animosities," *LF* (April/May 1997): 67–75.

112. S. Mydans, "Confined, Pol Pot Tells of Feeling 'Bit Bored,'" *NYT* (October 24, 1997); Mydans, "Two Khmer Rouge Leaders Spend Beach Holiday in Shadow of Past," *NYT* (January 1, 1999).

113. L. Kuper, *Genocide: Its Political Use in the Twentieth Century* (New Haven, Conn., 1982); G. Prunier, *The Rwanda Crisis: History of a Genocide* (New York, 1995); R. Verdier et al. (eds.), *Rwanda: Un génocide du XXe siècle* (Paris, 1995); D. Franche, *Rwanda: Généalogie d'un génocide* (Paris, 1997); T. P. Longman, *Zaire, Forced to Flee: Violence against the Tutsis in Zaire* (New York, 1996); T. P. Longman with Alison Des Forges, *Zaire, Attacked by All Sides: Civilians and the War in Eastern Zaire* (New York, 1997); and P. Gourevitsch, *We Wish to Inform You That Tommorrow We Will Be Killed With Our Families* (New York, 1998). See also T. P. Longman, "Christian Churches and Genocide in Rwanda," and C. de Lespinay, "The Churches and the Genocide in the East African Great Lakes Region," both in Bartov and Mack, *In God's Name.*

114. Citations from M. Danner, "Bosnia: The Turning Point," *NYRB* (February 5, 1998): 34–41. Other articles in this remarkable series by Danner in the *NYRB* include "Bosnia: The Great Betrayal" (March 26, 1998): 40–52; "Bosnia: Breaking the Machine" (February 19, 1998): 41–45; "America and the Bosnia Genocide" (December 4, 1997): 55–65. Danner reviews a large number of books concerned with events in the former Yugoslavia. See also M. A. Sells, *The Bridge Betrayed: Religion and Genocide in Bosnia* (Berkeley, Calif., 1996); Sells, "Serbian Religious Mythology and the Genocide in Bosnia," in Bartov and Mack, *In God's Name*; and S. A. Kent, "Writing the Yugoslav Wars: English-Language Books on Bosnia (1992–1996) and the Challenges of Analyzing Contemporary History," *AHR* 102 (October 1997): 1085–114. Emir Kusturica's extraordinary recent film *Underground,* provides some insight into the tangled web of Serbian history, myth, and violence. For background on Bosnia, Kosovo, and now also Chechnya, see N. Malcolm, *Bosnia: A Short History,* 2nd ed. (New York, 1996); N. Malcolm, *Kosovo: A Short History* (New York, 1998); and C. Gall and T. de Wall, *Chechnya: Calmity in the Caucasus* (New York, 1998).

115. P. Holquist, "State Violence as Technique: The Logic of Violence in Soviet Totalitarianism" (unpublished paper, 1998), p. 29. For recent attempts to grapple with this century's genocides and tyrannies, see, for instance, D. Chirot, *Modern Tyrants: The Power and Prevalence of Evil in Our Age* (New York, 1994); Y. Ternon, *L'état criminel: Les génocides au XXe siècle* (Paris, 1995). A recent study that fails to distinguish between the Soviet Gulags and the Nazi camps, despite its otherwise admirable moral commitment, is T. Todorov, *Facing the Extreme: Moral Life in the Concentration Camps* (New York, 1996).

116. Holquist, *State Violence,* p. 23, also citing T. Judt, "The Longest Road to Hell," *NYT* (December 22, 1997). See further in Bartov, *Murder in Our Midst,* pp. 72, 86–88, 142–44, 193–94, n. 6, and the sources cited therein. H. Wu, *Troublemaker: One Man's Crusade against China's Cruelty* (London, 1997), makes analogies to the Holocaust in speaking about Chinese camps, without, however, troubling to make

such important distinctions as can be found in Holquist. Bizarre links between Chinese oppression and Nazism are also present in the recent Hollywood production *Seven Years in Tibet* (1997), produced and directed by Jean-Jacques Annaud.

117. A. Weiner, "Delineating the Soviet Body National in the Age of Socialism: Ukrainians, Jews, and the Myth of the Second World War" (unpublished paper, 1997), pp. 2–7. See also Weiner, "Excising Evil: The Soviet Quest for Purity and the Eradication of the Nationalist Movement in the Vinnytsia Region" (unpublished paper, 1997); Weiner, *Making Sense of War: The Second World War and the Fate of the Bolshevik Revolution* (Princeton, N.J., 2000); N. Naimark, "Ethnic Cleansing between War and Peace" (unpublished paper, 1997). The papers by Holquist, Weiner, and Naimark cited in notes 115–17 will be published in revised form in *Modernity, Revolution, and Population Management in the Twentieth Century*, ed. A. Weiner (Stanford, Calif., forthcoming).

118. On trauma and memory, see C. Caruth (ed.), *Trauma: Explorations in Memory* (Baltimore, Md., 1995). See also many of the contributions to G. N. Arad (ed.), *Passing into History: Nazism and the Holocaust beyond Memory,* special issue of *H&M* 9 (fall 1997).

119. For the use and abuse of the traumatic memory of bystander groups that fell victim to policies of collective punishment, see, e.g., M. de Keiser, "The Skeleton in the Closet: The Memory of Putten, 1/2 October 1944," *H&M* 7 (fall/winter 1996); de Keiser, *Putten: De razzia en de herinnering* (Amsterdam, 1998); Farmer, *Oradour.* On the reworking of the memory of the Holocaust in France and Germany, see Wieviorka, *Déportation et génocide;* Rosenfeld, *Thinking about the Holocaust,* part IV; Bodemann, *Gedächtnistheater.*

Chapter 4

1. J. Taubes, *Ad Carl Schmitt: Gegenstrebige Fügung* (Berlin, 1987), p. 7, cited in T. B. Strong, "Foreword: Dimensions of the New Debate around Carl Schmitt," in C. Schmitt, *The Concept of the Political* (Chicago, 1996), orig. pub. as *Der Begriff des Politischen* (Munich, 1932).

2. U. Herbert, "Den Gegner vernichten, ohne ihn zu hassen: Loathing the Jews in the World View of the Intellectual Leadership of the SS in the 1920s and 1930s" (unpublished paper, 1996); and in much greater detail, Herbert, *Best: Biographische Studien über Radikalismus, Weltanschauung und Venunft, 1903–1989* (Bonn, 1996), part I. See also L. Hachmeister, *Der Gegnerforscher: Die Karriere des SS-Führers Franz Alfred Six* (Munich, 1998), chapters 1–7; M. Wildt, *Das Führungskorps des Reichssicherheitshauptamtes. Versuch einer Kollektivbiographie* (Hamburg, 1996).

3. L. Strauss, "Notes on Carl Schmitt: The Concept of the Political," in Schmitt, *The Concept of the Political,* pp. 81–107.

4. Testimony by Dr. David Wodowinski, in *The Attorney General against Adolf Eichmann: Testimonies,* vol. 2 (Jerusalem, 1974 [in Hebrew]), p. 1117, cited in D. Michman, *The Holocaust and Holocaust Research: Conceptualization, Terminology and Basic Issues* (Tel Aviv, 1998 [in Hebrew]), p. 232.

5. M. Bloch, *Strange Defeat: A Statement of Evidence Written in 1940* (New York, 1968), pp. 177–78.

6. See B. Lang, *Heidegger's Silence* (Ithaca, N.Y., 1996); A. Rabinbach, *In the Shadow of Catastrophe: German Intellectuals between Apocalypse and Enlightenment*

(Berkeley, Calif., 1997), chapter 3; A. Gleason, *Totalitarianism: The Inner Life of the Cold War* (New York, 1995), pp. 20–39, and literature cited there in, pp. 219–22, n. 30–48; *Telos,* special issue (summer 1987); D. LaCapra, *Representing the Holocaust: History, Theory, Trauma* (Ithaca, N.Y., 1994), chapter 5; Strong, "Foreword," and literature cited therein. See also T. Nevin, *Ernst Jünger and Germany: Into the Abyss, 1914–1945* (Durham, N.C., 1996); J. Herf, *Reactionary Modernism: Technology, Culture, and Politics in Weimar and the Third Reich,* 2nd ed. (Cambridge, 1984).

7. See, e.g., T. Todorov, *On Human Diversity: Nationalism, Racism, and Exoticism in French Thought* (Cambridge, Mass., 1993); A. Memmi, *Le racisme* (Paris, 1982); P. Sahlins, *Boundaries: The Making of France and Spain in the Pyrenees* (Berkeley, Calif., 1989).

8. On boundaries between epochs, see, e.g., R. Heilbronner, *Visions of the Future: The Distant Past, Yesterday, Today, and Tomorrow* (New York, 1995); between reality and the mind: P. Loewenberg, *Fantasy and Reality in History* (New York, 1995); between genders: J. W. Scott, *Feminism and History* (New York, 1996). On modern technological utopias, see, e.g., S. Kern, *The Culture of Time and Space, 1880–1918* (Cambridge, Mass., 1983); A. Rabinbach, *The Human Motor: Energy, Fatigue, and the Origins of Modernity* (Berkeley, Calif., 1990).

9. Nostalgia for a mythical past in antiquity is the leitmotif of Livy's *The Early History of Rome,* while making the (Germanic) barbarians into models of lost purity is at the core of Tacitus's *The Annals of Imperial Rome.* Nostalgia for a mythical past in ancient China characterizes Ssu-ma Ch'ien's *Records of the Historian* (New York, 1958). See also D. Lowenthal, *The Past is a Foreign Country* (Cambridge, 1985).

10. See, e.g., W. H. McNeill, *The Pursuit of Power: Technology, Armed Force, and Society since A.D. 1000* (Oxford, 1983); B. M. Downing, *The Military Revolution and Political Change: Origins of Democracy and Autocracy in Early Modern Europe* (Princeton, N.J., 1992); B. Moore, Jr., *Social Origins of Dictatorship and Democracy: Lord and Peasant in the Making of the Modern World* (Boston, 1967); B. Z. Kedar, "Expulsion as a Problem in World History," *Alpayim* 13 (1996 [in Hebrew]): 9–22.

11. M. Adas, *Machines as the Measure of Men: Science, Technology, and Ideologies of Western Dominance* (Ithaca, N.Y., 1989); M. Ferro, *Colonization: A Global History* (London, 1997); V. G. Kiernan, *European Empires from Conquest to Collapse, 1815–1960* (Bungay, Suffolk, 1982); D. B. Ralston, *Importing the European Army: The Introduction of European Military Techniques and Institutions into the Extra-European World, 1600–1914* (Chicago, 1990); D. Pick, *Faces of Degeneration: A European Disorder, c. 1848–c.1918* (Cambridge, 1989); I. Hannford, *Race: The History of an Idea in the West* (Baltimore, Md., 1996); E. Barkan, *The Retreat of Scientific Racism: Changing Concepts of Race in Britain and the United States between the World Wars* (Cambridge, 1992). See also C. Lévi-Strauss, *The Savage Mind* (London, 1966) and *Tristes Tropiques* (New York, 1976).

12. See, e.g., C. Essner, *Deutsche Afrikareisende im neunzenten Jahrhundert: Zur Sozialgeschichte des Reisens* (Stuttgart, 1985); S. Friedrichsmeyer et al. (eds.), *The Imperialist Imagination: German Colonialism and Its Legacy* (Ann Arbor, Mich., 1998); R. Aldrich, *Greater France: A History of French Overseas Expansion* (New York, 1996); M. K. Matsuda, *The Memory of the Modern* (New York, 1996), chapter 7; L. Lowe, *Critical Terrains: French and British Orientalisms* (Ithaca, N.Y., 1991); E. W. Said, *Orientalism* (New York, 1979).

13. For the German case and the links between the "gardening society," ecological thinking, "ethnic landscapes," and genocide, see Z. Bauman, *Modernity and*

the Holocaust (Ithaca, N.Y., 1991); J. Wolschke-Bulmahn, "Nature and Ideology: The Search for Identity and Nationalism in Early Twentieth-Century German Landscape Architecture," *AICGS* 17 (February 1996): 1–31; G. Gröning and J. Wolschke-Bulmahn, "Politics, Planning and the Protection of Nature: Political Abuse of Early Ecological Ideas in Germany, 1933–45," *PP* 2 (1987): 127–48; D. Inkelas, "Landscape Planning and the Development of SS Policy in Annexed Poland, 1939–1942" (unpublished paper, 1996); D. Dwork and R. Jan van Pelt, *Auschwitz: 1270 to the Present* (New York, 1996), part I. On Chinese gardens and utopian thought, see J. Stuart, "A Scholar's Garden in Ming China: Dream and Reality," in *AA* 3/4 (fall 1990): 31–51, and literature cited therein; W. Bauer, *China and the Search for Happiness* (New York, 1976).

14. P. Crook, *Darwinism, War and History: The Debate over the Biology of War from the* Origin of Species *to the First World War* (Cambridge, 1994); L. L. Clark, *Social Darwinism in France* (Alabama, 1984); E. Conte and C. Essner, *La quête de la race: Une anthropologie du Nazisme* (Paris, 1995); J. M. Effron, *Defenders of the Race: Jewish Doctors and Race Science in Fin-de-Siècle Europe* (New Haven, Conn., 1994); P. Weindling, *Health, Race and German Politics between National Unification and Nazism, 1870–1945* (Cambridge, 1989); R. N. Proctor, *Racial Hygiene: Medicine under the Nazis* (Cambridge, Mass., 1988); G. Aly et al., *Cleansing the Fatherland: Nazi Medicine and Racial Hygiene* (Baltimore, Md., 1994); M. Burleigh, *Death and Deliverance: "Euthanasia" in Germany, 1900–1945* (Cambridge, 1994). Some of the literature on recent debates on these issues is cited in O. Bartov, *Murder in Our Midst: The Holocaust, Industrial Killing, and Representation* (New York, 1996), p. 3, n. 2.

15. See, e.g., T. Head and R. Landes (eds.), *The Peace of God: Social Violence and Religious Response around the Year 1000* (Ithaca, N.Y., 1992); T. J. J. Altizer, *History as Apocalypse* (Albany, N.Y., 1985); D. G. Roskies (ed.), *The Literature of Destruction: Jewish Responses to Catastrophe* (Philadelphia, 1989); S. E. Aschheim, *Culture and Catastrophe: German and Jewish Confrontations with National Socialism and Other Crises* (New York, 1996); T. W. Adorno, *Negative Dialectics* (New York, 1973), esp. part III, chapters 2–3; H. Arendt, *Between Past and Future: Eight Exercises in Political Thought,* rev. ed. (New York, 1968), esp. chapter 3; R. J. B. Bosworth, *Explaining Auschwitz and Hiroshima: History Writing and the Second World War, 1945–1990* (London, 1993); R. J. Lifton and E. Markusen, *The Genocidal Mentality: Nazi Holocaust and Nuclear Threat* (New York, 1990).

16. See, e.g., H. Arendt, *The Origins of Totalitarianism* (New York, 1951); F. Furet, *Le Passé d'une illusion* (Paris, 1995); M. Burleigh and W. Wippermann, *The Racial State: Germany, 1933–1945* (Cambridge, 1991); R. J. Lifton, *The Nazi Doctors: Medical Killing and the Psychology of Genocide* (New York, 1986). See also E. Hobsbawm, *The Age of Extremes: A History of the World, 1914–1991* (New York, 1995); M. Mazower, *Dark Continent: Europe's Twentieth Century* (New York, 1999).

17. On the Soviet Union, see esp. M. Lewin, *Russia/USSR/Russia: The Drive and Drift of a Superstate* (New York, 1995); G. Hosking, *The First Socialist Society: A History of the Soviet Union from Within,* 2nd ed. (Cambridge, Mass., 1993); S. Kotkin, *Magnetic Mountain: Stalinism as a Civilization* (Berkeley, Calif., 1995); R. Conquest, *The Great Terror: A Reassessment* (New York, 1990) and *The Harvest of Sorrow: Soviet Collectivization and the Terror-Famine* (New York, 1986). On capitalism in crisis, see, e.g., B. Moore, Jr., *Injustice: The Social Bases of Obedience and Revolt* (Stamford, Conn., 1978); C. S. Maier, *Recasting Bourgeois Europe: Stabilization in France, Germany, and Italy in the Decade after World War I* (Princeton, N.J., 1975).

On demography, see M. S. Quine, *Population Politics in Twentieth-Century Europe* (London, 1996); J. M. Winter, *The Great War and the British People* (Cambridge, Mass., 1986). On gender, see M. R. Higonnet et al. (eds.), *Behind the Lines: Gender and the Two World Wars* (New Haven, Conn., 1987); M. L. Roberts, *Civilization without Sexes: Reconstructing Gender in Postwar France, 1917–1927* (Chicago, 1994); R. Bridenthal et al., *When Biology Became Destiny: Women in Weimar and Nazi Germany* (New York, 1984). On empire and decolonization, see, E. J. Hobsbawm, *Industry and Empire: From 1750 to the Present Day* (London, 1968); F. Fanon, *The Wretched of the Earth* (London, 1965); R. Girardet, *L'Idée coloniale en France* (Paris, 1972); J.-P. Rioux (ed.), *La Guerre d'Algérie et les français* (Paris, 1990). See also G. Kolko, *Century of War: Politics, Conflicts, and Society since 1914* (New York, 1994); J. L. Talmon, *The Age of Violence* (Tel Aviv, 1974 [in Hebrew]).

18. For some suggestive works on this theme, see J. McConkey, *The Anatomy of Memory: An Anthology* (New York, 1996); F. A. Yates, *The Art of Memory* (Chicago, 1966); P. H. Hutton, *History as an Art of Memory* (Hanover, N.H., 1993); M. Halbwachs, *On Collective Memory* (Chicago, 1992); J. Le Goff, *Histoire et mémoire* (Paris, 1988); P. Nora (ed.), *Les Lieux de mémoire,* 3 vols., paperback edition (Paris, 1997); J. R. Gillis (ed.), *Commemorations: The Politics of National Identity* (Princeton, N.J., 1994).

19. In this context, see O. Bartov, "'Seit die Juden weg sind . . .': Germany, History, and Representations of Absence," in *A User's Guide to German Cultural Studies,* ed. S. Denham et al. (Ann Arbor, Mich., 1997), pp. 209–26.

20. On collecting and nostalgia, see W. Benjamin, "Unpacking My Library: A Talk about Book Collecting," in Benjamin, *Illuminations,* ed. H. Arendt (New York, 1969), pp. 59–67. For an example from China, see W. Li, "The Collector, the Connoisseur, and Late-Ming Sensibility," *TP* 81 (1995): 269–302. On the aesthetics, politics, and theft of art in Nazi Germany, see P. Adam, *Art of the Third Reich* (New York, 1995); B. Hinz, *Art in the Third Reich* (New York, 1979); J. Petropoulos, *Art as Politics in the Third Reich* (Chapel Hill, N.C., 1996); A. E. Steinweis, *Art, Ideology, and Economics in Nazi Germany* (Chapel Hill, N.C., 1993); L. H. Nicholas, *The Rape of Europe: The Fate of Europe's Treasures in the Third Reich and the Second World War* (New York, 1994). For Polish views of Jews, see, e.g., S. Markowski, *Kazimierz: The Jewish Quarter of Cracow, 1870–1988* (Cracow, 1992 [in Polish and English]).

21. On the USSR, see R. Stites (ed.), *Culture and Entertainment in Wartime Russia* (Bloomington, Ind., 1995), esp. on Sergei Eisenstein's film *Alexander Nevskii* (1938), pp. 65–66; D. Bordwell, *The Cinema of Eisenstein* (Cambridge, Mass., 1993); P. Kenez, *Cinema and Soviet Society, 1917–1953* (Cambridge, Mass., 1992). See also J. Hay, *Popular Film Culture in Fascist Italy: The Passing of the Rex* (Bloomington, Ind., 1987), chapter 5; R. A. Rosenstone (ed.), *Revisioning History: Film and the Construction of a New Past* (Princeton, N.J., 1995). A good introduction to European art at the turn of the century, including the impact of colonialism, technology, and war, is R. Hughes, *The Shock of the New: Art and the Century of Change* (London, 1980). On the links between French national identity and colonial artifacts, see H. Lebovics, *True France: The Wars over Cultural Identity, 1900–1945* (Ithaca, N.Y., 1992). See also the extraordinary catalog of the 1986 Vienna Exhibition, J. Claire (ed.), *Vienne, 1880–1938: L'Apocalypse Joyeuse* (Paris, 1986). Paris also hosted an exhibition on "japonisme," or the impact of Japanese prints on French art.

22. For some discussion of the nature, purpose, and crisis of modern historiography, see, W. Dilthey, *Selected Works,* vol. 1: *Introduction to the Human Sciences*

(Princeton, N.J., 1989); R. A. Makkreel, *Dilthey: Philosopher of the Human Sciences* (Princeton, N.J., 1975); J. Ortega y Gasset, *History as a System and Other Essays Toward a Philosophy of History* (New York, 1941); N. Chiaromonte, *The Paradox of History,* rev. ed. (Philadelphia, 1985); R. Koselleck, *Futures Past: On the Semantics of Historical Time* (Cambridge, Mass., 1985); H. White, *The Content of the Form: Narrative Discourse and Historical Representation* (Baltimore, Md., 1987); L. Gossman, *Between History and Literature* (Cambridge, Mass., 1990).

23. On the Jewish idea of history, see Y. H. Yerushalmi, *Zakhor: Jewish History and Jewish Memory* (New York, 1989). On German historiography, see G. G. Iggers, *The German Conception of History: The National Tradition of Historical Thought from Herder to the Present,* rev. ed. (Hanover, N.H., 1988). On the historian's authority in ancient China, see W. Li, "The Idea of Authority in the Shih chi (Records of the Historian)," *JAS* 54/2 (December 1994): 345–405. On the memory, testimony, and representation of trauma, see L. L. Langer, *Holocaust Testimonies: The Ruins of Memory* (New Haven, Conn., 1991); G. H. Hartman (ed.), *Holocaust Remembrance: The Shapes of Memory* (Oxford, 1994); W. von Bredow, *Türkische Geschichte: Kollektive Erinnerung an den Holocaust* (Stuttgart, 1996); S. Felman and D. Laub, *Testimony: Crises of Witnessing in Literature, Psychoanalysis, and History* (New York, 1992); M. Blanchot, *The Writing of the Disaster* (Lincoln, Neb., 1986); S. Friedländer (ed.), *Probing the Limits of Representation: Nazism and the "Final Solution"* (Cambridge, Mass., 1992).

24. For some examples, see M. Eliade, *The Myth of the Eternal Return or Cosmos and History* (Princeton, N.J., 1954) and *The Sacred and the Profane: The Nature of Religion* (New York, 1959); J. Campbell (ed.), *Man and Time: Papers from the Eranos Yearbooks* (Princeton, N.J., 1957). On Jewish mysticism and preoccupation with mending the world, see G. Scholem, *Kabbalah* (New York, 1974); F. Rosenzweig, *The Star of Redemption* (Notre Dame, Ind., 1970); E. L. Fackenheim, *To Mend the World: Foundations of Post-Holocaust Jewish Thought* (Bloomington, Ind., 1982); E. Levinas, *Difficult Freedom: Essays on Judaism* (Baltimore, Md., 1990). On religious and secular communal or communist utopias, see I. Oved, *Two Hundred Years of American Communes* (New Brunswick, N.J., 1988); Y. Gorni et al. (eds.), *Communal Life: An International Perspective* (New Brunswick, N.J., 1987).

25. On colonial atrocities and links to later events in Europe, see S. Lindqvist, *"Exterminate All the Brutes"* (New York, 1996); J. Walston, "History and Memory in the Italian Concentration Camps," *HJ* 10/1 (1997); I. Hull, "Military Culture and the Production of 'Final Solutions' in the Colonies: The Example of Wilhelmine Germany" (unpublished paper, 1998), part of a larger project to be published in book form; C. Essner, "Zwischen Vernunft und Gefühl: Die Reichstagsdebatten von 1912 um koloniale 'Rassenmischehe' und 'Sexualität,'" *ZfG* 6 (1997): 503–19; T. Dedering, "'A Certain Rigorous Treatment of All Parts of the Nation': The Annihilation of the Herero in German South West Africa, 1904," in *The Massacre in History,* ed. M. Levene and P. Roberts (New York, 1999), pp. 205–22. See also V. N. Dadrian, *German Responsibility in the Armenian Genocide : A Review of the Historical Evidence of German Complicity* (Watertown, Mass., 1996).

26. On nationalism see, e.g., B. Anderson, *Imagined Communities: Reflections on the Origin and Spread of Nationalism,* rev. ed. (London, 1991); E. J. Hobsbawm, *Nations and Nationalism since 1780: Programme, Myth, Reality,* rev. ed. (Cambridge, 1993); L. Greenfeld, *Nationalism: Five Roads to Modernity* (Cambridge, Mass., 1992); E. Gellner, *Nations and Nationalism* (Ithaca, N.Y., 1983); G. Eley and R. G. Suny (eds.), *Becoming National: A Reader* (New York, 1996). See also J. L. Talmon, *Po-*

litical Messianism: The Romantic Phase (Boulder, Colo., 1985), and Talmon, *The Origins of Totalitarian Democracy* (Boulder, Colo., 1985). On the links between modernity, total war, and genocide, see D. Pick, *War Machine: The Rationalisation of Slaughter in the Modern Age* (New Haven, Conn., 1993); J. J. Reid, "Total War, the Annihilation Ethic and the Armenian Genocide," in *The Armenian Genocide: History, Politics, Ethics,* ed. R. G. Hovannisian (New York, 1992); R. G. Hovannisian (ed.), *The Armenian Genocide in Perspective* (New Brunswick, N.J, 1986); V. N. Dadrian, *The History of the Armenian Genocide: Ethnic Conflict from the Balkans to Anatolia to the Caucasus* (Providence, R.I., 1995); Bartov, *Murder in Our Midst.* On the emergence of the surveillance state, see P. Holquist, "'Information Is the Alpha and Omega of Our Work': Bolshevik Surveillance in Its Pan-European Context," *JMH* 69 (September 1997): 415–50.

27. The links between modern warfare and genocide can be gleaned from any major study of the latter. See, e.g., H. Hirsch, *Genocide and the Politics of Memory: Studying Death to Preserve Life* (Chapel Hill, N.C., 1995); L. Kuper, *Genocide: Its Political Use in the Twentieth Century* (New Haven, Conn., 1981); S. Totten et al. (eds.), *Century of Genocide: Eyewitness Accounts and Critical Views* (New York, 1997); R. J. Rummel, *Death by Government* (New Brunswick, N.J., 1994). On genocide as combined cleansing of racial pollution and asocial behavior, see M. Zimmermann, *Rassenutopie und Genozid: Die nationalsozialistische "Lösung der Zigeunerfrage"* (Hamburg, 1996); and as combined ethnic and class war, see B. Kiernan, "The Ethnic Element in the Cambodian Genocide" (unpublished paper, 1998). On ideological soldiers and war crimes, see O. Bartov, *Hitler's Army: Soldiers, Nazis, and War in the Third Reich* (New York, 1991); H. Heer and K. Naumann (eds.), *War of Extermination: Crimes of the Wehrmacht, 1941–1945* (New York, 2000); M. von Hagen, *Soldiers in the Proletarian Dictatorship: The Red Army and the Soviet Socialist State, 1917–1930* (Ithaca, N.Y., 1990).

28. For comparisons between Soviet and Nazi sociologically or racially motivated policies of population transfers and mass murder, see, e.g., the following works: S. Wheatcroft, "The Scale and Nature of German and Soviet Repressions and Mass Killings," *Europe-Asia Studies* 48/8 (1996); N. Naimark, "Ethnic Cleansing between War and Peace in the USSR," P. Holquist, "State Violence as Technique: The Logic of Violence in Soviet Totalitarianism," and A. Weiner, "Delineating the Soviet Body National in the Age of Socialism: Ukrainians, Jews and the Myth of the Second World War"—all three papers are to be published in *Modernity, Revolution, and Population Management in the Twentieth Century,* ed. A. Weiner (Stanford, Calif., forthcoming); A. Bullock, *Hitler and Stalin: Parallel Lives* (New York, 1992); B. Wegner (ed.), *From Peace to War: Germany, Soviet Russia and the World, 1939–1941* (Providence, R.I., 1997); and I. Kershaw and M. Lewin (eds.), *Stalinism and Nazism: Dictatorships in Comparison* (Cambridge, 1997). On other links and comparisons, see R. F. Melson, *Revolution and Genocide: On the Origins of the Armenian Genocide and the Holocaust* (Chicago, 1992); R. Secher, *Juifs et Vendéens: d'un génocide à l'autre* (Paris, 1991); and E. Malet (ed.), *Résistance et mémoire: D'Auschwitz à Sarajevo* (Paris, 1993).

29. On the bureaucratic nature of the Nazi genocide of the Jews, see R. Hilberg, *The Destruction of the European Jews,* 2nd rev. ed., 3 vols. (New York, 1985); H. Mommsen, *From Weimar to Auschwitz* (Princeton, N.J. 1991), esp. chapter 11. On technocrats and genocide, see G. Aly and S. Heim, *Vordenker der Vernichtung: Auschwitz und die deutschen Pläne für eine neue europäische Ordnung* (Frankfurt

am Main, 1993); G. Aly, *"Final Solution": Nazi Population Policy and the Murder of the European Jews* (New York, 1999). On historians and Nazism, see G. Aly, *Macht-Geist-Wahn: Kontinuitäten deutschen Denkens* (Berlin, 1997); P. Schöttler (ed.), *Geschichtsschreibung als Legitimationswissenschaft, 1918–1945* (Frankfurt am Main, 1997); K. Schönwälder, "'Taking Their Place in the Front-Line'(?): German Historians during Nazism and War," *TAJB* 25 (1996): 205–17; O. Heilbronner, "'... aber das "Reich" lebt in uns': Katholische Historiker unter dem Nationalsozialismus," *TAJB* 25 (1996): 219–31; S. Heim, "'Überbevölkerung' und 'Rassenkampf': Werner Conze und Gunther Ipsen" (unpublished paper, 1997); B. Mrozek, "Hitlers willige Wissenschaftler?" *Die Weltwoche* (July 3, 1997); M. Kröger and R. Thimme, *Die Geschichtsbilder des Historikers Karl Dietrich Erdmann: Vom Dritten Reich zur Bundesrepublik* (Munich, 1996); W. Oberkrome, *Volksgeschichte: Methodische Innovation und völkische Ideologisierung in der deutschen Geschichtswissenschaft, 1918–1945* (Göttingen, 1993); K.-H. Roth and A. Ebbinghaus, "Vorläufer des 'Generalplan Ost': Eine Dokumentation über Theodor Schieders Polendenkschrift," *ZfS* 21 (1992). On lawyers and judges, see Michael Stolleis, *The Law under the Swastika: Studies on Legal History in Nazi Germany* (Chicago, 1998); I. Müller, *Hitler's Justice: The Courts of the Third Reich* (Cambridge, Mass., 1991). On physicians, see M. Kater, *Doctors under Hitler* (Chapel Hill, N.C., 1989); H. Friedlander, *The Origins of Nazi Genocide: From Euthanasia to the Final Solution* (Chapel Hill, N.C., 1995); G. Cocks, *Psychotherapy in the Third Reich: The Göring Institute,* rev. ed. (New Brunswick, N.J., 1997).

30. See, e.g., H. Sluga, *Heidegger's Crisis: Philosophy and Politics in Nazi Germany* (Cambridge, Mass., 1993); A. D. Beyerchen, *Scientists under Hitler: Politics and the Physics Community in the Third Reich* (New Haven, Conn., 1977); T. Powers, *Heisenberg's War: The Secret Story of the German Bomb* (New York, 1993).

31. The most sustained criticism is M. Foucault, *The Order of Things: An Archeology of the Human Sciences* (London, 1970). Bauman, *Modernity and the Holocaust,* is a critique of the sociological profession. D. J. K. Peukert, "The Genesis of the 'Final Solution' from the Spirit of Science," in *Reevaluating the Third Reich,* ed. T. Childers and J. Caplan (New York, 1993), criticizes modern science; see, most recently, A. Beyerchen, "Rational Means and Irrational Ends: Thoughts on the Technology of Racism in the Third Reich," *CEH* 30/3 (1997): 386–402. B. Lang, *Act and Idea in the Nazi Genocide* (Chicago, 1990), is a philosophical critique, as is, of course, T. W. Adorno, *Negative Dialectics* (New York, 1973). H. Kaplan, *Conscience and Memory: Meditations in a Museum of the Holocaust* (Chicago, 1994), is a critique of modern political ethics. D. LaCapra's *Representing the Holocaust: History, Theory, and Trauma* (Ithaca, N.Y., 1994) and *History and Memory after Auschwitz* (Ithaca, N.Y., 1998) are critiques of the historiography and representation of the Holocaust. Yet by and large the academic disciplines have continued their nineteenth-century traditions without seeing twentieth-century utopias and genocides as anything more than a series of road accidents on the path to a better future, deeper understanding, and expanding knowledge, on the basis of the old and "proven" frameworks of learning, conceptualization, and progress.

32. See references above, chapter 3, nn. 109–17.

33. See, e.g., L. Ferry and A. Renaut, *Système et critique: Essais sur la critique de la raison dans la philosophie contemporaine* (Brussels, 1984); J.-F. Lyotard, *The Inhuman: Reflections on Time* (Stanford, Calif., 1991); D. J. Haraway, *Primate Visions: Gender, Race, and Nature in the World of Modern Science* (New York, 1989).

34. M. Horkheimer and T. W. Adorno, *Dialectic of Enlightenment* (New York, 1991); A. Finkielkraut, *The Defeat of the Mind* (New York, 1995); Finkielkraut, *Remembering in Vain: The Klaus Barbie Trial and Crimes against Humanity* (New York, 1992); Bauman, *Modernity and the Holocaust;* Arendt, *The Origins of Totalitarianism;* Bartov, *Murder in Our Midst.*

35. For examples of the consequent realignment and reconceptualization of history and historiography, see D. LaCapra, *Rethinking Intellectual History: Texts, Contents, Language* (Ithaca, 1983); S. Cohen, *Historical Culture: On the Recoding of an Academic Discipline* (Berkeley, Calif., 1986); J. W. Scott, *Gender and the Politics of History* (New York, 1988); L. Hunt (ed.), *The New Cultural History* (Berkeley, Calif., 1989); R. Cohen (ed.), *Studies in Historical Change* (Charlottesville, Va., 1992); J. Appelby et al. (eds.), *Knowledge and Postmodernism in Historical Perspective* (New York, 1996); P. Hamilton, *Historicism* (London, 1996). See also D. Harvey, *The Condition of Postmodernity: An Enquiry into the Origins of Cultural Change* (Oxford, 1989).

36. On coming to terms with inhumanity in the twentieth century, see, e.g., G. M. Kren and L. Rappoport, *The Holocaust and the Crisis of Human Behavior,* rev. ed. (New York, 1994); G. E. Markle, *Meditations of a Holocaust Traveler* (New York, 1995); J. K. Roth and M. Berenbaum (eds.), *Holocaust: Religious and Philosophical Implications* (New York, 1989); T. Des Pres, *Writing into the World: Essays, 1973–1987* (New York, 1991); J. E. Dimsdale (ed.), *Survivors, Victims, and Perpetrators: Essays on the Nazi Holocaust* (Washington, D.C. 1980); R. Moses (ed.), *Persistent Shadows of the Holocaust: The Meaning to Those Not Directly Affected* (Madison, Conn., 1993). On pain and torture, see J. Améry, *At the Mind's Limits: Contemplation by a Survivor on Auschwitz and Its Realities* (New York, 1986), esp. the chapter "Torture"; E. Scarry, *The Body in Pain: The Making and Unmaking of the World* (New York, 1985); E. Peters, *Torture,* expanded ed. (Philadelphia, 1996). See also J. Baudrillard, *The Transparency of Evil: Essays on Extreme Phenomena* (London, 1993).

37. In this context it is important to note that Primo Levi's memoir, known in its English translation as *Survival in Auschwitz* (New York, 1961), is called in the original Italian *Se questo è un uomo* (*Is This a Man?*), carrying the obvious association of the Christian *Ecce Homo.* See also Levi, *The Drowned and the Saved,* for further and more pessimistic ruminations on the humanity of man in inhuman circumstances.

38. See above, chapter 3, nn. 84 and 89. See also W. Laqueur and R. Breitman, *Breaking the Silence* (New York, 1986); B. Wasserstein, *Britain and the Jews of Europe, 1939–1945* (Oxford, 1988); M. Gilbert, *Auschwitz and the Allies* (New York, 1981).

39. See, e.g., J. Erickson, *Stalin's War with Germany,* 2 vols. 2nd ed. (London, 1985).

40. See above, n. 29, and chapter 3, n. 28.

41. J. Herf, *Divided Memory: The Nazi Past in the Two Germanys* (Cambridge, Mass., 1997); R. G. Moeller, "War Stories: The Search for a Usable Past in the Federal Republic of Germany," *AHR* 101 (October 1996): 1008–48; R. G. Moeller (ed.), *West Germany under Construction: Politics, Society, and Culture in the Adenauer Era* (Ann Arbor, Mich., 1997); D. Abenheim, *Reforging the Iron Cross: The Search for Tradition in the West German Armed Forces* (Princeton, N.J., 1988); D. C. Large, *Germans to the Front: West German Rearmament in the Adenauer Era* (Chapel Hill, N.C., 1996); F. Stern, *The Whitewashing of the Yellow Badge: Antisemitism and Philosemitism in Postwar Germany* (Oxford, 1992).

42. See above, chapter 3, nn. 89 and 102.

43. On Israeli-German relations, see M. Zimmermann and O. Heilbronner, *"Normal" Relations: Israeli-German Relations* (Jerusalem, 1993 [in Hebrew]); M. Wolff-sohn, *Eternal Guilt? Forty Years of German-Jewish-Israeli Relations* (New York, 1993); S. Shafir, *An Outstretched Hand: German Social Democrats, Jews, and Israel, 1945–1967* (Tel Aviv, 1986 [in Hebrew]). On relations with Austria, see H. Embacher and M. Reiter, *Gratwanderungen: Die Beziehungen zwischen Österreich und Israel im Schatten der Vergangenheit* (Vienna, 1998). On Yad Vashem, see J. E. Young, *The Texture of Memory: Holocaust Memorials and Meaning* (New Haven, Conn., 1993), chapter 9. See also see T. Segev, *The Seventh Million: The Israelis and the Holocaust* (New York, 1993).

44. See above, chapter 3, n. 88. See also M. Friedman "The State of Israel as a Theological Dilemma," in *The Israeli State: Boundaries and Frontiers,* ed. B. Kimmerling (Albany, N.Y., 1989); G. Greenberg, "Orthodox Jewish Thought in the Wake of the Holocaust: *Tamim Pa'alo* of 1947," in *In God's Name: Genocide and Religion in the Twentieth Century,* ed. O. Bartov and P. Mack (New York, 2000).

45. On church collaboration with the Nazis in Germany, see chapters by R. P. Ericksen, S. Heschel, B. Griech-Polelle, and D. L. Bergen, in Bartov and Mack, *In God's Name;* W. G. Jeanrond, "From Resistance to Liberation Theology: German Theologians and the Non/Resistance to the National Socialist Regime," in *Resistance against the Third Reich, 1933–1990,* ed. M. Geyer and J. W. Boyer (Chicago, 1994); for a survey of the literature, see R. P. Ericksen and S. Heschel, "The German Churches Face Hitler: Assessment of the Historiography," *TAJB* 23 (1994): 433–59. On France, see W. D. Halls, *Politics, Society and Christianity in Vichy France* (Oxford, 1995); E. Fouilloux, *Les chrétiens français entre crise et libération, 1937–1947* (Paris, 1997).

46. The best recent work on the conservatism of the 1950s and its impact on the younger generation in the 1960s and 1970s is D. Herzog, "'Pleasure, Sex, and Politics Belong Together': Post-Holocaust Memory and the Sexual Revolution in West Germany," *CI* 24 (winter 1988): 393–444. See also R. G. Moeller, *Protecting Motherhood: Women and the family in the Politics of Postwar West Germany* (Berkeley, Calif., 1993); and the comprehensive introduction by the editor to Moeller, *West Germany under Construction.*

47. Extensive extracts from the Vatican's first statement on the church and the Holocaust, issued on March 16, 1998, were published the following day in German translation by the *SZ* 63, p. 13. The statement expressed sorrow for the guilt of the sons and daughters of the church, not for any doctrinal, policy, or moral errors by the hierarchy. On the silence of the Vatican, see P. Blet, *Pius XII and the Second World War: According to the Archives of the Vatican* (New York, 1999); J. Cornwell, *Hitler's Pope: The Secret Policy of Pius XII* (New York, 1999). On how Hitler was "levered into power" by the conservatives, see I. Kershaw, *Hitler, 1889–1936: Hubris* (New York, 1998), pp. 377–427.

48. Generally on postwar American Jewry, see E. S. Shapiro, *A Time for Healing: American Jewry since World War II* (Baltimore, Md., 1992).

49. For some background, see A. Dowty, *The Jewish State: A Century Later* (Berkeley, Calif., 1998), esp. chapters 7–8 and literature cited therein; E. Sprinzak, *The Ascendance of Israel's Radical Right* (Oxford, 1991); M. F. Marty and R. S. Appleby (eds.), *Fundamentalism and the State* (Chicago, 1993), esp. chapters by Sprinzak and C. S. Liebman; I. Lustick and B. Rubin (eds.), *Critical Essays on Israeli Politics, Society, and Culture* (Albany, N.Y., 1991), esp. chapter by K. Avruch; E. Don-Yehiya,

"Jewish Messianism, Religious Zionism and Israeli Politics: The Impact and Origins of Gush Emunim," *MES* 23 (April 1987): 215–34; A. Arian and M. Shamir (eds.), *The Elections in Israel 1992* (Albany, N.Y., 1995); A. Willis, "Redefining Religious Zionism: Shas' Ethno-Politics," *ISB* 8 (fall 1992): 3–8. The biannual Hebrew-language magazine *Alpayim* has carried some important contributions to the debate over the nature of Israeli society and the conceptualizations of national identity surrounding the secular-religious split. See, most recently, issue 16 (summer 1998), with articles by the Supreme Court judges Haim Cohen (emeritus) and Aharon Barak (president); Rabbi Shmuel-Avishai Stockhammer; and professors Menachem Mautner (law), Yossi Yonah (education), and Baruch Kimmerling (sociology), all of whom write on the tension between law, liberalism, and Judaism in the state of Israel.

50. *The Order of Terror: The Concentration Camp,* trans. W. Templer (Princeton, N.J., 1997). Citations are from the translated version.

51. *Facing the Extreme: Moral Life in the Concentration Camps,* trans. A. Denner and A. Pollak (New York, 1996). Citations are from the translated version.

52. This term was used first by D. Rousset, *L'Univers concentrationnaire* (1945; Paris, 1965).

53. C. Lanzmann, *Shoah: A Oral History of the Holocaust* (New York, 1985), p. 200. On joyless reactions to the liberation by Jewish inmates in Auschwitz as described by Primo Levi, see above, p. 67, where he notes that they often realized only then that they had nothing to go back to.

54. *Facing the Extreme,* pp. 38–39.

55. *The Order of Terror,* pp. 162–63.

56. *Facing the Extreme,* pp. 17–18, 71–90.

57. *The Drowned and the Saved,* pp. 70–87.

58. *Facing the Extreme,* pp. 91–118.

59. Levi, *Survival in Auschwitz,* pp. 99–105; J. Semprun, *Literature or Life* (New York, 1997), pp. 58–77.

60. I. Kertész, *Fateless* (Evanston, Ill., 1992), chapter 8; Semprun, *Literature or Life,* chapter 1. Also compare Kertész, *Kaddish for a Child Not Born* (Evanston, Ill., 1997), and Semprun, *Literature or Life,* chapter 2, "Kaddish," for two entirely different perspectives. Even among politicals there were vast differences, of course. See M. Buber-Neumann, *Milena* (New York, 1988), on how former Communists were abused by Communist inmates in the women's camp of Ravensbrück. On the manner in which Jewish women were treated worse than other women inmates even in what they called a "good" forced-labor camp, see F. Karay, *Rockets and Rhymes: The Hasag-Leipzig Women Labor Camp* (Tel Aviv 1997 [in Hebrew]). In his harrowing tale of the experiences of the "politicals" in the camps, *The Human Species* (Marlboro, Vt., 1992), Robert Antelme notes that the Jews fared much worse. Although he barely survived, Antelme was eventually saved from post-liberation starvation and illness by the intervention of well-connected French resisters, among whom was the former Vichy official and future president of the Fifth Republic, François Mitterrand.

61. *The Survivor: An Anatomy of Life in the Death Camps* (New York, 1976).

62. Levi, *The Drowned and the Saved;* T. Borowski, *This Way for the Gas, Ladies and Gentlemen* (New York, 1967); Améry, *At the Mind's Limits;* Ka-Tzetnik, *Shivitti: A Vision* (San Francisco, 1989); Finkielkraut, *Remembering in Vain.*

63. Y. Arad, *Belzec, Sobibor, Treblinka: The Operation Reinhard Death Camps* (Bloomington, Ind., 1987).

64. Y. Arad et al. (eds.), *Documents on the Holocaust: Selected Sources on the Destruction of the Jews of Germany and Austria, Poland, and the Soviet Union* (Jerusalem, 1981), p. 433, for English translation and p. 434 for a copy of the original, hand-written proclamation in Yiddish. Ibid., pp. 301–4, for two calls for resistance by the Jewish Fighting Organization of the Warsaw Ghetto in January 1943.

65. Ibid., p. 433.

66. Ibid., pp. 461–71, for extracts from the diary of a Jewish partisan on the life of partisans and Jewish family camps in the forest, 1942–43, and the operations diary of a Jewish partisan unit in Rudniki Forest, 1943–44.

67. Y. Gutman, *The Jews of Warsaw, 1939–1943: Ghetto, Underground, Revolt* (Bloomington, Ind., 1989); S. Rotem (Kazik), *Memoirs of a Ghetto Fighter: The Past within Me* (New Haven, Conn., 1994). See also A. Paucker, *Standhalten und Widerstehen: Der Widerstand deutscher und österreichischer Juden gegen die nationalsozialistische Diktatur* (Essen, 1995); Paucker, "Jewish Resistance in Germany: The Facts and the Problems," *Gedenkstätte Deutscher Widerstand* (Berlin, 1991); K. Kwiet and H. Eschwege, *Selbstbehauptung und Widerstand: Deutsche Juden im Kampf um Existenz und Menschenwürde, 1933–1945* (Hamburg, 1984); R. Poznanski, "Reflections on Jewish Resistance and Jewish Resistants in France," *JSS* 2/1 (fall 1995): 124–58.

68. "Individual and Mass Behavior in Extreme Situations," *ASP* 38/4 (October 1943): 417–52.

69. See above, chapter 3, pp. 127–134, esp. nn. 92, 95, 98, and 100. See also below, pp. 185–212.

70. See above, chapter 3, n. 93. See also R. Moses (ed.), *Persistent Shadows of the Holocaust: The Meaning to Those Not Directly Affected* (Madison, Conn., 1993); J. E. Dimsdale (ed.), *Survivors, Victims, and Perpetrators: Essays on the Nazi Holocaust* (Washington, D.C., 1980).

71. In the present context, see, e.g., C. Caruth, *Unclaimed Experience: Trauma, Narrative, and History* (Baltimore, Md., 1996), and Caruth (ed.), *Trauma: Explorations in Memory* (Baltimore, Md., 1995); S. Friedländer, "Trauma and Transference," in Friedländer, *Memory, History, and the Extermination of the Jews of Europe* (Bloomington, Ind., 1993); E. L. Santner, "History beyond the Pleasure Principle: Some Thoughts on the Representation of Trauma," in *Probing the Limits of Representation: Nazism and the "Final Solution,"* ed. S. Friedländer (Cambridge, Mass., 1992); LaCapra, *Representing the Holocaust;* and L. Douglas, "Wartime Lies: Securing the Holocaust in Law and Literature," *YJLH* 7/2 (summer 1995): 367–96, his "Film as Witness: Screening *Nazi Concentration Camps* before the Nuremberg Tribunal," *YLJ* 105/2 (November 1995): 449–81, and his "The Memory of Judgment: The Law, the Holocaust, and Denial," *H&M* 7 (fall/winter 1996): 100–120.

72. H. Binneveld, *From Shell Shock to Combat Stress: A Comparative History of Military Psychiatry* (Amsterdam, 1998). See also A. Becker, *Oubliés de la grande guerre. Humanitaire et culture de guerre, 1914–1918: Populations occupées, déportés civils, prisonniers de guerre* (Paris, 1998), pp. 337–58; T. Bogacz, "War Neurosis and Cultural Change in England, 1914–1922," *JCH* (1989); E. D. Brown, "Between Cowardice and Insanity: Shell Shock and the Legitimization of the Neurosis in Great Britain," in *Science, Technology and the Military,* ed. E. Mendelsohn et al. (New York, 1988); J. E. Talbott, "Soldiers, Psychiatrists and Combat Trauma," *JIH* (1997);

N. Ferguson, *The Pity of War* (London, 1998), pp. 340–43; R. W. Whalen, *Bitter Wounds: German Victims of the Great War, 1914–1939* (Ithaca, N.Y., 1984), pp. 61–65, and sources cited therein, esp. S. Ferenczi et al., *Psycho-Analysis and the War Neuroses* (London, 1921).

73. C. R. Browning, *Ordinary Men: Reserve Police Battalion 101 and the Final Solution in Poland* (New York, 1992), chapter 18; S. Milgram, *Obedience to Authority: An Experimental View* (New York, 1974).

74. D. J. Goldhagen, *Hitler's Willing Executioners: Ordinary Germans and the Holocaust* (New York, 1996), part I. For a review of this book, see O. Bartov, "Ordinary Monsters," *TNR* (April 29, 1996): 32–38.

75. *The Weimar Republic: The Crisis of Classical Modernity* (New York, 1992).

76. *Modernity and the Holocaust.*

77. *The Origins of Totalitarian Democracy,* orig. pub. in Hebrew in 1952.

78. *The Origins of Totalitarianism,* first published in 1951.

79. E. Kogon, *The Theory and Practice of Hell: The German Concentration Camps and the System behind Them* (New York, 1950 [first published in German as *Der SS-Staat* in 1945]); L. Poliakov, *Bréviaire de la haine* (Paris, 1951); G. Reitlinger, *The Final Solution: The Attempt to Exterminate the Jews of Europe, 1939–1945* (London, 1953); R. Hilberg, *The Destruction of the European Jews* (London, 1961); J. Tenenbaum, *Race and Reich: The Story of an Epoch* (New York, 1956). See also Y. Gutman and G. Greif (eds.), *The Historiography of the Holocaust Period* (Jerusalem, 1988); I. Kershaw, *The Nazi Dictatorship: Problems and Perspectives of Interpretation,* 3rd ed. (London, 1993); D. Pohl, "Die Holocaust-Forschung und Goldhagens Thesen," *VfZ* 45/1 (1997): 1–48; Michman, *The Holocaust,* pp. 13–42.

80. D. G. Schilling, "Re-Presenting the Holocaust in the General Histories of World War II" (unpublished paper, 1998).

81. L. S. Dawidowicz, *The Holocaust and the Historians* (Cambridge, Mass., 1981), chapters 4–5.

82. S. Ettinger, *Modern Anti-Semitism: Studies and Essays* (Tel Aviv, 1978 [in Hebrew]); S. Almog (ed.), *Antisemitism through the Ages: A Collection of Essays* (Oxford, 1988); R. S. Wistrich, *Antisemitism: The Longest Hatred* (New York, 1992).

83. The best surveys of these schools are C. R. Browning, *The Path to Genocide: Essays on Launching the Final Solution* (Cambridge, 1992), chapter 5; M. R. Marrus, *The Holocaust in History* (New York, 1987), chapter 3; Kershaw, *The Nazi Dictatorship.* See now also U. Herbert, "Vernichtungspolitik: Neue Antworten und Fragen zur Geschichte des 'Holocaust,'" in *Nationalsozialistische Vernichtungspolitik, 1939–1945: Neue Forschungen und Kontroversen,* ed. U. Herbert (Frankfurt am Main, 1998); a revised version of this essay is in the English translation of this book, U. Herbert (ed.), *National Socialist Extermination Policies: Contemporary German Perspectives and Controversies* (New York, 1999). The most extensive and devastating critique of the *Sonderweg* theory, which also contains references to all major works in that genre, is D. Blackbourn and G. Eley, *The Peculiarities of German History: Bourgeois Society and Politics in Nineteenth-Century Germany* (Oxford, 1984).

84. See esp. I. Trunk, *Judenrat: The Jewish Councils in Eastern Europe under Nazi Occupation* (1972; Lincoln, Neb., 1996); Y. Gutman and R. Manbar (eds.), *The Nazi Concentration Camps: Structure and Aims. The Image of the Prisoner. The Jews in the Camps* (Jerusalem, 1984 [in Hebrew]); Y. Gutman and R. Manbar (eds.), *Patterns of Jewish Leadership in Nazi Europe, 1933–1945* (Jerusalem, 1979 [in Hebrew]).

85. See above, chapter 3, nn. 89, 100, 102.

86. Y. Elkana, "Bizhut ha-shihehah" ("In Praise of Forgetting"), *Ha-aretz* (March 2, 1988): 3. See also M. Zuckermann, "The Curse of Forgetting: Israel and the Holocaust," *Telos* 78 (winter 1988–89): 43–54; Zuckermann, *Shoah in the Sealed Room: The "Holocaust" in Israeli Press During the Gulf War* (Tel Aviv, 1993 [in Hebrew]), pp. 17–31; U. Ram, "The Map and the Board: Introductory Remarks to the History of Memory and Forgetting (a gesture to Yehudah Elkana's article 'In Praise of Forgetting')," *T&B* (1998 [in Hebrew]).

87. On the medical profession, biology, and eugenics, see Weindling, *Health, Race, and German Politics;* Proctor, *Racial Hygiene;* Aly et al., *Cleansing the Fatherland;* Burleigh, *Death and Deliverance;* Kater, *Doctors under Hitler;* Lifton, *The Nazi Doctors;* Friedlander, *The Origins of Nazi Genocide;* Cocks, *Psychotherapy in the Third Reich.* On scientists, see H. Mehrtens and S. Richter (eds.), *Naturwissenschaft, Technik und NS-Ideologie: Beiträge zur Wissenschaftsgeschichte des Dritten Reiches* (Frankfurt am Main, 1980); Beyerchen, *Scientists under Hitler;* Powers, *Heisenberg's War.* On other academics, see Aly and Heim, *Vordenker der Vernichtung;* M. Burleigh, *Germany Turns Eastwards: A Study of* "Ostforschung" *in the Third Reich* (Cambridge, 1988); Kröger and Thimme, *Karl Dietrich Erdmann;* Aly, *Macht-Geist-Wahn;* Oberkrome, *Volksgeschichte;* Roth and Ebbinghaus, *Vorläufer des "Generalplan Ost";* Schöttler, *Geschichtsschreibung;* Heim, *"Überbevölkerung" und "Rassenkampf";* Mrozek, *Hitlers willige Wissenschaftler?;* Conte and Essner, *La quête de la race;* Sluga, *Heidegger's Crisis.* On lawyers, see Müller, *Hitler's Justice.* On top SS men, see Herbert, *Best;* Hachmeister, *Der Gegnerforscher;* Wildt, *Das Führungskorps des Reichssicherheitshauptamtes.* On schools, see H. Scholtz, *Erziehung und Unterricht unterm Hakenkreuz* (Göttingen, 1985); G. Platner (ed.), *Schule im Dritten Reich—Erziehung zum Tod?* (Munich, 1983); H. Kupffer, *Der Faschismus und das Menschenbild der deutschen Pädagogik* (Frankfurt am Main, 1984). On art, see Petropoulos, *Art as Politics;* Steinweis, *Art, Ideology, and Economics in Nazi Germany.* On the media, H. Hoffmann, *The Triumph of Propaganda: Film and National Socialism, 1933–1945* (Providence, R.I., 1996); E. Rentschler, *The Ministry of Illusion: Nazi Cinema and Its Afterlife* (Cambridge, Mass., 1996); D. Welch, *The Third Reich: Politics and Propaganda* (London, 1993); O. J. Hale, *The Captive Press in the Third Reich* (Princeton, N.J., 1964).

88. Goldhagen, *Hitler's Willing Executioners,* p. 7. The term is of course taken from C. Geertz, "Thick Description: Toward an Interpretive Theory of Culture," in *The Interpretation of Cultures: Selected Essays* (New York, 1973), pp. 3–30.

89. For an extraordinary collection of documents and photographs, see E. Klee et al. (eds.), *"The Good Old Days": The Holocaust as Seen by Its Perpetrators and Bystanders* (New York, 1991), and *The German Army and Genocide: Crimes against War Prisoners, Jews, and Other Civilians, 1939–1944,* ed. Hamburg Institute for Social Research (New York, 1999). See also, e.g., A. Grynberg, *La Shoah: L'impossible oubli* (Paris, 1995); A. Adelson and R. Lapides (eds.), *Lodz Ghetto: Inside a Community under Siege* (New York, 1989); des Pres, *The Survivor;* Kogon, *The Theory and Practice of Hell;* Arad, *Belzec, Sobibor, Treblinka.* Y. Gutman and M. Berenbaum (eds.), *Anatomy of the Auschwitz Death Camps* (Bloomington, Ind., 1994); Dwork and van Pelt, *Auschwitz;* E. Ringelblum, *Notes from the Warsaw Ghetto,* 2nd ed., ed. J. Sloan (New York: 1974); A. Tory, *Surviving the Holocaust: The Kovno Ghetto Diary* (Cambridge, Mass., 1990). For only a few harrowing memoirs, see, e.g., I. Zuckerman (Antek), *Those Seven Years, 1939–1946* (Tel Aviv, n.d. [in Hebrew]); F. Stiffel, *The Tale of the Ring: A Kaddish,* 2nd ed. (Wainscott, N.Y., 1994 [1984]); M. Nyiszli, *Auschwitz: A Doctor's Eyewitness Account* (New York, 1993); C. J. Letulle, *Nightmare Memoir:*

Four Years as a Prisoner of the Nazis (Baton Rouge, La., 1987); S. Nomberg-Przytyk, *Auschwitz: True Tales from a Grotesque Land* (Chapel Hill, N.C., 1985). See also the controversial work, J. F. Steiner, *Treblinka,* 3rd ed. (New York, 1994).

90. For biographical details see D. Meron, "Between Books and Ashes," *Alpayim* 10 (1994 [in Hebrew]): 196–224.

91. For a brief history of the Jewish Brigade and its involvement in the *Brihah,* see H. Bartov, "The Flag and the Bridge," in *The Living Bridge: The Meeting of the Volunteers from Eretz Israel with the Holocaust Survivors,* catalog of an exhibit (Tel Aviv, 1983 [in Hebrew]). See also D. Ofer, *Escaping the Holocaust: Illegal Immigration to the Land of Israel, 1939–1944* (New York, 1990); I. Zertal, *From Catastrophe to Power: Holocaust Survivors and the Emergence of Israel* (Berkeley, Calif., 1998).

92. See H. Gouri, *The Glass Cage: The Jerusalem Trial* (Tel Aviv, 1962 [in Hebrew]), pp. 123–26, chapter entitled "Star of Ashes."

93. I will be citing here the recently reissued Hebrew edition of the sextet: *Salamandra* (Tel Aviv, 1994); *House of Dolls* [*Beit ha-bubot*] (Tel Aviv, 1994); *Piepel* (Tel Aviv, 1988); *The Clock* [*Ha-shaon*] (Tel Aviv, 1994); *The Confrontation* [*Ha-imut*] (Tel Aviv, 1989); *The Code: The Burden of the Nucleus of Auschwitz* [*Ha-tsofen: Masa ha-garin shel Auschwitz*] (Tel Aviv, 1994). Unless otherwise indicated, all translations in this section are mine.

94. Ka-Tzetnik, however, writes the following in his introductory paragraph to this volume: "*Piepels*—young lads who were chosen by barracks commanders in Auschwitz for sexual perversities. The author of this chronicle does not know where the term *Piepel* was derived from, who coined it, and from what language it originated. In any case, in Auschwitz it was a common term, such as the words *bread, mussulman, crematorium.*" See the Duden German language dictionary entry for "Piepel." There is also probably a connection with the Hebrew term *pipi,* used by children to denote penis (and urinating), probably from Yiddish but common in similar forms in many other European languages. *Piepels* are mentioned in various sources. See, e.g., Stiffel, *Tale of the Ring,* p. 196; E. Wiesel, *The Night Trilogy,* 3rd ed. (New York, 1988), p. 70.

95. It should be noted that many of these volumes were published under different names both in Hebrew, Yiddish, and in translation to other languages. There is also some reason to assume that, at least initially, Dinur wrote in Yiddish and his work was then translated into Hebrew. Thus, e.g., the first edition of his first published book after the war, *Salamandra* (Tel Aviv, 1946), notes that it was "translated from the manuscript" by Y. L. Barukh. The original language is not given, but since Feiner's volume of poetry in the early 1930s was in Yiddish, it appears likely that he was still using Yiddish when he wrote it in a D.P. camp in Italy. According to the original Hebrew edition of T. Segev, *The Seventh Million: The Israelis and the Holocaust* [*Ha-milion ha-shevii*] (Jerusalem, 1991), p. 2, the manuscript was indeed translated from a Yiddish manuscript by the writer Y. D. Berkovits, who received it from Zalman Rubashov, a poet later known as Zalman Shazar, the third president of Israel. These details are omitted from the English translation of Segev.

Most earlier editions and translations describe these books as "novels," and libraries tend to catalog them under "fiction"; Dinur has always rejected both of these terms as irrelevant to his work, claiming to be merely a chronicler (see more on this below). His work has been published in English, Yiddish, German, Polish, Russian, Portuguese, Spanish, and Arabic. The most widely translated volume seems to be *House of Dolls,* which is also the most pornographic. The best collection of Ka-

Tzetnik's writings in the United States is probably in the Widener Library at Harvard University.

96. Thus, for instance, J. E. Young, *Writing and Rewriting the Holocaust: Narrative and the Consequences of Interpretation* (Bloomington, Ind., 1990), mentions works of Ka-Tzetnik in the bibliography (categorized under "Fiction and Imaginative Literature"), but not in the index; M. Teichman and S. Leder (eds.), *Truth and Lamentation: Stories and Poems on the Holocaust* (Urbana, Ill., 1994), a five-hundred-page anthology, mentions Ka-Tzetnik in the bibliography (categorized under "Fiction") but includes no extract from his work; S. DeKoven Ezrahi, *By Words Alone: The Holocaust in Literature* (Chicago, 1980), makes no mention of him; nor does D. G. Roskies, *Against the Apocalypse: Responses to Catastrophe in Modern Jewish Culture* (Cambridge, Mass., 1984); nor does Roskies, *The Literature of Destruction*. No mention is made in L. Langer (ed.), *Art from the Ashes: A Holocaust Anthology* (New York, 1995); in Langer, *Versions of Survival: The Holocaust and the Human Spirit* (Albany, N.Y., 1982); or in Hartman, *Holocaust Remembrance*. Ka-Tzetnik does appear (under "Fiction") in the bibliography of A. H. Rosenfeld, *A Double Dying: Reflections on Holocaust Literature* (Bloomington, Ind., 1988), but the book lacks an index and I could find no mention of him in the text. The only essay on Ka-Tzetnik I could find in recent scholarship and anthologies on the Holocaust is H. Needler, "Red Fire upon Black Fire: Hebrew in the Holocaust Novels of K. Tsetnik," in *Writing and the Holocaust,* ed. B. Lang (New York, 1988). This essay, however, is far too sketchy to be described as a significant contribution to our understanding of Ka-Tzetnik. The best analysis I know is the above-cited article by Meron, "Between Books and Ashes," but it too deals with another matter, namely Dinur's destruction of his prewar poetry, to which I will return below.

97. In this respect, as in another discussed below, there are some striking similarities between Ka-Tzetnik and Wiesel. The difference is that Wiesel maintains the same rhetorical tone throughout his writing, whether it concerns postwar New York and Paris, prewar Sighet, or Auschwitz. This enables him to create a distance between the reader and the atrocities he describes, which in turn makes reading him somewhat less disturbing than reading Ka-Tzetnik's frenzied prose. This may be another reason for the former's popularity and the latter's obscurity.

98. One of the best analyses of pornography I know can be found in Vladimir Nabokov's 1956 essay, "On a Book Entitled *Lolita,*" in his *Lolita,* 5th ed. (Harmondsworth, 1982). For a more recent interpretation, see L. Williams, *Hard Core: Power, Pleasure, and the "Frenzy of the Visible"* (Berkeley, Calif., 1989). I would like to thank Dagmar Herzog for drawing my attention to this book.

99. On Israel and the Holocaust, see D. Porat, *The Blue and the Yellow Stars of David: The Zionist Leadership in Palestine and the Holocaust, 1939–1945* (Cambridge, Mass, 1990); Ofer, *Escaping the Holocaust;* Zertal, *From Catastrophe to Power;* H. Yablonka, *Foreign Brethren: Holocaust Survivors in the State of Israel, 1948–1952* (Jerusalem, 1994 [in Hebrew]); Segev, *The Seventh Million.* On forging Israeli national identity, see Y. Zerubavel, *Recovered Roots: Collective Memory and the Making of Israeli National Tradition* (Chicago, 1995); N. Ben-Yehudah, *The Massada Myth: Collective Memory and Mythmaking in Israel* (Madison, Wis., 1995); N. Gertz, *Captive of a Dream: National Myths in Israeli Culture* (Tel Aviv, 1995 [in Hebrew]); O. Almog, *The Sabra—A Profile* (Tel Aviv, 1997 [in Hebrew]).

100. This motif can be found, for instance, in Wiesel's "Dawn," in *Night Trilogy,* as well as in the early chapters of Ka-Tzetnik's *The Confrontation.* On revenge see

also B. Lang, "Holocaust Memory and Revenge: The Presence of the Past," *JSS* 2/2 (1996): 1–20, and Segev, *The Seventh Million,* pp. 140–52.

101. Television came to Israel only after the Six Day War of 1967. On television and the Holocaust in the United States, see the J. Shandler, *While America Watches: Televising the Holocaust* (New York, 1999). With some rare and important exceptions, the cinema hardly dealt with the topic, either in Israel or elsewhere (see, e.g., N. Gertz, "From Jew to Hebrew: The Zionist 'Narrative' in the Israeli Cinema of the 1940s and 1950s" [unpublished paper, 1997]). Radio, along with the newspapers, was the predominant medium of mass communication in those years, but provided only two outstanding examples of Holocaust representation. First, the live broadcasts of the Eichmannn trial in the early 1960s, which were closely followed by the whole nation and whose impact on the youngsters of the time is almost impossible to gauge, though it was doubtlessly profound. Second, the long lists of missing family members' names, for whom survivors were still looking, that were read daily on the radio, a terrifying, yet quickly routinized ritual that stamped the mind, quite unconsciously, with the sense of living after a great catastrophe.

102. Two such books, very popular in pre-1967 Israel among teenagers, can illustrate this type of literature: Y. Gutman, *Revolt of the Besieged: Mordecai Anielewicz and the Uprising of the Warsaw Ghetto*] (Merhavia, Israel, 1963 [in Hebrew]); and J. Ziemian, *The Cigarette Sellers of Three Crosses Square* (New York, 1975).

103. The word *Stalag* is derived from the German *Stammlager,* or prison camp. I should add here that this type of pornography was most probably read mainly by boys, whereas Ka-Tzetnik was read, I believe, just as often by girls. This would imply that boys read Ka-Tzetnik differently from girls. I have no way of ascertaining this assumption, however. To be sure, this would also be relevant to the fact that these boys later became combat soldiers who had to negotiate between their self-image as defending the survivors (*sheerit ha-pletah*) and their perceived need to become as tough and cruel as the enemy. (Women in Israel served in combat only in the 1948 war and even then in very small numbers.) I wish to thank Linda Mizejewski for drawing my attention to this important gender distinction.

104. *House of Dolls,* p. 229. Originally published in *Ba-mahaneh,* April 23, 1987. Parts of this letter are inscribed on a stone tablet on the site in Jerusalem, known as Givat Ha-tahmoshet (Ammunition Hill) where this soldier fell.

105. The issue of unfulfilled revenge is dealt with in a variety of manners by writers on the Holocaust. Wiesel's story "Dawn," in *Night Trilogy,* is about taking revenge against the wrong enemy, and in this case the protagonist actually ends up shooting the British hostage his Jewish terrorist group had taken in Palestine. Hanoch Bartov's novel *The Brigade* (London, 1968 [orig. pub. in Hebrew in 1965]) is also concerned with the impossibility of taking revenge, this time by young Jews from Palestine who were in the British Army, when the Allies occupied Germany.

106. The one exception might be Borowski, *This Way for the Gas, Ladies and Gentlemen.* But Borowski was a "privileged" inmate since he was not Jewish, which makes for a major difference in his perspective on Auschwitz.

107. P. Levi, *Ha-zehu adam?* (Tel Aviv, 1988), Hebrew translation of *Se questo è un uomo,* originally published in 1947 and hardly noticed, then reissued in 1958 to great public acclaim; published in English originally as *If This Is a Man* (New York, 1959), then as *Survival in Auschwitz* (New York, 1961). Interestingly, of the next two volumes in Levi's trilogy, *The Reawakening* (New York, 1987 [orig. pub. as *La tregua* in 1963]) and *Moments of Reprieve* (New York, 1987 [orig. pub. as *Lilit e*

altri racconti in 1981]), the former was already published in Hebrew in 1979, with a brief introduction by the author from which it is instructive to cite the following lines: "I am very glad and proud that my 'Reawakening' is being published in Israel many years after its birth in Italy. It is not strange that my first book (*Survival in Auschwitz*), of which the present volume is a sequence, was not translated into Hebrew: *Survival in Auschwitz* is the diary of a concentration camp, a far too familiar topic for yet another book on it to arouse any attention. Conversely, the events related here are less familiar: they took place on the margins of Europe. . . . This brief and happy period of the end of the Second World War, when a 'high wind blew over Europe,' and when, in the midst of the ruins and massacres, it was possible to breathe everywhere the greatest of hopes. . . . Perhaps precisely because of this characteristic, of a kind of journey upward, a reverse path to the infernal voyage that had led to Auschwitz, *The Reawakening* has become a popular book, in Italy and other countries in which it has appeared" (*Ha-hafugah,* 2nd ed. [Tel Aviv, 1990 (1979)], p. 5).

108. Primo Levi, *The Drowned and the Saved* (New York, 1988).

109. In addition to Levi's and Wiesel's works cited above, see Améry, *At the Mind's Limits.*

110. Dante Alighieri, *The Divine Comedy: Cantica I: Hell (L'Inferno)* (Harmondsworth, 1972), pp. 235–37 (Canto xxvi).

111. In this context we should also bear in mind the case of Paul Celan. See S. DeKoven Ezrahi, "'The Grave in the Air': Unbound Metaphors in Post-Holocaust Poetry," in Friedländer, *Probing the Limits of Representation,* pp. 259–76; J. Felstiner, *Paul Celan: Poet, Survivor, Jew* (New Haven, Conn., 1995).

112. For an analysis of the transformation of Wiesel's original Yiddish text, *Un di velt hot geshvign (And the World Kept Silent)*, published in Buenos Aires in 1956, to the first French edition of *Night,* published in Paris in 1958 as *La Nuit,* and the manner in which Wiesel changed the main drift of his text from a Judeocentric *J'accuse* to a universalist cry of outrage and despair, see N. Seidman, "Elie Wiesel and the Scandal of Jewish Rage," *JSS* 3/1 (fall 1996): 1–19.

113. See especially "Dawn," in *Night Trilogy,* which is highly reminiscent of both Dostoevsky's preoccupation with assassination in *The Possessed* and *Crime and Punishment,* related to his own traumatic experience of mock execution in his youth, and of Sartre's interest in waiting for an execution as expressed in the story "The Wall." This was also an interest voiced by Ernst Jünger when he served as an officer in Nazi-occupied Paris and conducted several executions of Wehrmacht deserters. See B. Engelmann, *In Hitler's Germany: Everyday Life in the Third Reich* (New York, 1986), pp. 238–39.

114. Blurb in all volumes. Segev, *The Seventh Million,* p. 3, cites Dinur's testimony from the court's protocol, meeting 68, June 7, 1961, as follows: "I was there for about two years. Time there is different from what it is here on earth. Every split second ran on a different cycle of time. And the inhabitants of that planet had no names. They had neither parents nor children. They did not dress as we dress here. They were not born there nor did anyone give birth. Even their breathing was regulated by the laws of another nature. They did not live, nor did they die, in accordance with the laws of this world. Their names were numbers. . . . They left me, they kept leaving me, left, . . . for close to two years they left me and always left me behind. . . . I see them, they are watching me, I see them. . . . " See also Gouri, *The Glass Cage,* pp. 123–26, whose description of the event carries a hint of irony. In *The Code (Ha-tsofen)* Ka-Tzetnik writes: "More than a hundred people gave testimony to the

judges during the Eichmann trial, and I am the only one who was paralyzed already after the second question: 'Is your name Dinur?' 'Yes,' I answer. 'What is the reason that in your books you hide under a different name?' Such a simple and conventional question, and yet the moment it goes through my ears and reaches my brain an explosion occurs there: Here they are about to combine two identities into one, and I have to declare and confirm this publicly! Therefore I escape to no-man's-land, become a 'vegetable' in hospital. How did Professor Bastiaans [the psychiatrist who treats Dinur with LSD] put it? 'Then a total separation occurred in your mind, I would call it *splitting*'" (p. 77). Wiesel writes: "At first I had a hard time getting used to the idea that I was alive. I thought of myself as dead. I couldn't eat, read, cry: I saw myself dead. I thought I was dead and that in a dream I imagined myself alive. I knew I no longer existed, that my real life had stayed *there,* that my present self had nothing in common with the other, the real one. I was like the skin shed by a snake" ("The Accident," in *Night Trilogy,* p. 246). This sense of two selves who cannot come to terms with each other is prevalent in many of the testimonies analyzed in Langer, *Holocaust Testimonies.*

115. See further in Segev, *The Seventh Million,* pp. 323–84. Also in *The Seventh Million* note the photograph of Ka-Tzetnik immediately after he fainted on the witness stand (after p. 404). See the prologue, "Ka-Tztnik's Trip," which provides some important information on Ka-Tzetnik (pp. 3–11; somewhat more detailed in the Hebrew original, *Ha-milion ha-shevii,* pp. 1–9).

116. *House of Dolls,* p. 230.

117. Survivors have often expressed anxiety regarding the effect they would have on members of their family who had not experienced the Holocaust, especially their children. Both Ka-Tzetnik in *The Confrontation* and Wiesel in "The Accident" are troubled by having polluted the soul of a woman who can never understand their Holocaust experience. Langer, *Holocaust Testimonies,* cites interviewees anxious about the effects of their experiences in the Holocaust on their children. See also H. Epstein, *Children of the Holocaust: Conversations with Sons and Daughters of Survivors* (New York, 1988). It should also be noted that many societies have treated soldiers returning from war as polluted by the violence of battle and have established elaborate rites of purification that the warriors were compelled to undergo before being allowed to rejoin society. For some important psychological insights, see Moses, *Persistent Shadows of the Holocaust.*

118. This was reflected most recently in the novel by Hanoch Bartov, *Regel ahat ba-huts (Halfway Out)* (Tel Aviv, 1994), which carries a sense of bewilderment at having grown up in the shadow of Auschwitz in Palestine without ever really acknowledging it.

119. This is echoed also in the closing pages of Wiesel's "The Accident," in *Night Trilogy;* in Paul Celan's poetry, most forcefully perhaps in his poem "Engführung"; and in Borowski's suicide soon after his liberation.

120. Note that the last volume of the sextet has three distinct titles. It is called *Ha-tsofen (The Code)* in Hebrew; *Shivitti* in English; and is subtitled *Masa ha-garin shel Auschwitz (The Burden of the Nucleus of Auschwitz).* The "code" refers both to the motto of all volumes, "[A.DM.A']," which is never wholly explained but may be related to tears (*dema*), man (*adam*), blood (*dam*), and earth (*adamah*), as well as to Ka-Tzetnik's attempt to decode the "secret" of Auschwitz through LSD-induced psychiatric sessions and mystical visions. *Shivitti* is derived from a verse in Psalms 16:8 that appears above the prayer column in synagogues, normally surrounded by

various coded words and incantations of kabbalistic derivation. The verse "shivitti adonai [yehova] le-negdi tamid" (I imagine God [Jehovah] always before me) is a central element of Jewish belief. This in turn is also related to the Hebrew title. Finally, the subtitle is related to a vision by the author whereby Ashmedai, or Satan, is being crowned as king of the universe instead of God, and his name is changed to Nucleus (so it appears also in Hebrew), "Born in the midst of the oven, in the mysterious laboratory of Auschwitz. Created from a new material, a potion distilled from the souls of 1,500,000 burned children" (p. 51). But Nucleus also seems to refer to nuclear, i.e., atomic (which in Hebrew reads the same, *garin*), as the smoke bellowing out of the crematorium's chimney is likened to "a fiery mushroom" (p. 106). Moreover, it refers to the splitting of the nucleus of man as well as of the atom, and Ka-Tzetnik speaks repeatedly in this volume of his own splitting, e.g.: "I do not faint, but take leave of myself. I have become two. What then and now— reality-of-one-time, multiplied into two—thus I-then and I-now, one identity, split into two" (p. 103).

121. This can of course also be seen in European cinematic representations of the Holocaust, especially in Italian and German films produced in the 1970s and 1980s.

122. *The Code,* pp. 22–24.

123. Ibid., pp. 77–78.

124. Ibid., p. 78.

125. It should be noted that in several earlier versions of Ka-Tzetnik's works and their translations the titles reflect his preoccupation with the Bird of Hol (*of ha-hol*), born of its own ashes, or the Phoenix. See, e.g.: *Ke-hol me-efer* (title page includes English title *The Phoenix Land;* now published as *Piepel*) (Tel Aviv, 1966); *Phoenix over the Galilee* (English translation of *Ke-hol me-efer,* later retitled *Piepel*), (New York, 1969); *Star of Ashes / Kokhav ha-efer / Ash-shtern* (text and title page in English, Hebrew, and Yiddish), (Tel Aviv, 1967); *Star Eternal / Ash-shtern / Kokhav ha-efer* (New York, 1971).

126. *The Code,* p. 112.

127. Ibid., p. 113.

128. Ibid.

129. The most glaring, almost comical use to which Ka-Tzetnik's work is put can be found in an addendum that accompanies four of the six volumes, whose title betrays its content: "How a high school student, addicted to drugs, was saved and healed." The boy was healed, of course, by reading Ka-Tzetnik, and his thankful father contributed a sum of money with which the "Ka-Tzetnik Prize for Holocaust Consciousness" was established. See also the introduction, appended to most volumes, by the Chief Rabbi of Israel, Yisrael Meir Lau, a Holocaust survivor. Yet in the closing pages of the last volume, *The Code,* Ka-Tzetnik asserts: "I write even on the subject called the 'Holocaust,' yet the moment I turn my gaze inward to that which flows day and night with my blood in my arteries, right away a sort of spool of colorful thread reappears very close to my eye, rolling away from me, returning very close to my eye and once more rolling away to an unfamiliar, endless, opaque and dark region—and back again" (p. 113).

130. I still recall one young leader of a Tel Aviv motorcycle gang in the late 1960s who boasted of the SS boots he had managed to procure in a flea market; to him (and other members of the gang who envied him for this precious possession) they appeared to enhance his masculinity and toughness.

131. See esp. Segev, *The Seventh Million*, pp. 396–404.

132. *House of Dolls*, Ka-Tzetnik's most explicit and widely translated book, is also the least autobiographical of his oeuvre, since by definition he could never have been to the women's camp where his sister was forced to become a prostitute for German soldiers. See also Wiesel's encounter with a former camp inmate who was a child prostitute in "The Accident," in *Night Trilogy*.

133. See further in O. Bartov, "Intellectuals on Auschwitz: Memory, History, and Truth," in Bartov, *Murder in Our Midst*.

134. Goldhagen, *Hitler's Willing Executioners*, p. 7.

135. For more details, see Bartov, *Ordinary Monsters*.

136. See, e.g., Goldhagen, *Hitler's Willing Executioners*, p. 218.

137. For an analysis of the reception of Goldhagen's book in Germany, the United States, France, and Israel, see O. Bartov, "Reception and Perception: Goldhagen's Holocaust and the World," in *History, Memory, Nazism: Hitler's Willing Executioners in European and American Self-Reflection*, ed. G. Eley and K. Canning (Ann Arbor, Mich., 2000).

138. Goldhagen, *Hitler's Willing Executioners*, p. 15.

139. E. Roll, "Goldhagens Diskussionsreise: Der schwierige Streit um die Deutschen und den Holocaust: Eine These und drei gebrochene Tabus," *SZ* (September 9, 1996); V. Ullrich, "Daniel J. Goldhagen in Deutschland: Die Buchtournee wurde zum Triumphzug," *Die Zeit* (September 13, 1996), which begins with the instructive statement: "The historians criticize 'Hitler's Willing Executioners.' The public finds the book liberating."

140. Goldhagen, *Hitler's Willing Executioners*, pp. 593–94, n. 53.

141. Meron, *Between Books and Ashes*, p. 196.

Conclusion

1. Martin Walser's October 1998 speech was made available on the Internet (www.boersenverein.de/fpreis/mw_rede.htm). For some responses, see: M. Maron, "Hat Walser zwei Reden gehalten?" *Die Zeit* (November 19, 1998); S. Friedländer, "Die Metapher des Bösen," *Die Zeit* (November 26, 1998); "Bubis nennt Walser und Dohnanyi 'latente Antisemiten,'" *FAZ* (November 29, 1998); R. Cohen, "Germany Searches For 'Normality,'" *NYT* (November 29, 1998): A10; M. Erte et al., "Schuld und Schlußstrich," R. Augstein, "'Wir sind alle Verletzbar,'" and R. Mohr, "Total normal?" and "'Moral verjährt nicht': Ignatz Bubis über die Auschwitz-Debatte und seine Auseinandersetzung mit Martin Walser und Klaus von Dohnanyi," all in *Der Spiegel* 49 (November 30, 1998); S. F. Kellerhoff, "Alte Männer im Streit? Deutschlands Historiker und die Debatte um Martin Walser," *Die Welt* (December 3, 1998); R. Leicht, "Warum Walser Irrt," *Die Zeit* (December 3, 1998); S. Boedecker, "Der Wunsch nach Normalität," and "Ein anderes Mahnmal?" *Die Woche* (December 4, 1998); N. Sznaider, "Wir Sind alle Fremde," *SZ* (December 5–6, 1998); J. Nolte, "Das falsche Schweigen: Kommentar," *Die Welt* (December 7, 1998); "'Es kommt darauf an, wie man Rituale mit Leben erfüllt': Salomon Korn, Präsidiumsmitglied des Zentralrats der Juden, über die Kontroverse zwischen Walser und Bubis," *FR* (December 11, 1998); G. Gaus, "Der normale Imperativ," *SZ* Feuilleton (December 12, 1998); W. Büscher, "Es gibt zwei Erinnerungen," *Die Welt* (December 12, 1998); K.-H. Bohrer, "Schuldkultur oder Schamkultur," and C. Leggewie, "Die Zukunft der Vergangenheit," *NZZ* Literatur und Kunst (December 12, 1998); U. Herbert,

"Nötig ist der nüchterne Blick auf die Vergangenheit," *BaZ* (December 15, 1998); I. Buruma, "War Guilt, and the Difference between Germany and Japan," *NYT* (December 29, 1998): A19.

2. *The Drowned and the Saved* (New York, 1988), chapter 3, "Shame."

3. *The Reader*, trans. C. B. Janeway (New York, 1997). Originally published as *Der Vorleser* (Zurich, 1995). Citations are from the translated version.

4. Ibid., p. 104.

5. Ibid., pp. 109–11.

6. Ibid., p. 113.

7. Ibid., p. 137.

8. Ibid., p. 119.

9. Ibid., pp. 128–29.

10. Ibid., p. 134.

11. Ibid., pp. 147–48.

12. Ibid., p. 157.

13. Ibid., p. 158.

14. Ibid., p. 163.

15. Ibid., pp. 170–71.

16. Ibid., p. 179.

17. Ibid., p. 160.

18. *Fragments: Memoirs of a Wartime Childhood,* trans. C. B. Janeway (New York, 1996). Originally published as *Bruchstücke* (Frankfurt am Main, 1995). Citations are from the translated version. The book won the National Jewish Book Award, the Jewish Quarterly Literary Prize, and the Prix de la Mémoire de la Shoah.

19. *The Painted Bird* (New York, 1965).

20. See, e.g., J. P. Sloan, "Kosinski's War," *TNY* (October 10, 1994): 46–53. See also S. R. Horowitz, *Voicing the Void: Muteness and Memory in Holocaust Fiction* (Albany, N.Y., 1997), chapter 4. Earlier evaluations of Kosinski in S. DeKoven Ezrahi, *By Words Alone: The Holocaust in Literature* (Chicago, 1980), pp. 152–58; L. L. Langer, *The Holocaust and the Literary Imagination* (New Haven, Conn., 1975), chapter 5. A. H. Rosenfeld, *A Double Dying: Reflections on Holocaust Literature* (Bloomington, Ind., 1980), part III, discusses other cases of "Deceptions and Corruptions," but makes no mention of Kosinski.

21. *Der Absender* (Zurich, 1995).

22. D. Ganzfried, "Die geliehene Holocaust-Biographie," *Weltwoche* 35 (August 27, 1998); see also Ganzfried, "Fakten gegen Erinnerung," *Weltwoche* 36 (September 3, 1998).

23. H. Raczymow, *Writing the Book of Esther* (New York, 1995); originally published as *Un cri sans voix* (Paris, 1985). D. Grossman, *See Under—Love* (New York, 1989); originally published as *Ayen erekh ahavah* (Tel Aviv, 1986). J. M. Rymkiewicz, *The Final Station: Umschlagplatz* (New York, 1994); originally published as *Umschlagplatz* (Paris, 1988). See now especially F. I. Zeitlin, "The Vicarious Witness: Belated Memory and Authorial Presence in Recent Holocaust Literature," *H&M* 10 (1998): 5–42.

24. Cited by J. Lau, "Ein fast perfekter Schmerz," *Die Zeit* 39 (September 1, 1998).

25. See, e.g., A. Aciman's enthusiastic review in *TNR* (January 19, 1998). For another negative aesthetic judgment, see R. Klüger, "Kitsch ist immer plausibel," *SZ* (September 30, 1998). I first read the book on recommendation by Saul Friedländer.

26. For some other discussions of this scandal, see, e.g., I. Hartwig, "Die heikle Affäre um Binjamin Wilkomirski/Bruno Doessekker," *FR* (September 10, 1998); M. Ebel, "Wie Wilhelm Tell zu einem SS-Mann wurde," *BeZ* (September 30, 1998); "In a Country Waking up to a New Future, These Men Have Become Potent Symbols of Germany's Nightmare Past," *The Independent* (September 30, 1998); N. Weill, "La mémoire suspectée de Binjamin Wilkomirski," *Le Monde* (October 23, 1998). For the two most comprehensive analyses in English, see P. Gourevitch, "The Memory Thief," *TNY* (June 14, 1999): 48–68; E. Lappin, "The Man with Two Heads," *Granta* (summer 1999): 9–65.

27. T. Borowski, *This Way for the Gas, Ladies and Gentlemen* (New York, 1967).

28. See, e.g., I. Kertész, *Fateless* (Evanston, Ill., 1992); I. Fink, *The Journey* (New York, 1992); A. Appelfeld, *Katerina* (New York, 1992). See also Appelfeld, "Buried Homeland," *TNY* (November 23, 1998): 48–61.

29. P. Levi, *The Drowned and the Saved* (New York, 1988), pp. 83–84: "I must repeat: we, the survivors, are not true witnesses. . . . We survivors are not only an exiguous but also an anomalous minority: we are those who by their prevarications or abilities or good luck did not touch bottom. Those who did so, those who saw the Gorgon, have not returned to tell about it or have returned mute, but they are the 'Muslims,' the submerged, the complete witnesses, the ones whose deposition would have a general significance. They are the rule, we are the exception."

30. *Wartime Lies* (New York, 1991).

31. *Fragments,* p. 154. See also Ben-Zion Tomer's quasi-autobiographical play on this theme, "Children of the Shadows" (1962), in *Israeli Holocaust Drama,* ed. M. Taub (Syracuse, N.Y.), pp. 127–85.

32. *Wartime Lies,* pp. 180–81.

33. Levi, *The Drowned and the Saved,* pp. 83–84.

34. Ibid., p. 86.

Index